Office Kaizen 2

Also available from ASQ Quality Press:

Office Kaizen: Transforming Office Operations into a Strategic Competitive Advantage
William Lareau

Learning Lean 5S: Quality Pocket of Knowledge (QPoK)
ASQ

Lean for Service Organizations and Offices: A Holistic Approach for Achieving Operational Excellence and Improvements
Debashis Sarkar

Profitability with No Boundaries: Optimizing TOC and Lean-Six Sigma
Reza (Russ) M. Pirasteh and Robert E. Fox

5S for Service Organizations and Offices: A Lean Look at Improvements
Debashis Sarkar

Lean Kaizen: A Simplified Approach to Process Improvements
George Alukal and Anthony Manos

The Executive Guide to Understanding and Implementing Lean Six Sigma: The Financial Impact
Robert M. Meisel, Steven J. Babb, Steven F. Marsh, and James P. Schlichting

Lean ISO 9001: Adding Spark to your ISO 9001 QMS and Sustainability to your Lean Efforts
Mike Micklewright

Root Cause Analysis: Simplified Tools and Techniques, Second Edition
Bjørn Andersen and Tom Fagerhaug

The Certified Manager of Quality/Organizational Excellence Handbook: Third Edition
Russell T. Westcott, editor

Enabling Excellence: The Seven Elements Essential to Achieving Competitive Advantage
Timothy A. Pine

The Quality Toolbox, Second Edition
Nancy R. Tague

To request a complimentary catalog of ASQ Quality Press publications, call 800-248-1946, or visit our Web site at http://www.asq.org/quality-press.

Office Kaizen 2

**Harnessing Leadership,
Organizations, People, and Tools
for Office Excellence**

William Lareau

ASQ Quality Press
Milwaukee, Wisconsin

American Society for Quality, Quality Press, Milwaukee 53203
© 2011 by ASQ
All rights reserved. Published 2010
Printed in the United States of America
15 14 13 12 11 10   5 4 3 2 1

Library of Congress Cataloging-in-Publication Data

Lareau, William.
   Office kaizen 2 : harnessing leadership, organizations, people, and tools for office
excellence / William Lareau.
       p. cm.
   Includes index.
    ISBN 978-0-87389-801-0 (alk. paper)
   1. Organizational change.   2. Organizational effectiveness.   3. Industrial efficiency.
4. Corporate culture.   5. Production management.   6. Waste minimization.   I. Title.
II. Title: Office kaizen two.

   HD58.8.L374 2010
   658.4'06—dc22

2010042280

Publisher: William A. Tony
Acquisitions Editor: Matt Meinholz
Project Editor: Paul O'Mara
Production Administrator: Randall Benson

ASQ Mission: The American Society for Quality advances individual, organizational, and community
excellence worldwide through learning, quality improvement, and knowledge exchange.

Attention Bookstores, Wholesalers, Schools, and Corporations: ASQ Quality Press books, video,
audio, and software are available at quantity discounts with bulk purchases for business, educational,
or instructional use. For information, please contact ASQ Quality Press at 800-248-1946, or write to
ASQ Quality Press, P.O. Box 3005, Milwaukee, WI 53201-3005.

To place orders or to request a free copy of the ASQ Quality Press Publications Catalog, visit our
website at http://www.asq.org/quality-press.

∞ Printed on acid-free paper

Quality Press
600 N. Plankinton Avenue
Milwaukee, Wisconsin 53203
Call toll free 800-248-1946
Fax 414-272-1734
www.asq.org
http://www.asq.org/quality-press
http://standardsgroup.asq.org
E-mail: authors@asq.org

Contents

List of Figures . . . . *xi*

Preface . . . . *xv*

PART I   **THE LANDSCAPE OF OFFICE KAIZEN** **1**

Chapter 1   **The Key Principle of Change in the Universe** **3**

Chapter 2   **The Topography of World-Class Methods** **13**

Innovation, Continuous Improvement, and Changing
    Processes 14
Waste 15
The Toyota Production System 18
Lean Manufacturing 22
Value Stream Mapping 23
Six Sigma 23

Chapter 3   **The Challenge of Change One: Human Behavior
as It Operates at Work** **27**

The Seven Human Needs 27
Different Ways of Viewing the World 32

Chapter 4   **The Challenge of Change Two: Automatic
Processing, Cognitive Maps, Dissonance,
and the Primacy of Action** **37**

Input, Processing, and Awareness 39
Cognitive Maps: A Leader's Greatest Challenge and
    Greatest Opportunity 43

                The Implication for Leaders.   52
                The Challenge of the Frozen Tundra of
                      Corporate Culture.   53

**Chapter 5   The Challenge of Change Three: Group and
               Organization Dynamics**. **57**
                Group Formation   58
                Propinquity.   59
                Leadership, Status, and Authority   61
                Conformity.   63
                Goals, Roles, and Norms   65
                Attribution   68
                Attraction   69
                Polarization   70
                Social Loafing   71
                Abilene Paradox.   72
                Idiosyncrasy Credits.   73
                Groupthink.   74

**PART II   THE METHODS AND TOOLS OF
                OFFICE KAIZEN** **77**

Chapter 6   The Structure of Successful Change **79**
                The Structures of Managing Change and
                      Leadership   84
                Structural Configurations Described   85

Chapter 7   Common Office Kaizen Tools and Methods **107**
                The Brown Paper Approach.   108
                Group Brainstorming Methods   109
                Standard Work   136
                One-Point Methods   137

Chapter 8   Office Kaizen Value Stream Mapping Concepts. **139**
                The Basic Structure of a VSM.   140
                The *OK2* Approach to VSMapping   147
                A Few Other Concepts and Symbols You May Need . . .   160
                Remember   163

Chapter 9   **Constructing an Office Kaizen Current State**
Value Stream Map **165**

  1. Prepare for the VSMapping Event   165
  2. Give the Team Members (Who Will Be Building
     the VSM) an Overview of VSMapping Concepts
     and Principles.   167
  3. Review and Refine the Charter of the VSMapping
     Team with the Team Members.   167
  4. Review the Level of Mapping That Will Be Used . . .   167
  5. Review the Scope of the Mapping   168
  6. Discuss the Definition of "Future" That Will Be
     Used in Implementing Improvements and the
     Investment Strategy behind Improvements   168
  7. Review the Steps in This Chapter So Team Members
     Can Anticipate What They Will Be Doing.   169
  8. Introduce the Kaizen Action Sheet (KAS) and
     Its Use   170
  9. Collect Preliminary Data   170
10. Construct a Rough Sequence of Activities.   171
11. Divide the Team's Work into Process Chunks
     and Assignments   171
12. Collect Detailed Information   172
13. Generate the First-Cut CS-VSM   176
14. Perform Communication Diagramming   176
15. Review the First-Cut CS-VSM with Workers
     from the Process.   176
16. Make Changes to the VSM   177
17. Review the Revised VSM with the Process
     Workers and Make Any Adjustments.   177
18. Construct Ancillary Analyses.   177
19. Identify and Sort Possible Improvement Ideas   178
20. Discuss the Improvements and Determine Final
     Classification   181
21. Review Sensitive and/or Bold Improvements with
     Appropriate People   182

Chapter 10   **Constructing an Office Kaizen Future State**
Value Stream Map and Action Plan **183**

  1. Select the Time Horizon for the FS-VSM   183

2. Select the Improvements That Will Generate the
   Forecast Shown in the FS-VSM. 184
3. Denote Improvements That Will Be Included on
   the CS-VSM. 185
4. Estimate the Impact of Improvements 187
5. Lay Out the Activity and Inventory Boxes of the
   FS-VSM. 190
6. Construct the Time Ladder. 192
7. Prepare a Summary Benefits Table for the End of
   the FS-VSM 192
8. Develop the Action Plan (AP) 193
9. Develop the Implementation Plan 196
10. Present the Findings of the CS-VSM, FS-VSM,
    and AP 197
11. Next Steps 200

PART III   THE MECHANICS OF SUCCESSFUL OFFICE
             KAIZEN IMPROVEMENT EVENTS. **201**

Chapter 11   **The Landscape of Improvement Actions** **203**

Chapter 12   **Preparing for Kaizen, Six Sigma, and
             Scramble Events.** **209**
             Preparing for Scrambles. 216

Chapter 13   **Conducting Improvement Actions That Last
             One Week or Less.** **219**
             Event Length 220
             Number of Teams. 222
             General Structure of an Event 222
             Detailed General Schedule for the Week. 225
             Final Comments on Conducting Weeklong
                Improvement Events 248

Chapter 14   **Conducting Follow-Up Actions on Events That
             Last a Week or Less** **249**

**PART IV   THE LEADERSHIP OF SIGNIFICANT OFFICE
KAIZEN TRANSFORMATION EFFORTS** **253**

**Chapter 15 The Secret Ingredient to Excellence:
Action Leadership** **255**
The Primacy of Action   258
Types of Leadership Action   260
Implementing Action Leadership   266

**Chapter 16 Transforming a Single Work Group, Section, or
Department** **273**
Detailed Implementation Steps and Schedules   276

Chapter 17 Transforming a Site **297**
Getting Started   301

**Chapter 18 Transforming an Organization with
Multiple Sites** **315**
Approaches That Guarantee Failure   315
What Has to Happen at a Site   319
The Recommended Approach for Enterprises with
Multiple Stand-Alone Sites   319
The Recommended Approach for Enterprises with
Many Sites That Are IWGs or Departments   330

Chapter 19 What's Next? **337**

Appendix   The Office Kaizen Team 21 . . . .   *339*
List of Abbreviations *347*
Index *349*

List of Figures

Figure 1.1   The three stages of change......................   4

Figure 1.2   The mechanism of persistent disequilibrium..........   11

Figure 2.1   Taiichi Ohno's original wastes...................   16

Figure 2.2   Office Kaizen wastes from *OK1*   17

Figure 2.3   The principal approaches and methods used in the TPS .   19

Figure 2.4   A push (panel A) and pull (panel B) illustration   20

Figure 3.1   The seven inborn human needs   28

Figure 4.1   Black rectangle for afterimage experiment   38

Figure 4.2   Two examples demonstrating higher-order automatic processing of visual information   38

Figure 4.3   Conceptual diagram of the stages of human information processing   39

Figure 4.4   A schematic of preconscious processing—cognitive map operation   46

Figure 6.1   The LBB........................   80

Figure 6.2   The LBB opened up.....................   83

Figure 6.3   The 15 structural configurations   85

Figure 6.4   Sample KGVFC......................   97

Figure 6.5   Sample KAS   99

Figure 6.6   Team 21 graph for a work group in a general office environment.........................   101

Figure 6.7   General level descriptions and the specific definitions for the T-metric of deadlines and commitments   102

Figure 6.8   The five-point scale used to assess weekly Team 21 progress   104

Figure 7.1   MAD example after categorizing   110

Figure 7.2   Close-up section of a MAD after final ranking   114

Figure 7.3   An example of a C&E diagram   115

Figure 7.4   An example of a line/run chart..................   116

Figure 7.5   An example of an X-bar and R (means and ranges) SPC chart   118

Figure 7.6   An example of a histogram   120

Figure 7.7   An example of a flowchart   121

Figure 7.8   An example of a spaghetti diagram   123

Figure 7.9   An example of a handoff chart for processing a commercial loan   125

Figure 7.10 A sample RACI chart   126

Figure 7.11 A sample Pareto chart   127

Figure 7.12 The terms and meanings of 5S   129

Figure 7.13 A portion of a sample 5S audit sheet   130

Figure 7.14 A 5S visual display   131

Figure 7.15 A sample portion of a cross-training matrix for a buyer group   133

Figure 7.16 A DILO of supervisory activities   135

Figure 8.1   The first two activities of a VSM for processing a new checking account   141

Figure 8.2   An illustration of lead and cycle times for multiple inputs to an activity box   146

Figure 8.3   A portion of the checking account process showing how a decision tree is presented and how a rework cycle is displayed   153

Figure 8.4   Flowchart of the process shown in Figure 8.3   155

Figure 8.5   An example of communication diagramming on a CS-VSM   159

Figure 8.6   Illustration of a supermarket kanban system   162

Figure 8.7   An example of a FIFO lane   163

Figure 9.1   KAS place markers shown on the VSM   180

Figure 9.2   An example of a relationship grid for classifying improvement ideas   181

Figure 10.1 An example of a CS-VSM with improvement loops . . .   186

Figure 10.2 An example of summary tables showing KAS contributions to improvements   189

Figure 10.3 An alternative FS-VSM format and the traditional format   191

Figure 10.4 An example of summary benefits table for the end of the FS-VSM   193

Figure 10.5 An example of an AP for an FS-VSM   194

Figure 11.1 General categories of events with some of their
characteristics 204

Figure 13.1 General structure of a weeklong event. 223

Figure 13.2 Example of an Office Kaizen waste checklist 227

Figure 13.3 An example of a KTS 228

Figure 13.4 An example of a KTDL 235

Figure 13.5 An example of a KSAP......................... 241

Figure 13.6 An example of a KFCL......................... 242

Figure 15.1 The challenge of creating outstanding leadership 257

Figure 15.2 Types of LActs: leadership touches, spontaneous
interactions, and orders 261

Figure 15.3 The relative impacts of the six types of leadership
actions 265

Figure 15.4 The flowchart of AL implementation. 267

Figure 15.5 An example of a LAM 269

Figure 16.1 Schematic illustrating the organization of
Chapters 16–18 274

Figure 16.2 Office Kaizen implementation schedule for a
single IWG 278

Figure 16.3 Office Kaizen implementation schedule for a
department 284

Figure 17.1 Office Kaizen implementation schedule for a site...... 302

Figure 18.1 Office Kaizen implementation schedule for a multisite
organization with large sites. 322

Figure 18.2 Office Kaizen implementation schedule for a multisite
organization with locations that consist of IWGs and/or
small departments. 332

Preface

The Japanese term *kaizen* has come to mean many things. It's hard to pin down a precise definition, even from native Japanese speakers, because it has morphed over time from a word to an icon of a business philosophy. Kaizen is a compound word: *Kai* means "small" and *Zen* means "good." To some, kaizen is a philosophy that contends that excellence and competitiveness are attained by pursuing many small improvements in waste reduction rather than seeking a smaller number of breakthrough improvements. Breakthrough improvements are not bad; they just cannot serve as the sole road to competitiveness. To others, kaizen represents a body of tools and techniques that improve processes by eliminating waste and thus making the processes faster, more efficient, and of higher quality. To still others, kaizen is viewed as an adjunct to lean manufacturing methods (the tools and approaches of the Toyota Production System [TPS]). As Chapter 1 shows, kaizen is a bit of all these, but it needs to be much more if it is to function as a strategy for creating maximum value in an organization over the long term.

Office Kaizen is, by definition and focus, the application of kaizen and its adjuncts to nonmanufacturing processes. Nonmanufacturing processes are those that involve paper, data, and people processes in areas other than the factory floor. Thus, Office Kaizen is usually thought to involve "typical" office areas such as purchasing, logistics, finance, human resources, quality control, engineering, planning, and so on. Factory processes are generally considered to be those that involve equipment, manufacturing lines, heavy machinery, and the like.

However, the distinction between office and factory is not as clear-cut as it might first appear. Few factory processes operate without extensive software, paper, and data support integrated into them in regard to materials, purchasing, engineering, plant maintenance, scheduling, and planning. The nature of modern machine processes demands that Office Kaizen approaches, however they are defined, be implemented side by side with other world-class tools to optimize the effectiveness of equipment. So, whether you're in a factory or a law office (yes, even a law office), you won't get to where you want to go (or, rather, where you *should want* to go) without using the methods of Office Kaizen.

The forerunner to this book is *Office Kaizen: Transforming Office Operations into a Strategic Competitive Advantage* (referenced from here on as *Office Kaizen 1*, or *OK1*). *OK1* presents a focused leadership system for structuring and maximizing the involvement and participation of intact work groups (IWGs) and ad hoc teams pursuing process improvements. *OK1* was focused in this manner because these two groups present the single greatest opportunity for obtaining kaizen benefits: fully engaging and maximizing the day-to-day efforts of employees. Properly focused IWGs (the seven people in an engineering work group, the four people in a customer service work group, and so on) are closest to the processes and can improve things at a very organic level. Ad hoc work stream teams (WSTs) provide an opportunity to pursue cross-functional improvements that are beyond the reach of IWGs. If you were to do only one "kaizen thing" in an organization's office and/or manufacturing areas, the structures presented in *OK1* are that one thing. Chapter 6 gives a brief overview of the concepts of *OK1* that are important to get the most out of *Office Kaizen 2 (OK2)*.

Yet, there is much more to leading a successful Office Kaizen initiative than maximizing the waste removal activities in IWGs and forming WSTs to implement more complex improvements. Office Kaizen will produce only a shadow of its potential unless managers and leaders do what is necessary to structure and sustain results. Results cannot be sustained unless leadership understands how to support and maintain significant cultural change. An organization that effectively utilizes kaizen (and/or lean manufacturing and/or Lean-Six Sigma) methods over the long term as part of everyday business is one that has dramatically changed its culture from what it was before. That so many organizations fail in implementing world-class methods suggests that many of the successes are based on happenstance or luck. Having the right people at the right time with the right approaches working on the right processes is an outstanding strategy when it occurs. However, it doesn't occur very often by chance. And even if lightning does strike, the luck that produces good kaizen results is almost never enough to keep things going or provide a model for extending the success to another location in the same organization.

Expanding on what *OK1* presented, *OK2* continues to forgo dependence on good fortune and completes the picture of what's required for a comprehensive, sustainable Office Kaizen implementation. The purpose is to provide predictable, defined structures and methods to replace circumstance and luck in the pursuit of excellence. *OK2* pursues specific objectives in order to complete the road map to kaizen success:

1. *Provide leadership at all levels with an understanding of how human motivation and group and organization dynamics influence what everyone does every minute at work.* Leadership's failure to more completely understand how and why people perceive and interpret reality, make decisions, and influence one another is by far the single biggest source of loss in business. Many billions of dollars are lost every year because leaders attempt to compel people to work against the dictates of basic human nature. Once management understands the inner compulsions and operating characteristics of individuals and groups, it is better able to harness the true human potential of its organization in every pursuit. This objective is critical to Office Kaizen, but it applies to every person, every day, in every process and in every type of initiative in every business.

2. *Provide leadership at all levels with an understanding of what cultural change is and how it can be most effectively led.* Many leaders view cultural change as something distinct and often preliminary, if it is not ignored outright, to process improvement. I've heard many times, often from senior executives, "We must change our culture before we focus on _____" (insert lean, Six Sigma, kaizen, project management, etc.). Or, the converse is often heard, "We don't have time for culture change; first we must make _____ (insert lean, Six Sigma, kaizen, etc.) work before we worry about culture." These views are incorrect and dangerous. Cultural change is achieved by using world-class tools within a framework of leadership structures. Any methodology will have a limited impact if its implementation is not pursued as part of an organized plan to effect cultural change, that is, the manner in which everyone in the organization thinks about and approaches work all day long. Every process improvement, instance of waste removal, project team action, and functional work group activity must be guided by the defined structure of an overarching cultural change initiative. If not, the benefits of the best tool use in the world won't be 10% of what they could be, they won't last, and they will not create any long-term change in the existing culture, except to make people more cynical. Make no mistake about it—all sustainable

successes demand a primary focus on cultural change as a strategic initiative that is enacted by the disciplined use of world-class tools and structured leadership. Those with a desperate need for bottom-line impacts should not despair—this approach is no less intense than a focus on fast results; in fact, focusing on culture with structure gets faster and more impressive results than tools alone.

3. *Present and explain why, how, and when the principal methods and tools of Office Kaizen can best be applied.* While leadership's understanding of human nature and cultural change can provide (if the understanding is applied) a solid foundation for tool usage, inefficient tool usage can discourage management and process workers, waste resources, and lead to poor plans and decisions. Chapter 7 presents instructions on how to apply what I consider the basic elements of the world-class kaizen "toolbox." Many parts of this toolbox are integral to Six Sigma and lean approaches as well.

4. *Provide guidance for planning, conducting, and following up on continuous improvement events.* A *continuous improvement event* (CIE; sometimes called rapid improvement events or kaizen blitzes) is a four- to five-day "blitz" in which a team of four to six people gives its focused, full-time attention to a process to analyze, test, and implement solutions. Most of the time the principal focus of a CIE is the removal of waste. This is because waste reduction is relatively easy to achieve compared with implementing innovations. CIEs are one of the most visible elements of a lean or kaizen initiative in offices and factories. However, as with most things that provide tremendous benefit, the best results can only be obtained by following best practices with unerring discipline. *OK2* devotes several chapters to planning, conducting, and following up on various types of events.

5. *Present detailed approaches for leading kaizen-based cultural change initiatives at various levels of the organization, from single work groups to corporate-wide efforts.* From what I've observed over the last 25 years, it's easy to conclude that many people believe that a lean, kaizen, and/or Six Sigma change initiative requires nothing more than a series of CIEs and some tools training. If this were true, almost every enterprise in the industrialized world would have a world-class culture. It takes a lot more than an occasional week of hoopla, excitement, box lunches, and a few process improvements—

however exciting—to create lasting change. Chapters 16–18 describe the structural and leadership requirements for transformations of everything from a single work group to an entire corporation.

6. *Provide insights into applying value stream mapping (VSMapping) in nonfactory settings.* VSMapping has become an almost mandatory analysis tool in the past 10 years. Despite its popularity, few references detail the unique methods necessary to make VSMapping fit requirements of office processes. Chapters 8–10 discuss the creation of current and future state value stream maps (VSMs) as well as improvement action plans for office processes.

OK2 is not intended to be a comprehensive, detailed how-to encyclopedia of all lean and kaizen tools for nonfactory applications. While many tools and techniques are discussed and usage details presented where they are important and not obvious, the primary focus of this book is to provide guidelines for method and tool applications within the context of leading successful Office Kaizen cultural change initiatives.

This book does not provide an in-depth review of lean manufacturing methods. A properly implemented lean manufacturing initiative involves many of the Office Kaizen methods discussed in this book insofar as many of the tools are effective in almost any environment. However, a number of specific lean manufacturing methods, such as total preventive maintenance (TPM) and single minute exchange of die (SMED), among others, are specifically designed for machine environments and have only tangential application to office settings. Other elements of lean manufacturing apply in concept to office processes but don't always work well in practice. One of these involves the concept of takt time. *Takt time* is the time period in which one unit of work must be completed in an activity in order to meet customer demand in a defined time period (a shift, a day, or a week), whether the customer is the next workstation or the final customer.

If every worker/machine/station in a process creates one unit of work at the takt time and immediately passes it (or it flows) to the next person/station, there is no buildup of inventory and no waiting for work at any station: The process will produce just what the internal customer wants. A central concern of lean manufacturing is to determine the takt time of a process and then modify each task in the process so that the work flows smoothly from station to station. This concept applies to any type of work, but it does not always work as well when applied in rote fashion to office processes.

For example, a factory worker or a machine often performs the same action to a great many consecutive "pieces" (units of work) that pass through the station. Each piece is essentially the same. In an office setting, a worker may appear to be dealing with the same situation when reviewing, for example, one of a succession of medical insurance forms to ensure that it has the proper diagnostic, payment, and provider codes. While each claim form may ask for similar information and appear to be an equivalent, some may be easy and routine and others may be very complex and unique. Complex claims take more time. Even more at variance with factory work, office workers are often required to do many other tasks at unpredictable times and for varying durations during the day, such as answer phones, call others for information, go to meetings, provide data to supervisors, consult with colleagues, and so on. Few office workers, except those in paper/data "factories" such as credit card processing, do only a single task all the time. Thus, a feverish focus on takt time in most office processes does not always produce the best return for the effort invested. This concept and other concepts that do not fit well in most office analysis situations are not discussed in depth in this book.

There are four sections of this book. Part I, Chapters 1–5, provides an overview of the Office Kaizen arena and the challenge that leaders and managers face when attempting to change their organizations. The information presented in these early chapters, particularly Chapters 2–5, is new, perhaps surprising, and hopefully stimulating for most leaders because the content is not typically discussed in the business press or business schools. These relatively new (with more supporting research arriving every day) insights into the mechanisms of human behavior and decision making can provide leaders with the knowledge to better guide and shape their organizations.

Part II, Chapters 6–10, discusses the basic tools and methods of Office Kaizen. Chapter 6 presents the concepts and mechanics of structural configurations: the organizational and leadership skeleton that provides the form and shape of world-class organizations. Chapter 7 presents an Office Kaizen toolbox that meets 80% of data collection and analysis requirements in both Office Kaizen and many general factory situations. The methods range from simple problem-solving tools such as Pareto charts and spaghetti diagrams to RACI charts and one-point lessons for office tasks. Chapters 8–10 complete the tools and methods presentation by reviewing the best methods for constructing and using VSMapping for office processes.

Part III, Chapters 11–14, drags you face down through every element and nuance of planning successful CIEs. If you apply the structures, forms, coaching tips, and insights of Chapters 11–14, your CIEs will be viewed as both improvement miracles and applied learning and leadership workshops.

Part IV, Chapters 15–18, describes the processes, structures, and leadership requirements to conduct various transformations in an organization. Chapter 15 is especially important, insofar as it describes a method that is central to successful change: action leadership (AL). AL is a method for structuring critical leadership actions in support of implemented process improvements, employee effectiveness, and a focus on bottom-line results. AL focuses a small but vital portion of leadership attention and involvement to those parts of the organization that seldom benefit from attention. The returns can be immense for everyone involved. AL is presented at this point in *OK2* because the earlier chapters provide the basis for many essential leadership actions.

Chapter 16 broadens the scope of implementation by describing the methods, schedules, and leadership approaches required to transform a single work group, a section, or a department. Chapter 17 describes the additional mechanics and approaches for implementing a comprehensive transformation at an entire site. Chapter 18 outlines the particular considerations that must be dealt with when a multisite organization attempts to transform itself. Finally, Chapter 19 offers a few final comments and observations.

Good hunting on the battlefields of waste. Come back with your completed kaizen to-do list (see Figure 13.4) or on it!

PART I

The Landscape of Office Kaizen

What challenges does a leader face when he or she begins an Office Kaizen change initiative? The leader's answer to this question determines the strategies and methods that are selected. All too often, a well-intentioned leader does what he or she thinks is required, but the Office Kaizen effort falls short. The leader did not know the right answer to the question.

Approaching an Office Kaizen transformation without the correct answer to the question is similar to the position of nineteenth-century scientists who contemplated space flight. They had little knowledge about the nature of space, the effects of radiation and weightlessness, how to provide compact heating, cooling and oxygen generation methods, and so on. Even if they could have conceived a way to propel a manned vehicle into orbit, the crew would have died.

Today's leaders who are interested in Office Kaizen are in a predicament similar to that of nineteenth-century space scientists. They have not had an opportunity to learn the specifics of the "space" they face: how and why human beings act as they do at work, the mechanisms that create resistance to change, strategies to deal with the resistance, the dynamics of groups and organizations, and the evolution of corporate culture. This section provides the basic knowledge of these areas that twenty-first-century leaders must have before they launch their transformation missions into Office Kaizen "space."

1

The Key Principle of Change in the Universe

It isn't often in the field of human behavior and the workings of organizations that clear, inviolate principles can be described. Yet, one such principle exists. This principle, which describes and predicts whether an attempted change effort will succeed, operates so well because it underlies every change in our universe. While psychologically based principles provide insights and general predictions, they can't predict specific cases. The key principle we are about to discuss is based on physics. If you understand this principle, you can easily determine whether a change of any kind will possibly succeed. If you do not adhere to the tenets of this principle, the change effort will invariably fail. It is harder to determine whether a change effort *will* succeed, because other factors (e.g., changes in leadership, inconstant support, lack of resources, the organization being bought or sold) can doom even an endeavor that adheres to the tenets of this principle at first. However, if a change effort follows the insights that this principle generates, success is possible and conceptually easy, although it's always hard work to achieve.

This key principle derives from chaos theory and the concepts and operations of self-organizing systems. An outstanding and monumentally insightful book (in my opinion) by Kevin Kelly, called *Out of Control: The Rise of Neobiological Civilization* (more recent editions have the title *Out of Control: The New Biology of Machines, Social Systems, and the Economic World*), explains the workings of this principle and many others that relate to it. While *Out of Control* deals with robotic, biological, and neobiological systems, its principles apply to organizational change just as much as they apply to ant colonies, ponds, prairies, and artificial intelligence. My explanations borrow freely from the work of Kevin Kelly as well as Stuart Kaufman, Christopher G. Langton, and many other pioneers in the exciting field of complexity theory and self-organizing systems.

3

Every system is composed of entities. An *entity* is the smallest logical operating unit in a system. For an ant colony, individual ants are the entities. In a solar system, the sun and planets (and planetoids—sorry about that, Pluto) are the entities. For our universe as a whole, galaxies seem to be the entities, although an argument could be made for stars. In the human body, cells are the entities. The actions of the entities in a system are constrained by their basic nature and the rules of the environment they inhabit. A tree cannot walk to a different forest, a worker ant cannot change itself into a queen ant, and a planet cannot change its orbit by itself. A system operates successfully when the entities create a series of interactions among themselves that make it possible for the system to maintain itself as it is in its current environment. It is the actions of the individual entities and their impact on one another that determine how the overall system operates, whether it successfully adapts to change, and whether it survives (maintains itself).

Figure 1.1 illustrates the three stages of change in a system. First, these stages and their operations are described in regard to a common experience. Then, we explore how these stages relate to and impact the organizational change efforts that are so often expected to make continuous improvement (or anything else) successful. Finally, we review the "rules" that derive from the operation of these stages in successful system adaptation in our universe. The necessity of adhering to these rules is incorporated into every aspect of the concepts and suggested implementation structures provided in the later chapters in this book.

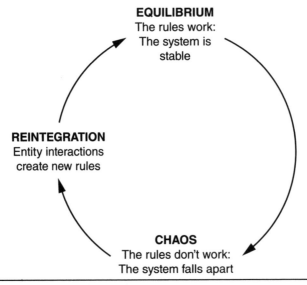

Figure 1.1   The three stages of change.

Every system strives to maintain itself and resist change. After all, if the system has been successful, why change anything? What evolutionary pressure could there be to make significant modifications to a successful system? When a system is successful at surviving in its present environment, the entities continue to interact as they always have; the system is stable by definition. The entities are not compelled to explore new rules for entity interaction. In fact, they have nothing to gain, and much to lose, by changing spuriously. This stage, shown at the top of Figure 1.1, is termed *equilibrium*. When a system is in equilibrium, its entities have a set of rules that have evolved to allow the system to survive. A system moves away from a state of equilibrium only when the external environment presents challenges that the entities cannot overcome using their current rules of interaction. This occurs in forests, ponds, glaciers, fisheries, ant colonies, human bodies, and businesses.

An organization at equilibrium resists pressure to change from any source. In effect, its entities are rewarded by feedback from the system (they get to survive) for maintaining the current status. This is a cardinal trait of traditional social and business organizations that are doing okay. These systems tend to be slower than molasses running uphill at 0°C when responding to threats on the horizon. Consider how long it is taking the US automobile industry to respond to crisis. Not only was there the inherent inertia of a stable physical system, the tendency to avoid reality was further fueled by the operation of human group dynamics, a powerful force in itself for preventing change (as Chapters 4 and 5 explain). This is why, although it is good for an organization to be in a position of equilibrium rather than a position of chaos or reintegration, a successful organization is likely to be very slow to respond to environmental pressure.

If a system's entity interaction rules are ineffective or inefficient in dealing with the external environment, the system is forced away from equilibrium and falls into chaos, shown at the bottom of Figure 1.1. The entities, experiencing the consequences of failure, begin to interact in other ways, trying new types of interactions within the constraints of the overall system. A Himalayan glacier can't relocate itself to one of the earth's poles to save itself from global warming. If the new interactions do not yield effective new rules, the system remains in chaos until it is killed off by the environment.

It is important to realize that the entities are always randomly experiencing new types of interactions even when the system is in a state of equilibrium. However, these "fringe" interactions, although they are always present, are not adopted en masse by other entities as new rules. This is because the system does not benefit from these new interactions and therefore does not provide feedback to the entities that encourages the new actions. The continuous generation of novel interactions provides a system with an "idling engine of change" that delivers a standby capability to quickly discover more effective interactions when the external environment changes. Successful, established organizations that are able to continually come up with novel approaches show that they are able to remain in equilibrium or persistent disequilibrium (to be discussed shortly) while revving up this engine of innovation from time to time.

However, once in chaos, the entities are forced to attempt to discover the beginnings of new rules that will work for them in the changed environment. The stage of chaos is critical to survival because it causes the system to send feedback to all of its entities that the old interactions are not working. Successful adaptation demands that failed systems pushed from equilibrium must descend into chaos and work through the reintegration stage before they are successful again. In Figure 1.1, a system cannot fall to the left and move from equilibrium to reintegration and then back to equilibrium. Without the frenzied, experimental interactions that occur in chaos, new rules cannot evolve.

This law of systems adaptation cannot be violated, either by human organizations or by physical ones. One common example where business organizations frequently attempt to move counterclockwise from equilibrium to reintegration and then back up to equilibrium involves continuous improvement (CI), lean, and Six Sigma initiatives. Rather than setting a structural framework for the desired initiative and then compelling workers, supervisors, and managers (the entities) to establish a set of new interaction rules via experimentation, management typically mandates a program of training and progress reports. Everybody is trained, given a few marching orders, and sent on their way, with perhaps special in-house facilitators who are expert in the tools of the selected initiative.

Management, not being familiar with the three stages of change, thinks it is doing the right thing. After all, it is what it sees most other organizations doing. And since organizations always claim that their initiatives are successful, an outside observer would assume the approaches are working. Often, management has an uneasy feeling that letting the workers and supervisors work it out among themselves will lead to chaos in the usual sense of the word (e.g., riots among the cubicles, casual Fridays every day). It does not understand that the chaos must be not only encouraged but also structured so that the entities are required to interact within a defined framework that increases their chances of success. The elements of this framework are discussed in Chapter 6.

There is no substitute for compelling entities to work it out among themselves, with all the mistakes and missteps that are inherent when a great many entities interact. In fact, mistakes are a critical part of teaching the entities what doesn't work. To get out of chaos, entities, through constant experimentation, must discover the beginnings of new rules that work in the changed environment. If this experimentation proceeds well enough to begin to find new, more effective ways to interact, the system enters a state of reintegration; it has a chance to develop a whole new set of rules. If the entities continue to evolve better and better rules faster than the environment changes, the system may move to a new state of equilibrium with new rules that work in the new environment. A system can arrive at the reintegration stage and still fall back to chaos, however, if sufficiently effective new rules do not evolve.

Even if some trusted, followed, respected, and acknowledged expert "knew" the correct new rules for entity interaction and system survival, the rules could not be applied as dictated policies even if every entity in the system worked hard to follow them. The entities, even if they could read, hear, and understand the rules, would not have worked out the countless minute and specific interactions that would govern the almost infinite number of possible interactions among themselves. This can only occur in messy trial-and-error interactions. Without these countless interactions, the entities might try to follow the dictated rules, but, not having actually learned through experience how the details work through use, their obedience to the rules would be only superficial and the system would not survive.

Consider the human body as an example. It consists of about 10 trillion cells, about 20% of which are bacteria that are not part of the human genome (we pick them up after birth but could not live without most of them). Think about how our bodies operate from moment to moment: These 10 trillion entities are constantly interacting in ways that are not well understood with our current science and technology. There is no conscious "you" controlling the interactions of these cells, or even the interactions among huge groups of cells such as the brain, kidney, liver, and heart. Almost all of the processes of life and thought (thought is discussed extensively in Chapter 4) proceed via an almost infinite number of interactions each day, only a miniscule proportion of which are under any conscious control.

The interactions of the cells of the human body are governed by the limits and guidelines established in our genome. Operating within these evolved constraints, every one of our cells has a very specific role and a limited number of ways in which it can interact with other cells. Needless to say, these rules are extremely effective: They keep 10 trillion cells functioning as a single system for a lifetime. A person never suddenly turns into a pool of mush at a street corner because his or her cells decide to take a vacation and move around randomly. Nobody in good health suddenly dies from walking to the door. A healthy body never "forgets" to breathe while it is asleep or distracted by TV. The human genome's design parameters permit the entities to work very well together almost all of the time.

These circumstances demonstrate why there will never be a fitness pill that will make it unnecessary for people to exercise in order to get in shape. While a pill might supply energy and/or enable faster repair of cellular damage (we already have drugs to do these things, although with some risks), there is no way that a pill of any kind would be able to mimic the effects of the almost infinite adjustments made by trillions of entities in a human body as they interact with one another quadrillions of times during just five seconds of exercise. The process of exercising and "getting into shape" requires that countless minute physical and chemical changes occur between and within entities (and subentities within cells such as mitochondria) as they do their jobs under the increased stress of unexpected exercise. We could not create a substance to mimic the results that the entities create among themselves, even if we understood exactly what happens when cells improve our physical conditioning (and we currently don't understand these processes very well, other than to describe results).

Let's consider what happens when a human system attempts to improve its physical conditioning and how that relates to the three stages of system adaptation shown in Figure 1.1. Let's say that Bill thinks he is in good shape but is told by his physician after his annual physical that he needs to take better care of himself. His doctor tells him to begin some light jogging and watch his diet. So, on the way home, Bill stops by a sporting goods store and picks up new running shoes and shorts. The next morning finds Bill standing on his front porch in his new shoes and shorts, ready to start jogging.

There are billions of muscle cells in Bill's left calf muscle. When Bill starts to take a step, these cells contract to lift his leg. They relax as the leg is lowered for the next push-off step. In the 20 years that Bill has been out of college, these cells have contracted and relaxed many, many times. Since Bill has done very little running or jumping since college, the contractions have not been strong; many of the calf muscle cells have not been required to do much work, and many have hardly been used at all (more intense exercise recruits a higher proportion of the cells). Bill has walked around the office, shopping centers, airports, his neighborhood, his yard, and his home at low speeds— nothing arduous. On this fateful morning, the calf cells don't know that Bill is standing on the front porch wearing his new running shoes. If the cells could think, they might assume that Bill was standing in the kitchen deciding what to eat for breakfast.

All of a sudden, Bill starts jogging. The calf cells get a command from the motor area of the brain to contract, but this time it's CONTRACT! relax CONTRACT! relax CONTRACT! relax CONTRACT! The cells have no choice but to obey, as that is a parameter that is built in. However, the interactions the entities have adapted to over the years concerning glucose processing, pain transmission, mitochondrial operations, lactic acid disposal, oxygen uptake, and so on, are not up to the task at hand. CONTRACT! relax CONTRACT!—the entities cannot dispose of the rapidly building lactic acid—relax CONTRACT! relax CONTRACT!—oxygen uptake cannot keep up with expenditures—relax CONTRACT! relax CONTRACT! relax C-NT-ACT!—the calf entities are suddenly awash in hormones secreted by the adrenal gland entities as the hypothalamus entities do what they can to keep up the muscle effort—rreellaaxx C-N—C-!—whole groups of entities can no longer contract—rrrllxxxx—_ _ _ _ R _ C!!!—. Finally, over 70% of the calf entities are not able to respond to contraction orders, and a massive cramp locks them all in a state of CC!!CO!!!NN!!T!!RA!!!C!TI!!!O!N!!! Defeated by the failure of billions of his out-of-shape calf entities, Bill stops and limps home, cursing his doctor under his breath and hoping that no neighbors see him.

If the calf entities had had a choice, they might have opted to leave the calf muscle when the jogging started, crawl down the leg, and seek out a new career opportunity in the leg of a dedicated couch potato who ignored the physician's orders. The parameters of cell design, the structure in which they operate, do not allow that. Some of the entities may have wanted to kill themselves after half a block of jogging, but there are very strict rules built into the genome about when a cell can end its life. Perhaps some of the entities with connections in the brain might have preferred to leave the calf and migrate up to the cortex for a job in corporate. After all, the brain entities don't move; all they do is process data from the rest of the organization—sounds a lot like corporate to me. However, cells can't go where they want; they must stay and work it out.

So, pushed out of equilibrium and thrown into a state of chaos by Bill's jogging, the calf entities have no other choice but to begin to interact in different ways if they are to deal with the feedback the system is giving them, as the jogging causes all sorts of problems. Each of the entities has no broader knowledge of the challenge than what it experiences from interactions with nearby entities; none of them understand what's happening except that they are suffering (well, they don't actually understand anything at all, but some degree of anthropomorphism is necessary for the story). Yet, as Bill continues to jog several times a week for the next few months, something almost magical happens. In a matter of a few weeks, Bill's entities begin to enter a state of reintegration. All of a sudden, they do their job as Bill jogs a mile or two with only mild discomfort.

In no time, the entities are able to handle the demands more effectively. Bound by the specific design principles of each type of cell, they influence one another in countless new ways. There will be mistakes, such as numerous sore muscles, perhaps shin splints, and a few calf cramps at night. But all of Bill's entities, from calf to lung to heart to back muscle entities, will become more efficient because they are required to work it out among themselves at the entity level. Three months after Bill started jogging, his system has entered a new stage of equilibrium: He can cruise along for several miles without a care—all made possible by forcing 10 trillion entities to work it out among themselves. This is a classic example of successful system adaptation to change.

Bill's system would have remained in equilibrium indefinitely if nothing had changed. But one day, Bill meets Jim on a run and Jim convinces Bill to join him in training for a marathon that is taking place in four months. To have any chance of completing the race, Bill will have to increase his mileage. Let's say that, prior to meeting, Bill and Jim each had been training about three miles a day for three to four days a week. They agree to start training together. Bill and Jim, feeling macho like many novice runners, convince each other that it would be fun to go on a 10-mile run to kick off their training regimen. This will almost certainly push Bill's and Jim's entities from equilibrium into chaos; it is simply asking too much of as-yet-undertrained-for-a-marathon entities. If Bill and Jim attempt to maintain their daily mileage, at 6–10 miles per workout (about 40 miles per week), their entities are likely to remain in chaos for several months, and they may be at risk for some severe setbacks. While they will eventually move into reintegration and then into a new state of equilibrium, there will be much pain and suffering.

It is well known in running circles that it is dangerous and painful to dramatically increase mileage in a short time period; chaos hurts in this case because pain is the system's feedback to entities that things are not working. Runners (and many other types of athletes) long ago discovered a key element of safely pushing the envelope toward improved system performance. This element, called *persistent disequilibrium*, is a critical tool for improving any system's performance without dangerously hurting it. It is illustrated in Figure 1.2.

The key element in persistent disequilibrium is pushing a stable system just a bit toward the edge of chaos, just a bit away from comfortable equilibrium. This forces the system to change and adapt without invalidating the

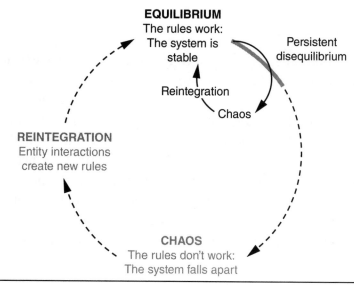

Figure 1.2 The mechanism of persistent disequilibrium.

entire set of rules that have been working. Persistent disequilibrium stresses the system a bit but does not risk casting all of the entities into chaos with the attendant risk of system chaos or failure. This is what happens when weight lifters add a few pounds to a workout or when runners like Jim and Bill add a mile to their daily workout once or twice a week for a couple of weeks and then add another mile a couple of times a week for the next two weeks. Eventually, they are running an extra 10 miles per week without casting their entities into chaos. Various portions of their system may be a little sore and tired from time to time, but there is little risk of systemwide failure.

This same persistent disequilibrium must be constantly applied to any system that strives for improvement. It is the central improvement mechanism for evolution. Aside from dramatic changes mandated by radical changes in the environment (e.g., whatever killed off the dinosaurs), life-forms evolve by generating a myriad of tiny, tiny modifications on a continual basis. Most come to nothing. However, every now and then, one of the random modifications makes it easier for the system (organism) to succeed in its present environment, even if there are not any dramatic challenges to its survival.

Human organizations have a profound advantage over inanimate and cellular-based systems. It is possible for the entities (people) in a human organization to understand the principles of system change and persistent disequilibrium. Unlike human calf cells, people in an organization can understand what is happening if they are informed and involved. As is discussed in later chapters, this can be used to accelerate and improve changes. When people are the entities, their effectiveness in adapting to change and producing more change can be increased if a few guidelines are followed:

1. The people must be allowed to experiment within acceptable guidelines, to try new things, and to test the limits to see what works. In a non-self-aware system such as most of the human body, the system gets feedback only when it begins to fail. In a self-aware system, the individual entities can evaluate whether a change might work for their part of the entire system. While they might be incorrect, given their limited perspective of the entire system, with appropriate information and feedback from management they will find many beneficial improvements. Of course, as we will see in later chapters, human assumptions and expectations can also be a liability in motivating people to change.

2. The people must be given detailed information about the results of their efforts and how their processes were improved or compromised by what they did. This is not usually the case in most human organizations. Self-aware entities cannot experiment effectively if they do not know the desired results in all of their details.

3. Mistakes must be viewed as precious learning moments. If we are encouraging entities to try new things within a framework of guidelines that everyone uses and understands, there can be no "bad" mistakes. Therefore, mistakes must be considered as valuable learning experiences to be discussed and dissected in order to discover why a good idea with good motivations did not work.

4. Energy must be devoted to continually encouraging the entities to push the envelope and ensure that established rituals and habits do not automatically censure or kill any new ideas. There must be a fine balance between maintaining persistent disequilibrium, challenging established practices, and improving the mechanisms that are set up to foster the generation of new ideas.

As you read the following chapters, consider how the operation of persistent disequilibrium would be engaged by the use of the tool or method. Think of the organization as a mass of entities that must be shepherded to come up with ways of working within the guidelines presented in the various chapters.

2

The Topography of
World-Class Methods

Before we go any further, it's important to establish how the concepts and methods of kaizen, waste, waste reduction, lean manufacturing, the Toyota Production System (TPS), continuous improvement, Office Kaizen, Six Sigma, value stream mapping (VSMapping), and various other tools and approaches relate to one another. It's not important for you to understand these relationships from the perspective of how (or if) to apply various tools to Office Kaizen, because this book will provide you with that guidance. It's important because we have to have a common foundation for our discussions. To some, Six Sigma includes almost all of these methods and approaches. They hold this view because they don't understand the concepts. Others may believe it because their organization's Six Sigma initiatives have absorbed some or all of these approaches. In the first case, they need to learn more. In the second case, they may be exactly right.

The same may be true of VSMapping. As this book discusses in Chapters 8–10, VSMapping is a very specific process charting, analysis, and improvement planning tool. The construction of a value stream map (VSM) has become an expected first step in many improvement efforts. Because many organizations start their improvement efforts with a VSM, any subsequent process activities are often considered to be part of the VSMapping approach. While this would seem wrong to someone without inside knowledge of these organizations' activities, if it works for them, fine. Since each reader has a different history with improvement tools and world-class methods, it's important to establish what we mean when we refer to one of these tools, methods, or philosophies. Not only will this make our discussions more cogent, it will assist you in dissecting what others mean when they speak of specific approaches or agglomerations of them.

You will shortly discover that the more you know, the harder it is to answer a simple question such as, "What is kaizen?" The correct answer depends not only on what you know but also on the questioner's breadth of knowledge. Often, the least complicated way to handle such a question is, "How about that ball game last night?"

INNOVATION, CONTINUOUS IMPROVEMENT, AND CHANGING PROCESSES

World-class methods are applied to make processes work better. There are only three ways to try to make a process better. The first is to simply outsource it and hope the supplier does a better job than your organization. That's not kaizen (or anything else), but it can lead to big gains if the supplier is better than its customer at what it does and if there are no other significant considerations such as shipping times, trade secrets, and so on. Buying other companies or product lines does just about the same thing but has many risks.

The second way is to discover a bold and radically new way to do something that provides a dramatic, stepwise improvement in quality, cost, speed, customer satisfaction, market share, and so on. This category of improvement is generally termed an innovation. An *innovation* is an improvement in the basic nature of a process, typically using technology. Examples include a new chemical that cuts the curing time of plastic by 50% and using websites to sign up customers (at least some of them) rather than using human customer service operators. (I'm not claiming humans always give great customer service; I'm just using it as an example. If you don't agree, press four and hold for our next available operator.) Generally speaking, business and society are in love with innovation as a primary mechanism for progress or at least the appearance of it.

It's easy to understand why. Innovation is exciting. A large number of executives and managers enjoy the challenge and thrill of betting the company, the year, or the quarter on innovations. Innovations are risky—at best, only 1 in 10 works and makes money. Thus, pursuing them provides a thrill akin to hunting wild boar with a spear. Those who lead successful innovations are viewed by the business world as bold visionaries. Everyone remembers Edison for the innovation of finding a filament material that made incandescent lightbulbs practical. Nobody remembers the lab assistants who prepared the thousands of experiments to find a suitable filament, or the names of the people who led the production changes that enabled lightbulb factories to be productive enough to make lightbulbs affordable.

But the main reason why leaders love innovation is because it is easy to lead. Innovation requires little cultural change and little change in how leadership runs an organization. Innovation can be put into gear by putting money into research and swinging for the fence. Nothing has to change in a traditionally run organization if a stream of sufficiently significant innovations can be realized. Of course, few organizations can keep it up for more than a few years, or a decade at most, because competitors jump right in and eliminate the advantage that the successful innovation created. More and faster innovations are required to stay ahead. Few traditionally run organizations can maintain a productive, creative environment when they get big and successful and/or their markets mature; it's hard to stay on the edge of persistent disequilibrium when things are working well.

The third and final way to change a process is to come up with a steady stream of small improvements. Any one improvement may not be earth shattering (such as eliminating a signature from a form), but when many of them are put together they can have a significant impact on overall performance. The difficulty with small improvements is that you can't get them on a reliable, ongoing basis unless you have a system in place to generate, support, and sustain the improvements. Since a small improvement usually involves changing a small bit of an employee's task, the employee has to be involved. For the employee to be continually involved, supervision has to provide a supportive environment to keep employees engaged. For this to occur, upper management has to provide the supervisors with the training, support, and resources to create and maintain an environment of engagement. It's a lot of work, but there's no other way—a continuous and sustainable stream of small task improvements requires significant changes at all levels. This is the one type of improvement that a competitor cannot easily replicate.

WASTE

Reduction of waste is the fundamental objective of most continuous improvement, kaizen, and lean methods. Waste is defined in factory environments as any effort that does not change the form or function of a product. This means that if an activity is not doing something to the product that the customer wants or needs, such as bending metal, molding plastic, assembling a circuit board, cooking a car tire, drilling, sanding, painting, and so on, the activity is waste. In nonfactory environments, the products are information and services rather than physical objects. The jargon Japanese expression for waste is *muda*, loosely meaning "junk," as in, "What's all this junk doing here on my desk?" In the last few years, waste has increasingly been referred to as "non-value-adding activity" because it sounds more sophisticated than "waste" in management circles and in financial discussions. They are the same thing.

The definition I prefer is:

Waste is energy and activity for which an all-knowing customer would not be willing to pay because the activity does not significantly improve the probability of getting a more reliable, higher-performing product or service over the long term at the best possible price.

This definition of waste focuses on long-term, sustainable gains and eschews short-term gains (e.g., cutting needed training funds to look good for a quarter) that create even more waste in the long term. Companies that compete only on price and/or continuously focus on short-term gains are always in trouble. Even if they survive, they will never be outstanding, and they are only a wink away from falling into chaos with the next environmental challenge.

Taiichi Ohno, the primary engineer of the TPS, defined seven types of waste for a factory environment. These are shown in Figure 2.1.

Ohno's wastes apply to offices as well as factories, but the names don't readily stimulate thinking about many of the complexities that can be hidden in office processes. To deal with this issue, *OK1* presented the "Office Kaizen Wastes," which are summarized in Figure 2.2. These 26 wastes focus specific attention on sources that often compromise office and administrative functions. The Office Kaizen wastes include office analogs of Ohno's seven wastes; these are shaded in the figure.

Category of waste	Name of waste	Definition
People	Motion	Reaching or walking
	Waiting	Of people or parts (not machines)
	Processing	Extra activity necessitated because a known best way of doing the work is not being used
Quantity (material)	Making too much	Work-in-process, or WIP. Resources invested in output that has been created between processes but is not being used immediately
	Moving things	Any transport of materials or product, such as forklifts, conveyors, rolling hampers, and so on
	Inventory	Raw materials and finished goods that are not being used
Quality	Errors	Defects

Figure 2.1 Taiichi Ohno's original wastes.

Category of waste	Name of waste	Definition
People	Goal alignment	Energy lost by different people/areas working at cross-purposes
	Assignment	Energy used to complete an unnecessary task
	Waiting	Of people or parts (not machines)
	Motion	Reaching or walking (searching, phoning, e-mailing, texting)
	Processing	Extra activity necessitated because a known best way of doing the work is not being used
Process	Control	Energy used for supervision or monitoring that does not produce sustainable, long-term improvements in overall performance
	Variability	Resources expended to compensate for and/or correct outcomes that deviate from expected or typical outcomes
	Tampering	Energy lost in compensating for arbitrary changes made to a process without proper study
	Strategic	Energy lost in processes that satisfy short-term goals but do not provide value to end-use customers/shareholders
	Reliability	Energy lost in dealing with unpredictable process outcomes
	Standardization	Energy lost because all don't do a job in the best way
	Suboptimization	Energy lost when internal processes and areas compete
	Scheduling	Energy lost in compensating for poorly scheduled activities
	Work-around	Energy lost by using unapproved, informal processes
	Uneven flow	Energy lost in dealing with the consequences of "empty spots" or too much work in a process flow
	Checking	Energy used for inspection (and rework)
	Errors	Incorrect process actions that must be repaired or scrapped
Information	Translation	Energy lost in unnecessary data changes/adjustments
	Missing	Energy lost in compensating for missing information
	Handoff	Energy required to handle information more than once
	Irrelevancy	Energy lost in dealing with unnecessary information
	Inaccuracy	Energy lost in dealing with incorrect information

Figure 2.2   Office Kaizen wastes from *OK1*.

Category of waste	Name of waste	Definition
Asset	Fixed asset	Equipment and buildings that are not maximally used
	Inventory	Energy invested in raw and finishing goods/information that is not being used at the moment
	Work-in-process	Energy lost in producing data or materials in the process stream that cannot be used at the moment
	Moving things	Energy lost in moving data, information, or product

Figure 2.2 Office Kaizen wastes from *OK1*. (Continued)

For example, "work-around" waste is very common. It is most often seen when someone develops or inherits a spreadsheet application that is then used for a task instead of the software that is "supposed to be used." Problems arise when data are downloaded from the company system, "run" in the spreadsheet, and then put back into the company system. Inconsistencies arise because the company system and the spreadsheet usually have different assumptions and calculations. *OK1* presents detailed explanations and examples of these 26 Office Kaizen wastes.

If Ohno's original seven wastes were used as a checklist for locating waste in an office, there's a good chance that many instances of Office Kaizen waste would be overlooked. The office-centric names of the Office Kaizen wastes speed up insights by using language that's specific to many office processes. This doesn't mean that the wastes in Figure 2.2 are etched in concrete or represent the ultimate truth; they are simply one version that helps in conceptualizing and searching for office waste.

THE TOYOTA PRODUCTION SYSTEM

The Toyota Production System (TPS) is a body of tools and approaches that began to evolve in the 1950s under the guidance of Ohno and Kiichiro Toyoda (the company changed the "d" in Toyoda to a "t" after World War II because it felt that the "d" made the name sound "too Japanese"). While the TPS is still evolving today, the framework was well established by the early to mid-1980s. It is a body of tools and approaches designed to attack Ohno's seven wastes. The primary methods of the TPS are shown in Figure 2.3. The shaded cells show the methods that have limited application to offices, in that they are very machine-oriented.

Category of waste	Name of waste	General approach to attack waste	Methods	Definition of method
People	Motion	Workplace management	Standard work	The best way to work that is used as the performance and training standard until a better way is discovered
	Waiting		Workplace organization	Clean, neat, and signed with everything in a labeled place; nothing unneeded left in area
	Processing		Kaizen	Working with everyone to continuously improve processes
Quantity (material)	Making too much	Just-in-time	Leveling	A smooth, easy flow of products from one station to another
			Kanban	A signal that signifies when and how much material can be moved and to where
	Moving things		Single minute exchange of die	Practices and procedures that eliminate waste from machine changeovers and setups
	Inventory		Preventive maintenance	Practices and procedures that ensure that equipment is kept in good condition so that running time is maximized
Quality	Error	Prevent errors	Jidoka	A set of best practices for providing for machines to self-check themselves as they operate
			Poka-yoke	A set of procedures to reduce the probability of errors by people and equipment

Figure 2.3   The principal approaches and methods used in the TPS.

For example, *single minute exchange of die* (SMED) is a set of best practices that eliminates waiting, motion, moving things, and processing waste (mainly) when it is necessary to change a die, mold, or drill bit on a machine. The basic waste-elimination strategy is the same as that applied in all kaizen activities, but the methods are very machine-oriented (e.g., "Reduce or limit the number of screw attachments for fixtures, jigs, and tooling," "Use multiple spindles on CNC machines"). It could be argued that preventive maintenance (PM) applies to offices if computers are considered the machines. PM techniques should be applied at server farms and on large mainframes, but they don't readily or economically apply to standard office desktops.

The methods shown in Figure 2.3, when applied not only as tools but as a philosophy to every department and process, are the TPS. This "complete coverage" emphasis is critical to understanding why the TPS works so well for Toyota. For example, purchasing personnel do not arrange for delivery of more than what the plants can use in a few hours in order to save money on large orders. They may pay a little more per piece when the materials arrive in smaller, more frequent lots, but they save big because the factory can be smaller (no space required to store extra inventory, plus less inventory control effort, less walking, and less transport needed), they handle the materials only once (less processing waste), and they don't risk having a large amount of bad material on hand if a defect is discovered. This sort of focus on waste reduction permeates the entire organization as an operating philosophy.

Pull versus Push

A key element in the TPS relates to push versus pull. This concept is important for understanding how VSMapping, discussed in Chapters 8–10, identifies waste in processes. Traditional business approaches rely heavily upon push for moving material to and through a process. Figure 2.4 illustrates the mechanisms of pull and push applied to a claims processing department in an insurance company. The process could just as well be filling prescriptions in

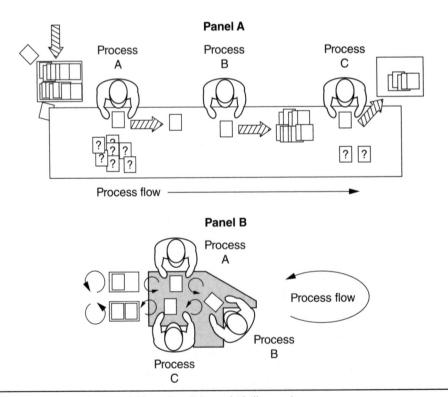

Figure 2.4   A push (panel A) and pull (panel B) illustration.

a hospital pharmacy or completing loan paperwork in a bank. The example shows the workers in close proximity, but they could just as well be in different parts of town or hundreds of miles apart.

Panel A presents a representative push situation. Striped arrows denote "push" in a VSM, so we might as well use them here; that is, each piece of paperwork is pushed to the next process without any input from the process or the worker who receives it. The items being pushed could be data files, but it is easier to display how it works with paper. As you can see, a large cart of folders has been pushed to the worker doing process A. The worker works on one at a time and then pushes the completed work to the worker at process B. When worker B finishes the work, it is pushed to the worker at process C. Worker C pushes completed work to the outgoing cart.

Several elements of a typical push system are evident in panel A. The first is the large amount of inventory. Everyone wants to look good in a traditional work setting by moving the work to the next station as quickly as possible, even if the next process cannot use it. Worse, traditional managers view the inventory as security, as in, "We've got plenty to ship!" Of course, the amount of inventory in the system has no relationship to what can be shipped—that is determined only by the speed (and quality) of the final process. The question marks on some of the folders denote a problem that cannot be solved right at the moment by a worker, so it is put aside. Since there are so many other folders to work on, the occasional problem folder is deliberately ignored. In fact, should a worker call a problem to a supervisor's attention, a typical response is, "I'll get to it later, just keep working." The result is that the problem never gets solved or the employee comes up with a "fix" in order to get the work off his or her desk. A further problem is shown by the folders on the floor near process A; when there is a lot of inventory in a process, it is easy for things to be damaged or lost.

A more subtle but very significant issue with push systems is also demonstrated in panel A. Note that worker C has a great deal of inventory in front of her. Is this because worker C is slow, because worker B is being carelessly fast or is very good, or is it some combination of these factors? Further, worker A has many problem folders in front of him, while B has none and C has only two. Is this because worker A is unskilled, nitpicky, or very perceptive about minor problems present in his task, or is it because workers B and C are passing along problems? These questions cannot be answered by simply looking at the illustration and/or counting inventory in a push situation.

Contrast the push approach with the pull philosophy in action in panel B. The curved arrows denote pull; that is, each worker calls for work to be passed to him or her by some signal. The incoming paperwork cart next to worker A holds two folders. When the cart is empty, that is a signal (called a *kanban*, the Japanese word for "store sign") to the upstream process that another two folders should be delivered. They are delivered only when the pull signal, the empty cart, is present. Worker A pulls his work from the cart when he is ready for it. That pull can be done only if worker A has no work in front of him (that is the pull kanban). Worker B works on one at a time and can pull in another piece (from worker A) only when she has none in front of her (her pull kanban). The same goes for worker C; worker C cannot pull from worker B unless she has no work in front of her. A folder cannot be pulled from worker C unless there is an empty spot on the cart. As panel B shows, the cart is full. This means that until the completed two folders after worker C are picked up and an empty cart is delivered, worker C cannot do anything with her completed work. This will stop workers B and A from doing more work after they complete the work in front of them.

The implications of this are that, in order for a pull system to work, each worker has to be well trained and the work must be balanced so that each worker (or process) can complete his or her work when the next process downstream is ready to pull it. This requires a lot of training and work analysis. A further benefit of the pull system is that its footprint (space taken up) is smaller, the amount of inventory in the system is greatly reduced, and the throughput time is much, much less. If each task in the panel B example takes one minute and we assume "first in, first out" (FIFO), it will take seven minutes for a new piece of work to go from the delivery cart to a pickup cart that is ready to be shipped. In the panel A example, it will take 57 minutes (given the number of folders displayed) for a new piece of work to move through the three processes—eight times longer.

A further benefit of the pull approach, if the workers are colocated, is that any errors can be dealt with quickly by the group if they are shown what to look for when they get work from the previous worker. If there is an error, it is passed right back to the previous worker to be repaired. This is called *successive checks* if the errors of interest are selected ahead of time, focused on for a few days, and then corrected. Then, if necessary, new errors are selected for attention. Successive checks enable a work group to correct its errors before any more are made. In addition, each person learns a little about the others' jobs. This facilitates further process improvements.

LEAN MANUFACTURING

Lean manufacturing is synonymous with the TPS, and it is also the term Womack, Roos, and Jones applied to the TPS in their 1990 book, *The Machine That Changed the World*. Most companies' lean systems are basically the TPS with all or some Japanese terms changed. Other names for lean manufacturing/TPS are flexible manufacturing, cellular or synchronous manufacturing, pull or flow manufacturing, and one-by-one manufacturing. All of these terms focus on the capability of a system with fast changeovers, small lots, and balanced work (everything moves between stations and workers at about the same pace) to rapidly produce different products on one or a small number of production lines with little inventory and few delays.

VALUE STREAM MAPPING

Value stream mapping (VSMapping) is a formalized and highly structured flowcharting approach that focuses on the time taken to move a product or service through the value chain. Properly done, VSMapping provides a clear view of how well a process can produce needed output in a smooth, even fashion. In recent years, VSMapping has become an almost mandatory initial step in analyzing a process prior to implementing improvements. It is popular partly because it works well. However, it has also become something of a fad. Many organizations "do" VSMapping because they are afraid of not having done it if someone higher up the management ladder asks. VSMapping is only an analysis tool. No matter what you find on one of them, the continuous improvements must still be formulated, implemented, and sustained. Chapters 8–10 explore VSMapping in detail.

SIX SIGMA

Six Sigma was developed as an improvement approach at Motorola in the late 1970s to deal with nagging quality problems. Sigma is the lowercase Greek letter for the letter *s* and is written as "σ." Statisticians use it as a symbol for a standard deviation. As σ gets larger, it signals greater variability in a distribution and lowers the probability (compared to a smaller σ) of guessing where the next score added to the distribution will fall. In almost all facets of business and life, you want σ to be small, which means that all the scores in the distribution are closer to the average of the distribution and thus easier to predict. For example, a critical characteristic in a pair of jeans is the waist measurement. If a customer buys a pair of jeans with a waist size of 34 inches, it is important to customer satisfaction to ensure that all of the jeans with a 34-inch waist label have a waste circumference very close to 34 inches. If not, many customers will be unhappy.

Let's say that a customer who buys a pair of jeans with a 34-inch waist label notices a variation of more than ½ inch each way from 34 inches.

This sets the specification limits at 33½ and 34½ inches. Although we would like to have all of the 34-inch-waist jeans be exactly 34 inches, this is almost impossible. Because of normal variation, every pair of jeans will vary slightly from 34 inches. Therefore, we will (in this example) settle for having actual waste measurements between 33½ and 34½ inches. For this to be true for 99.9% of jeans (meaning that only one pair in 1000 has a waist measurement outside the specification limits and thus is likely to be noticed as "bad" by a typical customer), the standard deviation for this distribution of jeans would be about 0.15 inches. This means that the average distance between any one waist size in the production run and the mean of 34 inches is 0.15 inches.

Motorola arbitrarily set the model for outstanding quality at six sigma (6σ) because it was a quality level almost unattainable at the time and thereby stood as a worthy performance goal for a world-class organization. Another reason is that the term *six sigma*, with its alliteration, sounds better than five sigma or seven sigma. A six sigma process has a distance of six sigmas between the mean of the process and the closest specification limit. This means that there is very little chance that normal processes will produce a product that falls outside the specification limits. In terms of the jeans with the 34-inch waist, a production process that produced a six sigma waist measurement output distribution would result in no more than about one pair of 34-inch-waist jeans in a million with a waist circumference outside the specification limit for that size. The σ for this level of quality would be 0.08 inches.

As first developed at Motorola, Six Sigma was heavy on process measurement, analysis, and improvement using statistical process control (SPC) methods, design of experiments, and general problem-solving tools to reduce variability in cell phone components, among other things. The problem-solving tools use many of the kaizen tools reviewed in Chapter 7. Six Sigma uses statistical thinking and techniques to attack specific problems created by unknown causes of variation. DMAIC (define, measure, analyze, improve, control) is one of the methods for organizing thoughts about process improvement. Six Sigma thinking posits that a process is impacted by known and unknown causes of variance. In the jeans example, known causes of variance would include the tension on cutting and sewing machines, sharpness of cutters, thickness of material, and so on. If all the known causes are controlled, waist measurements will be less variable, unless unknown causes of variation arise. Unknown causes of variance are those that occur without warning. In the jeans example, this would include such things as unexpected variability in the thickness of the material or a poorly trained operator running a machine.

Lean and kaizen methods assume that a significant problem in any process is waste, because waste is everywhere. These methods attack waste with comparatively little in-depth statistical analysis because waste can usually be easily found. The emphasis of Six Sigma is on eliminating a problem through rigorous process definition, metric development and measurement, process capability studies, and root cause analysis, followed by the installation of process improvements. The goal is to achieve (or begin to achieve) dramatic process improvements with an eventual six sigma (or better) objective.

Six Sigma Black Belts (SSBBs) are the general practitioners of Six Sigma. They are trained in both the theory and practice of using statistical thinking and problem-solving methods to fix a process or problem. Six Sigma training typically involves two to four weeks of classroom training separated by a number of weeks in the field during which the trainee works on a Six Sigma project in the actual work environment. If the teacher reviews the project as successful, the student is awarded a black belt. Most black belts are awarded by organizations that have developed their own internal programs, so there is a broad range of black belt skills and experience, depending on the rigor of the training.

Six Sigma Master Black Belts (SSMBBs) are trained in both typical black belt skills and the "soft" people and project management challenges of organizing and running complex, cross-functional problem-solving and/or improvement projects. SSMBBs typically lead improvement projects in a business area or unit. They work with business unit or site champions (executive-level sponsors) to select and direct projects in a portion of the organization. In a very large organization (with many locations), there is often a full-time SSMBB at headquarters who helps design large projects and provides technical assistance to SSBBs at various locations as required. In smaller organizations, an executive with either an SSBB or an SSMBB usually provides such assistance on a part-time basis. Many organizations also have Green Belts and Yellow Belts. Yellow Belts receive a day or two of training in problem-solving methods such as cause-and-effect (C&E) diagrams, Pareto charts, and so on. Green Belt training can last anywhere from a week to several weeks and might include SPC charting and capability studies, as well as problem-solving methods.

Typically, a Six Sigma project designed and directed by an SSMBB consists of several individual problem-solving and process control endeavors organized as one effort (e.g., to fix the quality problem in the paint department). The desired outcome may be lowered inventory, an in-control (statistically speaking) process, faster cycle times, lower costs, more machine uptime, and so on (or all of the above).

As you can imagine, once organizations started using lean and Six Sigma methods, a great deal of cross-pollination occurred. As a result, few Six Sigma programs do not have some lean DNA in them, and few lean programs have not absorbed some Six Sigma DNA. The challenge is that if all you know is the name of an organization's initiative, you don't know what tools and methods are actually being used.

3

The Challenge of Change One: Human Behavior as It Operates at Work

Effective leadership requires willing followers. Fear of the boss and the lure of paychecks can create acquiescence to management wishes, but they cannot create the enthusiasm, creativity, and participation that are the hallmarks of an outstanding organization. To get everything that employees can give, leaders must format their leadership approach and actions in a manner that is attractive and meaningful to employees' basic capabilities and needs as human beings. It is critical that leaders have a good understanding of the basic nature of human behavior. They must know what people need, how they are inclined to respond, and how they process information. In this chapter, we will review some of the basics of human behavior that, if properly addressed, can greatly increase the effectiveness of leadership.

THE SEVEN HUMAN NEEDS

Human beings have inborn needs that motivate, channel, and modify behavior. These needs, as they are pursued by individuals and groups, have a tremendous impact on how organizations and human society as a whole operate. The needs frustrate leadership that tries to ignore or sidestep them, and they support leadership that provides employees with avenues to satisfy them. There are many models and theories that describe human needs. I prefer a slight modification of control theory. The original control theory posits that people are always seeking, usually without being aware of it, to satisfy five basic needs. The seven needs of my slight modification of control theory are shown in Figure 3.1.

It is not important for our purposes whether these seven needs are the "real" human needs that future research may verify. You might be inclined to identify 10 needs or 3 needs if you thought about it for a while. The seven

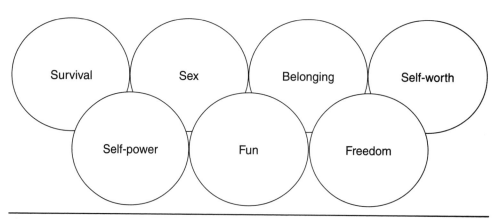

Figure 3.1 The seven inborn human needs.

needs are sufficient to demonstrate the power of innate needs and the ways in which they influence much of what we all do. As we discuss these needs, keep in mind that there is a range of each need's strength across people. While all humans appear to have all seven needs to some degree, some people are driven much more or much less than others by each of the various needs. Unlike Maslow's Hierarchy of Needs, which proposes sequential need hurdles, control theory stipulates that all seven of the needs presented in Figure 3.1 be simultaneously pursued.

Survival

Few people, except perhaps a small number who are very physically and/ or mentally ill, wish to die right now. It's easy to understand why. Everyone alive today is a genetic descendant of thousands of generations of prehuman and human survivors, those who struggled against all odds to raise offspring without medicine, science, reliable food and water supplies, central heating, prenatal care, refrigeration, transportation, and even without cable TV, personal music players, and cell phones. At the same time, they faced drought, disease, wild animals, floods, famines, prairie and forest fires, ice ages, short life spans, and infant mortality rates in the 90% range. As humans developed over the last few hundred thousand years, those who were too slow, stupid, weak, prone to illness, or not willing to keep struggling did not survive. Only those who strove against all odds (and were lucky) survived and produced offspring. Given this history, how can any manager say that his or her employees can't handle the work or aren't tough enough? Given the right leadership, any group of human beings can do almost anything because we are all the direct descendants of tough-as-nails survivors.

Sex

The pursuit of sex is hardwired into human beings by natural selection. In a primitive environment with high infant mortality rates, the bulk of resources, after ensuring basic survival, must be devoted to reproduction and child rearing. If a group of protohumans or humans (or squirrels or worms) did not have birthrates that exceeded their death rates, they did not pass their genes into the future. Every person alive today is a direct descendant of those who focused extensively on sex. This is why there are more than 6 billion people on earth now, with an estimated total of 12 billion to 20 billion by 2150. While almost everyone agrees in general that we have a population problem now, or will have one soon, the inborn urge to have sex and thus children is difficult to resist on an individual level—it is part of what we are.

Belonging

Human beings are born to work together and find satisfaction in groups. All people have an inherent need to be with other people. This tendency was wired into us long ago and is just as important as a strong sex drive in helping us survive as a species. Primates, protohumans, and humans who tried to make it alone or in very small groups did not survive. Those who formed groups had much better odds of surviving long enough to raise their offspring. The evidence of humans' need for contact with others is plentiful. When humans are deprived of human contact for long periods, they frequently become mentally ill and often psychotic (as prisons such as Pelican Bay in California demonstrate). People who live alone tend to die earlier, get ill more often, and take longer to recover. Babies who are held more gain weight faster and recover from illness and premature birth sooner than babies who are held less. People who have large, close, extended families during childhood tend to deal better with stress in adult life than those from smaller families with few nearby relatives. It's clear: Humans need to be around other people. They want to belong to a group, and they suffer when they do not. Think of what this means for leaders: Employees are seeking group membership. They need it. This means they must be allowed to function in effective teams and groups that get important work done. If not, they will find other groups that will accept them and provide their group belongingness fix. At work, these other groups can range from unions to groups of complainers, troublemakers, or those who simply go through the motions of work. Most of these alternative groups will generally not fully share management's goals. Employees need to belong. Good leaders provide them with opportunities for belonging to groups that assist the organization in meeting its objectives.

Self-Worth

Human beings crave feelings of self-worth; we all need to believe that we are valued for our unique qualities by those around us, particularly those we admire and/or those with whom we share similar values and attitudes. This provides validation of our selves as individuals. Without such validation, we suffer. People who lack close social contacts tend to be depressed more often and tend to have more difficulties with careers and forming new relationships compared with those with solid social contacts. Recent research discovered that a primary pain-processing center, the anterior cingulate cortex, is activated just as much from a social snub as it is from overt physical pain; the need for social acceptance is hardwired into us. The need for self-worth is active in people every day, especially at work. Our modern lifestyle of career chasing and job hopping has taken away traditional opportunities for self-worth provided by family relations living nearby and stable communities where people live for tens of years and provide social support for one another. Without realizing it and without seeking it, organizations have become the major default source for social and personal self-worth for many people. Ironically, this has occurred just as employees are increasingly being shown that they are disposable. This circumstance can greatly benefit both businesses and employees if work and organizations are modified to provide more opportunities for self-worth and group belongingness.

Self-Power

Human beings need to feel as though they have some control over their immediate surroundings; they need to believe they have self-power to look out for themselves. A well-known and often repeated experiment demonstrates the impact of merely the perception of self-power. A group of volunteer male subjects were told that they were participants in sensory perception research. Each of the subjects had one of his fingers placed in a sleeve that would deliver an electric shock sent from a computer. The subject was told that there were 10 levels of shock, ranging from 1, the least powerful, to 10, the most severe. The subject was then given one shock at each level from 1 to 10 as the experimenter called out the shock level. Level 1 was almost imperceptible, while level 10 was extremely painful. The subject was then told that he would be given a shock every few seconds and that he should try to guess the shock intensity and call out the appropriate number. The subject was then shown a button that was near his other hand. He was told that the more he pressed the button, the more he would reduce the intensity of the shocks. After receiving the 8th-, 9th-, and 10th-level shocks, subjects were very motivated to rapidly press the button.

A second group of subjects was taken through the same procedure with the same exact sequence of shocks, except that the function of the button was explained differently. The second group was told that the more they pressed the button, the more money they would receive. The potential money that could be earned was meaningful to the subjects. Thus, both groups were motivated to rapidly press the button. The secret of the experiment was that neither button was connected to anything; they were fakes. The results demonstrated that the subjects who thought they could reduce the shock levels by pressing the button reported shock levels that were one to three levels lower than the actual shocks. Just thinking that they could reduce the shocks made the subjects perceive the shocks as less painful. The subjects pressing the button for money reported the shocks as accurately as the subjects who were merely estimating the shock levels without any button to press.

This experiment, replicated many times over the years, demonstrates that if people believe they have some control over their situation, some self-power, they will find a situation less oppressive. The remarkable finding is that the amount of control does not have to be extensive. While it would be foolish for a leader to pretend to provide an opportunity for a self-worth need satisfaction that is empty, it is not necessary to let employees run rampant in order to meet their needs for self-power. They understand the realities of work and the constraints that exist. A wise leader finds as many situations as possible within these constraints to allow employees to satisfy their needs for feeling that they can make a difference. The structural configurations described in Chapter 6 create many of these situations.

Fun

Some theorists believe that humans are the only species that plays, but these people must have never owned a dog or cat or watched monkeys at a zoo. It is believed that people need to play in order to defuse tension, deal with a frustrating situation (as when satire is used to lambaste politicians and bosses), and increase bonds among a group that feels it is undervalued (as when a group of workers engages in a game of "ain't it terrible" as they complain about their organization and how they perceive their group's place in it). If people don't feel as though they can play around a bit at work, it is an indication that their frustration and anger are dangerously high. It is also an indication of an oppressive organization. The bosses may be keeping things under control but at a high cost in loyalty, enthusiasm, and commitment to getting things done. Fear can generate acquiescence, but it cannot create a highly productive work environment. As might be expected in our 24/7 world, fun is the least studied of the seven needs. Those organizations that bring in comedians for a few hours of entertainment under the guise of making work "fun" are missing the point; workers must find fun in one another, in their work, and in the organization.

Freedom

The need to have a choice in various situations is critical to human beings, if for no other reason than it allows us to attempt to manipulate a situation to our advantage. We have to move around in the world and make choices in order to eat, drink, procreate, find a job, and get ahead. The need for self-power provides the energy for us to make changes, but it might not be enough to drive us to find situations in which we can make a choice. The satisfaction of the need for freedom enables all the others. It is critical for leaders to provide employees with the maximum possible freedom that's appropriate in every situation. This enables employees to get the most of everything for themselves while providing management with what it wants. The structural configurations described in Chapter 6 create situations in which employees can enjoy appropriate levels of freedom in their day-to-day work.

So what do needs tell us? They tell us that employees are using their work life (and their home life—it's all the same as far as need satisfaction is concerned) to satisfy powerful compulsions that cannot be denied. This creates tremendous energy that has to go somewhere, much like a river raging through a canyon. A leader has only two choices: (1) direct this energy and benefit both the organization and the employee, or (2) let nature take its course and get only what the averaged need satisfaction of all employees produces.

DIFFERENT WAYS OF VIEWING THE WORLD

Need satisfaction doesn't explain everything about behavior. Although there is an infinite number of different combinations of need levels, many other characteristics influence how individuals behave. One of the most interesting influences on behavior is variously labeled personality, emotional, cognitive, or thinking type. There are many of these formulations. Each hypothesizes that there are a number of distinct ways in which people view the world and make decisions. Most of the approaches assume that a person's basic style is operating by their late teens due to genetic precursors, environmental influences, or both. We take a very quick look at two of these formulations, not to argue that either is the "truth" but to demonstrate the further challenges that face leaders when they attempt to transmit a clear message to a body of employees.

Enneagram theory argues that there are nine basic emotional ways of dealing with the world. They are numbered one to nine (the numbers are labels with no good or bad evaluation intended). Three of the nine basic types are summarized in the following list:

2. *Helper:* Helpers are emotionally expressive and focused on relationships in order to satisfy their primary drive: Live to give and receive love. They bring value to organizations by making everyone feel special, valued, and important. Less well-adjusted helpers can be manipulative with their caring, often working to make themselves more important to the organization by giving help with strings attached.

3. *Motivator:* Motivators are competitive and want to be admired. They place great value on winning and looking good while doing it. To the outside world, motivators seem to be confident as they further their careers. However, on the inside, motivators are often insecure and place great value on what others think of them. They can be excellent salespeople because, being so dependent on others' acceptance, they become expert at reading subtle cues of approval that they quickly cultivate.

8. *Confronter:* Confronters are the tough type; they are assertive and can be aggressive. Their source of energy is anger. They say what they think and are driven to make tough decisions. They are not bothered by breaking their own rules. They need a great deal of autonomy and can be defiant when it is not given. Confronters are adept in manipulating situations for their own advantage. They do not care if others don't like them, as long as they are respected.

Perhaps the most popular of the "type" perspectives over the last 40 years is the Myers-Briggs Temperament Typology. It hypothesizes four basic dimensions, each a continuum whose ends are denoted by letters: (1) E–I (extroverted–introverted), (2) S–N (sensing–intuitive), (3) T–F (thinking–feeling), and (4) J–P (judging–perceiving). A letter is assigned for the end of the continuum that a person is closest to. These four resulting letters combine to create 16 basic cognitive styles and a number of others when the score on a continuum is in the middle (denoted by an "X"). Short descriptions of a few of these 16 types follow:

ESTJ: Pillars of strength who know their community. Practical realists who like to organize and run activities and do it well. They are comfortable with passing judgment. This is the type that is thought of by Myers-Briggs devotees as describing most human social, business, and educational institutions.

ESFP: Fun-to-be-with performers who are outgoing, friendly, and fond of a good time. They are the most generous of all types. They can be impulsive and easily seduced. They love to work with people and are good in crises.

INTJ: Original minds with great drive for their own interests. They are the most confident of all types. They have "self-power" awareness. They can be stubborn, skeptical, critical, and independent, and they often make "stands" for minor details.

INTP: Quiet, reserved, and precise in language and thought. They are excellent teachers. They can appear impersonal and are impatient with small talk. They prize intelligence but can become intellectual "snobs" because of their own mastery.

ENTP: Alert, sensitive to possibilities, good at many things. Outspoken, love new, challenging assignments but are easily bored by routine. Great debaters, often argue both sides of an issue. Little respect for tradition.

ISTJ: Serious, practical, orderly, logical, matter-of-fact, and dependable. Steadfast guardians of society, they are implacable in following through despite protests, distractions, and problems.

ISFP: Natural "fine arts" artists. Quiet, impulsive, modest, dislike conflict, express themselves by action more than words. Enjoy "the moment" and do not care to lead. Loyal followers.

Readers can easily identify people they know (or perhaps themselves) in these very simplistic summaries of a few of the Enneagram and Myers-Briggs types. Several key insights may be gathered from these perspectives. The first is that employees are not a faceless, homogeneous group that attempts to carry out management mandates or even their own agendas in a rational, straightforward manner. Nor are they a group of people who have basically the same view of the world with slightly different "personalities." They are a heterogeneous agglomeration of markedly differing views of the world, seeking to find and reinforce what resonates best with their inherent views. Where one employee listens to an executive's speech and hears specific marching orders to start changing things, another hears just as strongly that things are pretty much okay and everybody should be cautious about change.

These "don't get it" employees (i.e., the ones who don't agree with management's intent) aren't incompetent or psychotic; in addition to the learning they have gained from their varying life experiences, they also view the world and everything that it presents through a different set of filters. This makes it even more urgent that leaders make it demonstrably, visibly, and consistently clear what they want and how they want it. Speaking louder won't do it. Speaking more often isn't enough. Everyone must see and hear direct, personal, face-to-face evidence about what the leaders want. They must see it daily and repeatedly from various sources and in various ways. If they do not get this information, their unique ways of viewing the world will not be sufficiently overwhelmed to force them to accept the reality of what is happening around them and what leadership wants them to do.

4

The Challenge of Change Two: Automatic Processing, Cognitive Maps, Dissonance, and the Primacy of Action

Human beings process and interpret a great deal of information automatically. That is, we assess the world and draw conclusions without conscious awareness; the reason why this is not obvious is because we are not aware that this processing is going on behind the scenes. Take a look at Figure 4.1. Stare at the black square for 30 seconds and then look away at a clear wall or a piece of white paper. You will see a shape like the dark square, only it will be lighter than the background with perhaps shaded edges. Now, tell yourself that the next time you stare at the black square and look away, you will not see the light shape; tell yourself that you forbid it to appear. Look at the black square again for 30 seconds and then look away. The shape is there again! You can't control the afterimage; it's automatically processed by innate visual system mechanisms. This is a very simple example of automatic processing.

Automatic processing occurs at all levels of human perception and cognition. Figure 4.2 presents two examples that demonstrate more complex (employing additional and "higher" brain areas) automatic processing of visual information. Look at the two central lines, A and B, in panel A. Does one look longer than the other? Most people "see" that B is longer. If you measure them, you will see that they are identical in length. Yet, they continue to appear different, even after you have measured them and know they are identical and try to see them that way.

The reason why this illusion persists is rooted in our distant evolutionary history. Creatures that were better at assessing the distance to threats (predators, cliff edges, etc.) and opportunities (food and sexual mates) were more likely to survive than those that were not as good. Rapid, accurate, automatic

Figure 4.1 Black rectangle for afterimage experiment.

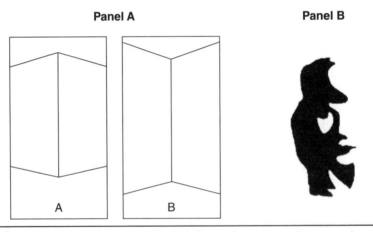

Figure 4.2 Two examples demonstrating higher-order automatic processing of visual information.

depth perception is critical to survival. Those who survive send their genes into the future. Automatic processing is woven into the visual interpretation system of every animal that depends on vision for survival. Evolution favored automatic channels that do this, even if the channels can sometimes be fooled, as in the Figure 4.2 optical illusions.

Panel B presents an example of more complex automatic processing that relies extensively on learned relationships for information. What do you see in panel B? Do you see a woman's face in partial shadow, or do you see a cartoon figure profile of a saxophone player? What makes someone see one but not the other? And even when you think it looks more like one than the other, your automatic processing sometimes flips the image to the other one. Let's take a look at how innate perceptual processes interact with previous experience to influence our perceptions and cognitions.

INPUT, PROCESSING, AND AWARENESS

Before we proceed, we need to make a few distinctions about levels of information processing in the human brain. A great many of our thoughts and actions are not decided consciously after careful consideration but are determined by parts of our brain that operate below our level of awareness. This fact and the processes that drive it have immense and profound implications for everyone who attempts to change human behavior. Figure 4.3 displays a very basic diagram that illustrates how this process, which is occurring in each of us all the time, operates. The sequence begins with stimuli that arrive at our sense organs. Our senses include vision, hearing, taste, smell, touch, and proprioception (awareness of where our body parts are in relation to one another) as well as stimuli from internal physiological states.

   Once the stimuli are received, they are subjected to hardwired physiological processing (such as giving us the impression that one line is longer than the other in panel A of Figure 4.2). At that point, the processed sensory information is "in the system" and is used for decision making, even if we are not consciously aware of it. For example, think right now about how the back of your left calf feels. When you think of it consciously, you can feel it. But when you are not directly attending to it, the sensations from it are processed at a low level and ignored (not passed to higher levels) if nothing is happening to your calf that compels your automatic processor to notify the conscious you.

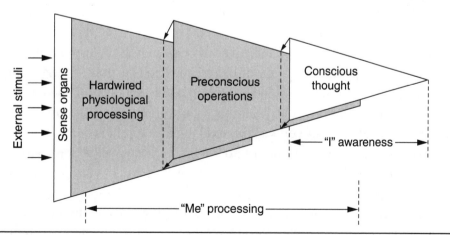

Figure 4.3   Conceptual diagram of the stages of human information processing.

The next step is what I call "preconscious processing" (many refer to this as unconscious processing, but I find that term too Freudian, as well as contaminated by 60 years of pop psychology concepts). *Preconscious processing* is automatic processing of sensory data so that their importance and significance can be assessed. Preconscious processing uses a number of hardwired filters and systems that are programmed to help us respond more quickly and efficiently to the environment. Dozens of these filters and systems are working behind the scenes all the time. For example, when we're not thinking about it or are asleep, our preconscious regulates our breathing.

If we are sleeping and somehow end up with a pillow or a blanket over our face and have difficulty getting enough oxygen, the preconscious rouses us a bit, without waking us, to get us to move. If that doesn't do it, the preconscious wakes us up in order to get the conscious brain to take over. If we are hungry but don't yet realize it, the preconscious will be on the lookout for the presence of food odors. If the preconscious detects strong enough odors, it will bring the information to conscious awareness ("Hey, I smell bread baking! I wonder where it's coming from?"). If we are not hungry, our conscious mind may not be aware of those same faint odors, but there will be measurable brain activity showing that our brain perceives the odors at a preconscious level.

Walking down a flight of stairs in a dark hallway is an excellent example of preconscious processing that employs what we have learned about the world. When we approach a darkened stairway that we have never used before, we are always a little careful with the first step or two, as we don't know exactly how high they are. After the first step, we proceed down the steps with nary a thought as to the location of the next tread, just as we do with familiar stairways at home. This is preconscious processing doing what it was intended to do: taking over a known and predictable task (almost all stairways have step risers of equal heights) so that our conscious selves can do other things that may have more survival value.

Almost all of us have experienced a very complex (and very frightening, in retrospect) example of the ability of the preconscious to control very complex behavior. How often have you been driving a car and all of a sudden realize that you're about to miss your customary, turn-off-there-all-the-time exit? Or you suddenly realize that you've "missed" the last 10 miles because you were daydreaming or listening to the radio? Who was driving the car? Your conscious mind wasn't driving, but somebody was because you didn't have an accident (hopefully).

Once we are familiar with and skilled at driving, we can do it on "preconscious pilot." It's not like the steering wheel was simply being held rigidly in place to drive the car in a straight line; few roads, even in Oklahoma or Texas, are perfectly straight for any distance. This means that our preconscious can steer the car a bit, apply the brakes, and even change lanes while we are thinking of other things. When an impending traffic event is different enough to require conscious attention, as when someone up ahead who has been on preconscious pilot suddenly cuts across four or five lanes to exit, we're roused out of our reverie by our preconscious because the situation is critical enough to demand conscious attention.

An example of preconscious processing that operates over a longer time period involves trying to recollect something that is just out of reach, such as trying to recall an actor's name from a show or movie. Often we can visualize the actor's face and some characteristics of the name, but we can't recall it. Failing to recall it, we stop trying and go about our day. All of a sudden, hours or even days later, while we're listening to the car radio or talking with a colleague or just reading the paper, the name pops into our consciousness. Where did it come from? How could you have "found" it when you weren't consciously looking for it? When you couldn't remember the name, the question was still being processed by preconscious mechanisms that are not well understood. When an answer was found that seemed to be important enough to register with some filter or awareness alarm, the preconscious pushed up the information to the conscious mind.

This conscious mind is the "I" awareness shown in Figure 4.3. "I" awareness is the conscious you; it is the you that has internal dialogs with itself and appears to make conscious decisions about where to eat and what to wear. It is what all of us think of as "me" even though the real "me" is composed of every segment of the processing chain. It is critical for leaders to realize that most of what seems to be their own and their employees' "I" awareness is heavily influenced and shaped second to second by preconscious processing (the "me" minus the "I"). When you are speaking with or interacting with employees, the overwhelming majority of both your and their reactions to what is happening is based on already-learned assumptions and expectations that are controlled by their preconscious, their "me."

A startling piece of research demonstrates the inherent and hidden power of preconscious processing. Researchers had volunteers place their heads in magnetic resonance imaging (MRI) machines. These machines show the exact spots of mental activity in the brain by identifying where blood is flowing. Blood flow increases where energy is being expended by brain cells as they do their work; the more brain cell activity, the more the blood flow and the more the MRI "lights up." With each subject, the researchers took a number of MRI scans. They did scans while the subjects were instructed to think about the word *pen*, when they thought about the word *cup*, when they reached with one hand for an actual cup, when they reached with the other hand for an actual pen, when they got ready to say *cup*, when they got ready to say *pen*, when they got ready to think about each word, when they thought about each word, when they said each word, when they got ready to reach for each item, and so on. The intent was to map the patterns of brain activity for any planned, intended, or performed aspect of thinking about, saying, and/or reaching for either the pen or the cup.

When the actual experiment started, the researchers told each subject, whose head was in the MRI machine, to randomly decide whether to reach for the pen or the cup. Subjects were told that as soon as they decided which one to pick, they should say the word as quickly as possible and simultaneously reach for the item as fast as possible. The resulting MRI pictures demonstrated that the motor area for moving the appropriate hand toward the selected object was activated before any of the higher brain areas involved in thinking about the object, getting ready to think about it, saying the object's name, and getting ready to say the object's name were activated. Think about this for a moment: Before the "I" consciousness of the subjects was aware that they would be reaching for the pen or the cup, a deeper level of processing had already made the selection and had started the process to reach for the appropriate item.

Other researchers have noticed this same type of phenomenon over the last 120 years using less advanced technology (e.g., electroencephalograms [EEGs] in the 1970s and metronomes in the 1890s). In every case, it seemed that before the "I" was aware of a decision, the "me" had already initiated action. The gap between the two is about ¼ to ¾ of a second. A common everyday instance of this can be recognized in patterns of typing errors. It has been known since the early days of the first typewriters that most typos do not result from simply hitting an incorrect key due to a motor skills error (at least after someone has learned to type at a basic level). The "me" of most people is typing ahead of their "I" as the "me" automatically predicts upcoming words and letters, sometimes incorrectly. You experience this yourself when your "I" all of a sudden realizes that a word or a few letters are incorrect or are going to be incorrect even as they are being typed, but it is difficult to immediately stop typing them; it takes the "I" a fraction of a second to regain control. By the time the "I" gets control of your fingers, you're halfway into the next word. This is caused by incorrect estimates and approximations about content on the part of preconscious "me" processing. The "me" gets the fingers moving before the "I" can process that an error is occurring and stop the fingers.

These findings demonstrate that there's more going on in our decision making and behaviors than simply conscious thought. What this implies is that preconscious processing works hand in hand with our conscious decision making in ways that are quite complex. The preconscious does a lot of the work and makes many decisions without the "I" awareness being informed (as with driving the car on "preconscious pilot"). Many of the conclusions we draw every minute are decided by the preconscious and announced to "I" awareness after they have been made. To each of us, cognizant of only our "I" awareness, it seems like we are consciously making decisions even though many of them are already foregone conclusions. The preconscious typically generates the action and an accompanying explanation/rationale that is based on past experience. This information is passed along to the "I" just as the action is performed, making it appear as though the "I" made a fast decision and acted immediately. It may be that people who are viewed as being very intuitive are simply more aware of what is going on in their preconscious and are perhaps able to shape its functioning in subtle ways.

COGNITIVE MAPS: A LEADER'S GREATEST CHALLENGE AND GREATEST OPPORTUNITY

Now we are prepared to look at the process by which the preconscious makes decisions as to whether to notify the "I" consciousness. Leaders of organizations face four challenges with regard to the operation of their employees' preconscious:

1. Ensure that employees are making preconscious decisions and judgments that are in the best interests of the organization.

2. Change existing preconscious values, hypotheses, and assumptions so that preconscious processing comes to the conclusions and motivates the actions that do the right things for the organization when the "I" conscious is not notified.

3. Ensure that each employee's "I" awareness is notified by his or her preconscious when automatic behavior doesn't conform to the values that are appropriate to the current situation in a world-class environment. To clarify the magnitude of the challenge this presents for leaders, we will discuss here the concept of the cognitive map.

4. Continue the first three challenges long enough so that the current traditional preconscious assumptions are replaced by world-class preconscious assumptions.

An individual's cognitive map is everything he or she knows about the world. It contains life theories (e.g., "Hard work is its own best reward"), learning (e.g., "It is bad to argue with the boss"), stereotypes (e.g., "Corporate types don't understand what we put up with every day out here in operations"), attitudes (e.g., "Life is wonderful"), life scripts (e.g., "Change jobs when the frustration gets too great"), and expectations (e.g., "Things will eventually work out"). It is important to realize that there is no such thing as "pure" information in the preconscious; *everything* in the preconscious is stored as part of a global heuristic that includes already-made value judgments, expectations, and priorities. The cognitive map and its heuristics enable fast decision making without "I" awareness, but it is not an objective, factual calculator—it is a social calculator closely attuned to the experience of each individual, especially in regard to interactions with other people and groups.

For example, consider the situation of waiting behind another car at a stop sign and both cars are signaling a right-hand turn. When the car in front begins to make the turn, the cognitive map of most drivers contains an expectation that the car in front will continue through the turn without stopping. This influences the preconscious to begin to pull up to a waiting position while the conscious "I" looks to the left to see when it will be clear to make the turn. Thousands of fender benders occur (and many more are narrowly missed) each year when the car in front stops midway through the turn for no apparent reason. Yet, 99.9% of the time, the automatic assumption is proved true when the car in front completes the turn once it has begun. When the expected assumption is true, it reinforces the strength of the existing associations in the cognitive map.

If one has recently had an accident or a close call in a similar situation, the "I" consciousness will be prodded into awareness in similar situations for a while. However, after a few days or weeks in which cars in similar situations continue to turn without stopping, the original "they'll continue to move once they start" automatic "me" assumption will once again be accepted and the preconscious will move the car ahead while "I" awareness looks left for oncoming traffic.

Now, transfer that same type of processing to a work situation. An executive tells his or her managers that they must focus their employees on speeding up cycle time for product and/or service delivery. With what part of their brains are the managers listening? If they are like most managers, they have heard many types of performance-related exhortations from executives in the past, most of which resulted in only a short-term emphasis on the issue in question. Their "me's" almost always decide that the rhetoric is the same old

hot air. In response, the managers' "I's" form a few teams, do a little process improvement, have a few reviews, and write up a glowing report, expecting that the executive's interest will quickly shift to something else. The employees of those managers have even more deeply ingrained expectations about such directions; they have heard countless managers and supervisors announce a push to improve this or that problem. And, being skilled social calculators, the "me's" of employees can sense an insincere supervisor who is just going through the motions. Most of these efforts die out after a short time with very few results and little but head nodding required of employees.

It is not that managers and employees do not consciously understand what leadership is telling them to do. Most of them understand all of it very logically and consciously. If asked, most will agree that leadership's emphasis is good business and needs to be addressed. The problem is that employees and managers are not logically and consciously making decisions from minute to minute each day. Whether they are reacting to small issues, prioritizing their time, giving direction, participating in meetings, deciding whether to take action about an issue, or resolving conflicts between what leadership has asked them to do and their own crises during a typical day, their preconsciouses are making value judgments. These preconscious value judgments are based on powerful assumptions that are maintained in their cognitive maps. These assumptions are built on past experiences that proved the assumptions correct. As long as the assumptions continue to prove valid more often than not, they will remain in force and dictate how the preconscious assesses everything it experiences. In other words, nothing will change in their preconsciouses, so they won't change their reactions and there will be little change in the culture of the organization.

Figure 4.4 shows how this process works from moment to moment. The width of the black arrows denotes the relative volume of processing through each channel in a typical person's cognitive map. For example, the very thick black arrows at the top of the figure show that almost all of the information impinging on us from moment to moment undergoes initial processing by the "me" (a very slight proportion may be processed by reflex action that is not immediately mediated by the brain). Thinner lines indicate less used processing options.

The initial processing is the first quick look at the information to determine whether anything imminently threatening is occurring: Is a nail sticking through our shoe into our foot? Is the car in front of us slamming on its brakes? Is the boss giving an impassioned speech about improving cost controls? This information is everything from sensory input (hearing someone speaking), to biological needs (hunger pangs), to expectations ("the car ahead will continue to turn the corner"). After the initial processing, the "me" generates a possible

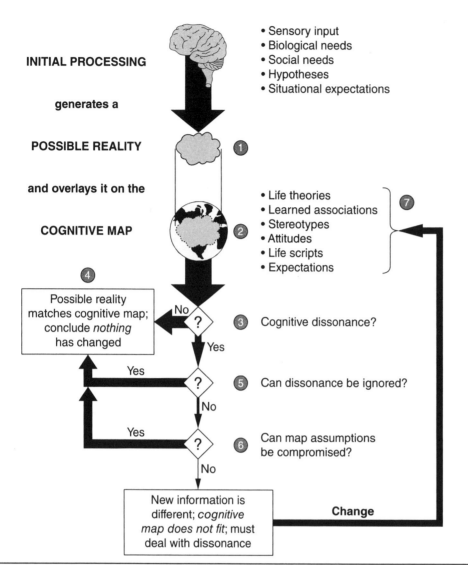

INITIAL PROCESSING

generates a

POSSIBLE REALITY

and overlays it on the

COGNITIVE MAP

- Sensory input
- Biological needs
- Social needs
- Hypotheses
- Situational expectations

- Life theories
- Learned associations
- Stereotypes
- Attitudes
- Life scripts
- Expectations

Possible reality matches cognitive map; conclude *nothing* has changed

Cognitive dissonance?

Can dissonance be ignored?

Can map assumptions be compromised?

New information is different; *cognitive map does not fit*; must deal with dissonance

Change

Figure 4.4   A schematic of preconscious processing—cognitive map operation.

reality. This occurs at point 1 in the figure. These possible realities are continuously generated; each is a temporary, situation-specific cognitive map that draws on everything that seems relevant to similar situations encountered by the preconscious in the past. It is critically important to keep in mind that preconscious decision making is driven by past assumptions that were assessed as effective at reducing pain, risk, and effort at that time. The preconscious is not concerned with identifying the most logical, rational course of action in a new situation. This is what the conscious "I" processing does, if it is called upon. As an aside, it is true that some people have developed a preconscious that contains many elements of logical analysis in specific situations (e.g., race car drivers, home inspectors). However, even some of these assumptions are tainted by subjective personal characteristics and values, and you never know when they are active!

Much of what we often regard as reaction time is the time required for the preconscious to determine how to handle information. This has been demonstrated by a massive amount of reaction time research over more than a hundred years. In one often-used approach, subjects are challenged to identify words flashed on a screen very briefly (in the range of a few thousandths of a second). For example, the subject might be shown the word *apple* printed in black on a white background for five milliseconds. Let's assume the subject is able to correctly identify the word. If the same word is printed in red, most subjects can identify the word faster, perhaps in three milliseconds. This is presumably because red is a color associated with apples, and this convergence of information makes it easier for the preconscious to identify the word via associations in our neural storage system. It is easy to make the same task more difficult for the preconscious. If the subject is shown the word *green* printed in red ink on a white background, it must be exposed much longer for correct identification than if the word *red* or *green* in black (or a red *red* or a green *green*) is shown on a white background. It takes more time for the preconscious to sort out the meaning of the word when it is paired with a divergent color that does not match the concept of the word.

Let's get back to the cognitive map. The possible reality for a moment is overlaid on the existing cognitive map at point 2 in Figure 4.4. This begins the process that will determine whether the preconscious will notify "I" awareness in order to deal with something unexpected or go with automatic, established preconscious assumptions. This is the critical moment for determining whether a specific leadership direction or example to do something different will succeed or fail in challenging existing preconscious assumptions. We are assuming that the leader is attempting to motivate people to do something different. This moment occurs hundreds of times a day in an organization.

The first step in the "fit" process is at point 3. The preconscious decides whether the possible reality is a close enough match to the cognitive map to lead to a conclusion of "no difference." If the possible reality matches the cognitive map, the preconscious ("me") determines that there is no cognitive dissonance, or conflict, and the preconscious assumptions are accepted (point 4). Note that the width of the line toward "No" (point 4) is very thick; this is the route that most decisions take. This is no surprise.

The human brain evolved to maximize survival value while minimizing energy expenditure, thus leaving the conscious mind ("I") free to deal with only the most critical events. It takes a great deal of energy for the "me" to counter well-established assumptions. Therefore, the preconscious takes every opportunity it can to ignore changes. This is woven into our genetics; it doesn't matter if this strategy is a burden in our current, fast-paced world. The "me" is operating more or less under the assumption that if a situation is critical enough, it will force its way past "me" to "I."

As the thickness of the lines in the figure shows, the preconscious does everything it can to deny changes—to live in a present that fits with a well-understood past in which the "me" can handle most of the heavy lifting. In the days of prehumans and up until the last 4000 years (more or less), the general features of the environment changed little from day to day and year to year. The same food was safe to eat (if not always plentiful), the same animals were threats or opportunities for food, and so on. Our preconscious processing was not developed to deal with the fast-changing world that our technology has created. In our modern world, a single poorly judged word in a meeting can spell job or customer loss. Our "me" processing is not finely tuned to deal with these distinctions unless it has been carefully conditioned by appropriate experience—thus the source of the advice to count to 10 if you are angry; it provides an opportunity for "I" awareness to take the controls from "me" operations.

If the "no difference" route is taken, the existing assumptions in the cognitive map are then used to generate an automatic value judgment and automatic preconscious responses. These preconscious responses (e.g., "We've heard this before," "It'll never work here") influence or determine consequent judgments and behaviors by "I" consciousness. (For example, "Okay, so it's another push for better quality. I'll go along if I'm asked to do something, but there's nothing I can do on my own. Besides, it'll probably die off in a couple of months, so why worry about it?")

If the possible reality does not match the cognitive map, cognitive dissonance occurs. This dissonance, or mismatch, suggests to the preconscious it may be necessary to notify the "I" consciousness so that it can deal with a situation for which there is no safe, automatic answer that fits. If such a suggestion were always enough to override the preconscious, leadership would be much easier; employees would make all of their decisions based on the current situation and its facts. Leading change would simply be a matter of describing the "here and now." Employees would pretty much always do what leadership asked (assuming that it was logical and safe in terms of current facts). Yet, this is not the way it works.

And it's a good thing it doesn't work that way. Stable cognitive maps that are resistant to change are key to individual survival and the stability of society. They enable our conscious "I" to attend to critical stimuli while our preconscious deals with the mundane. Over the past several hundred thousand years, humans and prehumans faced a world of harsh conditions in which dangers were well known. A well-developed and resistant cognitive map took care of routine processing while the conscious "I" attended to child rearing, food gathering, and defending against predators. In our current environment, strong cognitive maps support laws, customs, rituals, and traditions. If we rationally changed our cognitive maps with every observed modification in the environment, there would be no stable basis for a predictable society. Laws would change as fast as lobbyists could write checks to our elected officials, and there would be no basis for stable social norms. Stable and strong cognitive maps are the anchor of every culture. This is why the decision of "no difference" at point 3 in Figure 4.4 is a genetically selected tendency. This decision has the highest odds for success in situations where long-term stability is critical.

What has happened over the last 30,000 years is that our logical, cognitive, and social abilities to develop technology and complex organizations have outrun our innate information-processing mechanisms. If we want our employees to be able to adapt to our fast-moving, demanding world, we must provide them with enough evidence to continually make small modifications to their preconscious calculus so that their preconscious assumptions begin to correspond to the environment we are trying to create. To the extent that many, if not most, employees have not lived and worked in world-class environments, this new set of values must replace a great deal of what employees have learned in school, in other jobs, and in life in general. In effect, we must force their "I" to do enough work to establish new "me" assumptions. The only way this can happen is if leadership constantly forces the "me" of each employee to enlist his or her "I" in decision making, because the old "me" assumptions do not fit what the environment is presenting at the moment.

In those cases where there is cognitive dissonance at point 3, the decision-making process moves to point 5: Can the cognitive dissonance be ignored? As we discussed earlier, the inherent tendency is to ignore the dissonance and accept it as not important enough to override with "I" awareness (as long as the difference is not severe enough to present an obvious threat to survival). An example of this is the operation of flight simulators. Simulators are workstations that mimic the operation of aircraft. They are a comparatively low-cost way to train pilots, and they permit the practice of emergency maneuvers that are too dangerous to perform with actual aircraft. When the pilot is operating the simulator cockpit controls, which are identical to those of real aircraft, the windows of the simulator display computer-projected images that show what the pilot would expect to see if flying an actual aircraft. If the pilot banks the simulator, the simulator banks a bit in the expected direction and the outside view changes to show what the view would look like if the simulated plane actually banked as much as the control movement would generate in an actual plane.

Consider what happens when a pilot is in the simulator. The pilot knows that it is a simulator, because he or she saw it sitting in the middle of the hangar when entering the facility. The simulator looks like a big box sitting atop the gimbals and hinges that move it. The pilot knows how a simulator works. He or she has likely spent dozens, if not hundreds, of hours in such devices. Yet, when the pilot begins to operate the simulator, he or she is soon swept up in the reality of the exercise. As emergency scenarios are presented, the pilot's heart rate, perspiration rate, and blood pressure rise to levels generated in similar real-world situations. In every respect, the experience feels "real."

What is going on? From moment to moment, the pilot's preconscious is ignoring the small differences in reality (at point 5) and accepting all of the assumptions that have been established by previous flight experiences. When the pilot banks the plane sharply to one side, the difference between the expected physical sensation of a sharp bank and the slight tilt actually experienced is ignored. There is enough other information (the visual cues and instrument changes) to lead the preconscious to go along with established prior assumptions. As Figure 4.4 shows, the overwhelming portion of preconscious decision making at point 5 is to ignore any differences and make the conclusion of "no difference"—the flight experience is perceived as real.

If the difference at point 5 is too large to ignore, the preconscious moves to point 6: Can the previously established assumptions in the cognitive map be compromised a bit in order to arrive at an easy, low-energy-expenditure decision of "no difference" that does not require the "I" to be activated? A good example of how this operates has been demonstrated with an oft-repeated research study that was first conducted over 50 years ago. Volunteers were college-aged males who were placed one at a time in a small, sparsely furnished, warm, windowless room in the basement of a university building. They were assigned to empty a box of tightly packed wooden blocks one by one and repack the blocks one by one into a second, identical empty box. They were told to repeat the process back and forth between the two boxes until told to stop. They were left in the room for two hours. When the experiment started, they were told that it had to do with manual dexterity. In reality, the purpose of the task was to bore the subjects to the point of despair. Interviews conducted with subjects who had participated demonstrated that the task did just that.

After two hours, the experimenter entered the room and told the subject he was done. It was at this point that the actual research began. The subject was told that the boring nature of the task had led some subjects to complain about it on the way out of the lab, saying things such as, "That was the most boring experience in my entire life." The subjects were told that such comments had been overheard by subjects sitting in the outer office waiting for their turns to participate and that many of the subjects, upon hearing the negative comments, had declined to participate. As a result, the research was falling behind schedule. The researcher then offered the subject a deal: If he would say something about how interesting the experiment was and how much he liked it on the way out so that a waiting subject could hear it, the researcher would pay him. About 80% of the subjects agreed to lie. Half of the subjects were given a dollar for the lie, and the other half were given 20 dollars for the lie. When the research was first conducted in the early 1950s, a dollar would buy lunch or six or seven beers, and 20 dollars was a windfall.

The people waiting in the outer room were not subjects but other research assistants who posed as upcoming subjects. After the subjects lied in front of the research assistants and left the waiting room, they were paid their money and left. They believed that their involvement with the research was over. About a week later, the researchers called each subject to follow up. The subjects were asked a number of questions (e.g., "Have you had any dreams about blocks?" "Have you had any hand or finger pain or cramps?"). These types of questions were camouflage for the most important question: "On a scale of one (least) to seven (most), how interesting was the experiment?"

Those who were given a dollar for lying found the experiment, on average, two points more interesting on the seven-point scale than those given 20 dollars to lie. This experiment and numerous variations of it have been repeated many, many times over the years with the same general result: Those who get paid less to lie always rate the experiment as more interesting. Researchers can think of only one explanation. It is intimately involved with the preconscious and cognitive dissonance.

Aside from people with serious psychological problems and divorce attorneys for ex-spouses, everyone tends to think of himself or herself as good, moral, fair, and just. This is a basic preconscious assumption that most people use to interpret their own actions. Just think about what you told yourself the last time you deliberately drove by someone on the highway who appeared to need help: "I'm a great person but I'm in a hurry. Someone else will stop." Those subjects who agreed to lie had a similar problem to resolve: "Good people don't lie, but I'm a good person and I told a lie." The subjects who got

20 dollars to lie had an easy way of dealing with the unavoidable cognitive dissonance: "Who wouldn't tell a small, inconsequential, pearl white, innocent, after-all-I-did-the-experiment-why-should-they-get-out-of-it, and after-all-I'm-helping-the-researchers fib for 20 bucks?" Their preconscious concluded, "Sure, I lied, but it wasn't much of a lie and it was worth it! Almost any good, moral, just person would do the same!" This conclusion by the preconscious makes it easy to accept the dissonance as unimportant.

Those who lied for a dollar have a more difficult data integration and self-image challenge. Their preconscious must maintain their view of themselves as moral and upstanding, yet they lied for a lousy buck! Even though they did not know they were going to be called and asked about how interesting the experiment was, their preconsciouses were left to deal with the dissonance between their lofty views of themselves and the reality of their cheaply bought lies. Something had to give: Either the preconscious must revise its self-concept from "I'm morally good" to "I'm not so nice," or the experiment was actually a lot more interesting than it seemed to the conscious mind at the time, thus making the lie less "serious." During the week between their participation and the follow-up call, the preconscious "me" slowly and inexorably modified its view of the experiment until it got on average 28% more interesting than it was to someone who got paid the 20 dollars. The easily bought preconsciouses maintained their positive assumptions about their own integrity by reducing the severity of the lie. The only way to do this was by reinterpreting the experiment as more interesting.

If the cognitive dissonance cannot be dealt with by modifying the cognitive map assumptions on which it is based, the only remaining alternative is to conclude that the existing cognitive map is incorrect and must be modified. As the skinny "no" line leading out of point 6 in Figure 4.4 demonstrates, this option is not often selected. It is energy-intensive and requires that the conscious "I" be involved in an uncomfortable task. It requires that many of the underlying assumptions used by the "me" be changed. The preconscious knows that considerable tension and anxiety are created anytime new assumptions must be learned and integrated into the system, because only the "I" can start the process and it takes a while before the "me" responses become automatic.

THE IMPLICATION FOR LEADERS

One definition of a leader (otherwise known as someone who is trying to make kaizen work as part of a broad cultural change) is a person who compels others to do something new, to help them as a group go where they have not been before. To do something new requires the involvement of the conscious mind. The conscious is involved only when the preconscious cannot handle a situation with its existing assumptions. Employees can only be led (to something better) if the existing assumptions in their cognitive maps are compelled to change (assuming that the existing assumptions are "traditional"). New assumptions must be established, and further changes in the environment must quickly lead to the establishment of yet newer assumptions (if the leader continues to lead). This means that a much larger proportion of preconscious decisions will have to travel vertically in Figure 4.4, at least until the basic parameters of the new culture are established. The thin lines of the figure will have to be thickened, and the thick lines will have to be made thinner. This is the task of any leadership team that is laboring to transform a culture.

THE CHALLENGE OF THE FROZEN TUNDRA OF CORPORATE CULTURE

Think of each person's cognitive map as a block of ice. The block of ice is a set of established assumptions that is frozen in place. An organization's corporate culture is the operating characteristics of all the cognitive maps within in. That is, every organization is a frozen tundra made of blocks of ice side by side and stacked up. It doesn't matter what leadership wants or wishes the culture to be—the culture is what the frozen tundra does. If the culture is to be changed, the tundra must be melted down and refrozen into new, world-class ice.

Think of a person recognizing and adapting to a substantial change as requiring a portion of the block of ice to be melted so that it can be refrozen into the new ice of new assumptions that are more appropriate to the new environment. Every day, every cognitive map of every person encounters information that attempts to melt it. Think of each of these potential threats to existing assumptions as a lighted match thrown onto the surface of the ice. As the sizes of the various lines in Figure 4.4 show, most of the matches that land on the block of ice every day have almost no impact; the lit matches of small dissonances land on the ice and burn out. The little bit of ice that melts is quickly refrozen. The small dissonances end up having no effect, except to strengthen the "me's" tendency to ignore them in the future.

It's easy to think of situations where this occurs at work. Suppose an employee gets a memo or hears a speech about the necessity to pay more attention to safety. This usually occurs after a high-profile accident or the issuance of a report showing that the accident rate has increased or not gone down as much as hoped or promised. Rationally and consciously, the employee knows that safe behavior is in everybody's best interests. And no employee violates safety policy because he or she wants to get hurt. So, upon getting the memo or speech to be more safety-conscious, the employee's "I" makes a mental note to try to do better "at safety."

Yet, once back on the job, all sorts of signals are sent that it's okay not to worry too much about safety. People work without personal safety equipment and supervisors may say nothing about it (and often don't wear safety equipment themselves). Required quarterly safety briefings are not conducted as they were for a while after the last accident. In the parking lot, employees (including managers) exceed the speed limit, jaywalk, and don't obey stop signs. Everywhere, the employees' cognitive maps are supporting preconscious assumptions that scream, "Talk about safety, nod your head, and then do what's easiest, most comfortable, and fastest." Very rarely will an employee's "me" experience sufficient cognitive dissonance about safety to be forced to go straight to the bottom of Figure 4.4 and get the "I" involved to argue, "Hey, wait a minute. There's a safe way to work and I need to take the time to do it." Whatever safety matches (no pun intended) are thrown onto the block of ice, in this situation they have almost no impact on the existing culture.

Two mechanisms operate to keep each block frozen. The first is the inherent tendency of the preconscious to favor existing assumptions by ignoring small changes (point 5 in Figure 4.4), or, if they can't be ignored, changing the underlying assumptions of the existing cognitive map (point 6). This mechanism quickly refreezes what little melting occurs. The second mechanism is the influence upon any one cognitive map block from the hundreds or thousands of others clustered around it (the other people in the organization). The massed cognitive maps of an organization are a frozen tundra energy sink that can easily absorb the heat of a flamethrower, not to mention a few hundred matches. This self-perpetuating frozen tundra is an organization's self-perpetuating corporate culture.

If it is a typical organization, the summed preconscious assumptions support traditional management and work practices. If the frozen tundra is a world-class organization, the summed preconscious assumptions support enlightened, world-class practices. In either case, the tundra quickly refreezes even significant melting that impacts a particular block or number of blocks. This is why "hair on fire" change agents get eaten alive when they attempt to change an organization on their own. They cannot generate enough heat to melt enough blocks. After a while, they are turned to the frozen, dark side by peer pressure, negative feedback, and frustration. In order to get their own needs satisfied, they begin to give the frozen tundra what it expects: no changes.

The next chapter discusses the mechanism by which neighboring blocks of ice interact to ensure that existing blocks do not melt. That is why it is pointless to expect an organization to change or succeed in implementing something dramatically new when only a few cognitive maps have been changed or when a project kickoff launches a few thousand matches (e.g., speeches, banners, coffee cups, a few teams, posters) over a short time period onto the frozen expanse of ice. After a couple of months, all that's left is a frozen tundra littered with charred match remnants frozen to the tops of the blocks. If leadership is to be successful in changing its corporate culture, if the organization is to succeed at doing something different, a continuing, intense firestorm of matches must rain down on every cognitive map on a daily basis for years. Leaders must become fire chiefs—not the type who put out fires but the type who fuel an inferno of tundra-melting culture change.

5

The Challenge of Change Three: Group and Organization Dynamics

Human behavior in groups is more than individuals doing their "own things" while others are nearby. When more than one person is present, the interaction of the individuals creates a variety of very powerful influences that shape behavior above and beyond what is created by the sum of their individual tendencies and preferences. These forces are known as group and organization dynamics. *Group dynamics* are the forces that operate within a small collection of people. For reasons that will be discussed later in this chapter, a group is typically defined as fewer than nine people. *Organization dynamics* are forces that operate among groups of groups and between the organization and an individual. The tendencies and characteristics that these forces generate, the organization's own unique frozen tundra, are often summed up as *corporate culture*.

The grooming and maintenance of a corporate culture that fosters improved performance is a leader's most critical and most difficult challenge. It can't be done with speeches, "programs," and tools; it demands active, daily leadership from every leader at every level. This is doubly hard because the inherent tendencies of group and organization dynamics actively operate to pull an organization toward below-average performance, which reinforces traditional "me" assumptions. It should be no surprise to anyone who has worked in a number of organizations that the "let nature take its course" level of performance is almost always disappointing.

The normal resting state of human organization performance is fair to poor. This is because human societies did not evolve to operate large, complex organizations. They evolved to keep small organizations (20 to a few hundred people or so) alive in a brutal world. The demands of modern business and society (e.g., infrastructures, cities, nations) are orders of magnitude more complex than primitive survival challenges, yet they are powered by social behaviors that evolved millennia ago and cannot change as quickly as our technology enables the agglomeration of very large numbers of people in an organization. The development of a world-class organization requires that leaders devote immense effort to holding natural forces at bay. An examination of these forces will demonstrate just what leaders face when they attempt to move normal corporate culture toward excellence.

GROUP FORMATION

Humans are driven to form groups. The basic needs discussed in Chapter 3 cannot be fully satisfied without other people. It's easy to see that our inherent need for sex, belongingness, love, and human contact requires the presence of other people. A group is also essential for the satisfaction of power and freedom needs. While everyone wants some freedom, it's impossible to enjoy freedom from control without having a group whose control you can be occasionally freed from (but not so free that it's not there to provide support when you need it). Thus, inborn individual needs provide a powerful drive to form groups.

On a more basic level, the compulsion to form groups was naturally selected by a harsh environment that weeded out those who did not successfully form groups—individuals or even a small group could not survive long on their own. Therefore, every healthy human being alive today is compelled by genetics to need to be a part of a group, whether or not his or her "I" agrees or he or she likes it. This compulsion, if properly focused, can be a powerful mechanism to support leadership's objectives and enrich employees' lives.

If human nature is allowed to take its natural course, people will generally form groups of fewer than nine people. Most often, the groups will be four to seven. This number makes it easy for all members of the group to interact with one another and be close enough to give and receive subtle nonverbal cues as well as to feel as though they can reach out and touch one another. It is said in much of the small-group literature that the ideal number of group members is five to nine, often stated as seven plus or minus two. As groups get larger than three people, they are increasingly likely to break into smaller groups. It doesn't matter if a larger group is the official group (as with departments, sections, teams, or committees in an organization). When people are faced with a large group, they quickly form smaller groups within the larger group so that they can communicate more intimately and thereby obtain more belongingness and satisfaction.

This phenomenon is at work in every organization every day. There may be 20 people in the customer service department, but those 20 people will invariably form several smaller, much more tightly knit groups in order to provide each group member with sufficient need satisfaction. When people are required to work in a larger group (such as a project team of 25 people), performance will suffer because the inevitable informal, smaller groups will not communicate everything they know to the other small groups. People are, by design, not able to develop close bonds within such a large group. If forced to always interact as a single large group, the result will be more withdrawal, contempt for the group, conflict, and poor communication when compared with a smaller group.

The only way to get small group dynamics to work for you is to formally design a project or a department around teams of five to nine people. If the project requires 25 individuals, create five teams of 5 (or three of 6 and one of 7, for example), give each team specific tasks, and set up a formal process so that the teams can easily and frequently exchange information. In this way, there is little tendency for poorly defined small groups to do things that don't fit well with the big picture.

The same dynamics work with intact work groups (IWGs). An IWG consists of people who spend most of their day together working on similar tasks. Examples are groups such as the 6 people in the purchasing department, the 20 people working in production, the 15 engineers in the new products design group, and the 8 people working in human resources. To generate maximum effectiveness, each of these areas must be organized into teams of fewer than 10 individuals. For example, the 20 people in production could be formed into teams of 7, 7, and 6, and the 15 engineers could be formed into either three teams of 5 each or two teams, one with 7 and one with 8. These smaller groups provide much more opportunity for the IWG members to both obtain greater need satisfaction and take greater ownership of their jobs and assigned work areas/processes.

PROPINQUITY

Propinquity (pro-pin-qwi-tee) is the name given to the mechanism by which people tend to like things that are closer to them compared with things that are further away. The "thing" can be appearance, religious belief, nationality, economic status, political allegiance, neighborhood, type of car driven, and so on. Physical distance is the most powerful driver of propinquity simply because people who are nearby offer more opportunities for help, protection, need satisfaction, and information than do people who are farther away. In the past, the closest people were also likely to be members of the same group as well as close genetic relations.

It's easy to see propinquity in operation. For example, in our highly mobile society, many people do not know their neighbors very well. Yet, when they are driving down their street, most will not hesitate to wave at people in nearby yards because they assume that they are neighbors. And the neighbors, assuming that the waver is a fellow neighbor, wave back. Three blocks from their home, people hardly ever wave to others. Yet, if you live way out in the country, where there are comparatively few neighbors, people will routinely wave at other drivers on country roads a mile or more from their homes because they assume that the others are neighbors who are close by their standards. The same mechanism works to foster feelings of kinship within departments and sections of an organization. People in functional departments share the propinquity of not only physical proximity but also objectives, jargon, and leaders. These forces work to create strong feelings of identity and loyalty, even if most people are not aware of them.

Propinquity works (along with other dynamics discussed shortly) to strengthen group ties and enable the group to view itself as more significant and "better" than the overall organization. This enables the group to better satisfy its individuals' needs. However, at the same time, this process reduces communication and cooperation with other groups. A key challenge of leaders is to have strong, self-respecting groups that also have a clear understanding, driven by explicit metrics and instructions, about how they can each serve the overall organization and "nearby" groups from the comfort of their "home" groups. Do not make the mistake of thinking that so-called process-centered work groups and/or matrix-organizations as they are commonly practiced can be used to get the best of both worlds. It is a false hope that defies the facts of human nature.

A process-centered work group is one in which personnel from various traditional functional areas (such as product design, customer service, planning, operations, sales, and the like) are assigned to work as a team or department that focuses on one process or product. This is done to encourage the individuals to work together more efficiently and harmoniously than they did when they resided in discrete departments. It's a great idea in concept but rarely works in practice. Even if the people in the group report to the process or product manager of their new department, they know where their long-term career health is determined—the functional area they came from. Since so few organizations use process-centered work groups and those who try them tend to give up after a short time (remember, human nature is always pushing for more powerful, need-satisfying, and therefore more distinct and more homogeneous groups), employees know that the arrangement is most likely temporary. And there's still the issue of getting a specific process-centered work group to play nicely with other groups in the organization. It will also fall victim to the tendency to suboptimize (improve its status and outcomes at the expense of other groups and the greater organization).

Matrix-organizations are even worse. In these arrangements, personnel are lent or assigned by their home functions to participate on task forces, cross-functional teams, product groups, and the like. With excellent coaching and true leadership, these ad hoc groups can function well, but that is true of any group in any environment. However, such coaching and guidance are usually not provided in meaningful amounts. People still "belong" to their home departments and depend on them for career advancement and pay increases. There are all of the problems of process-centered groups and none of the benefits. The majority of matrix-organizations are simply traditional functional organizations that wish to appear as though they have more resources available than the organization is actually capable of providing. It's not uncommon for individuals in matrix-organizations to be on four to five "matrix" processes/projects at the same time as they hold down their regular job. Guess which responsibility gets the most attention?

LEADERSHIP, STATUS, AND AUTHORITY

Many people assume that strong leadership is anathema to world-class organizations. This is probably because they have seen too many instances of strong "bad" leadership in which bosses are arbitrary, emotional, vindictive, uncommunicative, unfair, and so on. Not wanting to be further victimized, many people assume/hope that world-class leadership is warm, fuzzy, comforting, permissive, and/or leadership by teams or committees. Nothing could be further from the truth or the reality of human group dynamics and internal needs. Humans are driven to crave leadership—strong, decisive, clear leadership. As with all other group dynamics, this craving is driven by evolutionary pressures.

As discussed earlier, our prehuman ancestors lived in very desperate times. If a group routinely spent a lot of time arguing and fighting about who would be in charge for a particular day or task, they were wasting time and energy that could have been devoted to more vital pursuits. In addition, if they were inclined to disagree, there would probably be a lot of disobedience, fights, arguments, poor organization, and lack of focus on critical tasks. They would gather less food, beat off predators less effectively, and, as a result, decrease their long-term odds of survival. As a result, natural selection weeded out groups that did not quickly and easily select leaders who would be followed.

All primate and human societies readily select and obey leaders, even if many of the members of the group or society do not like the leaders or agree with their decisions or capabilities. As the noted primate expert Frans de Waal has pointed out in his numerous books, this does not mean that followers and leaders are completely altruistic and straightforward at all times. Leaders and followers in chimpanzee (and other primate) societies frequently cheat on one another and the rules, but they do it carefully and selectively. We all know this is true of human followers and leaders. It is a universal primate (and likely a mammalian, if not life form in general) trait. It has even been observed in ant and bee colonies, where nursery ants (the feeders of the larvae) sometimes eat small portions of the food they're supposed to give to the larvae. This is probably an evolutionarily selected pressure relief mechanism that permits frustrated individuals to strike back against the group without threatening the group or their own survival too much.

Aside from a little cheating, humans and primates accord considerable respect and latitude to leaders. In return, leaders apportion considerable benefits to favored followers. In nonhuman primate groups, those followers closest to leaders have access to more and better food, better breeding partners, and so on. A look at the society pages of any major newspaper quickly confirms that human society's leaders usually have very attractive breeding partners, attend many sumptuous banquets, live in nicer homes, and drive more expensive cars. The most favored followers are those that do the most to satisfy leaders. The lessons to human leaders are clear. Followers are watching leaders every second and trying to determine what is acceptable and what isn't. It doesn't matter what leaders say if what they do is different. Followers give the most weight to what they see—actions—rather than what they hear. Leaders cannot fool followers by doing one thing and saying something else. Humans are tremendously insightful observers of other humans and cannot be long misled by talk.

A leader must also appreciate that acceptance by the followers does not mean that he or she is doing a good job as a leader. The absence of complaints means nothing. First of all, few people are willing to risk disfavor by pointing out poor leadership to a leader. (For example, an infamous job killer is an honest answer to the question, "Be honest with me, how am I doing as a boss?" The only safe answer is, "Boss, you're such a great leader that it intimidates many of us because we don't think we could ever be as good.") Further, most people in a group do not want to be the leader; the drive for authority is probably normally distributed. While many may daydream about being in charge, most people are content to do their part and let someone else do the leading. Therefore, even if the leader is doing a pathetic job, few will fight to take over even if there is an avenue for such a struggle; even fewer will tell the leader the truth about his or her performance. Leaders must realize that when they lead by words rather than by actions, they are training all of their followers to say one thing but do another. Leaders get exactly what they give, for better or worse.

CONFORMITY

The reluctance of followers to tell it like it is might cause some to infer that most people are spineless cowards. The fear that drives this behavior is fear of being kicked out of a group that one cares about and/or needs. Prehumans and early humans needed groups for survival. Groups did not survive if their members were not willing to subordinate themselves to the group most of the time (except for a little cheating). Everyone alive today is a product of this brutal culling process. Humans conform because conformity for the purpose of survival is hardwired into us. Just because it's often not life-threatening to be kicked out of a group doesn't change the hardwiring we were born with.

A pioneering experiment shows how pervasive this compulsion to conform is. Researchers arranged for a person to rush into a liquor store, pick up a case of beer, and noisily run off with it. This was done as real customers were waiting at the counter for the salesperson's attention. As the customers queued at the counter right next to the door, the salesperson, working with the researchers, would duck down briefly behind the counter as if he were looking for something. This was a secret signal for the "thief" to make his move and steal the beer. The salesperson then stood up and asked, "What can I do for you?" The purpose of the experiment was to determine what the customers would say about the theft, which they could not miss, and what impact the presence of other customers had on what they would say.

The researchers discovered that if one customer was present, he or she would mention the theft to the salesperson about 70% of the time. If two customers were waiting, either one of them or both would mention the theft only about 35% of the time. When three people were present, the group or any one of them would mention it about 30% of the time. With four or more, the numbers began to climb back up. What was going on?

The only explanation that made sense to the researchers (and to the many researchers who have duplicated and modified the experiment many, many times over the years) involved a very subtle but powerful conformity pressure. The moment of truth for the customers occurred when the salesperson stood up after the thief had left. When only one customer was present, there was a strong likelihood (usually 60%–80% across many studies) that he or she would mention the theft. The percentage of those not responding is probably the normal level of people "not wanting to get involved" for one reason or another. When two or three customers were present, it would seem logical to assume that the theft would be pointed out more often than if a single customer were present. Logically, there are two to three times as many people, and thus it's reasonable to expect two to three times the probability that someone would say something.

Conformity pressure changes everything. With one customer, the only determinant of whether the theft was mentioned, all other things being equal, was the personality and mood of the customer and his or her preconscious expectations about getting involved. The situation was much different when more people were present. When the salesperson stood up and asked, "What can I do for you?" everyone in the customer group waited in that first fraction of a second to see what the others would say. If nobody said anything right away, a group norm (expected behavior) of remaining silent was established. Given our inborn group tendencies, the tendency to not say anything is already primed. Someone who might have been inclined to say something might surmise, perhaps preconsciously, "Hmmm, what if I mention it and these guys don't back me up? I'll look like an idiot," or "Why should I get involved with having to wait for the police and give a report if these guys won't?" The "me's" did not want to do something different from the group, knowing what that usually means in terms of group approval. It seems incredible, but in that fleeting instant, with a very temporary group of individuals who don't know one another, a group norm can significantly influence whether people will report a crime.

Much the same conclusions were found years earlier when researchers faked a fight between two research assistants just as a stranger (the subject) rounded a corner and came upon the altercation. If no other passersby were present, the subject would attempt to intervene 70%–90% of the time (this was in the 1950s; you do so these days at your own risk). If there were other onlookers (research assistants) already watching the fight when the subject happened upon the fight, the odds of the new passerby saying or doing anything went down in direct proportion to the number of people observing. With a small group present, the strangers reported in follow-on interviews that they assumed there was a good reason for the fight or for letting it continue or else someone else would have already stopped it. Conformity pressures are always lurking in the background, pulling everyone in the direction of doing what others are already doing.

The lesson for leaders is obvious: Employees are going to conform to the existing norms of the organization by default (their preconscious assumptions). It takes a lot of effort, a Herculean amount of it, to entice people to go against the norms of the groups that satisfy their needs. There's no point in even trying if the effort is only going to be occasional or intermittent; it can't work.

GOALS, ROLES, AND NORMS

All groups have three basic operating parameters: goals, roles, and norms. Groups form (many groups spontaneously "form" themselves, rather than "being formed") in order to perform certain functions or goals. The goals of a group may be explicit and clearly stated, or they may be rather nebulous and difficult for even the group members to define. In fact, many members of informal groups may not even know they are in a group. For example, the annual community charity drive committee in your town or city most likely has very clearly defined goals and objectives. Most of the members could probably state the goals in a straightforward manner. Contrast that with the group from the marketing department that meets every day for lunch in the cafeteria. That group's members may not even realize that they are part of an established group. They would probably have difficulty arriving at a mutual agreement as to what the group's goals are. To one it might be companionship at lunchtime, to another it might be a forum for bitching about the company, and to a third it might be a means of selling his or her ideas on what the organization should be doing. When there is no clear agreement among members as to what the group's goals are, there are many opportunities for misunderstanding, disappointment, and frustration.

Roles are the second important characteristic of groups. Roles are specific sets of behaviors performed by group members. Each group has a fairly rigid and consistent set of roles occupied by group members. For example, the president of a company typically has a role that requires him or her to be "in charge," decisive, forceful, and experienced. In a family group, the father has a role that often requires him to teach the children masculine skills, to mow the lawn, and to take at least a passing interest in sports. Obviously, the role of father differs from family to family, but it is remarkably consistent over time within any one particular family. One person usually fulfills a number of roles at the same time. You could be a mother, a manager, an engineer, a member of a softball league, and a Jaycee all at the same time. Each of these roles requires a different and often conflicting set of behaviors.

Roles can be broken down into three basic types. The first type, the *enacted role*, is the actual behavior the person performs, what's really happening. The second type is the *perceived role,* the role that the individual perceives or believes he or she is filling. Finally, there is the *expected role*. This role defines the behavior that other group members expect to see from the individual. All of these roles will be the same for a specific individual in a given situation. For example, the president of a company could actually do what the ideal president does (the enacted role), feel that he or she is doing the right things (perceived role), and fulfill the expectations of the employees, the board members, and the stockholders (the expected role).

In reality, of course, things usually don't work out that well. This is generally because each of the groups you work with expects a different set of behaviors, and your estimates of what each of them expects may be off a little. When the amount of discrepancy between role types is more than average, it's called *role conflict* or *role ambiguity*. If there is sufficient role ambiguity or conflict among group members, the group is adversely affected. Morale tends to be lower, productivity suffers, and individual satisfaction decreases. Role conflict explains a great deal of what's euphemistically called "personality conflict" during termination interviews. The supervisor and the employee have conflicting views as to the expected role the supervisor wants to see and the perceived role the employee is striving to display. The important point is to realize that just because you think you are fulfilling a role (perceived role) as the best middle manager in the organization doesn't mean everyone else sees it that way. In fact, you may actually be doing the job as it ideally should be done (enacted role), but key people may expect more humility or more aggressive tactics (different expected roles). It's not what you do but how well you perform the expected role behaviors that is in the minds of the key players.

Do not make the mistake of underestimating the awesome power that role expectations play in shaping behavior and influencing peoples' evaluations of others' behavior. Just think for a moment of all the groups with which you interact during the day and the various ways you behave with each of them. You not only say different things as you move from group to group but you may also dress differently, use a different tone of voice, and display different body language. And you do these things more or less automatically once you've learned the norms of each group (the "me" again). Everyone else is doing the same thing and is also watching to see how you satisfy the behaviors they expect from you.

A famous experiment, perhaps the most famous in social psychology, demonstrates the power of roles to shape behavior. A group of male college students was selected to participate. The group was carefully tested to ensure that all final subjects were within the normal spectrum of psychological and medical well-being. Coin flips were used to separate the subjects into two groups. One group was designated as the prisoners and the other as jailers. A mock prison was set up in the basement of a campus building, and the prisoners and the jailers were left to their own devices as to how they would spend the week of the experiment. No other instructions were given. All they had to guide their behaviors was the presence of the "prison" and their own expectations of what prisoners and jailers were supposed to do.

The experiment had to be terminated early due to the surprising events that occurred. Almost immediately, the jailers began to brutalize the prisoners. They repeatedly rousted them out of their cells, made them walk blindfolded in a group to the bathroom, and herded them out of their cells for frequent inspections. The abuses were greatest when the researchers were not present (late at night) and the jailers could let their role-playing have complete expression. The prisoners, average college students who became prisoners only on the basis of a coin flip, did not rebel or argue with the jailers. Instead, they became docile, depressed, and compliant. Several of them broke down and cried when visited by friends and family members. Things got so bad that the experiment had to be stopped. Worse yet, none of the researchers had expected the role-playing to become so extreme. In fact, the researchers did not provide the impetus to stop the experiment, as they themselves had fallen into the role expectation trap (to them it was only an experiment, and thus they didn't see the problem). As the head of the study explained it later, a visiting graduate student was aghast at what was going on and was visibly shaken. Her reaction shook him back to reality and he terminated the study. He made this revelation in the preface to a book written by his wife, the then graduate student and now a well-known researcher in another area. Role-playing and expectations are even more powerful at work. People do it for a living, their egos are involved, and they've had years of practice.

The third important characteristic of groups is norms. Norms are the standardized rules of conduct for the group in general. They overlap to an extent with the behaviors expected from the specific roles people play. For some groups, norms are detailed and documented (as in norms for an air force bomber crew). For other groups, the norms are "understood" (as in most work groups). Norms serve several purposes. First, they provide group members with acceptable bounds for behavior; an individual doesn't have to endlessly deliberate about whether a certain behavior is okay—the group norms generally make it clear.

People obey group norms to get social approval (spoken or unspoken "pats on the back" from other group members). The more valued the group is in the eyes of the person, the more that person will conform to the norms in order to get accepted. This is why it's very important to let work group members assist in developing procedures and policies; if they help, they'll value them more and will obey them more often.

Compliance with group norms is dependent on a number of factors. The lower the self-confidence or self-esteem of a person, the more readily that person will comply with group norms. Persons who continually deviate from group norms will soon find themselves shut off from the group. If someone violates group norms, he or she will at first get a lot of attention from the group members (some of it unpleasant) as they attempt to bring him or her back into the fold. If the individual persists in the violations, he or she will end up out of the group. Major deviations from group norms are permitted only for individuals who have a high value to the group and/or those who have a history of compliance with group norms. An individual new to a group likely has relatively low perceived value and, as a result, has no maneuvering room: He or she will have to scrupulously obey all group norms without exception unless the expected role permits some deviations. Such is the case when a "mad scientist" type works in an engineering environment; he or she is expected to be absentminded, socially abrupt, and so on. If his or her performance is good, the strange behavior is accepted and even reinforced.

ATTRIBUTION

Attribution theories strive to explain how we perceive the causes of behavior, both our own and that of others. The central concern of attribution theory is whether a particular behavior is caused by internal factors such as personality type and mood or by external factors such as the expectations or presence of other people. In general, behavior that is unexpected or out of character for a particular person or situation is generally interpreted by observers as being caused by internal factors. Such "unexpected" information is assumed to contain more data about what the person is "really like." For example, if the president of the company sends a check and flowers to the sick spouse of a direct report, it's no big news; most employees would likely assume the executive was just doing what executives are supposed to do. There would probably be little said about his personality just because he sends flowers. On the other hand, if the same executive was reported to spend every weekend washing the bedsores of poor invalids on skid row, most everyone would assume it was the result of internal factors; the executive would most likely be perceived as one hell of a nice guy, salt of the earth, and so on.

The situation is reversed when we are attributing our own behavior. If you or I do something such as padding an expense account, we tend to attribute the cause of our behavior to external factors (e.g., "Everybody does it," "The company always screws me, so they owe me," "They know but don't care"). When we do something good, such as donating money to charity, we generally attribute the cause to internal factors (e.g., "I'm a prince," "What a guy").

Don't underestimate the power of attribution effects. They work with and on each of us. One researcher conducted a study that demonstrated just how powerful these influences can be. The scientist and his colleagues admitted themselves to a mental hospital as patients but acted as normally as they always did. The hospital staff did not know they were psychologists. Having been labeled as schizophrenics in their records, they soon found that all of their previously healthy behaviors were attributed to their mental illness. For example, if they wrote a letter, it was recorded in their chart as "writing behavior" and thus representative of their disease. If they talked as a group, it was "socializing behavior," not simply a discussion.

ATTRACTION

It's a well-worn adage that opposites attract. But as the earlier discussion of propinquity might suggest, this is not true. People like nothing better than to associate with and be around those who are very much like themselves. Imagine how pleasant it would be to spend an evening socializing with your own doppelganger; you'd have no disputes, no surprises, no arguments, and no misunderstandings. You'd share the same knowledge, have the same worldview, and you'd even understand each other's humor (or lack of it) perfectly. This is precisely why the number one determinant of successful relationships is similarity of attitudes. The same is true at work. This is why functional areas exist; people would rather be with their own kind—engineers with engineers, finance types with finance types, marketing and sales types out on the golf course together, and so on.

A research study conducted many years ago points out how perceptive people can be about attitudes. The researchers put a group of 20 paid volunteers in a simulated bomb shelter for 10 days. The room had no windows, no radio or TV, and no reading materials. The food was limited and bland, and the only drink was water (nonbottled). The room was hot and humid. There was only a small sink and a chemical toilet behind a curtain. Needless to say, the researchers had gone out of their way to create a very stressful and unpleasant environment. Through one-way windows, the researchers observed and logged every social interaction among the participants. Prior to the study, each participant had taken an exhaustive battery of attitude and personality tests. These were used to develop an attitude index that assessed how alike the people were to one another. At times during the study, a researcher would enter the room and confidentially interview each participant. One of the questions asked was, "If you could have any one person removed from this room, who would it be?" The interviews were conducted in whispers, so no one else could hear what was said.

The results were striking. Without exception, people selected individuals for removal who were most unlike them in their overall attitude index. This was true even if the two people (the rater and the person he or she disliked) had never spoken to each other during the experiment. Just hearing snatches of conversation and watching nonverbal cues was sufficient for the subjects to accurately discern who was most unlike them and thus the best candidates to recommend for removal.

Other research has shown that as people are perceived as having power and authority, their attitudes become ever more attractive to others and thus emulated by them. This mechanism allows the attitude copiers to share in the reflected status of the powerful one. With leaders at work, this aping of attitudes becomes even more powerful since leaders have tremendous influence over employees' futures. Leaders, just like everyone else, enjoy being flattered by having people act like them and accede to their implied wishes (including attitudes). Leaders must be very careful of the messages they are sending with both their "me" and "I" because, no matter what the leader intends, the followers are accurately determining what he or she really means. They will give the leader what the leader's actions are asking for, not what the leader says he or she wants.

POLARIZATION

Polarization is yet another social phenomenon that demonstrates how far people will go to look good to a group they want to be part of. *Polarization* (as in the plus and negative nodes of an electrical circuit) refers to the tendency for individuals in a group to put forward more extreme opinions and views than they would on their own (going further from the average of the distribution). This is caused by people who value the group wishing to appear to support the group more than the other members. This leads to the movement of average group view toward the extremes.

For example, in groups with social or racial prejudices, it has been shown that individuals will express views that are much more extreme than views they shared in private before the group assembled. In work settings, this mechanism can often be seen where there have been poor union–management relationships in the past. Even though working relationships appear to be reasonable to an outside observer, and individual union members and managers may work well together, homogeneous groups from either side present a much different picture. Groups of union personnel will describe the situation as horrible and will vent their spleen at management's abuses. Meanwhile, a group of managers will express similar views as to the union's culpability for the problems. In each case, group members are playing to the expectations of their own groups, upon which they depend for acceptance and support.

The key insight to leaders is that you can't trust a homogeneous group to give you honest feedback. The members will either pander to what they expect you want to hear or outbid one another to see who can most excellently demonstrate their support of the group. A leader must have many channels of communication available, including individuals and heterogeneous groups. Of course, if the leader appears to be happiest when hearing what he or she expects, there is little hope of getting the real story, no matter who is asked.

SOCIAL LOAFING

Social loafing is the tendency for members of groups to cut back on their efforts (or withdraw entirely) when the group becomes too large. As you may have surmised from the earlier discussion of group formation, a large group is one that approaches 10. The loafing occurs because a large group doesn't provide some of the individuals (not everyone in a large group loafs) with enough recognition and/or opportunities to be heard. The problem is twofold: (1) The group achieves less work and lower-quality output than one would expect from the number of people in the group, and (2) when individuals "loaf," they are demonstrating disrespect for the group and lowering its perceived value to others in the group, thus lowering others' inclination to work hard for the group and remain with it. This is yet another reason why ad hoc teams and IWGs must be kept to a maximum of nine, with five to seven being the ideal.

ABILENE PARADOX

The *Abilene Paradox* is a name given by Jerry B. Harvey to a particular (and common) instance of bad decision making driven by conformity forces. The paradox refers to the fact that a group of people can take a course of action that each of them privately thinks is a bad idea. It is caused in large part because nobody in the group will speak up and tell the truth. As Professor Harvey related the story in his article "The Abilene Paradox and Other Meditations on Management," an extended family is enduring a hot Texas afternoon in the 1950s on the porch of a house without air conditioning. One of them suggests that they drive to Abilene to eat in the cafeteria there. It was over 50 miles away with no freeways and in a car without air conditioning. The family members respond with, "Sounds like a great idea" and "Sounds good to me. I just hope your mother wants to go." The mother-in-law answers, "Of course I want to go. I haven't been to Abilene in a long time."

Four hours later, they return to the house, hot, dusty, soaked, and exhausted. The drive had been miserable and the food poor. Finally, one of them sarcastically says, "It was a great trip, wasn't it." The mother-in-law states that she didn't want to go but went along since the others wanted to. The husband and wife say they only went along to keep everybody happy. The wife added that she would have been crazy to want to go anywhere in that kind of heat. Finally, the father-in-law says he only suggested the trip because he thought that the others were bored sitting around on the porch.

Nobody stated the obvious when the suggestion to go to Abilene was made. Because nobody was willing to disagree with what they thought the group wanted, the initial suggestion gathered steam and became reality even though not a single person in the group agreed with the plan. In all groups that have any kind of history (and in many that don't, as in the liquor store example discussed earlier), there are strong forces operating to discourage people from disagreeing with a group's stated or even assumed desires. These forces operate on group members at the "me" level. Keep in mind that we are hardwired with a strong tendency to get along with all of the groups around us. While anyone can override this tendency in a given situation if his or her "I" is paying attention and can tolerate the group disapproval, there is constant, steady pressure from the preconscious to comply with group expectations.

The Abilene Paradox is often cited as being a common business world phenomenon. This is a mistaken interpretation. Abilene seldom operates in its full, classic glory at work. Work groups, unlike social groups, typically have at least one formally recognized person with higher status in the group. As we know from the earlier discussion about authority and leaders, people in a work group are often wary of disagreeing with the boss. This creates the same "don't say anything" result as Abilene if the boss wants something the group doesn't want, but the mechanism is more accurately described as "sucking up to the boss" rather than not wanting to disagree with the entire group. Of course, more than one dynamic is often at work in a situation.

IDIOSYNCRASY CREDITS

The pressures to influence people to defer to the stated or assumed norms are obvious and visible in all environments. Yet, the power of these compulsions can often seem less comprehensive and pervasive because of individuals whose actions appear to belie the power of conformity pressure; some people seem to revel in defying group expectations, and sometimes they get away with it. While some may simply be lacking in political or social awareness (and will pay a price for it), a few are immune to some extent from retribution because they have accumulated idiosyncrasy credits. These "idiosyncrats" earned these credits by having made contributions that are perceived as vital to the organization or a significant authority figure. A stereotypical example is the absentminded professor (or nerdy technical wizard) who acts and dresses strangely, sidesteps formal channels of authority, misses meetings, speaks without internal editing (even going so far as to actually tell the truth to executives!), and so on. This behavior is tolerated and sometimes even fondly perceived because of valuable past contributions (and hoped-for future contributions) by the professor or wizard.

The tolerance accorded those with idiosyncrasy credits demonstrates the power of leaders to flaunt some of the rules some of the time. In essence, group conformity pressures are overruled because one or more authority figures have decided that group norms are less important than the potential contributions of the idiosyncrat. These types of decisions are not usually "I" decisions; they are typically "me" operations.

While granting idiosyncrasy credits is a normal part of primate social processes, leaders need to be aware of the messages that permissiveness toward idiosyncrats sends to other members of the organization. Many people may be unaware of the contributions made by the idiosyncrat and may interpret the permissiveness as a general norm; that is, acting out and disobeying rules is okay. Younger and/or inexperienced employees often make this mistake. Equally damaging are the impacts on those who realize what is going on and view it as unfair. In almost every organization there are many, *many* people who make tremendous sacrifices and contributions but their efforts are little known to upper management. You can be sure that at least half of the "employees of the month" are not the best employees but simply those who had supervisors who made the effort to submit the nominations, thus also looking good themselves. These obscure performers view the leeway given to the idiosyncrats as undeserved special treatment. The resulting resentment and frustration come home to roost in the form of reduced effort and withdrawal.

GROUPTHINK

The term *groupthink* was coined by Irving Janis to describe what can happen when a tightly knit group that is isolated from outside information is under pressure to make an important decision. It is an extreme form of group conformity. In order for groupthink to occur, group membership must be highly attractive to the group members as a result of the belongingness need satisfaction and the status the group provides each of them. As a result, members will not risk disagreeing with what they consider to be group expectations. Going along with the group becomes more important to members than the content or quality of the decisions they are making.

As discussed earlier, when group members are vying for approval, they will often demonstrate their support for the group by stating positions that are much more extreme than their personal, private views (polarization). In a high-status group that is isolated, this competition to be seen as most supportive quickly moves the group to very extreme views. This creates ever-increasing pressure on anyone who expresses the slightest disagreement. Then, because the group hears absolutely no counteropinions, the group begins to think that it can do no wrong and that "any reasonable person" would agree with the group.

Groupthink can occur only if the group has the "luxury" of keeping out external information that would challenge its rationale and decisions. This pretty much limits the possible instances of groupthink to situations in which a group believes that it is threatened, can't take a chance with sharing data with others, or would be misunderstood, along with situations in which it believes that it is so unique and special that its operations must remain apart from society. Thus, groupthink is generally found in only very high-level corporate, military, government, and extremist groups.

Janis cites as an example the Kennedy administration's decision to invade Cuba at the Bay of Pigs. After the disastrous failure, members of Kennedy's cabinet each contended that they privately thought the decision was wrong but believed that everyone else wanted to do it and therefore didn't want to be the only one to disagree. While "pure" groupthink is rarely encountered in day-to-day business, its dynamics demonstrate the incredible power of groups to mold and channel group members' behavior.

One venue in which groupthink appears to operate at a moderate but constant level is within many boards of directors. The ongoing controversies that reach the press about executive compensation, loans, bonuses, fringes, back-dated stock awards, parties, multi-thousand-dollar shower curtains, and the use of chartered planes after retirement can be the result of groupthink processes. Most board members are members of several boards and may be high-level executives themselves. Board members and executives tend to be a fairly homogeneous group (e.g., very high income, mostly male, used to being listened to, and used to getting their views accepted). Therefore, it is not surprising that many boards are somewhat to completely lax about putting any limits on the senior executives who report to the board. In that situation, permissiveness and not asking too many questions appear to them to be perfectly reasonable, the very qualities they have come to expect from the boards to which they report. Further, since they all live in a similar environment of privilege and autonomy, it might seem "impolite" to ask too many questions of a peer.

As this chapter demonstrates, the multitude of forces operating "below the surface" in any organization or group is titanic, complex, and dynamic. If an organization is to move to a more effective corporate culture, leaders must be willing and able to control these forces and bend them to doing what is best for employees and the organization. In the best of cases, this type of effort requires at least 40% of executive and management time and attention. The remaining chapters demonstrate the most effective ways to control and lead these forces.

PART II

The Methods and Tools of Office Kaizen

All too often, the discussion of Office Kaizen methods is limited to the same basic problem-solving tools and value stream mapping (VSMapping) methods that have been used for years in factory applications. While the general concepts of the tools and VSMapping are valid in any environment, their applications to Office Kaizen environments require a slightly different perspective. This is particularly true of VSMapping. This section describes the best tools for Office Kaizen applications and also explores the details of planning, conducting, and following up on VSMapping efforts involving paper and data-driven processes.

This section also discusses an even more important set of methods: structural configurations. Structural configurations are a mix of leadership-mandated processes and cultural change mechanisms. They direct and focus the energies of an organization and its leadership to engage human capabilities and organization dynamics. Without these structures, problem-solving tools cannot create sustainable change.

6

The Structure of
Successful Change

This chapter discusses structural configurations: the established and expected standards, processes, and actions that compel employees to challenge unproductive preconscious assumptions and begin to establish the world-class assumptions that drive kaizen, lean, Six Sigma, and lasting cultural change. Some of these structures are discussed in more detail in *OK1*.

Most of us have been there. The carefully planned, logically reasoned, critical-to-success, "one of our key goals for the year" initiative is launched with fanfare, coffee mugs, and gleaming new posters for the hallways, stairwells, and meeting rooms. There may even be memo cubes, banners on the company sign out front, and laminated wallet cards with the initiative's objectives and values for employees to clutch closely to their bosoms as they work. After the hoopla dies off, the organization goes about its business, and the monthly reviews of the project indicate that everything is fine.

All of a sudden, after several months to as much as a year later, the roof falls in. The project is in dire straits: Goals are not being met, key individuals are no longer working on the effort (having been reassigned without executive knowledge), and there is no hope of reaching the goals within schedule and budget. Despite the business necessity of the initiative, its logical design, its ample resources, its executive blessing, and being carefully tracked by at least three different types of project management software by five different administrators and managers, the initiative is a failure. Time, money, and opportunity are irrevocably lost, and heads may roll.

To a naïve or first-time viewer or participant, it seems logical to assume that there must be one specific, discrete cause of the disaster that could have been avoided had it been identified. Perhaps someone entered a wrong date in a project management spreadsheet, maybe a key activity was omitted, maybe someone held a report for six weeks for a signature, perhaps the ever-famous "my dog ate the forecast," maybe the dollar-to-yen conversion rate changed, and so on. Alas, these types of occurrences, while as ubiquitous to every initiative as are ignored, faded project posters in a conference room, are almost never the cause of major program failures. What is the cause? It is human nature, operating without the benefit of effective leadership within the confines of the leadership black box (LBB).

The LBB nicely illustrates the disruptions caused by the lack of a structured leadership approach. Figure 6.1 displays the LBB and the situation that leaders of all organizations face. The top of the figure shows the mechanisms that executives use to direct their organizations. A formal or informal vision and mission drive the strategy of the organization. The strategy is pursued by an annual operating plan. In this plan are schemes for operating the day-to-day business and achieving planned projects that differ from, or are more significant than, customary day-to-day business operations. These special efforts include such things as developing new products or services, major cost or quality initiatives, software upgrades, new facilities, and so on. There will also hopefully be some thought and resources put aside for dealing with unplanned projects and circumstances (natural disasters, customer service crises, etc.).

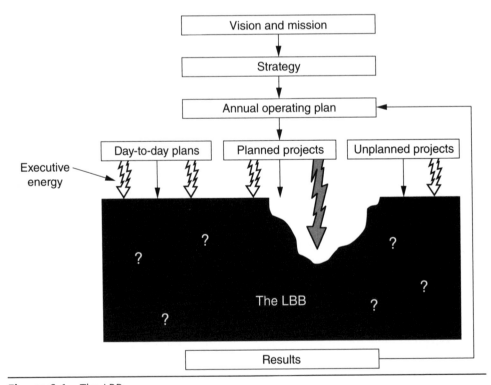

Figure 6.1   The LBB.

Once the annual plan is launched, the executives apply their energies to compel the organization to implement the plans as efficiently as possible. This is where leadership structures come into play—increasing the organization's ability to do what the executives require via better leadership and the resulting improved execution. Executives' energy and actions are represented by the "lightning" arrows in the figure. So far, this is textbook management.

The situation begins to deviate from the ideal when the rest of the organization gets involved in trying to do the work associated with the plans. Few organizations have defined procedures for each manager to use in order to evaluate, prioritize, and direct the myriad activities associated with both the annual plan and the employees' everyday work. There are always procedures for setting objectives and budgets, but there are never any procedures for what leaders must do every day to guide employees toward performing the most effective actions for their situations.

In other words, there are no standard leadership processes or structures. While there are countless documented business processes for many things, none exist to ensure that the intent of executives is properly implemented as the executives intended. In confidential interviews, senior executives concur that they are constantly amazed at how simple, clear objectives at their level can morph beyond recognition once they have traveled only two levels into the organization. Each of them has lived the example presented at the start of this chapter many times in their professional lives.

The LBB is an area of intense but confusing activity. Most executives and managers understand how it works in the same way that nonmechanics understand how automobile engines work: They can describe what's happening in general ("This is our proposal development group") but know few of the technical workings of day-to-day processes and how they interact with, confound, and complicate other processes. When the LBB produces good results, executives assume that their leadership and that of their managers was good and that the organization did as it was told. When a poor result is attained, executives assume that their leadership was good but that either the organization's business processes were faulty or the employees fouled up, or both. In reality, the business processes within the LBB are not the primary cause of major problems, although they can contribute to increased costs, quality lost, and cycle time. The failures are almost always a direct result of the absence of leadership structures to guide the implementation of changes and improvements while the day-to-day business rumbles along. The summed results of dozens or thousands of people each reacting individually, even amid good business processes and overall good intentions, are not leadership but chaos. The existence of value stream maps (VSMs), organization charts, and job titles serves to put a structured face on what is occurring (and may in fact create more efficiency), but it is still *leadership* chaos.

The large gray shaded arrow in Figure 6.1 shows what happens when executives are not happy with a major endeavor or when they are worried about an important effort that has just been launched. Executive energy increases and executives get "personally involved" to a deeper level in the organization. This is manifested by more frequent management reviews, demands for more frequent and/or detailed status reports, and/or red teams, tiger teams, war rooms, and the like. This extra effort does not eliminate the ambiguity; it merely compresses it a bit toward the bottom of the LBB. The executives can check on only so many things, and when they "check," it almost always causes many other problems.

Figure 6.2 opens up the LBB to demonstrate how the chaos of unstructured leadership creates damage to both initiatives and day-to-day work. The short white arrows represent the energy and actions of various managers, supervisors, and employees. The starbursts are places where conflicts, omissions, misinterpretations, adjustments, overlapping efforts, missed assignments, conflicting agendas, and the like occur. At the first few levels beneath the executives, there are relatively few problems. This is because there are fewer upper-level managers, and most of them are more experienced than lower-level employees in dealing with the top executives and interpreting their plans and intentions. They also have more frequent interactions with the top executives. These interactions enable the top executives and senior managers to catch a number of misconceptions and off-key decisions before they cause bigger problems deeper in the organization.

As activity descends into the organization, more people, processes, and departments get involved. There are fewer course corrections from senior executives, and more and more of the employees' actions deviate further and further from executive intentions. The number of problems begins to multiply exponentially, especially in larger organizations. The exponential growth of these problems is not shown in Figure 6.2 due to space constraints and a desire to present a clear diagram. As the area around the gray shaded arrow demonstrates, the impact of executive intervention often creates as many problems (these are the black starbursts) as it fixes; executives can make things happen fast in a specific area, but they often do so by taking resources from other processes and/or overriding established practices in nearby areas.

Keep in mind that Figure 6.2 is a vast oversimplification of reality. In any organization, the dynamics of processes and information flow in all directions

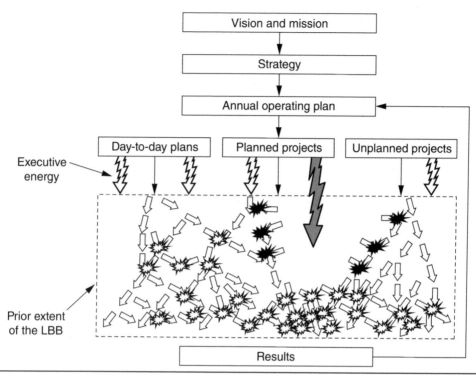

Figure 6.2   The LBB opened up.

within a three-dimensional space. The starbursts in the figure represent only a minute proportion of the disruptions that occur daily in every initiative and project in every organization.

When a problem occurs deep within the LBB, it tends to stay hidden (unacknowledged and uncorrected) for a longer time because it is the "property" of a specific group or process. The owners are justifying their decisions and actions and protecting their pride as well as trying to correct or control the "mistakes" they believe others have made. Executives are seldom aware of what is going on until poor results begin to come out of the bottom of the LBB. By then the damage is done and profits are lost.

A key for creating more effective leadership is to get all the arrows in Figure 6.2 running more or less parallel in the direction that leadership desires. This translates more of the organization's energy into results rather than friction and collisions. This is done by providing each employee with numerous presentations of irrefutable evidence as to proper direction and intent about daily work, key initiatives, and small improvements. With the proper structures in place, employees can't help but see and hear management do and say the right things at the right times at the right points in processes. Employees will monitor and chart metrics that require them to attend to their inputs to the critical processes they impact. Employees will be required, guided, and coached to constantly reexamine their assumptions about improving their work processes. No matter where they turn, whether it is a conversation with a manager or a glance at their area's metrics board, they will be confronted with clear, explicit direction and support for doing the things that best enable their work area to support the organization's overall objectives. Their "me's" will be constantly challenged and required to engage their "I's."

THE STRUCTURES OF MANAGING CHANGE AND LEADERSHIP

Structural configurations are established habits, practices, processes, expectations, and behaviors that compel employees at all levels to perform various repeatable sets of activities that focus them on critical processes, metrics, and issues. These mechanisms require employees, from executives to young new hires, to constantly reexamine their assumptions about improving their work processes.

All of the structural configurations presented in this chapter are world-class best practices. They have been distilled from a larger number of practices used at hundreds of organizations, including some of the best in the world; duplications and redundancies have been eliminated. These structural configurations represent the most parsimonious set that is absolutely required to achieve maximum results for effective leadership. If an organization properly installs and maintains the configurations that follow in this chapter, success is highly probable. If any of the structural configurations are omitted or compromised, the results will be significantly reduced—the elements presented are the minimum required for success.

Other practices and configurations can be added to the minimum set to provide "local flavor" and allow the organization to express its unique personality. For example, an added configuration that some organizations practice is having each executive take a small group of employees to breakfast once a month. This breaks down barriers, lets the executives get out their message face-to-face, and gives them a feel for the current psyche of the workforce. However, it is critical that none of the recommended configurations be omitted in favor of "better" or "other" ideas. The attempt to make such substitutions is usually resistance to trying something new and a desire to rename an existing activity as one of the structural configurations. Furthermore, it is critical that each of the recommended structural configurations (and any other "local" additions) be properly implemented and sustained. Merely going through the motions won't suffice to do anything except broadcast leadership's lack of concern and involvement and reinforce the worst existing traditional "me" assumptions of employees and management.

STRUCTURAL CONFIGURATIONS DESCRIBED

This section describes the nature and operation of 15 structural configurations. These fall into two categories, as shown in Figure 6.3. Configurations that fall under the Leadership of Significant Change umbrella serve to structure and manage large and/or focused changes. These configurations provide a means of ensuring that the executives responsible for the day-to-day operation of a site have a shared and agreed-upon ownership of and involvement in the allocation, direction, and guidance of change resources at the site. The configurations also provide for a large number of extremely effective leadership touches and direct actions (see Chapter 15). A site can be a manufacturing plant, a server farm, a back-office processing center, a research center, an administrative center, and so on.

The Team Metrics and Ownership System (TMOS), the other category of configurations, is a "pure" kaizen entity. TMOS elements enable many small improvements. These configurations are the structures that generate and support the ownership of day-to-day work processes by the employees and the removal of waste in each of the intact work groups (IWGs) throughout a site. TMOS is called the Lean Daily Management System (LDMS) in *OK1*. A

Leadership of Significant Change	Team Metrics and Ownership System
Executive Steering Committee	Daily work group meetings
Work stream teams	Visual metrics display
Work stream team leaders	Key goals visual focus chart
Work stream champions	Kaizen action sheet system
Charters	Team 21
Site improvement facilitator	Weekly continuous improvement meeting
Continuous improvement events	
Kaikaku events	
Gemba Wall	

Figure 6.3 The 15 structural configurations.

number of improvements to the LDMS motivated the name change so there would be no confusion between the contents of *OK1* and this book.

Leadership of Significant Change Elements

Executive Steering Committee (ESC)

The ESC consists of the top-level executives who own and direct the functions and processes at a site. In addition to the executive responsible for the overall site, a typical ESC consists of the heads of various departments such as operations, human resources, finance, sales, quality, customer service, and so on. By and large, the ESC will consist of the same people who would be called the site leadership team, the executive staff, or the management team. In unionized sites, it is wise to include an elected union official if he or she is willing. In the initial stages of many transformations, the union leadership is often reluctant to be so visibly and intimately involved with management in driving change (prior "me" assumptions at work). In that case, arrange to brief the union official immediately after each ESC meeting. Eventually, he or she will come around as the employees' "me" assumptions change. If there is a person at the site responsible for continuous improvement (or lean, Six Sigma, etc.), he or she should also be on the ESC.

The purpose of the ESC is to plan, guide, and direct all change efforts at the site. All too often, many of the functional or process heads at a site are not aware of the wide array of change efforts that are under way at the site. In most cases, each executive is operating with a different set of expectations, a different view of the current reality, and a different vision for the future. In such a situation, each executive runs his or her area of responsibility as a somewhat discrete entity, somewhat connected to the site's processes but serving mainly its own needs.

The ESC operates to ensure that every ESC member has a clear understanding of the change priorities at the site and how they are being addressed. In addition, the ESC approves any new change initiatives that cross departmental or process lines, provides resources to staff the change efforts, and reviews the progress of each change effort each week. Change efforts can include relocating a department, conducting a kaizen event, addressing a quality issue, improving customer service, introducing a new product, and so on. No longer will a department simply assume leadership of change on its own because its name seems related to the issue.

For example, in a traditional environment the information technology (IT) department would organize, lead, and staff any software upgrade projects. This would not happen with an ESC in place. The ESC would select a team leader (probably from IT) for the upgrade, assign a champion from the ESC (see "Team Champions" in this section), and have the team leader and the champion develop a charter and select team members who represent the processes and interests of other groups as well as the IT knowledge required. The ESC would approve or revise the charter, approve or revise the requested hours of effort assigned, and launch the effort. This same process would work for all but the very smallest changes: those whose impacts stay within departments and absolutely, positively don't impact anyone else's processes.

Think about what this means. For probably the first time, the management of the site will have a single, agreed-upon strategy for improvement and change. Further, they would have all discussed every allocation of the resources necessary to implement the changes. Each of the ESC members would understand a little about everything that was going on and a lot about the changes for which he or she would be the champion (see "Team Champions" in this section). Because the ESC reviews each effort each week and the champion checks on each effort a couple of times each week, there is almost no chance that an effort will have problems for very long before the ESC takes action.

The ESC must meet every week at the same time without exception. Remember, every employee is preconsciously attempting to support negative "me" assumptions—1 missed meeting out of 10 is all it takes to create the "Aha, I knew they weren't serious!" response from team members who report to the ESC each week. If an ESC member is traveling or otherwise disposed, he or she must send an empowered substitute. Those who might be used as substitutes should attend a number of meetings as totally silent observers to understand how the meetings work. The meetings must be carefully and tightly facilitated so that ESC members do not revisit old issues or discuss other business topics besides change efforts. The ESC meeting is only for reviewing and prioritizing suggested change efforts; drafting/revising charters; assigning champions, team leaders, and team members; and reviewing each change effort's progress. All other business should be addressed through normal channels such as the regular management meeting. Do not attempt to combine the ESC meeting with the regular management meeting. This always results in the ESC portion of the meeting being compromised.

Each week, each team (or the team leader if all team members do not attend—this is up to the team if the team champion or the ESC has not requested that all of them attend) gives a very brief update of its progress. These presentations should take place at the beginning of the meeting. No new overheads should be produced for these reports. If the team is on schedule and there are no problems, that is all that needs to be said, since the team's charter, with which all ESC members should be familiar, has already specified the schedule, deliverables, objectives, team membership, and the like. If there are problems, the team should briefly discuss a recovery plan, which has already been worked out with the champion before the meeting. The latter part of the meeting is spent reviewing proposed charters (see "Charters" in this section), generating objectives for new charters, following up on open action items, and setting priorities among the list of possible projects and teams.

The ESC meetings provide an opportunity for the ESC members to send a great many very effective direct leadership touches (see Chapter 15). ESC members are seen in the best possible light as involved coaches/leaders, and the employees relish their time in the spotlight.

An important structural configuration that dramatically improves the effectiveness of the ESC is the Gemba Wall, described later in this chapter. Without proper use of a Gemba Wall, an ESC sacrifices 30%–50% of its potential impact on driving change and improving operations.

Work Stream Teams (WSTs)

WSTs are ad hoc teams of employees, usually three to seven, assigned to a change effort by the ESC. The ESC determines the number of hours each member of a WST is permitted, expected, and/or assigned to work on the change effort. Not everyone on a team is assigned to work on the team for the same number of hours. Some team members participate only a few hours per week to ensure that the change effort is accommodating the concerns of their home departments. For example, while several IT people may be on a software upgrade team 20–30 hours per week, other members from operational work areas may be on the team for only a couple of hours each week to make sure that the installed upgrade will be easy for their compatriots to use. Because the ESC members run the site, the team members typically have little trouble getting free from their "normal" work for team duties. If they do have trouble, the team champion resolves the issue with other ESC members if the team leaders cannot get satisfaction.

It is important that team leaders and team members be hands-on process workers, not supervisors or managers, unless there is no other technical resource that can do the job. Teams loaded with managers and supervisors typically do not get as much done, because managers and supervisors tend to spend a lot of time directing others instead of actually doing team tasks themselves. It is important that the ESC meeting facilitator (the site improvement facilitator) be on guard to prevent the ESC from assigning managers and supervisors as team members and leaders unless there is absolutely no other resource with the required technical skills.

Work Stream Team Leaders (WSTLs)

Team leaders must operate as more than simply senior team members who coordinate meetings. WSTLs are responsible for checking on the task status of every team member every day and working with team members to resolve issues and stay on schedule. WSTLs must be high-energy "can do" people who work fairly well with others. It is not necessary that WSTLs be expert in the technical issues their team is attempting to resolve, although in some cases this may be desirable. It is always good practice for WSTLs to be experienced in the basics of problem-solving tools (cause-and-effect diagrams, Pareto charts, brainstorming techniques, meeting management, etc.). Each WSTL meets with the team champion (see "Team Champions" below) at least twice a week in addition to being at the team meeting with the champion at least once a week.

Team Champions (TCs)

TCs are members of the ESC who assist teams of several types (WSTs, kaikaku teams, and kaizen teams—see "Kaikaku Events" and "Continuous Improvement Events" in this section). Each member of the ESC typically champions two or three teams simultaneously once the ESC is up and running. The role of a TC is not to provide daily coaching to the teams (this is the role of the site improvement facilitator [see "Site Improvement Facilitator" in this section]) and the WSTL but to ensure that a team is on track and is getting the resources and support it needs. The responsibilities of a TC include leadership touches such as checking on the team several times a week to see if it needs help, checking to ensure that it is on schedule, and working with members if they are having problems. If necessary, the TC works behind the scenes with other ESC members to arrange new or different resources, resolve disputes between departments that may be impacting the team, and/or approach the ESC for changes in the charter.

It is important that a TC not be in charge of a department or process that a team will be working in or on. The role of the TC is to support the team's work and maintain the change leadership structural configurations, not tell the team what to do. If a TC runs an area being addressed by the team, there is always a tendency for the TC to preconsciously or consciously steer the team toward his or her biases. Also, the team members may hold back on being candid about issues that they fear (either preconsciously or consciously) will elicit a negative reaction on the part of the TC. A TC not directly involved with the areas or processes under examination is more likely to be neutral. Keep in mind that all ESC members are involved in approving the charters for all teams—the interests of every area and process that will be impacted by the WST should be adequately represented by ESC member input into the team charter and WST composition.

Being a TC not only helps the various change teams but provides tremendous benefit to the executive team. Over the course of championing a number of teams, each TC learns a great deal about the workings of parts of the organization of which he or she had little knowledge in the past. Over time, this knowledge changes each executive's perspective from that of an executive who leads an area/function to that of an executive who develops an informed, well-rounded organizational viewpoint. Experienced TCs are also closely in touch with the pitch and timbre of the organization culture.

In the course of being a champion, each ESC member also administers a great many direct leadership touches each week to the team members and an even larger number of positive indirect leadership touches to all of those who witness the TC working with the team. These touches by a group of TCs are invaluable in challenging the traditional "me" assumptions of employees.

Charters

Charters are contracts between the ESC and each team. They detail objectives, deliverables, resources required (including the time commitments of each champion, team leader, and team member), schedules, and planned activities. No team of any kind can begin work until the ESC approves a finalized charter. While some may initially contend that this requirement slows down changes, the opposite is the case. The effort that goes into producing a charter before beginning work is returned tenfold by the quality and speed of charter-supported initiatives. The charter ensures that all members of the ESC have reached consensus on the priority of the issues being addressed, the desired outcomes, the resources that are required, the objectives, and the general approach that will be used. Never again will an effort be pulled up short after a few weeks because an executive suddenly finds out that he or she has to provide a resource for 10 hours per week that cannot be spared. Never again will the executive team discover three months into a project that three departments have been trying to solve the same problem with different approaches, all unknown to one another.

Charters get their starts in many ways. Often, charters are born in the ESC, proposed by ESC members to address annual strategic goals or resolve operational issues that arise suddenly. These issues would arise in the course of normal business, management meetings, and so forth. They would then be referred to the ESC meeting: "Okay, let's develop a charter and get a team working on this in our ESC meeting on Thursday." If the issue is urgent, an emergency ESC meeting would be held following the current meeting. *Never do ESC business in a non-ESC meeting and vice versa.* When management generates the need for a charter, the ESC (or the appointed TC) generates objectives and a rough cut at the other sections. The TC, the team leader, and perhaps the selected team members then complete the charter and it is reviewed by the ESC. It is then either revised or approved. Charters can also come from employees of any level who approach an ESC member with a suggestion for a project.

A critical element of successful charters is specified and audited follow-on activities after implementation. That is, it is not enough for a team to implement an improvement. The team must also take responsibility for ensuring that the changes are supported after they have been implemented. The team must work with involved managers and supervisors (those who "own" the processes being improved) to design and monitor metrics that monitor performance. The team must also assign its own team members to audit involved work areas on a regular schedule to ensure that the changes are being maintained. If the changes are not being maintained, the team must work with the area supervisor and its champion to correct the problems.

Site Improvement Facilitator (SIF)

The SIF, perhaps also called the site lean leader, Lean-Six Sigma leader, Six Sigma leader, site improvement coordinator, and continuous improvement leader, is responsible for coaching the ESC, the champions, and the teams on a daily basis. The SIF also provides lean, kaizen, and continuous improvement training in real time to champions and team members if no other training resource is available. The SIF leads kaizen and kaikaku events and trains others to do the same. The SIF also monitors the performance of champions, team leaders, and team members (such as checking to ensure that each champion meets with his or her team once a week and the team leader two other times). The SIF also tracks and reports on the status of open action items from past kaizen and kaikaku events (see "Continuous Improvement Events" and "Kaikaku Events" in this section).

The importance of a good SIF cannot be overemphasized. Without a knowledgeable and high-energy SIF, the organization runs the risk of falling victim to small but steady degradations in the maintenance of its structural configurations. Each little slip, whether it is a champion who does not meet with the team as required, a team that falls behind its schedule without anyone saying anything, or a team leader who does not check on team members each day, reinforces the worse "me" assumptions of traditionally minded employees and decelerates the benefits the team should be attaining. The SIF also checks on the status of the structural configurations of the TMOS. Only a good, full-time SIF has the time and focus to make sure that all of these duties are performed consistently and correctly and that remedial coaching is quickly delivered. If a site has more than 100 employees, a full-time SIF is absolutely necessary. A site should have one full-time SIF for every 200–250 people. The investment in each SIF will be returned at least 10 times every year. The cost of not having an SIF is immense and would burn out your finance manager's soul if he or she looked upon it.

An SIF must have a basic, applied understanding of meeting management, basic problem-solving tools, lean tools, kaizen methods, basic project management techniques, organizing and coaching of kaizen and kaikaku events, value stream mapping (VSMapping), basic Six Sigma concepts (don't worry about the advanced statistical content; it is rarely used and if you need it, you'll know it and can get it easily), and process mapping *and* must have experience in implementing them in an applied environment. The SIF must be respected by the organization for what he or she knows and can do. The SIF will encounter tremendous resistance. He or she must be a high-energy go-getter who doesn't mind being at the front end of something new and daring and unpopular. At the same time, he or she must be able to work with all employee levels in a harmonious manner. It is imperative that the SIF be interviewed and selected by someone who understands the content of all the requirements and can determine whether the candidate will be able to do meaningful work immediately. An organization can develop an additional SIF from raw internal talent, but it is absolutely essential that the lead SIF be skilled and experienced. Many organizations make the mistake of trying to hire their first SIF "on the cheap"; this is one position that demands hiring and paying for the best you can get whether you can afford it or not, and you can't afford not to have the best in this position.

Continuous Improvement Events (CIEs or kaizen events/blitzes)

A CIE is a short, intense effort by a small team of three to six people usually working full time for a few days to a week to eliminate waste in a selected process and/or area. It is often called a kaizen blitz, a name developed by Toyota (which adopted the term *blitz* from German allies in WWII, who used the term to describe a high-intensity effort for fixing things in armament factories). The intent of a CIE is to study an issue or process using simple lean tools, determine opportunities to eliminate waste, and then implement the changes to eliminate the waste. The detailed preparation, conduct, and follow-up procedures and schedules of a CIE are discussed in Chapters 12, 13, and 14, respectively.

The emphasis on waste elimination, rather than the installation of technology or the spending of capital, is important. Taking waste out of a process is not risky to the product, process, or customers and yields immediate benefits. Just as important, each kaizen event provides the organization with a clear example of how improvement works and how quickly a small group of employees can make a big difference. Since ESC members are encouraged to attend short report-outs at the end of each day's efforts, the events provide an opportunity for a great many positive leadership touches. Of course, the team champion performs many leadership touches, as he or she is required to kick off the kaizen event, drop by a few times each day to visit the team, and attend each day's report-out.

Some misnamed CIE/kaizen blitzes are used for things other than identifying waste and implementing changes right away. This is often the case with VSMapping efforts. Many times, a large process cannot be mapped and attacked by a blitz in one week. When necessary, VSMapping is done as a separate effort. Often, a week or a few days are used to implement 5S (explained in Chapter 7). While every 5S action eliminates waste, it doesn't take much study or analysis to determine what to do. Therefore, while 5S eliminates waste and is extremely important as the often mandatory first step in an area, it is not strictly a CIE/kaizen event, because it is difficult to quantify the benefits of its waste reduction even though they are always present.

Kaikaku Events

A *kaikaku event* is a cross between a kaizen event on steroids and an intense WST project. *Kaikaku* generally means "transformation." It is a focused, planned effort that takes place over a period of several weeks to a few months. The purpose of a kaikaku event is to implement bold new processes, initiatives, and approaches. While a kaizen event focuses on waste elimination in a specific process or area in a short time, a kaikaku event typically involves a large area and more comprehensive objectives using new technology, innovations, and daring new ways of doing things. Waste elimination, while not the main focus of a kaikaku event, is always one of the desired outcomes. In fact, most larger kaikaku events require a few to many kaizen events as part of their project plan. Kaikaku events can be used to install new software systems and/or equipment or lines, reorganize an organization, design and launch a new product, reengineer an office process, design new office quarters, consolidate operations, or even transform a significant portion of an organization to a lean mode of operation.

Unlike a kaizen event, a kaikaku event is typically not a full-time endeavor by most of the team members. Most kaikaku events involve many simultaneous and overlapping work streams and kaizen events, often with built-in wait times as team members wait for information, technology or hardware/facilities, and other aspects of the project to "catch up." Team members work as required in the overall plan, sometimes full time for a week or a day, and sometimes only an hour or two a day for a week or two. The key to a successful kaikaku event is an unremitting sense of urgency and commitment. Management must be continually present and supportive in order to keep the team focused when there are delays or problems. It is all too easy for team members to begin to lose enthusiasm when a kaikaku runs into problems and they are not addressed quickly. The selection of a focused champion and the coaching and oversight of a skilled SIF are critical to kaikaku success.

Gemba Wall

The Gemba (Japanese term—*gem* means "real" and *ba* means "place"—meaning where the hands-on work takes place) Wall is where the status of all WSTs, kaizen events, VSMapping efforts, and kaikaku events and their supporting coaching, leadership, and management involvement are displayed. As large as 10 by 20 feet at a site with many employees and teams, the Gemba Wall shows, for each team, CIE and significant other activity; the names of the team champion, team leader, and team members; perhaps a team picture; and the team's charter including RACI charts, detailed schedules, status on schedule, deliverables, status of deliverables, open and planned action items, and the status of critical success factors (and what is being done to satisfy these factors—sort of failure modes and effects analysis for the critical success factors). The times and locations of upcoming critical events, meetings, and implementations (hands-on actions by the team or employees working with the teams) are also displayed. The purpose of the Gemba Wall is to provide a single, clear, publicly available display of how each effort is progressing. In a very large site or facility, more than one Gemba Wall may be necessary, each exactly the same (yes, it is a lot of trouble—it is always a lot of trouble to be world class).

A critical component of an effective Gemba Wall is the display of the leadership action matrices (LAMs) that track the mentoring, coaching, and leadership activities of champions, management, the site continuous improvement facilitator (CIF; discussed later in this chapter), and team leaders as they work with their teams to make sure that team objectives are met. LAMs are the action trackers of action leadership (AL—see Chapter 15) that specify defined and scheduled activities that are to be performed by various people. For example, a champion is required to meet with the whole team once a week and twice more with the team leader to provide in-person support and coaching as well as a challenge to team members' preconscious assumptions that management doesn't care. Each time one of these meetings is performed as scheduled, a "stoplight" is filled in on the person's chart to show that the action was done. Public display of such performance data provides powerful self-esteem and peer pressure elements to get everyone doing the right thing.

Do not place the Gemba Wall in or near the executive conference room. It must be available for viewing by the general employee population. A good solution is to hold the weekly ESC meeting(s) near the location where the Gemba Wall is displayed. In such a location, the attendance of the ESC members at the meeting provides the executives with an opportunity to administer a great many leadership touches as they come and go and are observed. If it is not too noisy at the location, the team update portion of the meeting should be held directly in front of the Gemba Wall so that team information can be referred to.

Team Metrics and Ownership System (TMOS) Elements

All of the TMOS structural configurations are focused on encouraging and enabling small, continuous improvements in IWGs of no more than nine people (a "TMOS group"). The size is restricted to assume maximum team spirit and commitment. If a work group has 10 or more members, it must be divided into at least two TMOS groups. Each TMOS group will have its own meeting with its own visual metrics display (see "Visual Metrics Display" in this section). If a group of 15 employees works collaboratively during the day as one large team, they would be divided into two or three TMOS groups, each with an identical board. If the TMOS groups work on different parts of the process (as in a bank processing center with little movement of workers between the groups), each TMOS group may have a unique set of metrics. I have installed as many as 250 TMOS groups in an operation with 1200 employees. Yes, it takes a lot of effort to set up these TMOS groups; it takes a lot of effort to be world- . . .

Daily Work Group Meetings (WGMs)

The single most influential structural configuration (if an organization were to install only one) is the daily WGM. This is a five-minute, stand-up meeting by a TMOS group as close to the start of the workday or shift as possible. It should be held in the work area if safety and noise considerations are not an issue. If the environment is noisy, it is absolutely mandatory that the group have earphones connected to the speaker's microphone. If people cannot hear easily, they cannot benefit from the meeting and will withdraw their involvement. Managers often contend that the expense of earphones is an unreasonable accommodation, but it is a small price to pay for complete engagement of the workforce. And yes, it is a lot of trouble to manage and maintain the headphones. Assign a team of employees to handle it.

The daily meeting is a "CNN"-type overview of what happened yesterday, what's likely to happen today, critical commitments, impending deadlines, meetings scheduled, the nature of the day's work (if it varies), a quick review of how the group's metrics are doing, announcement of any kaizen action sheets (see "Kaizen Action Sheet System" in this section) submitted, any change in Team 21 status (see "Team 21" in this section), and any other important announcements. The meeting is not a forum for problem solving or complaining. The meeting facilitator must be coached to cut off whining and long-winded expositions. The meeting must be short, snappy, and meaningful, or it will quickly become a burden. Properly run, it will become the catalyst for team ownership and commitment. Once one person in a group is able to run the meeting properly, others who wish to be facilitators are coached. When several or all of the group members are trained, the group can determine how to rotate facilitators.

Visual Metrics Display (VMD)

The VMD is a bulletin board (cork, white board, a piece of plywood, etc.) on which the TMOS group's information is maintained. The VMD should contain, among other things, the TMOS group's kaizen action sheet system, its key goals visual focus chart, its Team 21 chart, and other information that it or its supervisor/lead thinks is important. Other data may include attendance charting, cross-training status, production, safety and quality performances, and so on. Information that should not go on the VMD are social announcements, EEOC (Equal Employment Opportunity Commission) and safety posters, general memos on company policy, ads for selling personal items, personnel announcements, and the like. It is important that the VMD come to be considered a direct reflection of how the TMOS group is doing on its work and what its employees are doing to make their area perform better for the organization. A board cluttered with trivia and miscellany will not be viewed seriously.

Key Goals Visual Focus Chart (KGVFC)

The KGVFC displays the most important metrics of a TMOS group on a daily basis. The KGVFC should be used only for metrics that present significant challenges (it would not be used to simply track normal production unless output is a serious ongoing problem). Figure 6.4 presents a KGVFC as it might

Area/Process: Human resources

											Day of the month—June 2006																				
	No.	**Key metric**	**1**	**2**	**3**	**4**	**5**	**6**	**7**	**8**	**9**	**10**	**11**	**12**	**13**	**14**	**15**	**16**	**17**	**18**	**19**	**20**	**21**	**22**	**23**	**24**	**25**	**26**	**27**	**28**	**29**	**30**
Daily	A	Changes in benefits completed	Y	Y			R	G	Y	Y	R			Y	G	G	G	G			G	G											
	B	Requisitions entered	G	G			G	Y	Y	G	G			Y	G	G	G	G			Y												
	C	Review suppliers notified	Y	Y			Y	Y	Y	G	G			G	R	Y	G	G			G												
	D	Daily safety data collected	R	R			Y	Y	R	Y	R			Y	Y	G	G	Y			G												
	E																																
Weekly	F	Safety boards updated		Y					Y						G																		
	G	Cross-training (hours)		Y					G					R																			
	H																																

Performance level criteria

Legend			A	B	C	D	E	F	G	H
Green (G)		Goal completely achieved	100%	100%	100%	100%		100%	>10	
Yellow (Y)		Goal partially achieved	>75%	>80%	>90%	>90%		>95%	>5	
Red (R)		Goal missed	<75%	<80%	<90%	<90%		<95%	<5	

Figure 6.4   Sample KGVFC.

look at the daily meeting on the 20th day of a given month. This version has room for five metrics that are tracked daily and three that are tracked weekly, although not all spaces are used. The KGVFC is a "stoplight" chart in that a green-yellow-red color-coding system (but shown here in black and white) is used to assess whether the daily or weekly performance completely achieves goal (green or "G"), partially achieves goal (yellow or "Y"), or fails to achieve goal (red or "R"). The bottom of the KGVFC presents the criteria used for assessing the performance of each metric. At the end of each month, the work group and its supervision decide on the metrics for the next month. Some may be dropped, some may be added, and various performance levels may be changed if achieving "green" has become too easy.

The KGVFC is effective because it is simple, straightforward, visible, and "in the face" of the TMOS group every time they walk by the VMD. Often, the employees must take a daily performance number or two from a printed report or a computer screen and then place the appropriate colors on the KGVFC. Some managers, when first working with these charts, see the transfer as a waste of time. It is not. The data on the VMD create a single view of the current and recent situation, forcing the TMOS group to face the truth, good or bad, at least at every daily meeting and often many times during the day as they walk by. This is critical for challenging any false "me" assumptions about how they are doing or what's important. Metrics and performance data in computer reports or buried on a hard drive that must be deliberately accessed in order to be viewed are next to worthless in general and completely worthless for engaging a group of employees.

Kaizen Action Sheet System (KASS)

The KASS is a kaizen suggestion system maintained within each IWG. The purpose of the KASS is to provide each work group with a structured means to identify and eliminate waste in its own area and/or processes by itself, without having to go outside the work group for resources. This means that the suggestions submitted within the KASS cannot involve technology, plant maintenance, spending a lot of money (each work group should have a certain amount of petty cash or credits that it can allocate to its within-group improvements for signs, brackets, etc.), or changes that would impact another group's processes. Any of these categories of improvements, as well as safety issues, would have to be referred "upstairs" for possible action via management decree, kaizen or kaikaku event, or formation of a WST. Kaizen action sheets (KASs) are the means by which IWG members submit their suggestions. Figure 6.5 presents a sample KAS.

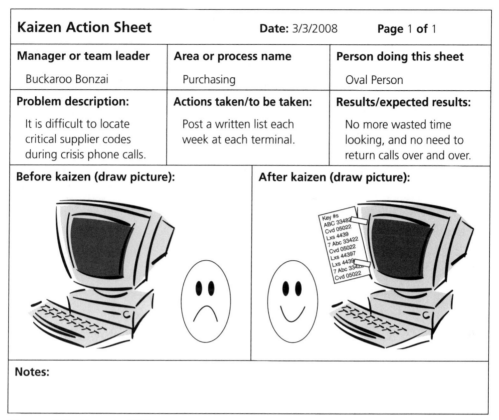

Kaizen Action Sheet		**Date:** 3/3/2008	**Page** 1 **of** 1
Manager or team leader	**Area or process name**		**Person doing this sheet**
Buckaroo Bonzai	Purchasing		Oval Person
Problem description:	**Actions taken/to be taken:**		**Results/expected results:**
It is difficult to locate critical supplier codes during crisis phone calls.	Post a written list each week at each terminal.		No more wasted time looking, and no need to return calls over and over.

Figure 6.5 Sample KAS.

The problem and the proposed solution are described in one or two sentences, the expected impact is noted, and before-and-after pictures are drawn. The pictures need not be sophisticated, but they are essential; they require the employee to think about the problem and the solution in a different manner (with a different part of the brain). This generates more involvement and ownership. It is best if each KAS is handwritten so that those without computers are not intimidated (and there's no value in spending time selecting fonts and clip art and doing endless revisions because anything computer generated is supposed to be "perfect").

The KASS operates via four folders or bins attached to the work group's VMD. Their labels and functions are as follows:

1. *Blank:* KASs are available at all times on the group's VMD, to be completed whenever an employee has an idea.

2. *Submitted:* A completed KAS is inserted into this folder. Each day at the WGM, the meeting facilitator announces each KAS in the submitted folder. The problem, suggested resolution, and identity of the

submitter are described. The solution is not discussed or evaluated at this time; this is handled at the weekly problem-solving meeting or among employees during available times during the workday.

3. *In progress:* After each KAS is announced, it is placed in this folder until it is implemented or the work group decides not to do it.

4. *Resolved:* When a KAS idea is implemented or turned down, it is placed in this folder. When the folder becomes full, the KASs in it are discarded. Do not collect the KASs and pass them around as "best practices." Do not enter them into a spreadsheet or count them. The best practice is implementing and maintaining the KASS, not the content of the ideas implemented or the number collected; almost any group doing the same work would come up with the same ideas if given the chance. The only ideas a work group will be enthusiastic about are the ones it generates. The key to success with the KASS is to allow each work group to operate its own system, to be involved, and to be committed to generating its own kaizen improvements. Ideas created by other groups will not be welcomed. Ideas involved with safety are an exception in which management may have to mandate adoption between groups (with appropriate discussion about work group–specific considerations).

Team 21

Team 21 provides an IWG with a long-term improvement plan that focuses on the quality, not the performance, of all of its processes. The appendix at the end of this book presents the graph template and the detailed level definitions for the Office Kaizen team. It requires a work group to assess itself and plan improvements based on selected T-metrics that evaluate the effectiveness of work processes and practices. The improvements are focused solely on kaizen, that is, small improvements based on waste removal. There are different sets of Team 21 for work groups in areas such as general office (or administrative functions), manufacturing, sales, engineering, and so on. The Team 21 approach can be constructed and/or customized for any work group, even those outside the mainstream of typical kaizen efforts, such as legal teams, research labs, and the like. Figure 6.6 shows the current Office Kaizen Team 21 status for an office work group and its goals for the next 12 months.

The first 20 T-metrics from left to right assess the work group's status against world-class performance levels. The square boxes inside the graph

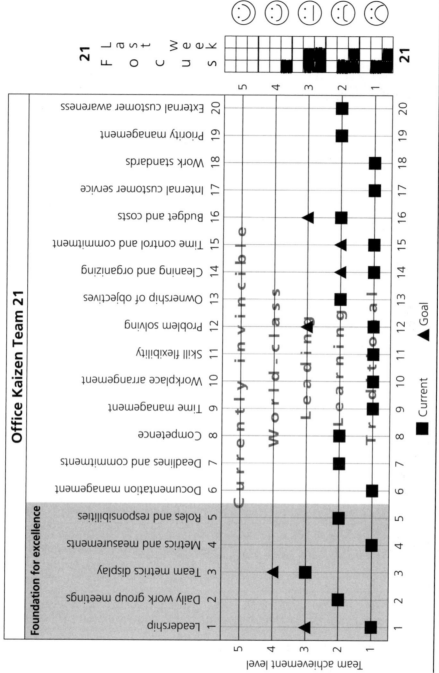

Figure 6.6   Team 21 graph for a work group in a general office environment.

show where the work group stands as of the last assessment. Each of these metrics is evaluated on a five-point scale. The general descriptions of the five levels of every T-metric and the specific level descriptions of the deadlines and commitments T-metric (number seven) from the Office Kaizen (general office/administration) Team 21 are shown in Figure 6.7. Every Team 21 has 80 specific definitions (four levels for each of the 20 metrics; the first level is not described since it is automatically "earned").

Given that any group automatically scores a 1 on each of the first 20 metrics, the minimum starting score is 20. The highest possible score is 100, a level of performance that is almost impossible (I have never encountered one in over 5000 work group assessments). In order to move to a higher level on any metric, the work group must meet every single aspect of the definition. The T-metric levels are designed to make it relatively easy to move from level one to two, harder to move from level two to three, very difficult to move from level three to four, and extremely difficult to move from level four to five.

If an IWG has not been doing anything structured and focused to improve its performance and is typical of most work groups, the group's initial assessment will be approximately 25–35, with an average of 30 across all industries (the example shown in Figure 6.6 illustrates a typical beginning score of 30: 11 ones + 8 twos + 1 three = 30). It is important that work groups

Level	General description	Specific definition for Office Kaizen T-metric 7: deadlines and commitments
5	Seamless, transparent automatic excellence	Firm schedules are always set and are never missed. Internal and external customers have full confidence that delivery will be on time, every time.
4	World-class, outstanding, not quite always automatic	The work group is skilled in using a structured system to manage deadlines and commitments (DCs). Every aspect of managing DCs is defined and understood; they are met at least 98% of the time.
3	System installed; frequent glitches but system works	The work group implements a structured system to manage DCs, and they are met at least 90% of the time.
2	Awareness established; first small steps taken	The work group begins to document and measure DCs; many DCs are regularly missed.
1	The usual mess, reactive, few or bad systems	Better left unsaid.

Figure 6.7   General level descriptions and the specific definitions for the T-metric of deadlines and commitments.

assess themselves, as managers almost always overestimate the performance of a work group that reports to them.

Prior to Team 21 implementation, the ESC sets a single three- to four-year goal for all IWGs at its site. An IWG can be expected, with proper supervision and coaching, to gain 10 points per year on any Team 21 metric. Given average starting points of about 30, a typical and appropriate three-year goal is 60 points, and a four-year goal is 70 points. Work groups that start lower than 30 will be able to pick up more points with the same amount of effort. The few work groups that start out with higher scores will have to earn fewer points, but each point will be harder to earn.

Once an IWG has assessed itself (after an introduction to Team 21 and an explanation of how it works) and a multiyear goal has been established, the work group selects the T-metrics and point levels on which it will focus in the coming year. It then selects the first T-metric on which it will work. Working as a group, they develop a plan to "pick up the point(s)" and post it on their VMD. The plans must be kept simple (10 action items at most), with specific group member names and dates attached to each action item. Given an approximate goal of 10 points per year, each work group that starts at about 30 points should set a monthly objective of picking up at least one point. This provides a cushion if they run into problems or are exceptionally busy.

Two points are critical to the success of Team 21:

1. Supervision must provide encouragement (leadership touches—see Chapter 15) and coaching to ensure that the plans are developed and attended to by the group.

2. The group must have some time to work on the improvement plans and the activities that are necessary to attain and sustain the improvements. The weekly continuous improvement meeting (see "Weekly Continuous Improvement Meeting" in this section) provides the time; management must provide the encouragement and coaching.

It is critical that the group work on its Team 21 a little each week. T-metric 21 helps motivate a work group and keep management informed visually by assessing the work group's efforts during prior weeks. Each Friday, one box in one of the levels of the T-metric 21 five-level "smiley-frowny" scale is shaded in by the team at its daily start-up meeting. The scale values are shown in Figure 6.8. After six to eight weeks of scoring on T-metric 21, it is relatively easy to assess whether the team has been seriously attending to its Team 21 performance on a weekly basis.

Level	Mood	Level description of last week's Team 21 effort
1	☹	No action taken on a plan to improve on any of the T-metrics (a plan is a posted list of team-developed actions that must be completed to improve by at least one level on one of the T-metrics).
2	☹	At least one action item on one plan was completed.
3	😐	At least three action items on a plan were completed.
4	🙂	At least four action items on a plan were completed, <u>or</u> one T-metric was improved by at least one point.
5	🙂	At least five action items on a plan were completed, <u>or</u> one T-metric was improved by two levels, <u>or</u> two T-metrics were improved by one level each.

Figure 6.8   The five-point scale used to assess weekly Team 21 progress.

Weekly Continuous Improvement Meeting

An IWG with the KASS and a Team 21 improvement plan will need time to work on improvements. Each TMOS group should move off-line to a meeting room for 60 minutes each week to discuss, plan, and implement improvements. If the environment requires continuous operations, the meetings can be held with alternating halves of the personnel or some other arrangement such as holding the group over for an extra hour after shift change once a week. However, even if it means paying for a mandatory hour of overtime each week for every employee, the meetings must be held (world class does not come without investment even though the returns are immense). These meetings should be facilitated to keep them on track and make the most of the time. Some organizations start with 30-minute meetings and increase the time to one hour if and when the number and complexity of improvement ideas being considered increase. The status of all improvement efforts must be displayed on the TMOS group's VMD. Often, when management is introduced to TMOS, it is reluctant to dedicate 30–60 minutes a week to a work group improvement meeting. If this time is not made available (and used wisely, of course), the work group will spend much more than an hour each week working inefficiently and/or dealing with problems that could have been solved. Go ahead, I know you're already thinking it: Becoming world class is not easy.

The weekly meetings should start and end in a conference or training room. It is best if each group always meets at the same time and place each week, as this creates healthy anticipation and some ownership of the meeting room time. Many organizations construct or dedicate rooms or leased trailers just for this purpose and equip them with projectors, flip charts, walls that permit taping of brainstorming ideas, and so on. Assuming eight hours a day of work time and one hour per meeting, one such meeting space can provide for 40 work groups, two enables 80, and three provides for 120 work groups. At an average of five per work group, three rooms can provide for a 600-person site even if they all work on one shift. During meetings, the work group will often move to its work area to explore or implement ideas that have been discussed and designed in the room.

Each room should also have process improvement supplies appropriate to the work group's processes. For example, the room might be equipped with sign- or label-making materials. A central store should hold materials that work groups may require for setting up kanban boards for forms, tabs for files, materials for putting together quick, temporary shelving, and so on.

7

Common Office Kaizen
Tools and Methods

Acountless number of tools and methods are involved with kaizen, lean, Six Sigma, and continuous improvement in general. Fortunately, the 80–20 rule applies here, as it does in most situations: 20% of all tools are used for 80% of the work. Since the proper use of the most commonly employed tools is central to determining the objective truth of a situation and engaging the participation and knowledge of involved individuals and teams, it is important to review how, when, and why these various tools and methods should be used. This will simplify the discussion as to how the tools are best applied to the conduct of the various improvement events described in Chapters 8–14.

While the earlier chapters should have made this obvious, I have found that one cannot emphasize it enough: The use of tools, however impressive the short-term results they obtain may be, does *not* create, lead to, or indicate the presence of world-class practices. If it did, practically every organization would be world class by this time. I have seen misbegotten pits of traditional mismanagement practices, waste, poor service, dangerous working conditions, and shoddy products that have been used to train everyone in dozens of lean, kaizen, and Six Sigma tools. Without proper leadership and use of the structural configurations discussed in Chapter 6, tools are only a bandage being applied to a badly infected, pus-oozing, gangrenous . . . you get the point. Tools and their applications look good, but alone they cannot do anything but delay dealing with the real problem. With good leadership and consistently supported structural configurations, the tools are, if properly used, a tremendous accelerator and enabler of process improvement of every kind, including leadership and structural configuration practices.

In 1985, Goal/QPC in Methuen, Massachusetts, published a booklet called *The Memory Jogger: A Pocket Guide of Tools for Continuous Improvement.* The booklet has been wildly popular, and millions of copies have been sold in many languages. In it, editor Michael Brassard presents the seven quality control tools. These seven tools include line/run charts, histograms, flowcharts,

Pareto diagrams, statistical process control (SPC) charts, scatter diagrams, and cause-and-effect (C&E) diagrams. Since you may encounter references to the individual tools as being part of the "seven," it will be helpful to know which ones they are. In the following sections, they are referenced with "7QC."

THE BROWN PAPER APPROACH

The brown paper approach is not a tool per se but more of a method or mode of presentation and discussion. Of course, given your understanding of pre-conscious decision making, an effective mode of presentation is itself a change tool. As Marshall McLuhan stated in his book *Understanding Media: The Extensions of Man* (New York: McGraw Hill, 1964), "We become what we behold. We shape our tools and then our tools shape us." The use of a group involvement/decision-making method that attempts to create consensus-driven results reinforces the best aspects of world-class organizations.

The *brown paper approach* uses large sheets of standard brown wrapping paper (from a roll) to display information and analyses. Most rolls of heavy-duty brown wrapping paper are 28 inches wide and come in various lengths, most commonly 50 feet (beware of the flimsy stuff; it tears too easily and falls apart). Always buy twice as much as you think you will need (unless your use of tools stops cold, you can always use it on the next effort). The team uses sticky notes or pieces of cut-up copy and/or colored paper that are attached with small pieces of masking tape (and are then permanently attached with transparent tape when all input is finalized). The use of the brown paper serves several important purposes:

1. It permits an entire team (and many observers during report-outs and presentations) to work on and view an entire process at one time. This is never easy with a computer, because when you move from screen to screen or slide to slide, you lose track of the previously viewed portions of the process.

2. When a computer is used, one person does most of the data entry work while other people stand around talking about other things or making phone calls. With the brown paper approach, each member of the team gets hands-on time creating and posting items. This involvement creates ownership of the work and a commitment to doing a good job.

3. The completed brown paper can be easily moved to other locations for display and explanation. When it is shown and explained to groups of employees, it is called an exposition display.

4. Most executives and managers are familiar with (and tired of) Microsoft PowerPoint presentations that have little impact any more. A brown paper creates instant interest because it is large, colorful, and enables the entire process to be viewed at one time.

5. Because a brown paper is handmade, it is not expected to be graphically perfect—little time is wasted selecting fonts and/or picking out cute clip art.

Everything in an event, analysis, or study should go on a brown paper. Resist the urge to work with a screen from a computer projector or enter things directly into a computer. Once data go into a computer, they are typically not fully processed by everyone or are changed by individuals without benefit of team input.

The edges of the front face of the brown paper should be covered by clear plastic packing tape, flush with edges. Do not buy the cheap brands of tape, as the tape is often hard to remove from the roll and shreds while unrolling. This clear tape strengthens the brown paper and protects the edges from tearing when the masking tape that attaches it to the wall is removed when moving the brown paper to another location. When joining brown paper sheets and/or adding extensions in the middle, join the sheets by taping on the back side with clear plastic packing tape.

Always use masking tape to attach the brown paper to a wall; it is easy to remove from the clear tape and usually does not remove paint from the wall. Once a brown paper has been finalized, the individual papers on it should be taped down with removable transparent tape. Again, the cheap tape is not worth the trouble it causes. And do not use the cheaper "permanent" shiny tape for attaching notes or taping them down permanently, because you cannot easily write on such tape and it rips the brown paper if you have to remove it.

GROUP BRAINSTORMING METHODS

Group brainstorming tools are those that are most helpful to a group that is collecting, conceptualizing, organizing, or refining information. Of course, as mentioned earlier, the use of a brown paper by itself for any group activity does this to a certain extent with any information because it is easy for many people to see the same thing and make contributions.

Modified Affinity Diagramming

Affinity diagramming was introduced in the mid-1980s in the *Memory Jogger Plus* book from GoalQPC of Methuen, Massachusetts (editor Michael Brassard learned of it from the Japanese, and some variants of it had been homegrown in some American advertising companies from the late 1940s onward). I prefer a slightly modified approach that I cleverly call modified affinity diagramming (MAD). MAD is a brainstorming, consensus-based, and consensus-building technique for gathering and prioritizing information about an issue or problem. It requires participation and thus builds involvement and commitment. It also builds teamwork and encourages innovative thinking. It can be used to generate ideas/content for everything from problem solving to annual planning. MAD works best with 10 or fewer people. When more than 10 people take part, it is often necessary to have the group work in sequence in smaller groups so that everyone can contribute (in larger groups, two or three people will always stay in back and not be involved).

Figure 7.1 presents the results of an MAD exercise conducted by the divisional management team of an electronics parts manufacturer that was having problems due to the dramatic reduction of defense-related business when the

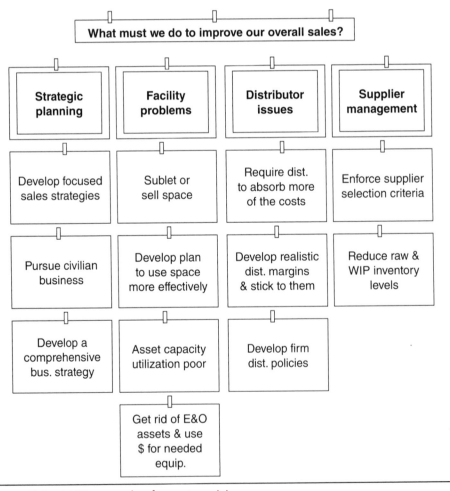

Figure 7.1　MAD example after categorizing.

Soviet Union collapsed. As do all of the tool examples shown in this chapter, Figure 7.1 displays "typed" content on posted sheets rather than what should always be handwritten content, for purposes of legibility.

Each person is given blank sheets (from either pads of large sticky notes or half or quarter sheets of copy paper), a bold, dark marker (use markers that will not bleed through if you are posting things on a wall), and colored dots. Do not use small sticky notes, as they cannot easily be read from more than three feet away. I find even the large sticky notes to be too small, but many groups use them. I have found that cutting a sheet of standard copy paper in half creates two 5½ by 8½ inch sheets that accommodate large letters that can be easily viewed from 12 feet away. The exercise is done on a sheet of brown paper about six feet wide by two widths high (56 inches) that is taped to the wall (refer back to "The Brown Paper Approach" section for instructions on how to prepare the brown paper).

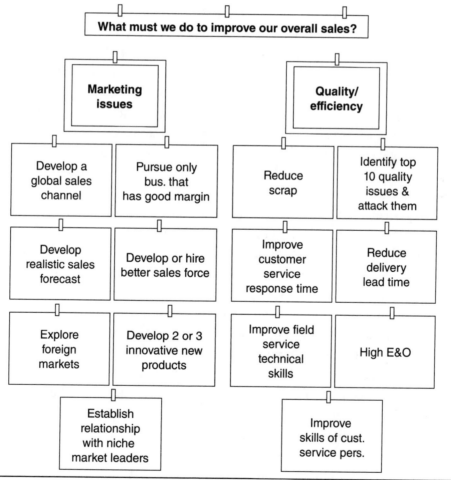

Figure 7.1 MAD example after categorizing. (Continued)

The process starts with posting a problem statement, issue, or question on the top of the brown paper. This statement should be written in large letters on a strip of white paper that is taped to the brown paper. It is important that the problem statement be as specific as possible. In Figure 7.1, the question is, "What must we do to improve our overall sales?"

The MAD process begins with the facilitator reading the problem statement. When a participant gets an idea, he or she simultaneously writes the idea on a sheet and calls out the idea. The "calling out" eliminates some of the duplication and stimulates others' thinking; it is not a request for approval or acceptance. The writing on the sheets should be as large and as dark as possible so that it is easy for others to read from a distance. Make large letters that take up as much of the sheet as possible, even if the letters must be distorted such as making them tall and thin. Each idea must also be a phrase. For example, "budget" is worthless; what about the budget does "budget" mean? "Develop budget for research" is much better. Each entry should include a verb and a phrase or a noun with several adjectives if "problems" are the issue. After a person writes down the idea, he or she walks the sheet up to the brown paper and tapes it up with a small piece of masking tape at the top middle of the sheet. Do not tape sheets to one another, as they tend to tear when they are moved. This active participation—the writing, the calling out, and the posting—is important for creating general buy-in from each person. Their actions are challenging preconscious assumptions that such exercises are useless and not worth the participation. This creates cognitive dissonance and the participant is forced to conclude that either he or she is a spineless coward for not voicing disdain for the activity or the activity and its participation are not so bad after all.

Every five minutes or so, the facilitator should read aloud the problem statement and each of the ideas that have been posted to that point. This helps participants come up with new ideas. When the group cannot generate any more ideas, the categorizing step begins. The facilitator instructs the group to move to the brown paper and move the sheets into categories of their choosing by moving them around *without any talking*. I have found that it is almost impossible to stop all the talking and joking around at this point, but it is important to try in order to minimize the status and hierarchy effects that talking creates. A category can have many sheets or only one. If a participant does not agree with the category of an item, he or she can move it. The work continues until all movement stops.

The facilitator then works with the group in a guided discussion mode to develop a name for each category. For example, sheets such as "Require dist. to absorb more of the costs" and "Develop firm dist. policies" appear to be distribution issues, so "Distributor issues" was picked as the category name.

This was written on a new sheet and then denoted as a category name by drawing a border around the edge. In some cases, the category name might be one of the sheets. If a sheet is selected as a category name, it is duplicated and the new one is posted above the category with a border drawn around it. This is done so that all sheets can be moved later and the category names will remain intact for other uses.

After the category names are completed, the facilitator reviews each sheet within each category with the participants in a guided discussion mode (sometimes heavily guided if the group is not doing well) to determine whether each sheet belongs in the category. Often, this step creates additional categories and results in the addition of new sheets and the elimination or combination of others. If participants add new items, everyone should have input on the category in which they are placed. Many of the adjustments are made because some entries are general statements of several specific issues of the same nature. An example of this would be when sheets such as "Develop compensation plan for sales," "Uneven compensation for different personnel doing the same sales job," and "Poor incentive compensation plan for salespeople" are generated. They might all be combined into one sheet and written as "Implement new sales compensation program."

Once the categories are established and vetted, the formal MAD is completed. A frequent next step that is useful for moving toward an action plan is to prioritize the individual sheets as an entire group. First, the logic for determining priority is agreed upon, such as most critical to profits, most important to customer service, and so on. Each participant is given a fixed number of colored dots (all one color). The number of dots is adjusted according to the total number of sheets generated. For 30–40 sheets with eight people, distributing 10 dots per person is appropriate. For more people and more sheets, the number of dots given to each person is adjusted but should not go above 15 per person. Each person is then instructed to put dots on those sheets that he or she thinks are important. Each person may put only one dot on a given sheet. The dots are then counted up, and the dot total for each one is written in a corner of the sheet. The final ranking of each sheet's total number of dots is written in very large print with a highlighter in the middle of each sheet. Figure 7.2 shows an example of a few sheets in the "Distributor issues" category from the Figure 7.1 example.

Any number of next steps can then be taken. The ranked items can be cross-referenced against ongoing and planned actions to determine whether the issues are getting the right attention. Action plans can be developed for each item. In some cases, the ranked items are then further evaluated against one or more focused categories. For example, each item could be assessed on the criteria of short-term profit impact, long-term sales, technological risk, and impact on

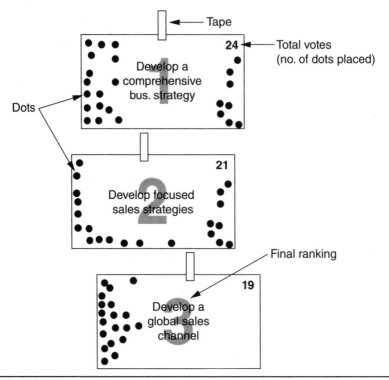

Figure 7.2 Close-up section of a MAD after final ranking.

customer satisfaction. These categories would run from left to right on a new brown paper, and the items would be listed on the left side, from highest ranked on the top to lowest on the bottom (using perhaps only the top 5–10 items). With 4 assessment criteria and 10 items, the matrix would be 4 wide by 10 high, not counting the items column on the left and the criteria row at the top.

Almost any method can be used to rate the criteria. While it can be cumbersome, I prefer having each person rate each item on each of the criteria, using a three to one range, where three is great impact, two is some impact, and one is slight or no impact. The rating can be done by giving each person dots and having him or her write the rating on the dots (dots should be a light color so the number can be seen). Almost any other method that suits the facilitator or the group can be used. This type of method is very powerful for creating buy-in to the results because everyone had input, knew they had input, and understood the process, and it wasn't just a meandering discussion.

7QC—Cause-and-Effect (C&E) Diagrams

Often called "fishbone" diagrams because their shape resembles a fish skeleton, C&E diagrams are an excellent way to explore the causes of a result or effect that is being explored. Figure 7.3 shows a "5M" C&E done by a

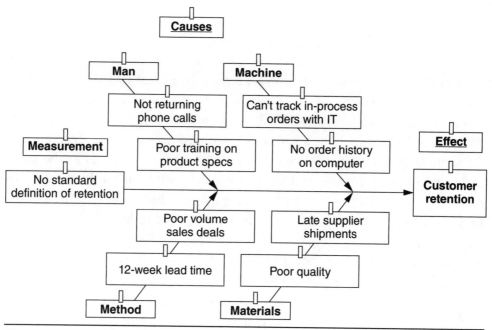

Figure 7.3 An example of a C&E diagram.

sales group to explore the cause of poor customer retention. 5M is a mnemonic aid that stands for man, machine, measurement, method, and materials. Given today's politically correct work environment, such a horrifically gender-insensitive label as "man" may be ill advised. Therefore, to maintain the handy 5M label, I suggest changing the first M from "man" to "mammal" (you could bring your dog in to help out!). The 5M are used as idea generators. You could use any five (or more) categories for a C&E diagram; the 5M are simply one traditional approach. The lines of the "fish" should be drawn on the brown paper. Everything else should be put on taped-on sheets so that they can be moved if it is necessary to make more room for input or activities such as rating the issues, as mentioned earlier.

As with the MAD process, use brown paper, white sheets, and masking tape to post content on a C&E. Use the same procedure as in the MAD process (i.e., each person writes, calls out, walks up, and posts his or her paper). In fact, an MAD could be used for the same purpose as a C&E, although an MAD is sometimes too time intensive and overly complex for a group facing a very specific issue. For example, it might be wise to use a C&E for an issue such as "Why are customer account numbers being entered incorrectly?" and an MAD for an issue such as "What can be done to improve customer service?"

7QC—Line/Run Charts

Line charts are the ubiquitous graphs for output, profit, sales, production, and so on, that are found on what seems like every other Microsoft PowerPoint slide in the world. Figure 7.4 shows a typical line chart (sometimes called a run chart) for the number of tissue sample tests processed by a pathology technician working a 12-hour shift. Each entry on the chart is the average of the three readings for that hour taken over three days for the same technician on the same shift. The figure graphs the mean (average) number of analyses for each hour on the y-axis against the consecutive shift hour on the x-axis. The round data point dots are often not shown on line charts, but they are helpful for easy viewing if only one or two items are tracked (otherwise, they tend to clutter up a graph).

Line charts are helpful for discovering/showing trends that would not be so apparent in a data table. In Figure 7.4, output is relatively high during hours 1–3 and 9–12 and drops during hours 4–8. One might conclude from the line chart that something very unusual is going on during hours 4–8; perhaps the technician is taking too many breaks or his or her breaks are too long, or perhaps the types of tests are more difficult during those hours. Guided only by the line chart data, a supervisor might conclude that something needs to be done to deal with the "problem" in the middle of the shift. Whether the

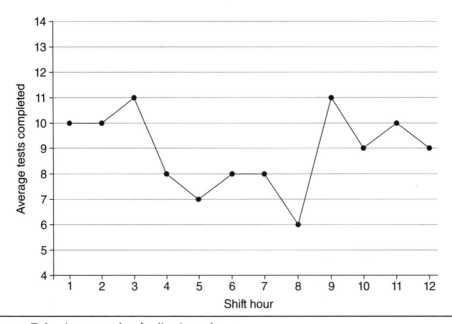

Figure 7.4 An example of a line/run chart.

remedial action would be to generate a C&E chart with lab personnel, make more careful supervisory "checks" on the pathology technician, explore additional technology that might improve performance, and so on, the supervisor is assuming that the trends shown on the line chart are real. As the next tool demonstrates, this is an incorrect assumption for this set of data.

7QC—Statistical Process Control (SPC) Charts

SPC charts are augmented line graphs that enable interpretation of the data as to whether the variability in a set of data is normal (common) or abnormal (uncommon). SPC charts were developed by Walter Shewhart at Bell Labs in the 1920s. W. Edwards Deming brought them into wide use in defense plants in the United States during World War II. After WWII, Deming took them (and statistical thinking) to Japan, where the Japanese used them to great effect. In the United States, SPC charts faded quickly after the war and then resurged in the early 1980s when they were thought by automotive executives to be a magic, instant-pudding answer to the problems of the automotive industry. While many organizations instantly joined the "SPC flavor of the month" club, a few were serious. Motorola was one of the serious ones, and its use of SPC eventually gave birth to Six Sigma.

Every set of data has normal or common variability. Whether it is the actual waist measurements in a lot of jeans labeled as waist size 34, the volatility of rocket fuel, or the placement accuracy of a brain probe, every set of data has normal variability: Normal variability drives the differences between measurements when things are completely under control and running smoothly. Naturally, in endeavors such as brain surgery and rocket fuel, it is hoped that the process can be designed and conducted so that normal variability is very, very small.

Abnormal or uncommon variability is created by differences that occur unexpectedly and therefore introduce more variability than would be expected under normal circumstances. Unexpected variability in brain probe placement could be caused by a voltage surge in the equipment, surgeon fatigue that is more than typical, anatomical anomalies in a patient, and so on. An SPC chart determines whether the variability of the data under analysis is expected and the result of normal variability, or if it has been impacted by uncommon or abnormal sources of variability.

Figure 7.5 displays an X-bar and R (which stands for "means and ranges") SPC chart for the same data displayed in Figure 7.4. There are many types of SPC charts. They all use the same basic logic and underlying statistical

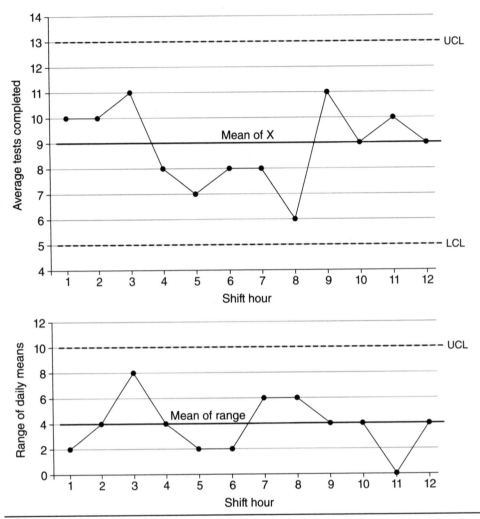

Figure 7.5 An example of an X-bar and R (means and ranges) SPC chart.

assumptions (while they are not complex, they are beyond the scope of this book) but vary in what types of data they analyze. An X-bar and R chart measures averages (from two or more measurements, typically not more than five), an individuals and moving range (Ind. and MR) chart assesses individual measurements (such as one lab technician's daily production each day for a month), a *p* chart measures the proportion of nonconforming (defective) items in a sample, and so on.

There are two graphs in an X-bar and R chart. In Figure 7.5, the top graph shows the means (of the three measurements taken for each hour of the shift) and the bottom graph shows the ranges (the highest mean for an hour minus the lowest mean for that hour among the three measurements taken that hour).

A typical X-bar and R chart would also show the data table of each hour's means and ranges. This has been omitted here.

The hoped-for results are that both graphs are "in control." That is, there must be no means or ranges outside the control limits (UCL = upper control limit and LCL = lower control limit) on the top and bottom graphs, respectively. These control limits are calculated from simple formulas that take into account the variability (the ranges) of the data and the number of measurements taken (how many measurements are used to calculate the mean for each hour of the shift). If all the means and ranges are within the control limits, it is possible that the process is in control; that is, there is not any uncommon variability. To make an absolute determination of "in control," there must also not be any other patterns that would indicate other out-of-control (or uncommon variance) conditions. One such pattern would be seven or more consecutive points on one side of the overall mean for that graph (the thick lines). Figure 7.5 has no points out of control and no other obvious out-of-control patterns. Therefore, it would make no sense to investigate what is going on in hours 4–8 from the data we have—there is no statistical basis to conclude that anything unusual is going on. The next step would be to collect more measurements for each hour (perhaps for 10 days of the technician's work) and then recalculate. If no out-of-control conditions are found, it is time to worry about something else.

Given this discussion, I hope it is clear that SPC charts should be employed whenever action is contemplated concerning what is found in line chart data. If the data are just FYI, there's no problem. However, it is foolish to take any action based on conclusions that the data do not support.

7QC—Histograms

Histograms are bar graphs showing the frequency distribution of measurements in a sample. If the shape of the distribution departs from what is expected, further analysis is indicated. Figure 7.6 displays a histogram showing the frequency distribution of the 36 shift means (each of 12 hours for three shifts) that were used to generate Figures 7.4 and 7.5.

The approximate shape of the histogram is roughly shaped like a normal or binomial distribution (hard to tell which with so few data points), which is generally expected if nothing strange is going on. The means at the two ends of the distribution are a bit of a concern, but since the control chart in Figure 7.5 was well in control, we have to conclude that the outliers (the means on the edges) are not a big issue, statistically speaking.

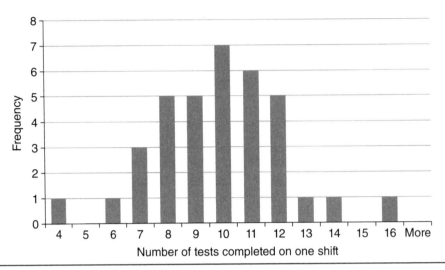

Figure 7.6   An example of a histogram.

7QC—Flowcharts

Flowcharts show the sequential steps of a process, often using standardized symbols such as those used in data processing applications. Figure 7.7 presents a typical flowchart. It shows the flow for deciding whether a new quote is needed for a revised customer order or whether the old quote can be modified. It then shows the steps taken to complete the revision. While the figure uses printed text, this is only for the sake of clarity in this example. It is always best if flowcharts are handwritten on white or colored paper that is taped to brown paper using the approaches explained in earlier sections of this chapter. You can make a set of shape masters and then photocopy them and cut them out if you wish. Use runs of tape and triangular sticky note cutouts to denote lines and arrows between shapes. This permits easy updating when the inevitable modifications occur.

Flowcharts always provide surprising insights into processes. Do not build flowcharts on a computer. If you need a computer copy, make it after all of the brown paper work has been completed and vetted. Do not develop flowcharts from existing charts or written documentation, as these sources are always lacking sufficient detail or are just plain wrong. The best approach is to walk the process, generally identify the sequence of steps, and then go back and walk the process again, speaking with workers, reviewing documentation, and never failing to ask, "Does that *always* happen?" when told what happens next. You'll discover that many processes that are thought to be fairly linear are, in fact, filled with "do" loops where the difficulties require the work to

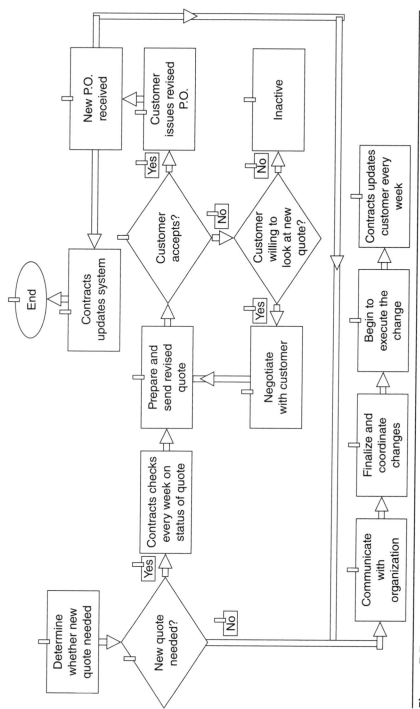

Figure 7.7 An example of a flowchart.

cycle back through previous steps for rework or additional input. You'll also find that different people take different actions at many points in the process. In effect, there is not a single process being used (there is no standard work, which explains a great deal about why you would be studying the process!). If there are several ways in which the process is being done, pick one for the flowchart. Make notes on the flowchart that call out dramatic deviations from what is displayed.

Several times during the construction of the flowchart brown paper, bring in groups of two or three people who do the process and have them review the process steps. They will point out many corrections and additions. After a number of groups have come through and given their feedback and you have made changes, bring them back in again. Be sure to include people from the process who did not give input in earlier discussions or questioning, if there are any.

It is helpful to attach copies of forms and computer screen shots beneath the various steps of a process. Prepare a double-high brown paper and use the top half for the flowchart and the bottom half for the forms/screen shots and other analyses, notes, and input related to the flowchart. Remember, the flowchart and the attached information will be used to tell a story to those who are unfamiliar with the process or parts of it (nobody knows the whole process). The more data and information you are able to display, analyze, and discuss, the more the audience and management will understand the issues you are highlighting and thus be more likely to agree to your suggested improvements.

Construction of a flowchart (or a value stream map [VSM]) is almost always a good first step in any analysis. The insights are always worth the trouble. Usually, if a flowchart is the principal process display, there will be a current state flowchart and a future state flowchart that shows how the process will operate if improvements are made. If the process was quite messy in the current state flowchart, there will be opportunities to reduce complexities and ambiguities by standardizing work, cross-training employees, changing job assignments, modifying or increasing authorization levels after training, and so on.

Spaghetti Diagrams

A spaghetti diagram identifies movement waste by showing the movement paths of data, paper, parts, and/or people within a site and/or process. Usually, a spaghetti diagram is developed to show movement for one process cycle (e.g., all of the walking and data transfer during month-end financial closing) or a certain time period (e.g., all of the walking in the customer service department during a four-hour period). Figure 7.8 displays a spaghetti diagram

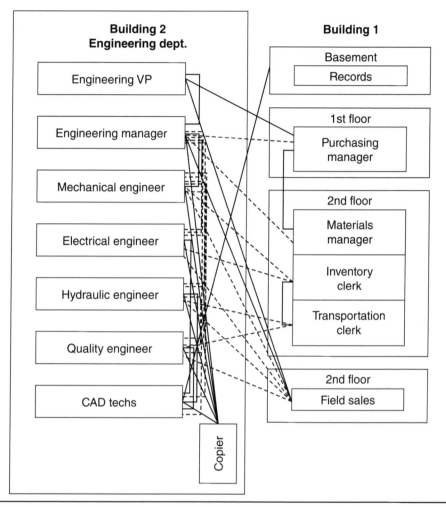

Figure 7.8 An example of a spaghetti diagram.

showing data flow (dashed lines) and walking (solid lines) for the movement required to process one engineering change.

The diagram should be drawn on a large sheet of white paper that is affixed to a brown paper. If there is a scale model diagram of the facility, it is okay to use it as the template (just make sure it represents the current layout, including furniture, equipment, plants, and anything else that might cause more walking). Each time something is moved or moves, a line is drawn between the two locations. In general, the line patterns are thickest where the potential opportunities for eliminating waste are greatest. For example, there is a great deal of communication with and walking to and from the CAD techs in Figure 7.8. Perhaps the CAD techs should be in the middle of the office rather than at the back of the department (probably because of hierarchy concerns).

Other information can also be discerned. Note that each of the engineers is sending information to the field salespeople. Should the information be combined, reviewed, and approved within the engineering department before several pieces and versions are sent by various engineers? Which group, the design engineers or the field salespeople, is better suited to figure out how a number of analyses, quotes, and drawings fit together? These are some of the questions that a spaghetti diagram can generate. Perhaps a field sales liaison could be located in the engineering office to help work out a method for more properly organizing and coordinating information between areas. This could be done in a blitz or with a work stream team (WST).

Handoff Charts

Handoff charts are a relative of spaghetti diagrams. Handoff charts display the transfer of data or materials between departments, areas, sites, and/or people. The paths taken and the distances traveled are not explored on a handoff chart, only the fact that a transfer took place and the number of times a transfer was made. Handoff charts are typically used to expose and explore the impacts of process dispersion in which different functions, location, or separation of tasks creates inefficiencies.

Figure 7.9 displays a handoff chart for processing a commercial loan in a bank. The individual lines show every handoff in processing a single loan. In some handoff charts, arrows are used on lines to show the direction of the transfer. Lines with arrows on both ends would represent one instance of information or material sent back and forth. Some add arrowheads at the ends of each line to show additional movement in the two directions (the lines would look like this: << ——>>>>). I don't think this has the impact of many separate lines, but suit yourself. Various types of dashed lines can be used to differentiate data from paper from parts, and so on. Color is not advised, because some people are color blind and because the colors do not photocopy well; thus a presentation to higher-ups could be cheapened if a low-quality copy or picture is used.

RACI Chart

RACI is an acronym for responsible, accountable, consulted, and informed (and yes, it could be ARCI, ICAR, RACI, etc.). It is a visual means of developing group input and consensus about roles and responsibilities in a process. It is a matrix that displays people, departments, or functions on one side and activities on the other axis. Each activity on a detailed process flowchart or VSM would

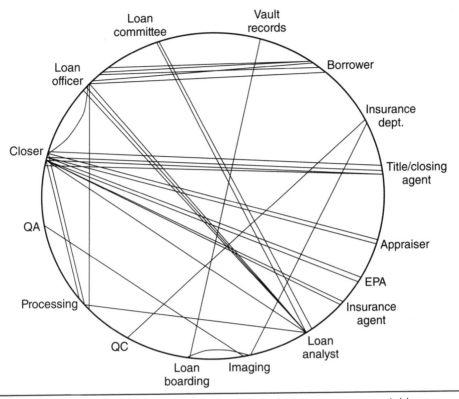

Figure 7.9 An example of a handoff chart for processing a commercial loan.

have a corresponding activity line on a RACI chart. Figure 7.10 displays a RACI chart for customer service and production scheduling activities.

The *R* stands for "responsible." These are the people or functions in a process that do the hands-on work of an activity. It is always best to identify a specific person, if possible. If a group or function is identified with an *R*, you cannot be sure that a specific person actually has the *R*, rather than whoever is available at a given time. This would make it difficult to identify training needs and skill deficits and plan improvements. For example, in Figure 7.10, P. Tommy maintains equipment contracts (line four). This means that he does all the hands-on work involved. There must be at least one *R* on each activity line. If there are a lot of them, there could be a problem. If everybody thinks he or she is a doer, there may be no one who really focuses on the task. Or, several people may each be doing a part of the activity, in which case the activity should be broken down into the constituent smaller activities.

The *A* denotes the person in authority. This is the person who owns the process, who is accountable if those with an *R* do not perform, and who might be able to authorize changes in the process unless that authority lies further

Tasks/actions	People				
	P. Tommy	B. Banzai	J. Bigboote	K. King	M. Margolis
Update customer contact list	A/R		I	C	
Run product availability report	A/R	C		C	I
Restock office supply cabinet	I	R	A		
Maintain equipment contracts	R		A/C	I	
Attend weekly business unit meeting		R	A/C		I
Approve pricing changes			A/R		I
Print management reports	C	R	A	I	I
Liaison with A/R	R		A/C		
Distribute current full-rate report	R	C	A		
Manage conference room bookings	R		A		
Track department metrics			A/R	C	

R = Responsible; the doer   C = *Must* consult before
A = Accountable; the owner   I = *Must* inform after

Figure 7.10 A sample RACI chart.

up the management ladder. There can be only one *A* on each activity line. It is not uncommon to discover processes that have no known *A* or many *A*s for an activity. In the figure, P. Tommy has the *A* for the first two activities, and J. Bigboote has the *A* for all the remaining tasks. It is okay for a person or function to have both the *A* and the *R* for an activity, as J. Bigboote has for approving pricing changes (line six).

The *C* denotes a person who *must* be consulted before the activity in order for it to be done properly. Here the "must" is critical. If there are too many *C*s for an activity, it is usually an indication that everybody is involved but only for political or hierarchical reasons. If the task can proceed effectively, legally, and accurately without the *C*, it should be eliminated.

The *I* denotes "informed." Analogously with *C*, the *I* is placed where someone *must* be informed after the *R* completes the task, in order to avoid difficulties with the results of the activity in question (such as when another area is impacted). Too many *I*s mean that time and effort are being wasted on e-mails, phone calls, visits, and so forth, and that there is a temptation for people to tamper and meddle where they are not needed. Further, for both *C*s and *I*s, there should be a standard manner of performing the *C* and the *I* that is always followed.

A RACI chart can also serve as a quick and dirty cross-training matrix. If the RACI shows that only one person has the *R* for an activity, it is a good idea to check and see how many other people currently have the skill to do the task, even if they are not assigned the *R*. A lone *R* without a backup means that the process will stop, slow down, and/or risk errors if the person who normally has the *R* is out sick, on vacation, or traveling. The same is true for *C*s and *I*s as well.

Pareto Charts

The Pareto chart is named in honor of Vilfredo Pareto (1848–1923), who was an eminent economist and democratic activist. His work on Pareto's law of income distribution led to the naming of this chart after him. A Pareto chart displays the frequency or percentages of various types of events on one axis (usually the y-axis) and the types of events on the other axis (usually the x-axis). It's a basic, generic bar graph in which the percentages or frequencies are shown in order from greatest to least, from left to right. The Pareto chart in Figure 7.11 shows the percentages of various types of errors made by customer service representatives at a bank branch when opening new checking accounts.

Many types of data approximate the 80–20 rule on a Pareto chart. As Figure 7.11 shows, the two mistakes of "missing customer signature" and "incomplete address" account for about 73% of all errors in creating new checking

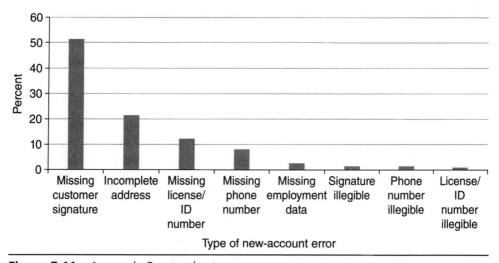

Figure 7.11 A sample Pareto chart.

accounts. With this information, it would be a good idea to closely examine why so many signatures were missing. As it turned out in the actual situation in this example, a new sign-up card had been introduced in the bank branches but new training (and/or notification of the change) had not arrived at all locations. The new card had the customer's signature block on the back side, while the former card had been one-sided. Newer account representatives would get involved with the client and occasionally forget to get the signature; the empty signature block had been a reminder in the past but was no longer present on the front side. The incomplete address problem was also related to the new form; some of the address blocks were too small, and account representatives and/or customers were leaving off information or abbreviating it in order to fit the space constraints of the form. Of course, the better (although longer term and more expensive) approach would be to enter the data directly into the computer with screen prompts and entry constraints.

In the short term, the correct actions would no doubt include some training on the new card at the branches as well as a redesign of the size of the address block.

5S

The tools and methods discussed to this point have been pure analysis tools. That is, they provide a lot of information about what is going on but do not lay out a specific remedy (although many suggest remedies). 5S can be a bit different. It can be used as an analysis tool, but it is primarily a method for structuring improvements related to workplace efficiency. 5S is a technique developed at Toyota (and now used by many others) for focusing a work group or area on good housekeeping and workplace organization. The name 5S is derived from five Japanese words. For your use in jargon supremacy struggles at work, the five Japanese words, their English counterparts (and an English counterpart that starts with an "S" where the clearest translation does not already start with an "S"), and a brief description of the desired actions and results of each *S* are shown in Figure 7.12.

Human beings are very territorial. They feel as though "their space" is special and they want to be proud of it and have it reflect well on them. This is just as true at work as it is at home. If a work area is dirty, disorganized, or difficult to work in, employees will not want to "own it" and will not take as much pride in it and the work they do in it as they would like (even if they do not know it; remember the preconscious). Therefore, a very wise first step in a work area improvement effort is to get it cleaned up and organized. This helps establish pride in the area and ownership of the follow-on improvement

5S name	English meaning	Required actions/results
Seiso	Cleaning (scrub/shine)	Clean and remove all dirt and debris.
Seiri	Clearing up (straighten)	Sort and arrange work-in-process; remove/store unnecessary tools/equipment; fix or remove defective equipment, material, and/or information. Dispose of what is not needed.
Seiton	Sort	Sort and organize all tools, equipment, files, data, material, and resources for quick, easy location and use. Label all locations and tools and equipment.
Shitsuke	Standardize	Perform all training and work according to established and documented procedures that are posted (and used) in the work area.
Seiketsu	Sustain	Keep it up and focus on it at all times.

Figure 7.12 The terms and meanings of 5S.

efforts. This is usually done in an intensive period of a day or two to a week in which every part of the work area and its equipment is cleaned, organized, and labeled, and old, unused, or broken things are removed *by the workers in that area* with appropriate facilitation. It often takes more than a few days to resolve the shitsuke issue of standard work being posted, much less used. Standard work has not existed in practice in 99% of work areas I have visited for the first time, even if they claim to have it.

After or while the cleanup is in progress, a 5S checklist for auditing the area is developed. It should be applicable to all areas of the facility with little modification. The audit is conducted by the supervisor, workers, a 5S cross-functional team, and plant management or a similar group established by the 5S implementation team facilitating the 5S event. A portion of a sample audit sheet for seiri (clearing up or straightening) for an office area is shown in Figure 7.13. The audit sheet scoring format can be yes-no, a five-point scale (like the example), or any other method. Keep it simple and easy to use. The audit should be done once a week, less often does not provide the emphasis to keep it alive. Each work group that has a visual metrics display (VMD) should use it to show its audit sheet and results graph.

The results of the audit are shown on a chart posted on the VMD for the work group (see Chapter 6). The score is shaded in on the display, and observations are written on it as well. Some contend that it is not necessary to show the graph if the audit score is posted as a table. They are wrong. We process most of our information visually. The always-underlying agenda in

	2. Set-in-Order	1 = Little or none	2 = Poor	3 = Fair	4 = Good	5 = Outstanding	Score
1	General postings are clean, undamaged, and neatly displayed	X					1
2	Aisles, emergency equipment, and exits not obstructed	X					1
3	Emergency medical supplies clearly labeled				X		4
4	Material on bulletin boards/PVD is well organized and neat	X					1
5	Movable equipment in designated areas	X					1
6	Supply cabinets/closets are neatly arranged and labeled	X					1
7	Wall decorations are neatly arranged	X					1
8	Wires beneath/behind desks are neatly bundled and labeled			X			3
9	Telephones are labeled with emergency numbers	X					1
10	Storage/supply areas contain no discarded/broken materials	X					1
11	Shelves are clearly marked for contents	X					1
12	Cleaning supplies are neatly stored in labeled locations	X					1
13	Documents are neatly stored in labeled locations			X			3
14	Responsibilities for document maintenance are displayed	X					1
15	File drawers are accurately labeled	X					1
16	Shared equipment stored in labeled location with tracking system	X					1
17	Offices and rooms are clearly labeled	X					1
18	Tools in general areas are labeled and in labeled locations	X					1
19	File cabinets contain no broken/discarded equipment/ documents	X					1
20	Desk surfaces hold only current work in process	X					1
						Average	1.4

Figure 7.13 A portion of a sample 5S audit sheet.

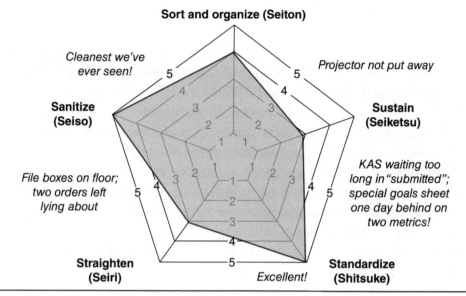

Figure 7.14 A 5S visual display.

any part of an improvement effort is to challenge traditional preconscious assumptions. While it is easy to walk by an audit form and not process the impact since it cannot be quickly and easily read from more than a couple of feet away, it is much more difficult to avoid processing a colorful chart that is easily interpreted. Specific encouragements, kudos, and admonishments are written directly on the visual 5S display. Whoever is doing the daily work group meeting (WGM; see Chapter 6) should refer to the 5S visual display each day to reinforce needed attention to specific items (and challenge existing preconscious assumptions). An example of a 5S visual display is shown in Figure 7.14.

Cross-Training Matrix

A cross-training matrix (also called a skill versatility chart/matrix) is similar to the RACI chart in format. Specific tasks are listed on one axis, and individuals who work in the area under study are listed on the other axis. The purpose of this matrix is to demonstrate "coverage" of tasks, that is, who and how many in a group can do each task. One hallmark of a superior work group is one in which almost all the workers can do a great many tasks. This provides coverage for absences, enables people to be quickly reassigned to handle fluctuations in task demands, and ensures that everyone in the work group is aware of how each person's work impacts the ability of the entire work group to do a good job.

It is important to enter tasks and not jobs. A job may have many tasks. If the matrix evaluates jobs (a group of tasks) rather than specific tasks, it is useless for guiding training and having an accurate picture of how well the tasks in a process are matched with skilled workers. For example, a customer support representative enters orders. There are very complex orders that involve credits and special shipping arrangements, and there are very simple, straightforward orders that anyone can enter. Orders may be faxed in, sent by e-mail, or taken over the phone. Being able to do the easy orders does not ensure that the workers can also process a complex order with customs forms and registrations. Being able to enter a faxed order may be much easier than doing it in real time on the phone. The difficulty levels of different categories of orders demonstrates why it is often necessary to break a task into subtasks or complexity/difficulty levels on a cross-training matrix.

An entry is made in each intersection that displays the relative skill level of each individual on each task. At its most basic level, the matrix can display whether an individual can do a task without help or guidance and at the same speed and level of quality as that of a worker skilled at the task. This is a good first step and/or a quick analysis tool to accompany a flowchart or VSM. However, in order to be most helpful, a fully developed matrix would have a method for displaying relative skill levels of each task. Often, each intersection displays a circle with quadrants that can be filled in as the individual more completely masters the task.

Figure 7.15 displays an example of a portion of a matrix for buyers. In this example, a completely filled-in circle demonstrates that the team member meets all performance requirements for the task and can train others. Three quadrants denotes that the worker meets performance requirements but may not be ready to train others. Two quadrants filled in shows that the worker can do the task but does it slower than a skilled worker. One filled quadrant denotes a worker who can do the task but is slow and requires a lot of help. The various skill levels could refer to output per hour and/or the quality of the performance.

Almost any sort of scheme for showing skill levels is okay as long as it is objective and easy to define and measure. When developing the approach, involve the workers and someone from personnel to ensure that legal problems are avoided (and if the area is in a union shop, a union representative to ensure no problems with work agreements). The numbers on the right side show the percentage of coverage for each person, that is, how many of the

Team member	Process or task								%
	Manual intake	Account setup	Order prep	..	Pricing	Metrics mnt.	Scheduling	SSU mtg.	
John Bigboote	●	●	●	..	●	◕	●	●	96
Paco Perez	●	◑		..	⊕	⊕	◔	◑	13
⋮	⋮	⋮	⋮	..	⋮	⋮	⋮	⋮	⋮
Rashid Faldi	●	⊕	⊕	..	◔	●	●	◕	42
Mary Jones	●	◑	⊕	..	●	◔	●	●	56
Task flexibility (%)	100	50	42	..	56	37	86	80	62
Task coverage	9/9	1/9	2/9	..	3/9	4/9	6/9	2/9	

Figure 7.15 A sample portion of a cross-training matrix for a buyer group.

quadrants on a line are filled in for that person. A higher percentage indicates that the worker is more valuable, in that he or she is more "flexible" across tasks. The percentage number on the second row from the bottom shows task flexibility, that is, how many of a task's quadrants are filled across all workers. This displays the depth of skills and knowledge among the workers for the task. The ratio number on the bottom (e.g., 2/9 for order prep) displays how many people (two) in the work group of nine people are fully skilled in each task. Note that the example displays nontechnical tasks as well, such as "SSU mtg.," which denotes the ability to run the daily WGM (see Chapter 6).

The matrix should be displayed on the work group's VMD so that it can work every day to create the positive, preconscious peer pressure and self-esteem needs that encourage people to learn more tasks. Supervisors should be evaluated on how well they improve the various numbers from month to month. When appropriate and not in conflict with company policy and/or union agreements, an individual's level of cross-training could be used to prioritize vacation and/or schedule preferences. It is not a good idea to try to financially reward people for mastering more tasks. This always turns out to be more trouble than it is worth because the amount of increased pay can never be very large. It is better to depend on the pride, self-esteem, peer group pressure, and supervisor approval that the visual display creates when people improve their performance and everyone sees it.

Day-in-the-Life-Of (DILO) Studies

A DILO is an analysis of what a person, machine, part, product, or process does or experiences over a certain period of time. The time period most often studied is a workday, shift, or other interval of interest, such as the amount of time it takes to produce an engineering change, complete a loan application, or produce an inventory status report. The process of conducting a DILO consists of monitoring the subject/object of interest and recording what happens.

The first step in doing a DILO is to determine which categories of activity will be measured. This often requires some initial observation and then discussion as to what the DILO should be evaluating. If the categories get too broad, the DILO might not be much help. The category of "working on the computer" would be too broad for a data analyst who spends most of the day sitting at a monitor. Better categories for computer work for that DILO might be "producing budget status reports," "inputting daily reports," "reconciling records with audit findings," and so on. On the other hand, the category of "working on the computer" might be okay on a DILO for a supervisor who spends most of his or her time on the floor with employees. The best approach is to do an informal preliminary DILO by observing the subject or a few subjects and writing down the various things that happen.

A further consideration is what sampling period to use. A decision must be made as to whether the observations will be assigned to the nearest minute, the nearest five-minute interval, and so on. Once that is determined, the length of the study must be selected. Will the study cover one shift a day each day for a week or three shifts a day for three days? The proper selection must be based on what you are interested in assessing. There might be a big difference between what a supervisor does on first shift and what he or she does on third shift. Combining the data will hide the differences between shifts. If data are gathered on one shift, will they always be from the same supervisor for a number of days, or will the data be collected across many supervisors? It depends on what you are investigating.

A DILO study can be a very powerful means of challenging false impressions about existing conditions. For example, many supervisors believe that they spend a great deal of time interacting with their direct reports. Usually, the facts demonstrate that this is not true. A DILO showing average findings for seven supervisors on the first shift over five days is shown in Figure 7.16. Observers shadowed supervisors as they did their work. The objective of the study was explained, and while the observers were instructed to interact minimally with the supervisors, they were permitted to ask questions if they could not tell what a supervisor was doing (e.g., "giving safety feedback" or "dealing with a discipline issue"). The observers checked off each activity on a data sheet as it occurred and wrote down how many minutes (to the nearest whole minute) each activity consumed. These times were then added up at the end of the observation period.

As Figure 7.16 demonstrates, supervisors spent a lot of time expediting parts, dealing with problems, and touring the area, which is a euphemism for simply walking around with no specific purpose. It was called "touring" so that it would not seem as negative to reviewing management as "visiting other supervisors" and "getting coffee" might be; never forget that you'll have to work on improvements with these supervisors later. The purpose of this DILO

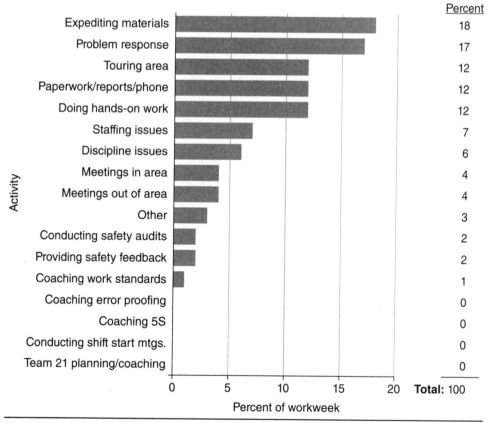

Figure 7.16 A DILO of supervisory activities.

was to set a baseline against which lean supervisory activities would be measured six months later. As you can see from the bottom five lines, there was little focused world-class behavior such as that described for TMOS in Chapter 6.

If a DILO is done for an order, invoice, report, or even an insurance claim being processed, the information will supplement what is found on a VSM. It all depends on what you are interested in analyzing. You can get a lot of texture from a DILO, but a DILO combines like activities so you can't tell at what point in the process various things are happening. In a VSM, you can see exactly where the delays and inventory are, but you may not get as much detail on specific tasks unless you plan for that level of detail before the VSM is developed. This is why it is often necessary to use more than one tool or approach.

STANDARD WORK

Standard work is defined as the best way to do the job that is currently known. The "best way" can be defined in many ways. A useful description is that standard work is the safest way to complete the task with outstanding quality that meets the output needs of the organization and provides superior customer satisfaction. Needless to say, this is often not explicitly defined in most office tasks (and a great many factory tasks as well). That is, there are people who do a great job, but the way they do it evolved by itself and, even if it is superior, is not an established standard for everyone.

The lack of standard work contributes to a great many errors and significant variability in process outcomes. If five workers each do a task in a slightly different manner, it is often difficult to determine the cause of the mistakes. Worse yet, when those five train the next five, the differences between them usually become greater as the new workers add their own well-intentioned embellishments. For these reasons, standard work is a bedrock principle of world-class work environments. It is usually developed by a kaizen blitz team or a WST involving the workers, their supervisor, the process customers, and so on. The team analyzes the performance requirements of the task. They review how everyone does the task and then decide the single best way to do it. This is often accomplished by the group constructing a flowchart of the process and discovering the different decisions, job aids, and judgments that the various workers employ. The final determination of the best way might require some experimentation and testing. Once the best way to do the task is determined, it is documented and perhaps accompanied by a flowchart and RACI, and everyone is taught the same method. A cross-training matrix is developed, and periodic audits are done to make sure that people are sticking to the standard work procedure.

When I do standard work for an office task, I prefer to have the following:

1. A step-by-step sequence of task instructions

2. A quality standard for any significant intermediate outputs and the final product

3. A detailed flowchart of the process

4. A simple cross-training matrix (showing which individuals can or can't do each task element)

5. A RACI

After things settle down and sustainability is no longer a problem, a more comprehensive cross-training matrix can be developed. Taken as a group, this information provides an excellent basis for making sure that all elements of the tasks are completely understood and that new people can be easily trained and evaluated.

ONE-POINT METHODS

One-point methods are an element found in total preventive (or productive) maintenance (TPM) within the Toyota Production System (TPS). An important part of TPM involves freeing up maintenance technicians to do the more technical work of maintenance, such as developing new equipment specifications, overhauling existing machines, improving equipment efficiency, and so on. One way to do this is to teach equipment operators to do some of the less technical aspects of equipment maintenance, such as routine checks of brushes, fluids, belt wear, tensioning, and so on. The first step in doing this is to break down the less technical maintenance tasks into short "one-point lessons." Each one-point lesson takes 5–10 minutes to teach and covers a single aspect of a task. A one-point lesson consists of step-by-step written instructions with detailed pictures, screen shots, tables of settings, and any needed code numbers or reference information. The operator is shown how to do the one-point lesson using the written instructions and the other aids. He or she is then observed the next time the task needs to be done. If there are problems, the training is repeated.

One-point lessons can be a powerful and relatively pain-free method for increasing coverage of critical skills in office environments. Once standard work has been defined for a task, it is relatively straightforward to break it down into a number of one-point lessons. A posted cross-training chart will indicate the most critical "holes" in the coverage. Starting with the most critical tasks (those that would cause the most problems if not done or not done well), identify the workers who need cross-training. Each day, a worker can be shown a one-point lesson or two for a task he or she has not yet mastered. If 10–15 minutes are devoted each day to this sort of training, the entire work group can be cross-trained in almost all tasks in three to four months. Of course, this will not happen if adequate resources are not devoted to developing standard work, one-point lessons, flowcharts, RACI, and the cross-training matrix.

8

Office Kaizen Value Stream Mapping Concepts

This chapter introduces the concept of value stream mapping (VSMapping), with particular emphasis on VSMapping used in office, data, and administrative environments. This chapter also explains basic VSMapping conceptual and construction principles, that is, what a value stream map (VSM) does and the various factors that influence its construction and use. Chapters 9 and 10 explain the methods and approaches for building a current state VSM (CS-VSM) and a future state VSM (FS-VSM) (and action plan), respectively, using the techniques introduced in this chapter.

VSMapping made its big entrance onto the business stage in 1999 with the publication of *Learning to See*, a VSMapping workbook for manufacturing processes written by Womack and Jones. In the span of a few years, the construction of a VSM has become an almost mandatory beginning element of many lean, kaizen, and Six Sigma projects. It has largely supplanted flowcharts as a first-step analysis tool in many situations. A VSM can provide a clear and incisive view of what's going on in a process. Its display of delays (most of them caused by inventory and batching) provides a nice overview of many of the problems in a process. Even better, a CS-VSM not only demonstrates where problems must be addressed in order to improve a process but also suggests an approximate priority for planned interventions. Perhaps most important, a VSM provides a single perspective on the process that everyone who participated in its construction can agree with (or at least accept as being reasonable). Again, as we found with preconscious assumptions, the medium/method is often an important part of the message (i.e., the value of working together).

A VSM is a highly stylized form of flowcharting. It focuses primarily on the time spent performing the various activities of a process and the time wasted by having data, paperwork, products, and/or parts waiting to be worked on before, between, and/or after each activity. In the course of mapping these times, a VSM highlights the portions of a process that are causing delays (whether it is the waiting of parts, material, paper and/or data, or the time required by various work steps). In effect, a VSM determines how long it will take to do the activities in a process and then adds the time it would take to work off the inventory between the activities (i.e., to work through work-in-process [WIP]). Insofar as waiting and inventory are associated with traditional "push" processes and all of the usual wastes associated with them and caused by them, a VSM can be a very effective first step in scoping out a process and prioritizing improvement opportunities that will move the process toward a pull approach.

If you haven't done a VSM in the past, things may appear very complex. Don't worry about it. Work through the examples and it will become clear (eventually, that is; there is no substitute for the learning that takes place when you actually suffer through a couple of VSM constructions in real time when it is all new to you). While this is not a detailed VSM how-to book, I have tried to provide enough examples and explanations to get you going. If you are comfortable with a little ambiguity and experimentation, you should be able to construct a great VSM for your own purposes with the information given. Take your time and carefully read and reread this chapter and the next two while you are working on your VSM. If you are in a large company and your first VSM may be viewed by internal experts and/or executives, it is wise to get your hands on a VSM example that meets the corporate standard (if there is one) or was viewed favorably. Make sure that your VSM will respect the customs they value. There are many, many approaches to VSMapping and iconography. Most of the approaches commonly used in office VSMapping are poorly adapted from manufacturing VSMapping and just aren't going to work well when you try to apply their insights. However, if the experts in your company have a technique they like, they are not going to be happy with you if you try something different that they are not familiar with—tread carefully.

THE BASIC STRUCTURE OF A VSM

Figure 8.1 presents the first two activities that are part of a bank's process for opening a new checking account. The striped arrows designate "push" activities. That is, the upstream activity (person, machine, computer, work group, etc.) pushes work to the next step, whether the next step is ready to work on it right away or not. These first two activities are "Collect data from applicant" and "Fax data to proc. center" (the back office).

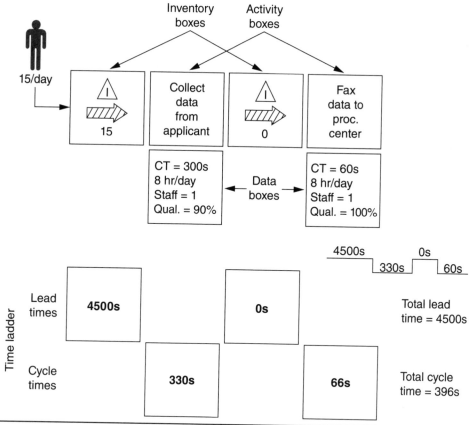

Figure 8.1   The first two activities of a VSM for processing a new checking account.

For VSMapping purposes, an activity is a discrete task that is usually done as a single unit of work and that is not normally broken down further so that two people could do different parts of it. Also, an activity ends and a new one begins when it is possible for the work to stop at a logical point (and go into WIP inventory) and then be started later at the next step. This is the level of detail that is most useful in Office Kaizen VSMapping (and those for factories as well). Higher levels of assessment are not very useful in most tactical process improvement activities.

Higher-level assessments (such as when a single activity box might be "Complete work at processing center") are typically used when a strategic issue such as outsourcing or site or product consolidation/transfer is being studied. For strategic issues, the details of individual activities are often not important. However, if activities are combined in a single activity box, a great deal of information can be lost for process improvement efforts. For example, if five activities in a VSM were to be lumped together as one (such as collapsing

10 processing steps into one activity box that might say, "Complete all back office data entry and verification"), the details of the process would be hidden and potential improvements in each of the constituent actions would be harder to spot. Such a combination of steps has other undesirable impacts that will be discussed later. One particular danger is that a sufficient number of small improvements can sometimes obviate the need to take strategic action—always go for kaizen first.

In Figure 8.1, the first activity requires a financial representative to speak with the applicant and write information by hand (yes, even in this age of computers!) on the checking account application form/card. While this could be handed off to another employee midtask, it would be inconvenient and disruptive for all concerned; it just isn't normally done. Therefore, filling out the application is considered a single activity even if it is only the first part of a string of seemingly continuous activities done by the representative. After this activity, the information could be left in a file, in an inbox, or on the desk for faxing at a later time. As a result, the faxing of the data is a separate activity, even though in this case it is almost always done right after the first activity (why this is obvious from the VSM will be explained later).

Beneath each activity box is a data box. The data box contains the cycle time (CT; which is hands-on work time) of the activity in the box above it and any other information important for understanding the process and identifying improvement issues. Some data boxes contain a lot of information, and some contain only a few items, such as in our example. It is always important to record the quality level of each activity if it is known so that the impact of poor quality can be incorporated into throughput and time calculations. For example, there is a 90% yield on the first activity; 10% of the applications have errors that must be corrected. If the consequences (added work and corrections there or downstream) of poor quality are not accounted for with specific steps later in the VSM, their impact must be included in the cycle time for the activity at the point where the defects occur (more on this later).

In between the activity boxes are inventory boxes. The triangle is the established symbol for inventory in a VSM. It can be paper, computer files, physical parts, and so on. The amount of inventory is written under the triangle. In this case, the inventory number represents the number of application "packages" (the application form and any attachments) waiting to be worked on at that point in the process.

Before proceeding, it is important to note that all of the examples concerning VSMapping in Chapters 8–10 are graphically illustrated as if they are being created with sticky notes attached to a brown paper. This approach makes changes to the VSM easy to accommodate without making a big mess. An added convenience of using the sticky notes is that the process lines can easily be laid out in a straight line and the time ladder can easily be lined up with the activity and inventory boxes. This makes it easy for everyone to follow the sequence of steps when the VSM gets complicated by "do" loops.

The time ladder is shown at the bottom of Figure 8.1. The convention has become that the lead times are shown on the upper level of the time ladder and the cycle times are shown on the lower level (as if the activity box is "pushing down" the time line). Thus, the sticky notes for the cycle time row are placed on the lower level of the time ladder. In a traditional VSM, where lines are drawn on the paper rather than posted with sticky notes, the time ladder is drawn on the paper in the form shown directly above "Total lead time = 4500s" in the figure.

The VSM starts at the left. The person figure conveys that people walk into the bank to open an account. The "15" below the person shows that this happens 15 times each day. The volumes used on a VSM are typically those for a single shift or an entire workday, whatever makes more sense as long as the same standard is used for the entire CS-VSM and the estimated FS-VSM that is created after improvements are identified. If the new-account requests arrive by e-mail or fax, a different symbol (you pick it) would be used, such as a couple of sheets of paper with an "e" and a lightning bolt through them or "fax" written on them. If several routes of arrival are possible, each corresponding symbol should be shown with the appropriate number of items below it (such as 15/day walk-in, 2/day faxed, and 4/day by e-mail). Each may have different cycle times and there would then be several stacked inventory and activity boxes at that point. The overall cycle and lead times on the time ladders would be an average of the multiple activity types and inventory levels. (An example of this is shown in Figure 8.2 on page 146.)

The 15 new-account applications go into inventory. Inventory in many office processes does not "stack up" as it might in a manufacturing operation. In this case, each of the 15 customers typically sits down with a financial representative and fills out the paperwork as soon as he or she comes in (or after a brief delay if the financial representatives are already busy with other customers). However, a VSM assumes that the inventory arrives all at once and then must be processed. This ensures that the maximum total waiting time for the 15 daily applications will be accounted for. That is, since it takes 300 seconds on average to complete an application with a customer, there are 4500 seconds of possible waiting time in a typical day/shift (15 × 300 seconds). While most of this waiting time may not actually occur very often, it could. For example, if each of the next 14 customers arrived just as the only financial representative available was beginning to open an account with the first customer, there would be about 4500 seconds of waiting time. The representation of this "hypothetical" waiting time is important to put on the VSM if contemplated improvements would impact the number of financial representatives available or change the amount of other work they might have to do.

Cycle times for an activity should always be based on actual observations. If the activity is not being done when the VSM is constructed, have the activity simulated by an employee using the actual forms, data, and so on. If this is not possible, then work with the employees who do the activity and make a guess (it's not the best option, but if you must do the VSM at that time, you have no choice).

Note that the "Collect data from applicant" data box in the figure shows the cycle time as 300 seconds. This is the time required to obtain the necessary information from an average checking account applicant. The 15 accounts per day multiplied by 300 seconds produces the 4500 seconds shown in the lead time box on the time ladder directly below the inventory box. Note that the cycle time shown on the time ladder for the first process is 330 seconds. The difference between 330 and 300 seconds represents the extra work required to process the 10% of the accounts that have mistakes on them. The extra 30 seconds, 10% of 300 seconds, is the added work that an employee will spend on average to correct the problem(s). In this case, the 30 seconds was an approximation made by the VSM builders and the employee who does the job. This added work would not be included at this point if a latter part of the VSM explicitly included the rework. (Figure 8.3 on page 153 demonstrates such a situation, and shows how decision trees are handled in a VSM.)

The second activity box in Figure 8.1 is "Fax data to proc. center." The data box shows that the cycle time is 60 seconds. Note that the cycle time on the time line for this activity is 66 seconds. This 66 seconds represents the 60 seconds for faxing each application plus an additional 10% of 60 seconds faxing back applications that are returned to the branch for rework by the processing center. The lead time for the inventory box between the two activity boxes is 0 seconds. This is because, as mentioned earlier, the typical procedure is to immediately fax the completed application to the processing center. Since the fax machine is located right next to the desk where the account application is filled out, there is virtually no lead time involved between the two activities. You could get super compulsive and put in a lead time of a second or two (the fax number of the processing center is on auto-dial), but the builders of this VSM didn't consider it important. However, be careful of making too many such assumptions on a large map; the seconds can add up.

It is important to appreciate that the overwhelming majority of time a VSM identifies as waste in a process is *not* wasted or inefficient hands-on work time. In the push example (Panel A) of Figure 2.4 in Chapter 2, it took 57 minutes to get a new piece of work all the way through the system from start to finish. Only three minutes of this time was hands-on work time (one minute for each of the three processes), termed *cycle time* in a VSM; 54 of the 57 minutes is the total waiting time (*lead time* in a VSM) of each new folder that arrives, assuming that inventory levels stay the same and everything is processed "first in, first out." Most VSMs have cycle time (hands-on work time) percentages of 1%–5% of total process time (which is lead, or waiting, time, plus cycle time). The majority of improvement opportunities discovered in a VSM are typically focused on reductions of waiting time via the reduction of inventory accumulation.

This focus on reducing lead time is right in line with the basic philosophy of kaizen and lean: Remove waste as much as possible with low-technology methods. There is little danger of ruining an output or negatively impacting customer service by reducing waiting time. Attempting to significantly reduce cycle time, on the other hand, can easily compromise an output because a change in the hands-on work method or technology could easily impact employee actions and work steps as well as employee skills and training concerns. These impacts can have significant effects on quality. This is always a very real danger when new technology is applied to reduce cycle times without careful study. Consider the problems that a simple change in the sign-up card for a new checking account caused in the bank example discussed earlier. The very low risk of attacking lead time provides an ideal way to make the customer happy because he or she gets the product or service quicker and the organization gets faster throughput with little risk. Where a cycle time problem is caused by a lack of task knowledge, job aids, bad input, or insufficient training, improvements to these task-related elements generally have only a positive effect on the output, insofar as the purpose is to see that the task is done correctly as designed.

Figure 8.2 illustrates how a VSM handles several simultaneous inputs to a process. Let's suppose that a branch gets, on average, 21 new accounts per day. Fifteen are opened by people arriving in person, two present themselves via faxed information on a form that an applicant picked up from the branch, and four applications arrive via e-mail after an applicant filled out an online form on the bank's website and the application was routed to the branch nearest the applicant's home address. These three paths are represented by the person figure, the two sheets of paper with "Fax" on the top page, and the single sheet with a lightning bolt and an "e," respectively.

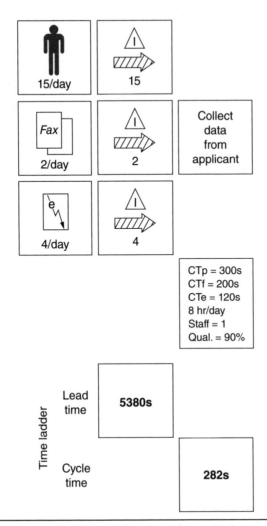

Figure 8.2 An illustration of lead and cycle times for multiple inputs to an activity box.

Data collection shows that it takes, on average, 300 seconds to open a walk-in account, 200 seconds to open an account submitted by fax, and 120 seconds to open an account submitted by e-mail. The overall quality rate is 90%. This information is shown in the data box. If the quality levels varied per type of account presentation (as they most likely would), this would require an additional adjustment in the final calculation of the overall cycle times. The calculation of the weighed cycle time is:

In-person cycle time	#	Fax cycle time	#	E-mail cycle time	#	Subtotals Person	Fax	E-mail	Raw total
(300s × 15) +		(200s × 2)	+	(120s × 4)	=	4500s	+ 400s	+ 480s	= 5380s

The 5380 seconds is the total time to process all 21 incoming applications. The rework time for 10% errors must then be added and the resulting adjusted total must be divided by 21 to arrive at the weighed cycle time per application:

$$\underset{\text{total}}{\underset{\text{Raw}}{5380s}} + \underset{\substack{\text{rework} \\ 538s}}{\underset{10\%}{538s}} = \underset{\substack{\text{total} \\ 5918s}}{\underset{\text{Adjusted}}{5918s}} \quad \frac{\underset{\substack{\text{total} \\ \text{Number of} \\ \text{applications}}}{\text{Adjusted}}}{} = \frac{5918s}{21} = 281.8s \cong 282s$$

This is the basic weighing procedure that is used whenever there are multiple simultaneous activity or inventory boxes that feed into the next element.

THE *OK2* APPROACH TO VSMAPPING

Now that some basic VSMapping methods have been introduced, a couple of significant conceptual differences between most office processes and typical factory/production processes must be discussed. These differences are conceptually subtle, but they significantly change the nature of the steps taken to improve the processes being studied with the VSM.

Presentation of Demand

The first difference between factory and office applications involves the point at which a demand for output is presented. In factory environments, the end of the process is where the demand is most often conceptualized to begin. The ideal of a world-class lean environment is that product is pulled through the process from the end of the process—nothing is produced before it is needed. This concept ignores the processing of the order information that is used to send a demand signal to the end of the production line, but, as they say, that's another process.

When a customer orders a product, it is a signal that the factory must deliver or, as quickly as possible, produce and then deliver the product. If the organization is truly lean, the production line has just produced, is just about to produce, or can very quickly produce and deliver/ship what is needed. If this occurs most of the time without the factory having more than a minimum amount of finished goods and/or in-process inventory, the factory is demonstrating the essence of flow or just-in-time production: responding to customer needs quickly without the waste of excess inventory.

The situation is conceptually different with most office and administrative processes. For example, in the case of a paper or electronic order for a product, the demand begins at the start of the process when the electronic, phone, or fax order is received. The process owners have little or no control over how often and/or how much the process will be driven by incoming orders, and each order's requirements must be entered into the process at its start. This is true of customers opening bank accounts, an engineering department producing a new product design for sales, and a finance department having to execute the monthly closing of the books. All of these processes are driven from a demand presented at the start of the process by some sort of customer. The primary consideration in these cases is to operate the process as quickly as possible to complete all of the work put in at the start, all the while minimizing waste and maintaining quality.

This sounds a lot like the factory situation, but it is much different in terms of what it portends for process improvements. In the factory, any inventory in the system that has not already been ordered is waste. In most office processes, the inventory in the system is an incomplete version of the output that has already been ordered. That is, a customer puts the paperwork or data in the system and wants the work on it completed as soon as possible (such as a loan application or an order for a discrete product). The partially done work is, in a sense, already owned by the customer of the process. The customer, whether opening a bank account, ordering a new product design, or in a hurry to see the results of the monthly closing, is waiting for his or her already-demanded product to be finished. While this difference may seem slight, it is important for how to best use and construct a VSM in an office environment.

In a factory setting, a CS-VSM is constructed to identify inventory and waiting waste. It is assumed that the process will pull from the end of the production line. The focus is on locating waste areas/issues that can be reasonably addressed within the planned implementation period so that there will be less inventory in the system once improvements are made. Once improvement opportunities are identified on the VSM, various Toyota Production System (TPS), Six Sigma, and other general continuous improvement methods are used to attack the waste. The improvements may involve any of the following: preventive maintenance, 5S, changeover improvements, workplace organization, installation of pull systems, variance reduction, and so on. An estimate is made of the likely impact of each of these improvements and then an FS-VSM is constructed that shows how the process will operate when the various improvements have been implemented. The primary emphasis is on using TPS methods to reduce inventory, which reduces waiting (lead) time and thus reduces costs and total process time.

In office settings, the in-process inventory cannot typically be reduced without negatively impacting customer service. With the exception of completely wasted steps, such as having to obtain an unnecessary signature or filling out a duplicate form, every piece of inventory in the process is a partially completed final output. A bank loan officer is not going to refuse to enter a loan application from what seems like a qualified borrower. An engineering manager could refuse to begin work on a new product design request from the company president, but that might lead to career issues in most environments.

The same is true for customers opening new checking accounts. A branch office could decide to process only five new accounts per day and hold the rest (first in, first out) in a file drawer for tomorrow, but neither the customers nor the bank would be served well. While it is always prudent to pursue the mandates of the TPS in every process where they apply, the main challenge in most office environments is not in reducing the absolute inventory in the process but in speeding up the process so that all of the inventory put into the process can be quickly completed and passed back to the customer. As a result, the Office Kaizen approach in this book is one that focuses on the unique demands of VSMapping in office processes. The primary difference, for those familiar with *Learning to See* and lean, is that Office Kaizen VSMapping focuses somewhat less on (but still uses) kanban and heijunka (a board that displays kanbans) and somewhat more on cross-training, task simplification, and work balancing. In both cases, the desire is to move things through the process as quickly as possible while minimizing waste. In an office setting, most of the waste is created by the people and the systems that cannot efficiently or quickly enough process the already-ordered, partially completed product in the system.

Type of Information Used

In a factory-oriented VSMapping approach, it is often recommended that you use "snapshot" data. That is, you measure what is in the process at the time you obtain the data for the VSM. This is usually a big mistake for both factory and Office Kaizen VSMapping applications for two reasons.

First of all, who is to say that the situation at the instant of collecting data is representative of the operation of the process as a whole? Everyone who has worked in an office or a factory, even a factory that is constantly pumping out a single product all the time, has observed dramatic fluctuations in output and quality from hour to hour or day to day across most workstations.

Even if things normally run pretty well, problems are not uncommon. How do you know if what you are collecting is typical? If you construct a VSM based on data that are not typical, your subsequent improvements may not be on target (and might not even be needed!). Anyone who knows anything about sampling theory and statistics would not be confident that taking a single measurement of status would accurately predict any characteristic of a process.

The second issue involves the manner in which most office work differs from typical production work. In a factory setting, the work is more or less constant in terms of tasks performed (within the bounds of the processes' normal variability). A machinist setting up and running a CNC machine performs a fairly consistent assortment of tasks from day to day, even if the parts being machined change. Inventory and cycle times may change for the machinist, but this goes to the sampling issue discussed earlier.

The same is not true for most office jobs. Except for production-type office jobs, which have narrowly defined standard work such as coding charge account or credit card bills, few office jobs involve only one task or two. In fact, most office workers in personnel, accounts payable/receivable, customer service, sales, purchasing, production scheduling, quality, research, legal, engineering, and the like have a wide variety of tasks among which they constantly shift. It would be foolish to assume that the condition of a process and its activities, inventories, lead time, cycle time, and so on, at any one time would be representative of an entire day, much less a week or more.

Further clouding the situation is an element that I call "process lead time." Lead time is the waiting time allocated toward processing inventory that is between activities. Process lead time is often included in cycle time because it appears, at first blush, to be hands-on work time. Actually, it is lead (waiting) time. For example, suppose you had been observing several clerks in accounts payable and timing their activities. You gave each of them five bills to pay and told them to tell you when they had completed their work. The five bills for each clerk were selected from existing accounts with no problems.

The typical assumption in this case is that the average cycle time of the five "typical" bills would give you a good measurement of cycle time for non-complex bills. Yet, how does the VSM handle the situation when someone asks one of the clerks a question? Or the clerk answers the phone? Or the clerk has to visit the restroom? Or get coffee? Or go to a training class for four hours? Or the clerk has to reconcile his or her account status when the boss calls? If the worker starts a piece of work that then sits on the desk or in an open computer file for 20 minutes while he or she is doing something else, how do you account for the part of the 20 minutes that is consumed by the other tasks not being studied by the VSM? If cycle time is the actual time it takes to do the work, how do you reconcile the total time the work sits on the desk with the amount of true cycle time that it takes to do the work?

One solution often proposed is to take the number of items processed by the activity in a given time period (often called "the demand") and divide it into the total time period. As you can imagine, in most office jobs, this cycle time ends up being a grossly inflated estimate of the actual cycle time to do a piece of the work if the worker does anything else. This is because all of the process lead time is assumed to be cycle time. This doesn't work for me.

So what do you do? The safest practice is to determine demand by reviewing a few months to a year of data (whatever is required to get a complete understanding of a normal cycle of the specific business process) and then compute averages for demand. This will determine how many units of work go through the process per day, per week, and so on. Then, cycle times must be determined by actually timing the activity at least 5–10 times. Get the pure cycle time (no interruptions or diversions); that's the highest level of performance that can be expected. Make sure you're not observing the best or the worst worker or the easiest or hardest piece of work. Test your estimate by checking with workers and supervisors. Then, once you're sure you're pretty close, use those cycle times to calculate lead times at each station.

Take the same approach to determine the inventory counts throughout the process. Set them as averages rather than "point in time" measurements. In many office processes, WIP changes cyclically throughout the week and often the month and sometimes the year as well. The data describing the number of inventory items waiting before an activity on a Monday at the beginning of the month may well be different from a Friday at the end of the month. I find that a general average is the best measure. However, if the reason why the VSM was initiated is due to something such as inability to meet demand at the end of the week, it is best to use data from that period of the week so that improvements will provide a solution to the presenting problem.

However, do not pick just any end of the week; get several points of data and average them. If the consequences of not being able to handle a lot of work at any time are extreme, take the largest inventory levels for that time period and design a VSM that deliberately focuses on the worst case. Then, once the FS-VSM shows what has to be done, you can be fairly confident that the improvements will protect the process from failure. Of course, you would also have to consider what to do with the extra resources that would not be needed during the other times of the week.

This process will give you the best "pure" process and lead times you can get. That is, you'll know about how long it takes to get a month's or a year's work done in terms of cycle time and lead time. The impact of other activities, tasks, and interruptions will not be included. That's why, in almost any office VSM, you cannot optimize a single process recklessly such as by taking workers out if you find that there are too many of them present for the amount of cycle time they consume for one of many tasks. You may see that you're overstaffed for the process on the VSM, but this is because the workers are doing anywhere from 1 task to 10 other tasks during the day. This is why you must serially optimize most of the processes in a work area if you are seeking overall effectiveness improvement—you cannot risk causing more problems with your "cure" for one or two processes. You must fix all or most of them, and then your overall solutions will gradually come together in terms of improvements and resources. In effect, you will be following the laws of chaos as discussed in Chapter 1; that is, pursue consistent disequilibrium and do not risk system failure by changing too many things at once. Of course, most office VSMs attempt to fix one process at a time. Therefore, you must be very careful to consider the impact of changes in that process on other activities the workers perform.

If there is tremendous seasonality in the demands or with in-process inventory at various points in the VSM, note this in the appropriate data box. If necessary, compute two or more separate lead times for the various peaks or valleys of inventory during very large seasonality variations. Better yet, but much more work, do two or three separate VSMs. Since extreme variability would require different sets of standard work, different VSMs make just as much sense. In that case, a great deal of any improvement strategy would be to facilitate changing the resources, schedules, and work assignments as the process moved from one level of demand to another.

Figure 8.3 presents the portion of the checking account process that deals with reviewing the checking account application materials at the data center, dealing with errors, and entering the information into the computer. Starting from the left, the first inventory square shows that 100 new accounts are presented to the data center every weekday from the branches (this is a daily average over an entire year). It takes 60 seconds to review each one, and, as we noted in Figure 8.1, 10% have a quality issue. The first lead time box shows 6000 seconds (100 applications taking 60 seconds each). This assumes that one person is doing the processing. If two people are typically doing the processing, that fact should be noted in the data box. The cycle time shown on the time ladder should be 60 seconds but the drop off interval would be 30 seconds

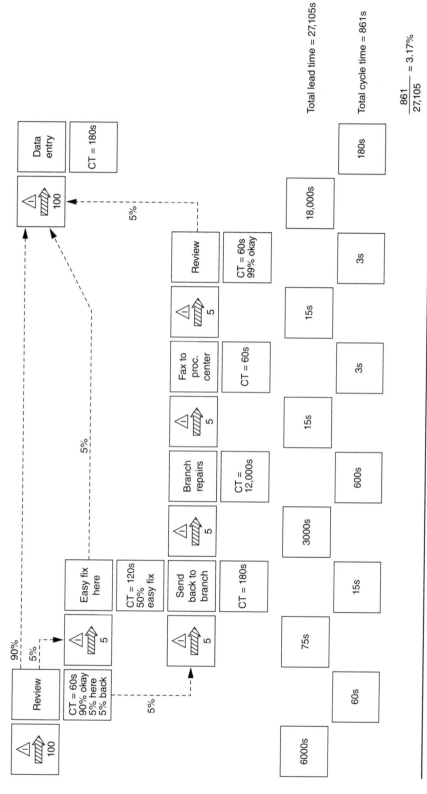

Figure 8.3 A portion of the checking account process showing how a decision tree is presented and how a rework cycle is displayed.

since two applications would be processed each minute. Note this in the data box. If the number of people varies between activities and/or during the day in a process, you'll have to estimate what the average staffing per day would be. If that is the case, be careful to note the actual number of people and people/hours that typically perform each activity and whether they do it full time, half time, and so on. Make careful notes in the data boxes so that it will be easy to explain how the cycle and lead time numbers were derived. Just as important is having the information to recalculate times when other information is discovered. You may think you'll remember the details, but take it from me, after building another couple of dozen activity boxes, it won't be easy to remember what happened earlier, especially if several people are making changes. Write all of the details in the data boxes!

Please keep in mind that this example assumes that the process will be empty at the end of the day. This is unrealistic, of course, but permits easy-to-understand calculations. The only difference between the examples and an actual situation would be that the inventory boxes would have varying amounts of inventory, depending on the averages that were obtained during data collection. These different inventory numbers would change the multiplier used to calculate the lead times from their corresponding cycle times.

The decision tree begins at the review activity. During the review, the employee classifies an error as either an easy one that can be fixed at the processing center (such as a missing zip code) or a difficult one that requires the branch to contact the customer and enter the data (such as a missing social security number for a completely new customer). The flowchart of this process is shown in Figure 8.4 for reference purposes. If the error is an easy one, the application is passed to the repair person who is represented by the "Easy fix here" activity box. Only 5% of the 100 applications per day take this route. The typical easy repair takes an average of 120 seconds. The other five problems (the other half of the 10% of 100 applications that have problems) have more complex errors. They are sent (faxed) back to the branch to be repaired. This takes 180 seconds, as the data box notes. Those five complex errors are then sent through the activities of "Branch repairs," "Fax to proc. center," and "Review," in that order. These activities take 12,000 seconds, 60 seconds, and 60 seconds, respectively.

The 12,000 seconds (3 hours and 19 plus minutes) of cycle time for the repair at the branch can be misleading. As we discussed earlier, this cycle time contains a lot of process lead time. Each repair took anywhere from one minute to a day or two to resolve, depending on how long it took for a financial representative at the branch to contact the customer by phone and get the cor-

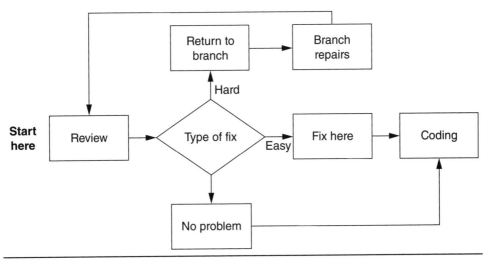

Figure 8.4 Flowchart of the process shown in Figure 8.3.

rect information. The actual work time for even the most complex repair takes only five or so minutes, including the phone calls, once the correct information is obtained. Most of the cycle time of this activity is actually process lead time since the application would simply sit on a desk between calls. However, since the entire task of "Branch repairs" is lumped into one activity box, the granularity of lead and cycle time within the box is lost.

As mentioned earlier, this is a common occurrence when an activity box is used to account for a task that has many subtasks. I ran into a particularly demonstrative example of this while working for a company in Russia. We were asked to look at its process for investigating, analyzing, and then purchasing other companies, as our client was constantly buying smaller enterprises. One box on the VSM was "Legal department reviews." The cycle time was six weeks. This made the percentage of cycle time for the entire process about 20% of total time (cycle time plus lead time). Of course, the bulk of time the paperwork spent in the legal department was lead time, but since all of the legal process was lumped into an activity box, there was no way to separate lead time from cycle time. We were not allowed to investigate the legal process since it was "busy" for several months. The best approach for both the bank and the Russian company's VSM would have been to dissect the activity box into its constituent processes. With cooperation from the legal department, a great deal of lead time, possibly weeks, could have been taken out of the process.

The VSM in Figure 8.3 is an example based on an eight-hour workday. If something sits overnight, no lead time accumulates between 5:00 p.m. and 8:00 a.m. unless a portion of the process deals with activities that are staffed for a longer time period. Any deviation from the accepted "day" for an activity should be noted in the activity's data box and included in various calculations. If the passage of overnight or nonstaffed shift time is critical, as when something sitting overnight causes a negative customer impact, it may be necessary to incorporate that time on the VSM as well. I would not recommend adding this "sitting" time to lead time. Instead, add a row to the time ladder that shows the added overnight time as a separate item. Use a different color of paper for that time line so that it stands out. That will enable analyzers and improvers to quickly locate the trouble areas caused by off-hours delays when such time is important.

In Figure 8.3, the two activity boxes for the two options for repairs (easy and hard) are shown directly above each other. This arrangement visually demonstrates that there are two different but simultaneous paths the application could take after the review activity. To calculate the various lead and cycle times on the time ladder, it is once again necessary to compute weighted averages. These averages adjust the times shown in the activity boxes by the proportions of applications that take each path. Thus, the cycle time on the time ladder below the "Easy fix here" and "Send back to branch" activity boxes is calculated by:

$$\frac{\text{Fix it here}}{\text{cycle time}} \quad \frac{5\% \text{ of}}{100} \quad \frac{\text{Send back}}{\text{to branch}} \quad \frac{5\% \text{ of}}{100}$$
$$120\text{s} \quad \times \ 0.05 \ + \quad 180\text{s} \quad \times \ 0.05 = 6\text{s} + 9\text{s} = 15\text{s}$$

The calculation of the lead time before the two activity boxes uses a similar approach. Five applications each wait 120 seconds (for "Easy fix here") and five applications each wait 180 seconds (for "Send back to branch"). Each of these totals is multiplied by the 0.05 because only 5% of the applications take each route as shown here:

$$\frac{\text{Fix it here}}{\text{cycle time}} \quad \frac{5\% \text{ of}}{100} \quad \frac{\text{Send back}}{\text{to branch}} \quad \frac{5\% \text{ of}}{100}$$
$$(120\text{s} \ \times 5 \text{ items} \times 0.05) + \ (180\text{s} \ \times 5 \text{ items} \times 0.05) = 30\text{s} + 45\text{s} = 75\text{s}$$

Of course, the lead time could have simply been calculated by multiplying the weighed total of 15 seconds of cycle time by five, which equals 75 seconds.

The five "send back to branch" applications are then worked on at the branch, each one taking 12,000 seconds on average. The weighed cycle time is calculated as:

$$\begin{array}{ccc} \text{Fix it at} & 5\% \\ \text{branch} & \text{of} \\ \underline{\text{cycle time}} & \underline{100} \\ 12{,}000\text{s} & \times \ 0.05 \ = 600\text{s} \end{array}$$

Thus, every single application is "taxed" 600 seconds in cycle time because 5% require so much time. This enables one single cycle time ladder to represent each of the 100 applications.

The lead time on the time ladder above cycle time is simply five times the 600 seconds, or 3000 seconds.

Faxing the application back to the processing center takes 60 seconds. The time ladder cycle time is:

$$\begin{array}{ccc} \text{Fix it back} & 5\% \\ \text{to branch} & \text{of} \\ \underline{\text{cycle time}} & \underline{100} \\ 60\text{s} & \times 5 \ \text{applications} \times \ 0.05 \ = 3\text{s} \end{array}$$

Every application that hits the system has 3 seconds of cycle time added to it because 5% of the applications must be faxed back to the processing center. The time ladder lead time prior to the faxing is calculated by:

$$3\text{s} \times 5 \ \text{applications} = 15\text{s}$$

The next step is review at the processing center. This second review is the same as the first one, but another activity box is added to the VSM. Nothing ever goes backward in a VSM, unlike in a flowchart that may have "do" loops that fold back on themselves.

Note that in a VSM, when a "do" loop or a decision tree occurs, the activity and inventory boxes are shown as being lower. This visually displays that the process takes more than one route.

If a step is repeated, another activity box and lead time box are added. The review takes 60 seconds per application, but it is only done to 5% of the applications, leading to a time ladder cycle time of:

$$60\text{s} \times 0.05 = 3\text{s}$$

The time ladder lead time is calculated by:

$$3\text{s} \times 5 \ \text{applications} = 15\text{s}$$

The last part of the Figure 8.3 VSM shows where all of the 100 applications come back together at data entry. It takes an average of 180 seconds to enter each application, and this cycle time is placed on the time ladder. The time ladder lead time is:

$$180s \times 100 \text{ applications} = 18,000s \text{ or 5 hours exactly}$$

The total cycle time for the entire VSM shown in Figure 8.3 is 861 seconds (14 minutes and 21 seconds). The total lead time is 27,105 seconds (7 hours, 31 minutes, and 45 seconds). Cycle time is 3.17% of lead time. This percentage is a bit higher than most office processes, but a big part of it is caused by the 600 seconds of cycle time added to every application for each branch repair that, as discussed earlier, contains a lot of process lead time.

If an item has more than one "do" loop cycle, you have a choice to make. You can either add additional lead time and activity boxes for each loop or factor the extra time for the additional loops to the last loop (the last set of activity and lead time boxes) you show. For example, if any errors were discovered at the processing center after the branch corrected them and returned them, you could add another "do" loop or simply put the small extra bit of time on the first "do" loop. In the Figure 8.3 example, the yield for the returned applications after repairs was estimated at 99%. The 1% with errors was ignored since it was only a "feeling" on the part of the process workers; they said that errors did happen after correction, but they couldn't remember the last one.

Communication Diagramming

Communication diagramming refers to the part of a VSM that displays where, how, and when information flows to and from activities and computers, counters, people, and so on. This is being presented in a separate step because such information is very important but is often omitted in a VSM. These communications, if missing, redundant, in excess, or poorly conceived, are often a significant source of waste. Changes in communications can provide an avenue for significant potential improvements. The communication paths are drawn above the activity boxes with lines of various types (dashed, doubled, etc.). Symbols are often put on the lines to represent the types of communication (e.g., a fax, hand carry, electronic transfer). When representing these lines on a first-cut VSM, denote the path with a strip of masking tape with the appropriate line drawn on the tape; this makes it easier to make changes without ruining the brown paper itself. After the CS-VSM has been fully reviewed, the taped lines can be replaced with lines drawn on the brown paper itself.

Figure 8.5 displays an example of communication channels on a CS-VSM. The activity boxes of the simplified VSM are labeled A–M. For ease of view-

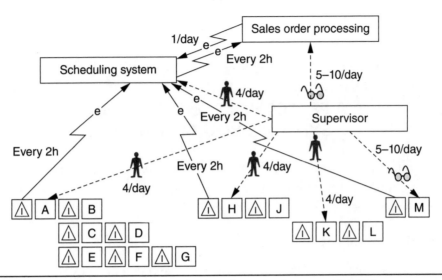

Figure 8.5   An example of communication diagramming on a CS-VSM.

ing, the data boxes are omitted, as is the time ladder. The dashed lines with the person walking represent data being delivered or collected by the supervisor, who walks to the person(s) doing the activity. If the transaction was done by phone, the line might have a headset superimposed on it. The choice of symbols is up to the teams. Of course, it is best if a site always uses a consistent set of symbols so they become easy to interpret after a few VSMs have been constructed.

As the figure shows, the supervisor visits activities A, H, and K four times per day to transmit scheduling information and obtain production data. The supervisor also visits the scheduling office/system four times per day to get information on what has to be completed and to get updates about the status of any changes. The details of these transactions would be included in data boxes in extra notes placed on the bottom of the VSM. The dotted lines with the eyeglasses represent look-sees, where the supervisor makes in-person checks on what is going on. The look-sees are different from the data collection/dissemination "walking figures" insofar as the look-sees are usually informal status checks driven, most likely, by anxiety. If they are required to operate the system, the walking figure would be a better choice given the definitions used here.

The solid zigzag lines with the "e" represent electronic transfers of information. The inventory stations next to activities A, H, and M (in this case, a server that automatically logs in customer files) each report status electronically to the scheduling system every two hours.

The situation depicted in Figure 8.5 is typical of data-intensive office processes. Without a clear picture of who knows what, when, and how, it would be difficult to make changes without creating even worse problems.

A FEW OTHER CONCEPTS AND SYMBOLS YOU MAY NEED

While you may not encounter them often, a number of VSMapping concepts that are common in factory settings may be useful in Office Kaizen settings from time to time.

Drop Off Interval (DOI)

All of the calculations in this chapter and the next calculate cycle time on the assumption that only one person at a time does an activity. This is the situation in a majority of office processes. However, some activities, especially in back offices that process large volumes of work, are done by several to many people at the same time. When you encounter one of these instances, the concept of DOI and its relationship to cycle time will be important.

The *DOI* is the period between outputs from an activity. If an activity is being done by one worker, the DOI is the same as the cycle time. That is, if it takes a worker 10 minutes to review a loan package, the DOI and the cycle time are each 10 minutes. If there are five workers doing the reviews at the same time, the DOI is two minutes; on average, the work group produces five reviews every 10 minutes. The formula for the calculation of DOI in this example is:

$$\text{DOI} = \frac{\text{Cycle time of one worker}}{\text{No. of workers performing the activity}} = \frac{10 \text{ minutes}}{5} = 2 \text{ minutes}$$

If the number of workers in an activity changes during the day, the number of workers figure will have to be weighted in order to generate an average number of workers doing the activity. All VSMs should *always* use cycle time—the time it takes one worker to do the process. Record the number of people who actually do the task at the same time in the data box for the activity along with the current DOI of the activity. These data may be important if staffing changes are contemplated as part of the improvements.

Kanban Board

A *kanban board* is a location that signals the presence of incoming work that is available to an activity and/or needs to be produced. In a factory, a kanban card may represent a large piece of equipment such as an engine waiting to be worked on. In an office setting, where the "work" represented is not physically large, the kanban board may actually hold the work itself, rather than cards. Examples are a kanban board for insurance applications awaiting approval or a board with purchase orders awaiting a buyer's attention. Kanban boards sometimes have kanbans for only one type of work/inventory. Others have many types and are organized into categories of urgency, effort, complexity, time required to complete, and so on, so that workers can deal with them in an organized manner rather than just letting things pile up while they work on whatever they happen to grab. These are called heijunka boards. Usually, the board is designed so that it can hold only a certain number of each type of work. When the number in a category exceeds the board's capacity, no more is accepted. This is a signal to all concerned that attention must be paid to the problem right away. Figure 8.6 (page 162) presents the VSM symbol for a kanban post in the legend. The following description of a supermarket describes how a typical kanban system works.

Supermarket

A *supermarket* is a particular kind of kanban board/location with kanbans that regulate the flow of materials between two activities. Mr. Toyoda chose the name after visiting American supermarkets, which he noted, "provide only what you need, when you need it" and what is taken is replenished, hopefully, before you need it again. Figure 8.6 presents a VSM-formatted illustration showing the operation of a supermarket. The illustrated supermarket is in the real estate closing office of a large bank. The two activities diagrammed are the preparation of generic closing packages (the package of standard forms with the bank's boilerplate information already filled in) and the finalization of the closing package that adds the borrower's and the property's unique information.

As the illustration shows, about 35 mortgage loans are closed (the demand) each day. There are four categories, or "buckets," in the supermarket of closing packages: loans that will be closed in 90 plus days, in 90 days, in 60 days, and in 30 days. Each category has a column with slots (similar to those in a time-card rack but larger) with the number of slots equal to the predetermined inventory level shown below the supermarket symbol.

When a closing technician is notified of a customer requirement, he or she withdraws the appropriate form from the supermarket rack. In this case, the withdrawal kanban is simply the technician's personal removal of the form since the supermarket is in the same room. In a bank with a poorly arranged process, the withdrawal kanban might be a phone call, an e-mail, or even an actual paper kanban sent through the interoffice mail, all of which would be very inefficient compared with having the two activities right next to each other. When

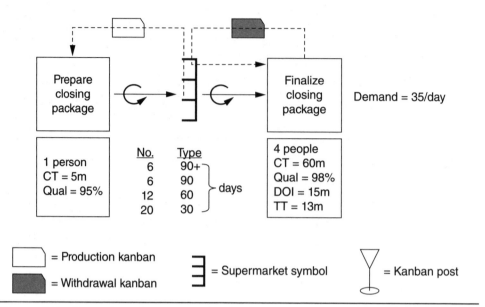

Figure 8.6   Illustration of a supermarket kanban system.

the administrative loan assistant observes an empty slot in one of the columns where one of the closing technicians has withdrawn one, he or she prepares a replacement. The assistant's observation of an empty slot serves as the production kanban. As with the withdrawal kanban, the production kanban might be a phone call, a paper kanban, and so on, if the two activities are not adjacent.

This system makes it easy to ensure that the closing technicians always have what they need and that there is never too many packages of any one kind prepared in advance of need. As an indication of what a VSM can show, a closer examination of the data box for "Finalize closing package" indicates a problem. Since the cycle time to finalize a package is 60 minutes, the DOI for the activity is 15 minutes with four technicians working. However, the takt time (TT) for the process is the 450 minutes of work time per day divided by 35 packages, which equals 13 minutes (rounded up). This means that, on average, the technicians will be falling behind by two minutes times 35 packages or 70 minutes each day. Of course, if this were a typical office process, there wouldn't be a supermarket already in place, and the problems that might motivate the VSMapping exercise would be the failure to keep up with closing, too many of one type of package and not enough of another, and so on.

First In, First Out (FIFO) Lane

A *FIFO lane* is a type of self-regulating kanban system that presents work to an activity. The work is done by the receiving activity in the order of "first

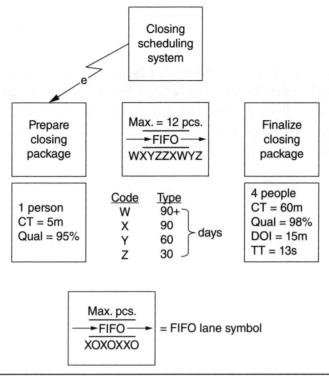

Figure 8.7 An example of a FIFO lane.

in, first out." A FIFO lane is typically used instead of a supermarket when there are a great many variations and/or the inventory is very expensive, perishable, or breakable. A FIFO lane is a great way to minimize inventory if it can keep up with demand. Figure 8.7 presents a FIFO in the place of the supermarket that was presented in Figure 8.6. The use of four different letters beneath the "FIFO" label shows the number of different item types that are in the FIFO lane; in this case, four. The listing below the FIFO box is information for the VSM reviewers. The FIFO is actually a better solution because the generic closing packages can be prepared very quickly; there is no need to build up a lot of packages in front of the closing technicians *unless* the closing administrative assistant is going to be absent for more than an hour or two, which could be the case as he or she has other duties.

REMEMBER . . .

Keep in mind that the VSM is an idealized, highly structured depiction of a process. It strives to take all of the times into account as though it were all "first in, first out" in every activity and inventory box. This is not always the way it works in reality; some applications could sit on a desk for days in the processing center, while others might be handled immediately, such as work for a VIP client. However, without the formalized structure of a VSM, it would be hard to analyze any process in terms of cycle times and lead times. The key insight is to realize that a VSM is a distorted "but as close as we can come" linear depiction of reality. As long as the same distortion assumptions are applied reliably and in both the current and future VSMs, any inaccuracies should be minor if the VSM is constructed by knowledgeable employees.

9

Constructing an Office Kaizen Current State Value Stream Map

Now that Chapter 8 has presented the mechanics of value stream mapping (VSMapping), this chapter presents the approach for doing the work that is required to collect data and build the current state VSM (CS-VSM). The general logistics of a VSM, kaizen, and/or lean event are discussed in Chapter 11. This chapter concentrates mainly on distinct issues as they pertain to VSM construction.

1. PREPARE FOR THE VSMAPPING EVENT

The secret of any process improvement effort is similar to that required for successful brain surgery: *preparation, preparation,* and then *more preparation.* Prior to the CS-VSM effort, you must have a team, a team leader, a champion, and a charter that has been approved by the Executive Steering Committee (ESC). Chapter 6 provided a general overview of the ESC structure and the procedures by which it operates. *Office Kaizen 1 (OK1)* provides more detail for those who are completely new to the process or who require more detail. If you have not formed an ESC, it is critical to get approval (or at least acquiescence) for the planned VSMapping effort from all management personnel whose areas will be impacted by the event. This includes all departments in which you will be collecting data and all of the supervisors of all team members you'll be using for the event. Before you start, develop a charter with either the ESC or a sufficiently influential group of executives or senior management. If you don't have their buy-in at the start, you run the risk of having team members kidnapped for "critical" tasks during the event or encountering resistance to pursuing the improvement opportunities you'll be identifying.

While the next preparation item may seem obvious, my observations indicate that, to many people, it is not. Make sure you have ample work space reserved for the duration of the VSMapping event. There's nothing like the negative impact on the team(s) of being kicked out of a conference room in the middle of an event that you have described to them as being "very important to the future of the company" in order to make room for a weekly weight-loss meeting. You'll need a room or two or three, depending on the number of teams that will be working and the sizes of the rooms, with a lot of clear wall space for hanging brown papers. Arrange to have all the supplies you'll need on-site before you start. Each team should have the following supplies:

- A copy of the layout of the site/facility that encompasses the process to be studied

- At least 10 rolls of heavy (standard) brown wrapping paper (usually 28 inches wide and 50 feet long)

- At least 12 rolls of transparent adhesive tape (not glossy, so you can write on it)

- Two rolls of masking tape

- Six rolls of clear plastic packing tape (high quality)

- At least 20 pads of square sticky notes in different colors

- Several pairs of scissors

- One pack each of red, green, and yellow stick-on dots (¾ inch)

- A yardstick or a long straightedge

- At least 10 markers in several colors

- A few pencils

- Access to a nearby copier (make sure a couple of reams of paper are available)

- About 50 sheets each of various colors of paper

- Three calculators (nothing fancy, just for performing simple calculations)

- Three stopwatches

- A flip chart and a stand with at least one spare pad of paper (ruled, if possible)

- 50 kaizen action sheets (KASs)

- Any personal protective equipment required in the work area

- Dry-erase board with erasable markers, or blackboard with chalk

- Digital camera

- Laptop computer and input device for digital camera media

- Digital projector

- Extension cords with ample outlets

Put all the smaller supplies in a box so they are ready to move to the project room. Have a copy of each team's charter for each team member along with a team copy of supporting phone numbers, floor plans, office locations, and so on, that are related to the process the team will be examining.

It is important to make sure that the champion and a few members of the ESC or involved management team are present at the kickoff to make appropriate comments and show support. These individuals should also be present at each day's summary meeting (discussed in Chapter 12). In addition, the champion needs to be available for consultation during the week on an as-needed basis. Chapter 12 discusses when to notify the various personnel.

2. GIVE THE TEAM MEMBERS (WHO WILL BE BUILDING THE VSM) AN OVERVIEW OF VSMAPPING CONCEPTS AND PRINCIPLES

This can be done by reconstructing the examples in Chapter 8 on a white board or by using an "approved" example for the organization's VSM materials (if any). It's not essential to provide a detailed "face down through the cactus" workshop; you only need the participants to understand the big picture of what they'll be doing. As mentioned earlier, they'll learn most of what they need by doing.

3. REVIEW AND REFINE THE CHARTER OF THE VSMAPPING TEAM WITH THE TEAM MEMBERS

The approved charter for the team may not be as detailed or as specific as required. Or it may not be described in a manner that is clear to the team members. Have each team carefully read the charter and modify it as required. It is important to make sure that the team does not change the intent or focus of the charter. If there are any questions about whether the intent of the charter is being changed, have the champion discuss it with the team(s).

4. REVIEW THE LEVEL OF MAPPING THAT WILL BE USED

In almost all cases, each activity box will represent one task (e.g., reviewing an application, entering a test result on a spreadsheet). In a select few cases, the level of mapping will require that an activity box represent several activities (such as when site consolidation is being considered and/or when processes or lines may be moved, combined, or divided). Give each team an example of what one of its boxes may look like by using an actual task from the process the team will be mapping.

5. REVIEW THE SCOPE OF THE MAPPING

The scope should be clear from the charter, but often it is fuzzy before the VSM is constructed. Therefore, have each team specify the first and last activity boxes of its VSM insofar as it understands the charter and its process at the moment. This might change as the team members collect data (there are almost always additional and/or different initial and finishing activities than are apparent at first glance), but at least they'll probably be close and sensitized to the issue. Tell them to check with the coach if they decide that the chosen beginning and ending activities have changed from the initial estimates. If it appears that the suggested changes conflict with the charter, have the team confer with its champion and the coach.

Another aspect of scope involves how far to pursue processes within and outside the organization. In most cases, the scope usually stops at the points where process steps are done by customers and suppliers. If the issue is sufficiently severe and appropriate, customer and/or supplier personnel may be on the team(s). In that case, it may be possible to include in the VSM some of the activities that take place at the customer and/or supplier location. However, be very careful, as recalled information about what happens in a process at another location may be inaccurate. That is, the representatives of the customer and/or the supplier may not be sufficiently knowledgeable about their processes if they are not hands-on workers in that process. And if they are hands-on workers, their knowledge may not extend to processes in which they have not worked lately. If there are any questions about what is appropriate, consult with the champion. Of course, it's always best if these issues are worked out before the charter is written and/or the event begins.

6. DISCUSS THE DEFINITION OF "FUTURE" THAT WILL BE USED IN IMPLEMENTING IMPROVEMENTS AND THE INVESTMENT STRATEGY BEHIND IMPROVEMENTS

There are several issues here. While the identification of changes is not formally done until after the CS-VSM is completed, team members will begin to generate improvement ideas as soon as they read their charter. It is a good idea to frame their thinking with a little realism right from the start. Let them know about the definition of "future" as it pertains to the future state VSM (FS-VSM) that will follow the CS-VSM. This is, of course, something that the charter should state. If it does not, work with the champion to come up with an answer on the spot, if possible. If the FS-VSM future is two weeks, that presents a very different set of limitations than improvements that have a six-month future. Generally there are several "futures." Typically, the action plan that accompanies the FS-VSM (see Chapter 10) will outline improvements that are expected to be implemented in at least two to three time periods such as one month, six months, and a year.

A second consideration is the investment strategy that the organization desires and/or is forced to accept. If the enterprise is short of cash or needs immediate relief from whatever issue prompted the VSMapping exercise, management will most likely be looking for big returns in a short time from little to no investment. If there is no short-term crisis, the enterprise may be willing to consider medium- to long-term investments if the returns are sufficient. However, the emphasis is always on cheap, fast improvements (the essence of kaizen) and then on medium- to longer-term fixes. After all, short-term improvements typically target waste reduction and cost little. There's no point in not getting them right away. If enough of them work well, they may eliminate the need for some of the more expensive long-term improvements.

7. REVIEW THE STEPS IN THIS CHAPTER SO TEAM MEMBERS CAN ANTICIPATE WHAT THEY WILL BE DOING

The goal of any VSMapping exercise is not only to develop a VSM and potential improvement ideas but also to develop analysis and VSMapping skills in employees. Consider everyone on the team(s) to be future facilitators and/or trainers. This means that you must give them enough information so that they can properly place every aspect of the VSMapping event (or kaizen event, 5S event, etc.) in a well-organized cognitive structure so that they can recall and use the information effectively in the future. Provide all of the attendees with access to training materials, forms, templates, and so on, for future use. Most often these are most economically provided online. For those who do not have such access, make a resource available for them to obtain paper copies.

8. INTRODUCE THE KAIZEN ACTION
SHEET (KAS) AND ITS USE

If the KAS (or the organization's/site's version) is not used in the organization, introduce it at this point and specify that *every* suggestion that comes to mind must be captured at that moment on a KAS. The KAS for each team must be deposited in a specific place (e.g., on an outlined and labeled spot on a table, in an envelope hanging on the wall). Chapter 6 explains how to use KASs. The requirement for KASs will ensure that nothing is lost. If KASs are not used, a great many ideas that pop into peoples' minds will be forgotten as the team(s) gets into the detail work of building its VSM.

Have a large number of KASs available that are already numbered in one corner of the sheet. As needed, have the coach of the event make more copies and number them. While it is not important that all KASs be used in order, the numbered sequence makes it easier to ensure that a large number of ideas are not misplaced.

9. COLLECT PRELIMINARY DATA

At this point, the team(s) should be ready to begin its data collection activities. It is important to assign specific time periods and assignments to each team so that valuable time is not lost while the team(s) is getting comfortable. It is best if the team members get to know one another by doing work rather than struggling to determine what to do as they get to know one another. After a day or so of the coach's direction and structure, most teams will be conditioned to working hard in a focused manner. The facilitator can then focus on being a coach and advisor rather than a task master.

The preliminary data collection steps are as follows:

a. *Obtain a layout of the facility/site:* If this wasn't taken care of beforehand, each team should do this as it walks around. If there are existing facility layouts, take them along on the "walk the process" step and make annotations as to what has changed. These annotated drawings will be used to create spaghetti diagrams of walking routes, data/ materials flow, and so on.

b. *Walk the process:* Each team should be assigned to walk its assigned process as a group. Give the team a definite time to be back in the team room. The purpose is not to collect detailed data but to determine the general layout of the process, the locations where work is done, the people and computers involved, and the general sequence of activities. Exact detail is not important at this point, but a general understanding of how the process flows is important because it will guide how the team divides up its work. The team should ask plenty of questions but not go into detail about times, numbers of items, and so on. Very useful questions at this point are, "What happens next?" "Who gets the work after you?" and so on.

10. CONSTRUCT A ROUGH SEQUENCE OF ACTIVITIES

After walking the process, each team should return to its work area and develop a rough sequence of the activity steps in the process. This should be done on sticky notes placed on brown paper (the same paper that will be used to construct the VSM) so that the notes can be easily adjusted. It also gets the team used to using the sticky notes and thinking of each note as a discrete activity or inventory location. This step is not shooting for accuracy; the objective is to allow the team to get an idea of the big picture and be able to estimate how much work needs to be done in each portion of its process's data collection efforts.

11. DIVIDE THE TEAM'S WORK INTO PROCESS CHUNKS AND ASSIGNMENTS

Unless the team leader is experienced, it is vital that the coach/facilitator assign very specific responsibilities to the members of each team. It is essential to have each team develop a RACI chart (see Chapter 7) on a brown paper that shows the function of each person on the team on various tasks. This not only keeps track of who's doing what but also helps the team learn how to use a RACI chart in real time. If possible, assign the team members to work on assignments in pairs. An extra team member can go with one of the other teams. However, do not assign people to work in groups of three unless you have to, as it is usually a waste of resources; the third person often has little to do. The pairing of team members helps them develop more insights into the process through discussion, and it also helps build team bonds. The coach should change team pairs for different assignments during the first two days so that everyone gets to work with most, if not all, members of the team.

12. COLLECT DETAILED INFORMATION

This step is where the nitty-gritty work of a CS-VSM and ancillary analyses is conducted. If this step is done thoroughly and with focus, the physical construction of the VSM will be as painless as it can be. Answers to the following set of questions should provide the bulk of the information required to construct the CS-VSM and the other analyses that are listed after the questions. Begin the questioning at the very first activity that defines the beginning of the scope. Then, proceed in order down (or up, if you're starting at the end of the process) the process, one activity at a time. If the team is divided into subteams, different teams can start at different spots in the process.

- *Information collection questions:* For every single activity, always ask the following:

  1. From what function does the activity get the work that arrives?

  2. How does the work get here from there? (e.g., mail, fax, carried, intranet, or internet)

  3. Where does it come from? (location)

  4. Where does the work wait before the activity?

  5. How much inventory is typically waiting to enter the activity? (each "piece" of inventory represents the raw material for the activity to produce one unit of output)

  6. Does the inventory vary during the day, week, month, quarter? If so, by how much?

  7. Is the inventory status communicated to other activities, people, computers, and so on?

  8. How often is this communication made?

  9. How do the people who do this activity get the input work? (e.g., somebody places it on their desk, they open a file)

  10. How many units of work are delivered to the activity at once?

  11. How many pieces of work are processed at once in the activity?

  12. Describe the activity in detail.

  13. Is this the only activity that can occur after the previous activity or while waiting in inventory?

  14. Can anything else happen?

15. What happens if there is a problem? Where does the work go?

16. What is the quality, percent good or bad, of this activity?

17. How is quality assessed?

18. Where are the quality data kept?

19. How often are they updated?

20. Who updates them?

21. What is the inspection procedure? (e.g., every piece, every tenth piece, when a problem appears)

22. Who conducts the inspection procedure?

23. Does this activity do its own rework?

24. If yes: How do rework or repair items arrive at the process?

25. If yes: Where and for how long are they held before the process receives them?

26. Is quality data on this process communicated?

27. If yes: How often, how (e.g., by computer, on report form), and by whom?

28. What are the types of things that go wrong in this activity?

29. What do you think are the causes of mistakes in this activity?

30. How many people do this activity at the same time? (get names; these are the *R*s that will be used in the RACI chart of the process)

31. How many people are trained to do this activity? (get names)

32. How many shifts and/or hours per day is the activity done?

33. Does the staffing ever change? If so, when and how?

34. Where does the work go after this step? (get names and locations of the places where the inventory waits for the next activity/process step)

35. How does the work get there?

36. Is the status of activity completion reported?

37. If yes: How often (e.g., after each piece, once a day), how (e.g., by computer, on a report form), to what (e.g., computer, person), and by whom?

38. Is the actual work product or parts of it (for data/information) communicated by the activity?

39. If yes: How often (e.g., after each piece, once a day), how (e.g., by computer, on a report form), to what/whom (e.g., computer, person), and by whom?

40. Who is the owner of this activity? (this is the *A*, for "authority," for the RACI chart of the process)

41. Who, if anyone, must be notified of the status before this activity is performed? (this is *C*, for "consulted," for the RACI chart of the process)

42. Who must be informed after this activity is performed (other than those covered in the earlier questions)? (this is the *I*, for "informed," for the RACI chart of the process)

43. What work instructions are there for this activity?

44. Where are the work instructions? (show me)

45. Are the work instructions used for training?

46. Who does the training?

47. How often are the work instructions changed?

I find it helpful to create a form with the questions and answer blocks or lines beneath each question. Keep a supply of questions for each team and keep the master available in case more copies are needed. This method (1) provides a means to ensure that the data collectors don't forget any questions, (2) provides a standard data recording format that is easy for anyone involved with the analysis to use to efficiently locate data, and (3) provides future teams working on the process with a well-organized package of information to supplement the VSM.

On the top of the first page, provide boxes for the activity name, final selected cycle time, cycle time measurements, and inventory level as well as who was interviewed/observed for the activity and who collected the data. Answers to some of the questions from the list may seem obvious in some simple and/or straightforward activities, but ask anyway. You'll be surprised at the complexity hidden behind even the simplest activities. And, often, a question about one issue and the answer to it will uncover information about something else that would not have arisen otherwise but is important to the analysis.

Any work samples, copies of job aids, and so on, should be placed in a folder with the activity's name on it. For those activities with work samples and related information, the question/answer packet should also go in the folder.

Remember to promote the use of KASs for every improvement idea at several points each day of the event. If someone on the team says, "What if . . .?," immediately tell him or her, "Put it on a KAS." If a process worker makes a suggestion, stop and put it on a KAS right away.

- *Activity cycle times:* It is essential to time each activity with a stopwatch. Take at least 10 measurements of the activity if possible. If times cannot be measured in the activity in real time, simulate the activity using real forms, screens, and actual workers. If that is not possible, interview several people who do the task and have them estimate how long it takes (do this without others nearby so that peer pressure is not operating to fudge the numbers one way or the other). If there are dramatic differences between them, explore the reasons why. If there are shift, weekly, monthly, or quarterly variations in the complexity of the activity, make notes. At some point, given the charter, the team (and perhaps the coach and the champion as well) might have to make a determination as to how to come up with a number.

- *Inventory counts:* As Chapter 8 discussed, many people determine the amount of inventory waiting before an activity by taking a "snapshot" of what is present at the instant they make their observations. This can be misleading. A better approach is to determine what is typically present on average. This is done by interviewing workers of the receiving activity (after the inventory). As with cycle times, if there is variability in the amount of daily, weekly, or other types of inventory, a decision will have to be made as to how inventory will be represented so as to best serve the charter.

- *Work samples/forms/screen shots:* At each process step, the team members should collect samples of work input and output from the activity. These can be copies of paperwork, computer screen shots, copies of job aids (such as checklists or work standards), and so on.

- *Data box information:* Before data collection begins, the team must decide what minimum data will be collected for each of the data boxes. The focus of the charter should provide sufficient basis to identify key metrics. If not, work with the coach to identify them.

13. GENERATE THE FIRST-CUT CS-VSM

The first step for each team is to create an exact sequence of process activities. This is done by placing sticky notes on the brown paper to represent each activity box and its accompanying data box and incoming inventory box. Use different colors for the activity and inventory boxes. As shown in Chapter 8, place the inventory symbol (triangle with a capital "I") in each inventory box. Place the activity's inventory count and cycle time in the activity's data box. Place the time ladder below the inventory and activity boxes (leaving enough vertical room in the event that choice points require the insertion of additional rows). Don't worry about putting cycle or lead time numbers on the time ladder at this point; they may change. Also, fill in the data boxes for each process with the two to seven key metrics that have been determined beforehand (e.g., cycle time, inventory count, quality level, staffing, number of shifts).

14. PERFORM COMMUNICATION DIAGRAMMING

Place communication lines on the VSM with masking tape (with lines on the tape). Show all movement of reports, data, look-sees, and so on. Make sure that all teams in the event (if there is more than one team) use the same symbols for faxes, hand-transmitted data, electronic transfers, and so on. If an organization or site standard does not exist, create it. If there is a standard, use it.

15. REVIEW THE FIRST-CUT CS-VSM WITH WORKERS FROM THE PROCESS

As soon as the first-cut CS-VSM has been constructed, bring in groups of two to five process workers and supervisors at a time and give them a guided tour of the process. If the process is sufficiently large, two or three groups can work on it at once, provided they start at different points and have a team member accompany them. The group is looking for three things:

- Is the sequence of activities, choice points, and "do" loops accurate? Are there any activities, choice points, or "do" loops (where the process stream "drops" down a level) missing, duplicated, or mistakenly included?

- Are the cycle times accurate?

- Are the inventory counts accurate?

In each instance where the reviewers do not agree or raise an issue with what is on the VSM, state the issue and the suggested answer (if any) on a sticky note (in a different color or with a dark border so it is easy to visually discern) and place it on the VSM at the appropriate point. Do not change the VSM contents until all of the reviewers have finished their inspections and the VSMapping team gets together (next step).

16. MAKE CHANGES TO THE VSM

After all the reviewers are done, the team should discuss each discrepancy and come to a decision. In some instances, it may be necessary to revisit the process and collect more data. Once the sequence of activities, cycle times, and inventory amounts have been determined, the time ladder boxes should be filled in by calculating cycle and lead times.

17. REVIEW THE REVISED VSM WITH THE PROCESS WORKERS AND MAKE ANY ADJUSTMENTS

Once again, bring in groups of process workers and guide them through the VSM, paying special attention to any areas that were sources of contention on the first review. Make any adjustments as required. Encourage the process workers to suggest improvement ideas as they review the VSM. Make a KAS for each suggestion right away. Write the number of the KAS on a sticky note on the map at the location of the proposed improvement.

18. CONSTRUCT ANCILLARY ANALYSES

Ancillary analyses accompany the VSM and enrich the insights that the VSM provides. The following are the most helpful, although many more could be useful in certain situations:

- *Spaghetti diagrams:* As Chapter 7 explained, spaghetti diagrams show the routes that paper, data, material, and/or people take to complete an action. The elimination of excess walking, data transfers, and paper shuffling is always a key element in Office Kaizen efforts. When the typical CS-VSM spaghetti diagram is created, it screams, "Why is all this stuff moving around so much?" Such insights are much more difficult to see on a VSM than on a spaghetti diagram.

Use the data obtained during the interviews to construct a spaghetti diagram for the entire process. While spaghetti diagrams can show data, paper, and material movement, they are typically used in office venues for showing paper and/or people movement. The amount of waste varies exactly with distance, which a spaghetti chart clearly displays. If the process is very large, it may be necessary to construct more than one spaghetti diagram (e.g., one for people, another for data).

- *Handoff chart:* As Chapter 7 showed, handoff charts are very good at showing transfers of information (data or paper) and materials. As with spaghetti diagrams, they very powerfully and simply show the main paths where information is passed between and among various areas, sections, departments, and/or people.

- *RACI diagram:* Process RACI diagrams (explained in Chapter 7) are different in focus from the RACI diagram the team uses to manage its own work. In effect, every activity on the VSM will contribute one row (or column, if the functions and people are shown across the top of the RACI chart). That is, the activity will have a column (or row) in which one or more workers will have the *R* (if several people do the activity at once and/or at different times), one column/row could have the *A* (by the rules of a RACI chart), and one or more may have an *I* or a *C*. Remember, the CS-VSM is a view of what is, not what should be, so some activities may have no *A* or even no defined *R*(s).

- *Cross-training matrix:* It's great if the team can create a rough cut of the cross-training matrix for the activity (or the entire work area), as shown in Chapter 7. This is very important if change activities or changes that move people are considered. In most environments, these matrices do not exist (especially in office environments), so the RACI chart will have to suffice as a rough approximation.

These ancillary tools, coupled with the VSM, will provide the team with a depth of insight into the process that few people could have imagined. Better yet, they will provide the team with the details that are necessary to generate a plethora of relevant improvement ideas.

19. IDENTIFY AND SORT POSSIBLE IMPROVEMENT IDEAS

Once the teams get to this point, most of the "face down through the cactus" work will have been done. If the analyses have been done properly, the team will be brimming with improvement ideas. If the coach has done his or her job properly, most of the ideas will be on KASs. It is important to structure the team's identification and sorting of possible improvements so that time and insights are not wasted. The following method works very well:

a. Have a supply of extra, numbered KASs ready for any spontaneous improvement ideas that the team generates.

b. If all of the reviewers' improvement ideas on the VSM have not been placed on a KAS, do so at this point.

c. After all of the KASs have been gathered, it is important for the team to review each one and make sure that everyone on the team understands exactly what the KAS means. If the wording is vague or general, ask the originator what he or she meant and determine what the KAS should say to make it focused and specific. If the team doesn't know what it means, most others won't, either. Further, the team can't afford to waste time by sorting and classifying foggy or unclear KASs.

d. Gather the entire team at the VSM. Have the team take the pile of filled-in KASs and write the number of each completed KAS on a sticky note of a different color (or a different shape such as a starburst) at the location on the VSM where the KAS applies. Attach the actual KAS at the bottom of the VSM (below the time line), beneath the location of the numbered note to which the KAS corresponds. An example of this approach is shown in Figure 9.1, where gray round notes are used. If they are not stick-on, small pieces of masking tape can be used to attach them.

e. Create an additional set of numbered stick-on shapes to represent the KAS shapes that have been placed on the VSM. They needn't be the same color or shape as the ones on the VSM; keep them simple and easy to create. These shapes are to be sorted onto a grid such as the one shown in Figure 9.2, which uses taped notes on a three by three grid to relate estimated impact on process time (the main focus for the project) to implementation time frame. The use of implementation time frame is almost always a key factor. The other factor could just as well be short-term cost reduction, risk, or scope of quality improvement.

The first column of Figure 9.2 shows the KAS that the team thinks can be completed in the week of the event. If the event is a "pure" VSMapping event

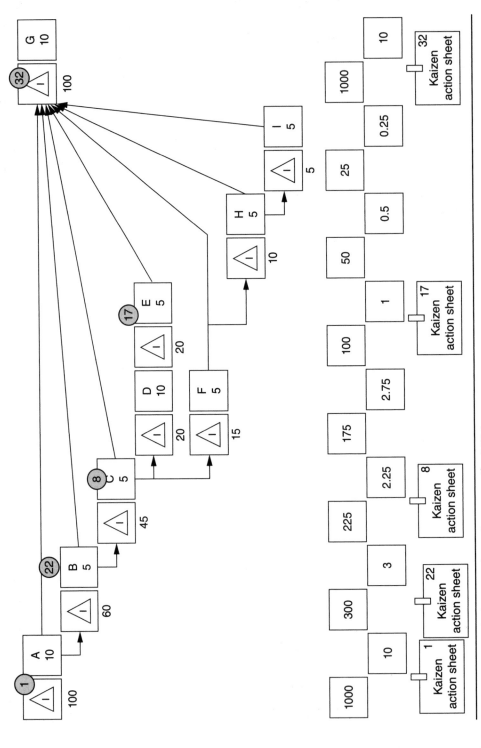

Figure 9.1 KAS place markers shown on the VSM.

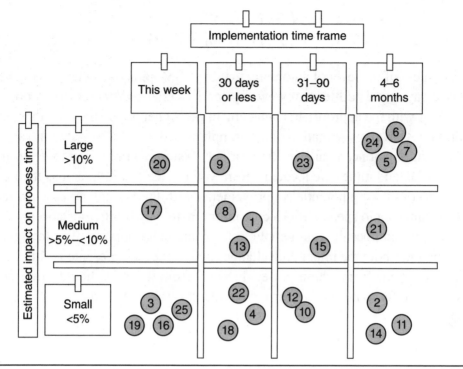

Figure 9.2 An example of a relationship grid for classifying improvement ideas.

in which the CS-VSM, FS-VSM, and an implementation plan will be developed, there may not be time, resources, or the intent to come up with changes during the week. Despite the intent, it is a good lesson in urgency and kaizen practice to have each team come up with at least one thing they can fully implement during the week.

20. DISCUSS THE IMPROVEMENTS AND DETERMINE FINAL CLASSIFICATION

At this point, most of the decision making will have been done as a result of discussions and classifications. The team, led by the facilitator or team leader, should make a final reality check review of each KAS and its classification. Can each KAS be done in its selected time period? Is the impact of each KAS realistically estimated? If two sheets are very close in focus or method, make sure that they truly are separate KASs and not merely duplicates of the same idea. It's better to take another 15 minutes of review than to find out later that something was amiss and a lot of work was wasted.

21. REVIEW SENSITIVE AND/OR BOLD IMPROVEMENTS WITH APPROPRIATE PEOPLE

Regardless of the level of autonomy that the VSMapping team has been given, it is always good politics to review any controversial and/or dramatic proposed changes with the appropriate management personnel before they see them in a formal review or presentation of the completed CS-VSM, FS-VSM, and action plan. You're not necessarily asking for permission; you're trying to determine where the land mines are located before you prance gleefully across the field. Prior to discussing potential improvements with the various process owners, each team should speak with its champion; there may be circumstances where the champion doesn't want people to have any extra opportunities to register complaints about the impending changes before they are presented. The champion is the one from whom power flows (or from whom it should flow), so it is best to refer to him or her for judgments in cases such as these.

10

Constructing an Office Kaizen Future State Value Stream Map and Action Plan

Most future state VSMs (FS-VSMs) are constructed immediately after completion of the current state VSM (CS-VSM). This is the best approach because the insights and complexities created or encountered during construction of the CS-VSM will be fresh in the minds of the team. No matter how detailed the notes, kaizen action sheets (KASs), and ancillary analyses; no matter how fine the construction of the CS-VSM; and no matter how extensive the team discussions have been, much information will be lost if construction of the FS-VSM is held off for another week or even a few days.

Even worse is the handoff of the construction of the FS-VSM to a team that did not construct the CS-VSM. One or two team members may need to drop out, and while they can be replaced, it is essential that both the CS-VSM and the FS-VSM be done by most of the same people. Keep this in mind when staffing the project and developing the schedule. Unless the process is incredibly long and/or complex, 32 hours over five days is usually sufficient for a team to do both the CS-VSM and the FS-VSM and the action plan.

The following sections describe the steps for constructing the FS-VSM.

1. SELECT THE TIME HORIZON FOR THE FS-VSM

The bottom-line concern in selecting the time horizon for the FS-VSM is, which improvements and their impacts will be used to create the FS-VSM? That is, which projected improvements will be implemented to change the CS-VSM process and drive the recalculations of cycle and lead times that will go into the FS-VSM forecast? As discussed in Chapter 9, there may be several meaningful (to the management team as expressed in the charter) futures to a CS-VSM: current week, one month, three months, and one year. In cases where the improvements are strategic changes and/or involve extensive capital expenditures, computer resources, or relocations of staff and equipment, a short-term future may be six months. In many other cases, a long-term future may be three months.

On some rare occasions, more than one FS-VSM may be required. The key is to work with the champion to determine what will best make the case for needed improvement resources to the management team. At the same time, it is important to guard against making the FS-VSM construction process a complex, labor-intensive exercise in VSMapping technology, options, and bells and whistles instead of what it should be—one step in the organization's continuous improvement journey.

The approach I prefer is to set a future of two to three months (unless the charter says otherwise) and wrap all of the improvements done in that time into a single FS-VSM. While a three-month-horizon FS-VSM may not overtly call out the isolated impact of the improvements made in the first two to four weeks versus those created in months two and three, any categories of improvement horizon can be listed separately on the VSMapping summary, and their impacts can be presented without creating a separate FS-VSM to showcase them. Later in this chapter, a technique for presenting several futures on a single FS-VSM is presented in the event that it might be needed.

2. SELECT THE IMPROVEMENTS THAT WILL GENERATE THE FORECAST SHOWN IN THE FS-VSM

After the rankings and ratings of the potential improvements are done in a manner similar to that presented at the end of Chapter 9, the team should be well prepared to select the improvements that are appropriate for the FS-VSM horizon. In Figure 9.2 from the previous chapter, a three-month horizon would mean that all of the improvements in the first three columns (i.e., "this week," "30 days or less," and "31–90 days") would be candidates for inclusion in the FS-VSM. The only open issue for the team is to decide whether all the candidate improvements will be included. If all the improvements are not going to be included for some reason, and there is some unease about the selections, it is wise to have the team check its assumptions by developing additional selection (or omission) criteria and using them to further screen the improvements that made the first cut. Some additional criteria might be ease of implementation, complexity, cost, technology risk, short-term impact, disruption of the workforce, and so on. Most often, an additional, formal matrix rating exercise is not required; a simple discussion usually suffices.

3. DENOTE IMPROVEMENTS THAT WILL BE INCLUDED ON THE CS-VSM

Those who review the CS-VSM must be able to easily determine which improvements were implemented in order to create the FS-VSM. The easiest way is to simply circle the selected KAS numbers with a bold marker or attach an extra label to each KAS included in the FS-VSM with a check mark or some other character. Another way is to simply remove from the CS-VSM all of the KAS numbers that will not be implemented in the construction of the FS-VSM. This approach has the benefit of eliminating disputes/discussions with observers about nonselected improvements. On the other hand, the removal of any KAS removes information that may be important to future teams and/or work groups that review the VSM outputs.

A common approach in planning the FS-VSM is to mark improvement loops on the CS-VSM. An *improvement loop* is a group of improvements that focuses on a part of the process and/or implementation strategy within a specific time period and/or using a specific improvement methodology. For example, IT systems changes may involve many parts of the process that have to be changed at the same time, thus making them an "IT loop." Improvements in a loop are often done sequentially or are attacked individually by a dedicated implementation team. This makes it easy to plan the improvement strategy, assess the overall impact on an area or a process, and determine whether more improvements have to be implemented in order to achieve the charter requirements. Loops can be circled on the CS-VSM, labeled (e.g., data center loop), and then presented as discrete sections of the implementation plan. Figure 10.1 shows a CS-VSM with improvement loops marked and labeled, along with those KASs that were selected for implementation (denoted by check marks). If there is no particular reason/logic that compels segmentation of improvements into loops, it's not necessary to include loops.

For ease of illustration and viewing in Figure 10.1, the communication graphing lines, data boxes, and push/pull arrows, as well as activity titles and detailed information in activity boxes on the CS-VSM, have been omitted. Keep in mind that many KASs may relate to communication improvements. Their numbers would be attached to the appropriate line and/or starting or ending point of the communication, depending on what the improvement targets. There may be one or two improvement loops dedicated to communication issues, and communication improvements may be included in other loops. If it is difficult to draw a loop because its elements are spread out across the process, either omit the loop outline or label its constituent improvements

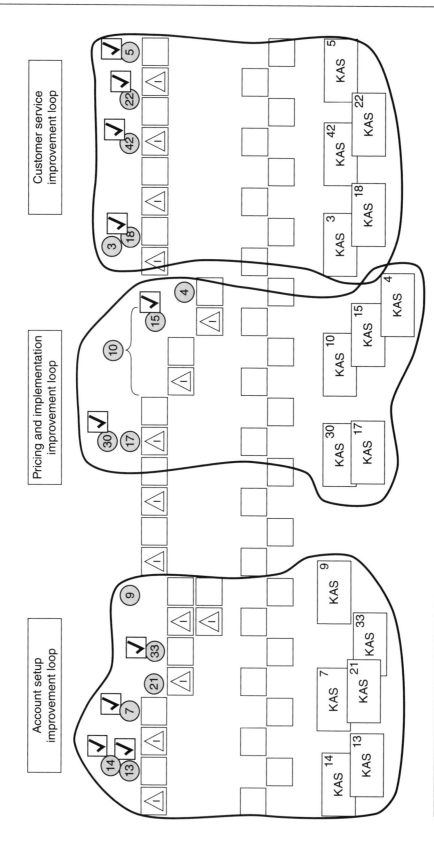

Figure 10.1   An example of a CS-VSM with improvement loops.

with a different color or shape so that viewers can easily see which KASs are included in that loop. The communication loops are simply a convenience for viewing and explanation. Details about planned improvements are included in the VSMapping action plan, which is described later in this chapter. It is important that items on the improvement plan be easily traceable to the appropriate KAS and areas of the FS-VSM.

4. ESTIMATE THE IMPACT OF IMPROVEMENTS

The next task for the team is to estimate the impact of each KAS that is to be included in the FS-VSM. It is best to be guided by the principle of conservative optimism in estimating benefits: Be enthusiastic but realistic. The team should not allow itself to get carried away by the excitement of the VSMapping event. It is better to undercommit to projections a bit and then be seen to overachieve with results, rather than commit to a lot and then do a great job but fall a little short of projections. Each KAS included in the FS-VSM can have one or more of the following impacts:

- Eliminate an activity and all of the cycle time and inventory associated with it.

- Eliminate an activity and transfer some or all of the cycle time and inventory associated with it to another activity.

- Improve an activity and reduce cycle time and/or inventory associated with the activity.

- Combine and/or add one or more activities that result in overall improved cycle time, inventory levels, and/or quality performance.

- Improve inventory methods (e.g., batch sizes, delivery frequency, and inventory staging and handling procedures such as supermarkets) to reduce lead time.

- Improve workplace organization methods (e.g., 5S methods—see Chapter 7) that improve performance across many activities. Be careful not to promise too much from 5S and/or visual systems. It isn't because there will not be improvement. The problem is that it may be difficult to specifically show where and when the visual system elements and/ or 5S impacts occur, especially if there are other improvement efforts under way that will impact the same area. It's best to simply state that the 5S/visual systems improvements will increase the benefits from other improvements and that they are necessary for that reason.

As the expected impact of each KAS is determined, make a note of the expected improvements on the KAS itself so that it will be easier to construct the FS-VSM. If there are more than 20 KASs, it will be helpful to make a separate listing of the included KAS by number and the expected improvements in cycle time, inventory, lead time, and quality levels (and any associated reductions in rework or repair). Place each benefit in a separate column. When each column is summed, it will be easy to compare and verify that all the expected improvements have been correctly included in the finished FS-VSM. Figure 10.2 presents a version of this summary sheet.

For ease of explanation and presentation, a number of ridiculously oversimplified assumptions have been made concerning the VSM upon which Figure 10.2 is hypothetically based:

- Every activity in the VSM has a cycle time of two minutes

- The process runs 450 minutes per day, meaning that every activity processes 225 units of work per day

- Every defect must be rerun, and it takes the full two minutes of cycle time to rerun or repair the defect at the activity where it occurred

Figure 10.2 shows reductions in time and pieces as positive numbers. If a KAS should actually add time, as it might do as one part of reorganizing a number of activities, the addition of time would be shown as a negative. If it helps you to reverse the signs, it's your VSM and your analysis. Keep in mind that every improvement must be converted to either cycle time or lead time for the purposes of the VSM. Also remember that the VSM shows the impact of every activity on the cycle and lead times of a representative single piece/unit of work/product/service going through the process from beginning to end.

The left two columns of the top table present the KAS reference number and a short description of the improvement, respectively. The third column presents the time horizon in which the improvement is planned. These data are used in the bottom table of the figure (which might always be required). The next two columns present the impacts of quality improvements. The "Quality pieces" column presents the number of pieces of defective output that a KAS eliminates. Each piece that does not have to be reworked or redone contributes to a cycle time savings of 2 divided by 225 pieces per day = 0.0089 minutes. Thus, KAS 2 is estimated to be able to eliminate 120 defects, which results in a total cycle time improvement of 0.0089 minutes × 120 = 1.07 minutes for the process represented by the FS-VSM. This cycle time is shown under the

KAS #	Shorthand KAS description	Time horizon (d)	Quality		"Pure" cycle time improvement (m)	Total cycle time (m)	Inventory pieces	Lead time (m)
			Quality pieces	Cycle time (m)				
1	Check set	5	60	0.53	0.13			
2	Standard work	50	120	1.07		1.07		
3	Supermarket	14		0.18		0.18	124	248
4	Layout change	21			0.50	0.50		
5	Lot size (no. of files)	5					24	48
..	..	..	..	..	..	..	..	..
38	Create pricing cell	90	90	0.80	0.33	1.13	175	350
39	Install pull in records	14					100	200
40	Error proofing	18	75	0.67		0.67		
	Totals		2433	21.627	5.01	26.64	1887	3774

Savings by time horizon	Type of improvement	Improvement horizon (d)				
		1–6	7–30	31–60	61–91	Totals
	Cycle time	3.24	1.21	2.50	19.69	26.64
	Lead time	53	1231	1714	776	3774
	Totals	56.24	1232.21	1716.50	795.69	3800.64

Figure 10.2 An example of summary tables showing KAS contributions to improvements.

"Quality" column because the improvement derives from not having to process the 120 pieces. The next column is "'Pure' cycle time improvement"—that is, the estimated savings that result not from eliminating a defect but from eliminating waste from the hands-on work that goes into each piece. As the figure shows, KAS 4 is estimated to be able to reduce hands-on cycle time by half a minute per piece (presumably through reducing the walking, reaching, searching for things, and so on, as a result of layout improvements).

The table at the bottom separates the projected improvements from the 40 KASs into columns based on four future horizons. The breakout of short-term versus longer-term improvements is very helpful if there is pressure to show some quick improvements (and if there are short-term improvements to show—which is almost always the case). If the KASs are put into a simple spreadsheet, they can be easily sorted and summed into whatever future buckets are necessary. However, it's always better to avoid spreadsheets and computers if you can and construct a representation of the figure with sticky notes on brown paper. If there are a great many KASs, have the categories of savings run down the left side of the brown paper and put the KASs along the top, one to each column. If you are creating different savings futures, use different-colored sticky notes for each future so it will be easy to pull out the numbers you need. Never underestimate the impact that a brown paper presentation can have on reviewers.

5. LAY OUT THE ACTIVITY AND INVENTORY BOXES OF THE FS-VSM

The impact of improvements is easiest to see and provides the most dramatic visual impact when the FS-VSM is presented directly below (or above) the CS-VSM (assuming that both are presented in the same briefing). It is good practice to not have them both on one doubled- or tripled-width brown paper taped together into a single piece. It is best to have them on separate brown papers so that they can be presented one at a time during a briefing and can be used individually later on.

There are two basic approaches for the general construction of the FS-VSM, as shown in Figure 10.3. The most common approach is to simply construct the FS-VSM with each activity placed right next to the inventory boxes before and after it. Typically, this results in an FS-VSM that is much shorter than the CS-VSM. This can be very impressive to some reviewers, but it is often difficult for reviewers who are not expert in the process to determine exactly where and how the improvements shown on the FS-VSM impacted the CS-VSM activities.

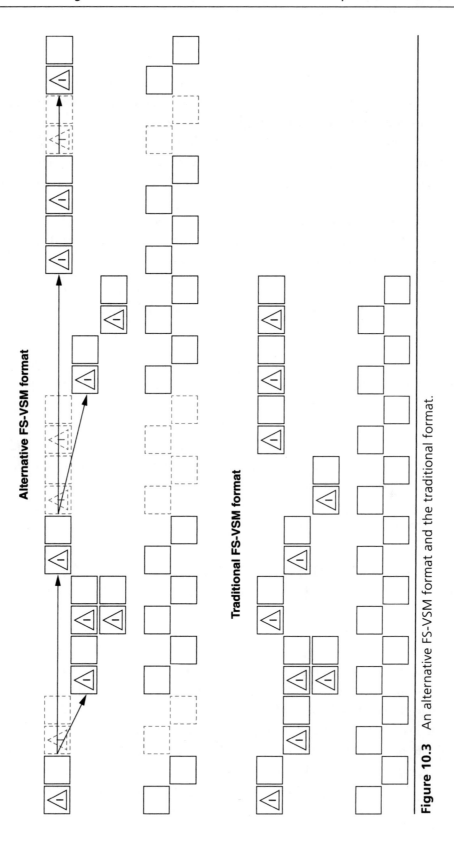

Figure 10.3 An alternative FS-VSM format and the traditional format.

An alternative approach can be very effective, although it violates "pure" VSM presentation traditions. Then again, if you can't violate some traditions in a continuous improvement event, when can you? The alternative approach is that the FS-VSM is constructed so that activities included on both maps are shown directly above (or below) each other.

This means that if activity boxes from the CS-VSM are eliminated due to improvements, the FS-VSM should show the "holes" where activities have been eliminated. Figure 10.3 shows both the traditional "compressed" format and the alternative "missing tooth" format, with the missing boxes represented by dashed lines. Both are based on the CS-VSM in Figure 10.1 that was improved by removing a number of activity boxes. Keep in mind that both of these illustrations are "stripped down" examples.

6. CONSTRUCT THE TIME LADDER

The cycle times selected for the future state activities should be written in each activity's data box. If an activity is performed by more than one person at a time, also enter the drop off interval (DOI) in the data box. Don't forget that all activities in a VSM use the cycle time and not the DOI. The inventory amounts selected for each inventory box should be placed in the activity's data box (the data box beneath the activity box to the right of the inventory box), and the number of pieces of inventory should be written beneath the inventory symbol on the inventory sticky note. The lead time for the time ladder should then be generated by multiplying the pieces of inventory prior to each activity by the cycle time of the activity box.

7. PREPARE A SUMMARY BENEFITS TABLE FOR THE END OF THE FS-VSM

It is important, especially if there are large estimated savings to be displayed, to dramatically showcase these estimates at the end of the FS-VSM. The summary benefits table should go right after the last activity box of the VSM. Figure 10.4 presents one suggested style with sticky notes. The "purest" form of this sort of summary presents only the cycle and lead time data. While you don't want to load the summary table with so much data that it's overwhelming, employ it to send the message that will best sell the action plan the team will be presenting. The example shows metrics such as numbers of handoffs and reworked files because these were some of the concerns, other than time and quality, that were on the management team's mind when the VSMapping exercise was launched.

	CS-VSM	FS-VSM	Improv. (units)	Improv. (%)
Lead time	7,495m	3,721m	–3,774m	–50.4
Cycle time	102.5m	76m	–26.5m	–34.9
Inventory pieces	4,323 pcs.	2,436 pcs.	–1,887 pcs.	–43.6
Rework (defects)	5,449	3,016	–2,433	–44.7
⋮	⋮	⋮	⋮	⋮
Handoffs	432	265	–167	–39

Figure 10.4   An example of a summary benefits table for the end of the FS-VSM.

Comparisons of data could just as well have involved numbers of activities with defined standard work, data files required/touched, feet of walking required, cross-trained employees, total paper pages/screens required, and so on.

8. DEVELOP THE ACTION PLAN (AP)

The AP for the FS-VSM is the general road map for how the various improvements will be implemented. Figure 10.5 displays a typical AP. At the most fundamental level, the AP assigns each selected KAS to a team and presents the status of its implementation vis-à-vis the established schedule. Some teams may handle many KASs, while some may handle only one, such as in instances when the implementation concerns a large effort over many months. As you

Improvement loop	KAS #	Objective	Overall goal*	Week 1 Beginning date: May 4, 2008 Schedule**										Champion/ team leader	Status code***
				1	2	3	4	5	6	7	8	9	10		
IT	5	Screen change	It works											Keiger/Bronsky	C
IT	2	New calculation	No errors											Keiger/Bronsky	C
IT	19	2 new input stations	Installed											Skinner/Rogers	P
IT	15	Upgrade SW	Installed											Keiger/Bronsky	C
IT	7	Summary report chg.	Installed											Fleugel/Horn	PL
Laboratory	11	Supermarket	Zero late											Piper/Taylor	C
Laboratory	3	Standard work	No errors											Piper/Bea	C
Laboratory	16	Kanbans to analysis	<4h process											Piper/Taylor	C
Laboratory	12	Cross-training	Zero unstaffed											Piper/Fife	P
Billing	10	5S office	Zero lost											Hope/Gary	C
Billing	14	Daily start-up mtg.	Established											Calwell/Nino	C
Billing	8	Status board process	Zero late											Calwell/Nino	C
Billing	4	Cross-training	Zero unstaffed											Hope/Gary	P
Billing	20	FIFO lane for posting	Zero late											Parry/Kate	C
Billing	18	Standard work	No errors											Freud/Jung	PL

Figure 10.5 An example of an AP for an FS-VSM.

Improvement loop	KAS #	Objective	Overall goal*	Schedule** Week 1 Beginning date: May 4, 2008											Champion/ team leader	Status code***
				1	2	3	4	5	6	7	8	9	10			
Order proc.	13	5S office	Zero lost												Swihart/Gear	C
Order proc.	1	Supermarket	Zero late												Swihart/Lander	C
Order proc.	9	Standard work	No errors												Swihart/Goodrich	C
Order proc.	17	Create 3 input types	No errors												Swihart/Smith	C
Order proc.	6	Cross-training	Zero unstaffed												Freulich/Smythe	P

Now

*See team charters for detailed/other metrics.

**Schedule symbols

Plan △ Actual ◣

Start

Progress ↑ ------ (if off schedule)

Completion

***Status codes

C = complete   P = in progress   PL = in progress late

NYS = not yet started   OH = on hold   X = cancelled

Figure 10.5 An example of an AP for an FS-VSM. (Continued)

can see from the figure, the AP has been put into a spreadsheet format (for the purposes of presenting this example). However, it is better to create a brown paper version of the AP and display it prominently, where it can be seen by many employees. Of course, each team is responsible for updating its portion of the display. It is even better if the FS-VSM is also displayed in the same area.

At the left of Figure 10.5 is a column for identifying improvement loops, if any are specified (often they are not). This helps observers make the connection between the loops on the FS-VSM and the KASs on the AP. The next two columns identify the KAS number and provide a short description of its focus, respectively. The next column, "Overall goal," describes the condition that must be attained in order for the KAS to be completely implemented. For example, KAS 12 in the laboratory loop is concerned with cross-training. As the "goal" column shows, the end result of KAS 12 being successfully implemented will be zero unstaffed tasks at any time in the laboratory due to lack of trained personnel. The details of what goes into the effort to arrive at this goal, including metrics and more detailed schedules, are found in the team charter that supports the implementation of the KAS. Work stream teams (WSTs) and team charters were discussed in Chapter 6.

The center of Figure 10.5 provides a simple general schedule for the implementation of each KAS. All that is shown are planned and actual start and completion times with a progress arrow showing where things stand at the time (note the "now" arrow between weeks four and five). More-detailed task schedules would be found on the Gemba Wall (discussed in Chapter 6), which displays all of the detailed information for each WST. While most of the KAS efforts in the figure have been completed or are on schedule, three of them (number 19, number 7, and number 18) are having issues. This means that they are behind schedule, which can be seen because their planned completion triangles are not filled in and an "overrun" dashed line runs past the missed completion date triangle. This sort of public display provides a little extra motivation for the champion and the team to get back on schedule and also demonstrates to the employees that the organization is candid about problems.

Finally, the last two columns display the names of the team champion and the team leader and the current status of the KAS implementation effort, respectively.

9. DEVELOP THE IMPLEMENTATION PLAN

The AP is not an implementation plan. The AP summarizes assignments and shows progress. The implementation plan is much, much more: It is the combined team charters of the WSTs (Chapter 6 again) that are tasked to complete all of the selected KASs. A *major* failing of many kaizen events, FS-VSM implementations, and Six Sigma efforts is that management assumes that assigning a champion and a team leader and setting a few schedule dates are adequate to focus resources and get results. For anything but the smallest tasks, this is not the case. The structures described in Chapter 6 are critical to making sure the FS-VSM is maximally realized. After the Executive Steering Committee (ESC) is formed, it must assign champions, review and approve charters and team members, review each team's status each week, compel champions to do their coaching duties with the team, compel the team to maintain its Gemba Wall and AP boards, and so on. Without such efforts, the FS-VSM and the AP will create only a tiny part of what could have been realized.

10. PRESENT THE FINDINGS OF THE CS-VSM, FS-VSM, AND AP

The specifics of each presentation will vary, sometimes quite a lot, depending on the nature of the audience, the urgency of the issues to be addressed by the proposed FS-VSM, the customs of the organization, the politics, and so on. However, a good general format/agenda is as follows:

a. *Introductory comments:* These are the "why are we here," "what got us to this point" observations, along with whatever support the speakers may wish to convey, given by the champion and other executives.

b. *Introduction of the team:* The team stands in front of the room and each member is introduced by the champion.

c. *Presentation of the agenda:* The team leader goes over the agenda (displayed on a brown paper or a flip chart), naming each element of the agenda, who will present it, and the allotted time. It is essential that team members present all the elements of the work. The items on the agenda are this list.

d. *Charter review:* Explain the motivation for the event, the problem statement, the objective, and the schedule, from the event charter.

e. *Description of data collection:* Describe what the team did to collect data, such as visiting the work areas, timing the processes, having employees from the areas review the VSM, interviewing various workers, and so on.

f. *Construction of the CS-VSM:* Two to four (depending on the length of the VSM) team members describe portions of the map. This should not be a detailed, every-activity-included description but rather a discussion of various important and relevant issues and activities. The intent is to give the audience a sample of the current state of the process and how the map describes it. Do not describe any of the KASs at this point—they are covered in step p. Be sure to mention the reviews of the map with process workers—how many times reviews were done and who did them (put their names on the VSM under the title "reviewers" at the start of the VSM).

g. *Handoff diagram:* If a handoff diagram was constructed, explain what it shows and what it means.

h. *Spaghetti diagram:* If a spaghetti diagram was constructed, explain what it shows and what it means.

i. *Standard work study:* If a standard work study was done, explain what it shows and what it means.

j. *Cross-training/skill versatility matrix:* If a cross-training matrix was constructed, explain what it shows and what it means.

k. *RACI chart:* If a RACI chart was constructed, explain what it shows and what it means.

l. *5S survey:* If a 5S survey was performed, explain what it shows and what it means.

m. *DILO chart:* If a DILO chart was constructed, explain what it shows and what it means.

n. *Statistical and other data:* If any control charts, Pareto charts, C&E diagrams, or other tools were used, they are presented and their implications discussed.

o. *Main findings/summary of the CS-VSM and other analyses:* The summary should be four to seven bullet points on a brown paper or flip chart (one page) that sums up the general situation, since many people may get lost in the bushes if the process is complex and/or lengthy.

p. *KAS and the KAS selection process:* This starts with a description of what a KAS is (if KASs are not already used in the organization), how they are denoted on the CS-VSM (see Figure 9.1), and the technique that was used (if any) to choose which ones would be incorporated into the FS-VSM (see Figure 9.2).

q. *Construction of the FS-VSM:* This description, like the discussion of the CS-VSM (step f), should not drag the audience face down through every activity. It should highlight where major changes are predicted to dramatically change the process seen in the CS-VSM. Do not present the summary benefits table (the comparison of the CS-VSM and FS-VSM that is shown at the end of the FS-VSM; see Figure 10.4) until all of the other analyses, if any, are presented. If the summary benefits table is attached to the end of the FS-VSM, place a cover sheet of brown paper over it, attached with small pieces of masking tape, so that you can keep it under wraps until the appropriate part of the presentation.

Steps r–z are estimations of what the g–o CS-VSM analyses would be if the improvements selected for the FS-VSM were implemented. Remember the concept of conservative optimism: There is no upside to showing inflated hopes and dreams in detail if they might not be realized.

r. *Handoff diagram*

s. *Spaghetti diagram*

t. *Standard work study*

u. *Cross-training/skill versatility matrix*

v. *RACI chart*

w. *5S survey*

x. *DILO chart*

y. *Statistical and other data*

z. *One-point lessons*

aa. *Summary benefits table:* As shown in Figure 10.4, this is where the overall summary estimates are described.

bb. *AP:* Take the audience through the most salient points of the proposed AP.

cc. *Next steps:* This is best done by the team leader and the champion. They should describe what needs to be done, including assigning champions, developing charters, setting up weekly status checks, establishing the Gemba Wall, and so on. If the organization is already doing these things, it is a good idea to just mention them so that everyone realizes the work is not over yet.

dd. *Questions:* This is the usual question-and-answer session with all of the team members in the front of the room, each answering a question or two.

Do not be intimidated by the vast number of possible agenda items. A team of four or five can easily get them done. My advice is to do as many ancillary analyses as you can that directly address critical concerns listed in the charter. When I am faced with a choice between (a) allowing teams to take a lot of breaks and spend time loafing and socializing and (b) giving teams a really tough workload that stretches them to the limit, I go for "b" every time. They'll feel prouder of their final product, they'll learn more, the process and workers will benefit more, and the team will look like heroes (you included!).

It is essential to have the team rehearse the presentation several times. The entire team doesn't have to do the whole presentation in sequence from item "a" to "dd" every time; that would take too long. Have each person do his or her assigned portion in front of a couple of other team members at least a few times. The first time, the listeners should jump right in with comments and corrections or advice in real time, and the second time they should wait until the end. The team leader and the champion should move about the room and sit in on as many of these as they can. It is important that each person not ramble on and use up more than the exact time allocated to his or her portion. After the team members have rehearsed their portions individually, the entire team should do the presentation from beginning to end.

Be sure to have people stand in front of what they are talking about and point out where the issues they are presenting are represented on the maps or other analyses. If someone is having a tough time during the final presentation, the team leader and/or champion should jump in and help.

11. NEXT STEPS

Once the AP has been completed, it is important to do a follow-up CS-VSM of the now-proved process to determine the actual results. The entire team does not have to be assigned to the task since only the CS-VSM is going to be constructed. Two or three people should be able to do it in a day or so. This is a good time to have a team member or a continuous improvement facilitator (CIF) work with a couple of the workers from the process to do the new map. If the results are good enough and there are other, more critical issues to address, nothing else needs to be done. If the process is still not good enough, it is time to start over and go through all the steps required to construct a new FS-VSM and AP.

PART III

The Mechanics of Successful Office Kaizen Improvement Events

The most visible, well known, and popular element of Office Kaizen initiatives is the continuous improvement event (CIE), also known as a kaizen blitz or a rapid improvement event (RIE). While they can't sustain a transformation effort by themselves, CIEs are extremely powerful if they are applied with focus and energy. All too often, however, the results of CIEs are only pale shadows of what they could be. This section shows a leader how to use the tools and many of the structural configurations described in Part II to plan, conduct, and follow up on (sustain the results) outstanding CIEs that not only create tremendous value but also serve as valuable teaching and cultural change mechanisms.

11

The Landscape of Improvement Actions

Improvement actions are defined in this chapter as any structured efforts to make changes that occur outside the normal day-to-day, "do the work" activities and processes of an organization. Improvement actions run the gamut from 5S activities that might last only four hours, to kaizen blitzes (continuous improvement events [CIEs] that start on Sunday evening and run through Friday afternoon [although I don't recommend that schedule]), to work stream team (WST) efforts that can last a year or more in extreme cases. While there is a great deal of latitude in how an improvement action can be structured, a number of best practices have proved themselves over time. This chapter briefly discusses the landscape of improvement actions so that the following chapters are clear to readers unfamiliar with the terminology. Chapter 12 discusses the event preparation process, and Chapter 13 describes the details of conducting events. Finally, Chapter 14 describes what must be done after an event is concluded in order to ensure that the benefits of the event are sustained.

Improvement actions can have many foci, from waste reduction to technology implementation to 5S to Six Sigma methods. Improvement actions have an even larger variety of names: CIEs, RIEs, kaizen blitzes, kaizen events, value stream mapping (VSMapping) events, Six Sigma events, workplace organization events, and so on. My perspective on the general categories of events and their characteristics is shown in Figure 11.1. Because of the constantly changing nature of improvement practices and the continually melding and interbreeding of methods, it is often difficult to tell exactly what an improvement action is about, solely on the basis of how it is labeled. Therefore, Figure 11.1 categorizes the improvement actions as if they are somewhat "pure"; for example, a Six Sigma event primarily applies Six Sigma methods, while an RIE focuses mostly on lean tools. The assumption of a defined focus makes it easier to discuss the specifics of planning and executing the various

Event/ improvement action type	Purpose	Principal mechanisms	Length of event	Size of each team
Kaizen blitz, rapid improvement, continuous improvement	Find and eliminate causes of waste	Lean tools and systems, TPS work sheets, general data collection tools, and ancillary mechanisms such as spaghetti diagrams and flowcharts	4 to 5 days	4–6
Six Sigma	Find and eliminate sources of uncommon process variability	Tools for data collection, root cause analysis, and statistical analyses	4 to 5 days	3–6
Scramble	Quickly investigate and remedy a specific issue and/or implement a narrowly focused change	5S, workplace organization, kanban, layout changes, and preventive maintenance actions	4 hours to 2 days	4–6
CS-VSM	Construct a CS-VSM to identify opportunities to reduce process throughput time	VSM and ancillary methods such as spaghetti diagrams, handoff diagrams, and cross-training matrices	1 to 3 days	4–6
FS-VSM and AP	Construct an FS-VSM and develop an AP to eliminate process throughput delays	VSM methods and improvement team organization and assignment	1 to 2 days	4–6
Work stream team	Perform any type of improvement and/or change required and approved by the Executive Steering Committee	Any of the methods included in this table	2 weeks to 1 year	4–6
Kaikaku	Implement a stepwise and/or significant change in work methods and/or technology, often involving new software and/or new equipment	All of the above plus IT, engineering, and/or plant maintenance methods	1 to 9 months	6–25
Six Sigma project	Eliminate process variability	Many of the other tools in this figure, plus tools for data collection, root cause analysis, and statistical analyses	1 to 6 months	3–10

Figure 11.1 General categories of events with some of their characteristics.

events when there are differences in what they require for optimal implementation results.

Common event types are shown in the left-hand column. The next four columns list the purpose, principal mechanisms, ranges of lengths, and typical number of team members involved, respectively. The figure is divided into three areas. The first area, consisting of rows one through three, presents actions that are conducted in a week or less. It is segmented and bordered by thin, solid lines. The second area, rows four and five, is segmented by thicker solid lines. It contains VSMapping events. The third area, rows six through eight, displays improvement actions that take more than a week and can run to a year or more for very complex tasks (such as implementing skill versatility tracking at a site). This area is bordered by thick, dashed lines.

Row 1 is the ubiquitous kaizen blitz/RIE/CIE. Chapter 6 gave a little background on kaizen events. It is the most common improvement action conducted, so much so that some organizations label almost any improvement action as a kaizen. Kaizen events are usually four to five days in length with a team of four to six people. These events focus on finding and eliminating waste in a week or less. That is, the problems are located and analyzed, and improvements are installed in the same week. This fast pace necessitates the focus on waste elimination using low-technology methods since it is almost impossible to make product, equipment, and/or software changes in a few days. Conversely, it is usually easy to manipulate visual signals, workplace arrangements, work instructions, job aids, task orders, standard work, specific worker actions, the locations and amount of inventory/information, and other factors that do not impact the form or function of the product or service.

Kaizen events are often conducted as stand-alone affairs to address a particular problem (such as portions of an improvement loop or a complex KAS [kaizen action sheet] issue). Ideally, there is an overall plan and strategy (such as working to implement a future state VSM [FS-VSM] or a corporate strategy) in place that guides the selection of issues and the design and prioritization of events. Kaizen events are often used to supplement WST efforts (displayed in row six). For example, a WST may be implementing work group start-up meetings throughout a facility over a six-month period. A CIE could be employed to speed up the installation of visual metrics displays (VMDs) or the daily work group meetings (WGMs) every now and then to provide a little excitement or get an area started quickly. It might help to think of a WST effort as a large military action and the CIE/kaizen events as intense, short-duration artillery barrages or air strikes used to overcome difficult challenges and/or speed up the overall advance at critical times.

The second improvement action shown in the figure is a Six Sigma event. While Six Sigma work is most often conducted under the rubric of a Six Sigma project (the bottom row), Six Sigma events of a few days to a week are often conducted to set up and run experiments and/or conduct focused data collection as part of a Six Sigma project, with the project time in between the Six Sigma events being used to collect more data, analyze findings, set up further data collection, confer with engineers and process staff, and so on.

The third row presents scrambles. A *scramble*, as the name implies, is a very short event of a few hours to perhaps two days that is typically used to get something done, such as organize a filing system, employ 5S to overhaul an invoice-processing area, install a previously designed supermarket, make layout changes, or introduce a new procedure to an office group and train them. Often, the personnel in a scramble are the workers in an area who have some scheduled downtime and are using the opportunity to implement things that cannot be done while work processes are under way.

One danger of scrambles is that management can begin to see them as inexpensive ways to get things done compared with a weeklong kaizen event. Scrambles are great for quick, planned, already-agreed-upon implementations where the task is straightforward once the trigger has been pulled. However, they cannot substitute for the observation and analysis of a longer kaizen event. Four to five days are required for a team to study a problem, explore options, collect data, soak up the possibilities, try out a few things, and then implement the selected improvements. A scramble does a very poor job in that role.

The fourth and fifth rows deal with VSMapping events. Row four shows that it typically takes one to three days to do a current state VSM (CS-VSM). The length of time is dependent on the size and complexity of the process. Row five shows that it typically takes one to two days to develop an FS-VSM and an action plan (AP). Most of the time, the CS-VSM, FS-VSM, and AP are done in one week as a single seamless event.

Rows six through eight describe the three improvement actions that take longer than one week. While they have different names, traditions, and foci, each of these three improvement actions is a variation of a WST event, the mechanics of which were described in Chapter 6. A WST is a cross-functional (to some degree) group chartered by the Executive Steering Committee (ESC) to achieve specific goals with defined and approved personnel, resources, schedules, and deliverables. The WST is coached by a champion from the ESC, and the ESC reviews the team's status weekly. This is exactly how a kaikaku and a Six Sigma project should be organized.

A kaikaku is an effort to achieve a stepwise, dramatic improvement much more rapidly than normal processes usually allow. It is used when time and results are critically important. Chapter 6 described how and when to use a kaikaku event.

A Six Sigma project should simply be a WST with a Six Sigma focus. This is often not the case. In the first 10–15 years of Six Sigma operations, Six Sigma was allowed, in many organizations, to operate as a separate entity that mysteriously went about doing "Six Sigma things." The aura of Black Belts (BBs) and Master Black Belts (MBBs) and "statistical methods" often led many to view the method as something akin to medieval alchemy, as in, "It's complicated, so let's leave them alone and hope they make us world class." The problem was that many of the projects were not focused on priorities that management would have selected, and many projects did not include sufficient input from the process workers involved. The inherently cross-functional nature of a WST and ESC involvement in charter approval would have eliminated most of these issues. The bottom line is that Six Sigma projects, just like all others, benefit from more input and participation if they are done in a structured manner.

12

Preparing for Kaizen, Six Sigma, and Scramble Events

This chapter deals with pre-event preparation procedures for improvement actions that last one week or less. This time period is the most well known and popular improvement action time span. The first five improvement actions described in Figure 11.1 in the last chapter typically take one week or less. The short time period of a weeklong (or less) event makes it critically important to carefully plan and prepare. Since there is so little time to recover from miscues or make dramatic adjustments in resources, personnel, access to work areas, information needs, political considerations, and the like, it is vital to make sure there are no surprises other than the usual process analysis and problem-solving issues.

The procedures for preparing for events lasting one week or less are shown in the following list. While the procedures refer to one event (i.e., one team of four to six with a team leader), it is possible to simultaneously run a number of events (i.e., several teams, each with a leader, and each working on a different problem, process, part, or issue) simultaneously. Simultaneous teams shouldn't be conducted the first time an organization runs an event. After a few people have been trained and can act as co-coaches, running a few events/ teams at once should not be an issue. Scrambles, being short, intense events that are often conducted by a work area and led by its own supervision, do not typically require as much extensive preparation over an extended period. Scrambles are discussed at the end of this chapter.

Five Weeks in Advance

1. *Select a management sponsor:* It would be ideal if there were already an Executive Steering Committee (ESC) formed, in which case it could simply assign a champion. The champion would then select a team leader, and the two of them would get things moving. Most organizations are not in that position yet. So if a possible sponsor or

informal champion can be found and recruited, do it as soon as possible. Otherwise, get two or three enthusiastic people to work with you to get the event-planning process started. They don't necessarily have to be the same people who will make up the event team.

2. *Determine the event focus:* It's best if every event is focused on a critical issue so that results will contribute significantly to the organization and reinforce the effectiveness of continuous improvement efforts. Thus, you must find a problem whose solution will make a difference to the organization's leaders. The difference could be in cycle time, inventory reduction, waste reduction, or quality. Generally, several of these areas will be positively affected by anything you do. If your organization has already conducted improvement events and is doing them the right way (i.e., using the structural configurations discussed in Chapter 6), there will be an existing list of management-prioritized issues for future events. If so, use that list. Unfortunately, the majority of organizations don't have such a list. Often, events are generated almost randomly. In other cases, each department selects and operates events on its own, and there is no central list that the site management team has agreed upon. If this is the case, try to assemble as many of the department lists as you can.

3. *Prioritize the lists of issues:* Regardless of where you get the candidate issues, use the techniques described at the end of Chapter 9 (see Figure 9.2) and the accompanying explanations to prioritize the issues. In most cases, the raw issues lists will not be as discrete and specific in identifying problems as those generated by the kaizen action sheet (KAS) approach. Before attempting to prioritize the issues, make sure they are defined and specific enough so that it's clear what is being ranked. For instance, "problems with customer order processing" may be a serious issue for the customer service department but may be too broad for a weeklong event. You could improve all sorts of things and still fail to address what was "meant" by the stated issue. Talk to people about what the "problems" really are if they are not sufficiently specific. When developing the ranking criteria (e.g., cost, risk, short-term impact, customer retention), be sure to examine the organization's stated objectives for the current planning year.

4. *Review the selected issue(s) and draft the charter with the process owner:* Meet with the owner of the area in which the event will be conducted. If there is more than one person and/or area involved, meet

with each of them individually and describe your issue selection process. Have them suggest a couple of people from their area who would be great to have on the event team. If they have serious objections, find out why. If you can't get them on board without destroying the purpose and intent of the event (unless they come up with something better), pick another topic and work with its process owner(s).

5. *Determine the executive approval process:* If the event is going to be successful, you will need resources and support. It's always best if these two vital elements come from the on-site person with the most authority. Find out who has to say yes and what person or group must approve an event.

6. *Present your case to the approval executive or the ESC:* Take your prioritized list of issues to the ESC, management team, or ranking executive. If you don't get the approval you need, find out why. If it's political and another person or department has to buy in first, go see that person. If it's the first event in the organization, it's often necessary to do a lot of legwork to get started. Thankfully, almost everyone in management has heard of continuous improvement events (CIEs) and wants to be seen as progressive, so the odds of being shut out are much smaller than they used to be.

Four Weeks in Advance

7. *Reserve space for the work room(s) and the final presentation room:* This is often the most difficult task. When you try to reserve space all day long for a week or so, you come in close contact with what people really care about at work: weight-loss meetings, book clubs, exercise classes, the bowling league, meditation classes, and so on. Do not underestimate the disruption that is caused by having to clear out the room at lunch, even for one day. You must have the room full time, 24 hours a day until the event is over (at least one hour past the formal end time). The best option is a single large room in which the team (or teams) can do its work and hang it on the walls and also make its presentations. If there is only one team working, it is not too much trouble to use a small conference room for the workdays and a different, large room for the final presentation. It is essential that there be enough wall space in the room or in the nearby hallways to hang many, many brown papers.

8. *Develop a draft charter:* Once you have approval to run an event, develop a draft charter. The draft charter requires a problem statement, a quantifiable objective or several of them, a start date and a general schedule for the week (see Chapter 13 for a sample schedule), a recommended champion, and a team leader. The charter should also state the scope of the event, that is, what areas, processes, and functions are thought to be involved. If some of the recommended team members can be named at this point, add them. Be sure to leave a spot or two on each team for personnel from the impacted areas. Work on the draft charter with the sponsor and any others you've been working with. If you are relatively certain that you will get approval, this step can sometimes be combined with the prior step.

9. *Review the draft charter with the process owners:* Take the draft charter to the owners of the process and get their reactions. Also, have them provide the names of employees in their area(s) who would fit well with the objectives of the team. At the end of this meeting, all of the recommended team members should be identified.

10. *Get draft charter approval:* Take the charter back to the approving person or group for sign-off. Make sure this individual or group reviews the prospective team members who have been recommended.

11. *At the same time, get approval for lunches, snacks, and so on:* It is very important to have lunches brought in during the event. Otherwise, team members will tend to wander off, "get some work done," "take a few calls," and so on. Over the course of a few days, many hours of productive work can be lost because team members have to forage for meals and refreshments. Also, team members break their focus on the work if they leave for lunch or disappear for an hour. It then takes extra time to get refocused on what they were doing. The best approach is to tell everyone in the event that lunches will be "working lunches" during the event, with a 15-minute break to check e-mail messages, take care of personal issues, and so on. It's also a good idea to have coffee, soft drinks, water, and the like, available all day long during the event. This cuts down on the extended social breaks that naturally occur when people leave to get refreshments. It's better if they get social reinforcement from one another in the team room. Further, having goodies helps the team members view their participation as a special activity, thus increasing their involvement and commitment.

12. *At the same time, confirm executive availability for daily briefings, the final presentation, and the kickoff meeting on the first day:* Make sure that the approving executive or management team knows when they will have to be available for the event kickoff, daily briefings, final presentations, and so on. They don't all have to attend every time (which would be great, but don't expect it), but a consistent and ample executive and management presence is essential. It rewards the team, keeps the members enthusiastic, and teaches management about how events and improvement tools operate.

13. *Finalize the working charter:* The working charter is the version of the charter that will be presented to the team on the first day of the event. It is a 95%–100% final charter (on the first morning of the event, the team may make some minor adjustments). In addition to having a completed list of team members, a team leader, and a champion, the charter should have a scope, a list of sequenced activities, a schedule for the week, a list of deliverables (as understood at the time), and metrics that will be measured to determine progress.

14. *Check that all necessary supplies are available or on order:* It's always best if the team leader buys the supplies and vouchers them to the organization so that the team gets exactly what it needs and enough of it. If that's not feasible, be as specific as possible with the order. It might not seem like a big deal before the event, but having to use a roll of thin brown paper instead of thick brown paper can cause a lot of aggravation since the thin paper rips more easily. The same consideration applies to cheap plastic tape that shreds when you try to unroll it. The basic supply list for most events is given at the beginning of Chapter 9.

    If a future state VSM (FS-VSM) has been constructed, arrange to have it hung in the room for the start of the event. If only a current state VSM (CS-VSM) has been constructed, it should be hung if it is reasonably current.

    For a kaizen event, the nature of the process may dictate some additional supplies and equipment. Kaizen event teams may need Toyota Production System (TPS) forms, 5S rating sheets, and so on. The coach/facilitator/lean leader will know which additional forms are most likely to be needed and where to get them if the organization is not already using them. Because kaizen events involve detailed study of work activities, it is often a big help to film activities while collecting data. This makes review easier than having to observe processes over and over (although repeated observation is required for timings, it is easy to verify timings from a video). If this is the case, the following additional items will be needed:

a. Digital video camera and spare media

b. Laptop with media input device from digital camera

c. TV for showing any videos or DVDs that may be appropriate for training or during final presentations

d. Materials and handouts for overviews of lean tools and/or methods

e. VCR if any VCR tapes are being used

f. Sufficient extension cords and outlet boxes to accommodate these additional electronic devices

While the office supplies are generally purchased, make sure that the videos, camera, TV, and the like are properly reserved and/or volunteered by individuals or departments.

For a Six Sigma event, the team may need various control chart forms, linear array recipe books (for designed experiments), and so on. The Six Sigma Black Belt (SSBB) coaching the event is the best source for determining what is needed and where to get it.

Three Weeks in Advance

15. *Notify selected team members, their supervisors, and the supervisors of the areas in which the team will be working:* The team leader and the champion should visit with the managers of the involved people and processes and let them know that it is important to notify everyone of their involvement in advance of the event. Once events are a common occurrence in the organization, the team leader can do this without the champion. In the beginning, however, the champion's presence will help encourage participation. The manager of each area may want to be the one who notifies his or her people of their involvement. If the manager is going to inform them, the team leader and the champion should provide a short write-up or outline so that the manager or supervisor can explain what will happen during the event. It's even better if the champion and the team leader can be at the notification session(s) so that they can answer any questions about the event. It is just as critical

to notify employees' supervisors that their people and area have been selected for the event. They should be told to make plans to replace the team members during their participation in the event.

16. *Send a notice to the process workers in the areas affected:* This should come jointly from the management of the area(s), the champion, and the team leader. If the organization is doing daily work group meetings (WGMs), the announcement should be made in the meetings of the areas involved and in nearby areas (so that they will know what is going on when the event is under way). The explanation should have a short statement of what the event will be focusing on, the names of the team members, and a statement of support. A copy of the charter can be attached and referenced so that future team members will have seen one before they actually work on one. If the organization is internet savvy, the information can be posted online, but it should also be mentioned in meetings and posted on visual metrics displays (VMDs; discussed in Chapter 6) and bulletin boards throughout the work areas.

17. *Check the room reservations again:* Make sure you haven't been pre-empted by a lunchtime hobby club.

18. *Arrange for refreshments:* Place your order(s) now or work with the individual who usually does it to make sure he or she can get what you need (as when you have attendees pick a sandwich from a menu at the start of the day and then place the order as a group for delivery around noon). Don't forget the coffee, water, sodas, ice, cookies, and so on.

Two Weeks in Advance

19. *Arrange for message board input:* Since almost everyone has a cell phone these days, the message board isn't as critical as it used to be, but it doesn't hurt to have one. It also serves as an "in-out" board so that team members can leave notes to other team members as to what they are doing when they are away from the room. A flip chart sheet should be labeled "Messages" and posted in an area where all team members can easily encounter it. A good spot is near the refreshments. Notify all areas that have personnel in the event to post any messages for team members on the board.

20. *Check with the supervisors of the team members:* The team leader must visit with each supervisor of the selected team members and make sure it is okay to have the team member off the job and on the event. The

team leader should also talk with each team member to keep him or her updated and to ensure that there are no schedule conflicts. I've had team members not mention upcoming vacations, surgeries, and so on.

21. *Check on the supplies:* If they are being ordered, check the status. If the team leader is doing the ordering, make sure it is done this week.

The Week Before

22. *Stage all supplies near the room:* Assemble all the supplies in boxes and make sure that they are available and locked up near the work room.

23. *Send another notice to the process workers in the areas affected:* Same procedure as in step 16.

24. *Send an e-mail to the executive/managers:* Remind them of the kickoff times, daily briefing times, and final presentation times for the event.

25. *Check on the room reservations.*

The Day Before

26. *Confirm management attendance at the kickoff meeting.*

27. *Check the room:* It's best if the room (or rooms) can be set up the night before (or early that morning if the event is starting on a Monday) and then locked until the coach arrives to greet the teams and the kick-off guests. If the room is in use for a night shift or a weekend shift, arrange the room early in the morning or just prior to the event.

28. *Make a final check of the supplies:* Make sure they have not been moved or tampered with and are ready to go. Check on the presence or scheduled delivery of all electronic equipment.

29. *Make a final check on the refreshments order.*

30. *Get a good night's sleep.*

PREPARING FOR SCRAMBLES

Scrambles are very task oriented. That is, they focus on a narrow issue, objective, or set of actions. They're referred to as scrambles (by some people), as opposed to kaizen events, because they are quick and intense. They range from a few hours to two days, although 90% of scrambles are one day or less. I think it is a mistake to treat something longer than a day as simply a scramble. If the issue is important enough to consume a couple of days, it requires more attention to planning and preparation than what is typically allocated to a scramble. All or only a few of the workers in an area can be involved. Most of the participants in a scramble effort are drawn from the work area involved, although it is not uncommon for an engineer or maintenance technician to participate if the effort involves this person's skills.

Compared with a kaizen event, a scramble has very little problem solving and/or data collection. This is because most of the analysis and decision making have already been conducted, and all that's left to do is the work itself. Often a work group will use a scramble to get some things done when they know they will be off-line for a few hours or a day. Scrambles are often used to tie up loose ends from a kaizen event.

The following are examples of scramble objectives:

- Perform 5S in a work area, conference room, or office area

- Organize files, workstations, and equipment

- Label areas, machines, workstations, and parts/tooling locations

- Train process workers on one-point lessons in real time

- Install kanban, supermarkets, staging areas, or flow lanes that have already been designed and whose need has been determined

- Install one or several primary VMDs that have already been designed (content/format has been determined)

- Install a 5S audit in a work group

- Train a work group to hold a daily work group start-up meeting

- Train a team to conduct a 5S audit

- Install shadow boards and workplace organization fixtures in a work area

- Install an error-proofing (poka-yoke) device in a needed area

Some longer (one day or so) scrambles may focus on several of these objectives for a small work area, a small group of machines, or a large single machine.

Every scramble should have a charter that has a champion, a team leader, team members, an objective, a scope, and a list of planned activities. The charter doesn't have to be more than half a page long if the scramble is straightforward. If the scramble is organized and handled within a department, it should be approved by the department manager, discussed with the supervisor(s), and announced to the workers at least a couple of days in advance. If the scramble is part of the ESC improvement plan/priority list, the champion and the team leader of the scramble should notify area management (who should already have been involved in the development of the charter), who will then inform the area supervision and employees.

If the scramble will take place when an opportunity occurs at the spur of the moment, such as when the computers are down for an hour or two, the workers should be told that one or more scrambles are being held in reserve in the event that time becomes available. The charters for them should be posted on the work group's VMD or in the work area if the Team Metrics and Ownership System (TMOS; see Chapter 6) is not in place.

Scrambles don't require a multiweek preparation period unless special resources are required. For example, a popular objective for an office scramble is to have a few people take half a day and develop first-cut standard work for a specific procedure. If the procedure involves laws and regulations (as in some areas of banking, such as internal audit), it is important that content personnel be available during the scramble. Make these arrangements ahead of time.

While it may not take weeks, a scramble focusing on general 5S (cleaning, organizing, arranging, signing, and so on) will require cleaning supplies, rags, labeling supplies, painting materials and supplies, file drawer organizers, hanging folders, and so on. Operations that have not been doing 5S may not have a lot of these materials on hand, so they will have to be ordered. While a scramble is often over quickly, the planning still takes some time to do it right.

13

Conducting Improvement Actions That Last One Week or Less

This chapter provides detailed procedures for executing improvement events of one week or less that are more complex than scrambles. These actions are typically called kaizen blitzes, rapid improvement events (RIEs), or continuous improvement events (CIEs). Events longer than one week are, by definition, work stream team (WST) efforts (these are described in Chapter 6). While value stream mapping (VSMapping) activities often take a week or so, they are discussed in detail in Chapters 8, 9, and 10. Six Sigma events are somewhat different from waste removal events and are discussed in a separate section of this chapter.

A successful CIE requires a great deal of focus and structure—much more than that required for shorter or longer improvement actions. A scramble of four hours to a day or two is usually so narrow in scope that its objective more or less defines the work in detail (e.g., organize the files in the sales department). And because the time is so short, there is minimal probability that the team will wander too far off track. A longer action such as a WST implementing a skill versatility system in customer service over a period of six months will undergo many variations of intensity and focus over the life of the effort. The team has plenty of time to plan what it will do, and if it gets off track a bit, it has plenty of time to recover. Further, with longer improvement efforts, it is very difficult to specify in advance exactly what will or should happen at a particular point in time; every WST and kaikaku effort has a different set of objectives, deliverables, tasks, and suddenly appearing challenges.

A weeklong event, on the other hand, has only a very short time to get a great deal of work done. Every minute is precious; any distractions or poorly executed or off-target tasks waste time that cannot be replaced. This is why what might seem to be "overengineering" of the event is, instead, vital to attaining maximum results (which includes "teaching" participants how to run a proper improvement event).

EVENT LENGTH

The most common duration of a CIE is four full days of work over a period of five days, or about 32 hours. Typically, an event will start at around noon on Monday, run from about 8:00 a.m. to 5:00 p.m. Tuesday through Thursday, and conclude around noon on Friday. This arrangement will be referred to as "an event week" for the remainder of this chapter. Obviously, these hours are a "day shift" schedule. Even if there is a night shift (or many shifts), it is recommended that weeklong improvement events be held during the day shift. This is because of the availability of management at report-outs and the greater amount of support resources and personnel typically present on day shifts. Of course, if the focus of an event is such that everything the team might need is available (and management and the champion are available to attend kickoffs, daily status meetings, and the wrap-up presentation), shifts other than the day shift can work.

The weeklong schedule is popular because it provides a few hours for people to get settled in on Monday and also provides time to get a little regular work done after the event on Friday. However, this is not the reason why I recommend this schedule. It is very difficult for people to pay intensive and fruitful attention to anything new and unfamiliar for a full 40 or more hours. If the event is tightly organized and coached as this chapter recommends, the attendees will be completely wrung out by noon on Friday. Keeping them longer during the week and/or for the extra half-days on Monday and Friday will not produce more work or better-quality work. Instead, output will suffer.

A week in an event is not like a week of normal work. In an event, people are forced to work in close quarters with little private staring-into-the-computer or random socializing time in the hallways; they are "on" every minute. In addition, they are often working with a number of people they do not know well or at all and must constantly be monitoring their actions and those of others in order to facilitate a pleasant working environment. At the same time, they are learning and using tools that might be new to them. Finally, they do not have their normal roles, norms, and status in organization structure to fall back on (the absences of which are a good thing because it opens their eyes to different ways of thinking). All of these factors increase the energy expended by the team members and the stress they feel. They can only take so much and continue to do good work. On the positive side, all of these circumstances tend to drive teams toward greater creativity and enthusiasm than what they might attain in their normal jobs.

Events shorter than a week are *not* recommended. If, during the planning stage, the event does not appear likely to provide enough work to keep a team busy for a week, the scope of the event should be expanded. While a week-long event is stressful and exhausting, the length serves another very important purpose that a shorter time period cannot provide. People need time to cognitively process their experiences. At night, while they are sleeping, each team member develops different insights and perspectives about the day's experiences and learning as the happenings of the day are integrated into his or her cognitive map. This is a completely subconscious, innate process that cannot be compressed or rushed. Even with a full weeklong event, there are only four nights when this vital processing occurs.

These considerations are even stronger arguments against holding events that are conducted across shifts. They do not work. Often, a manager from a multishift operation will suggest that an event be run over a two- to three-day period, with each shift passing the work to a team on the next shift. This suggestion is often promoted with a statement such as, "And there will be even more work time devoted to the event than having one team work a full week." The problems with this approach are many and profound. First of all, there is little ownership of the project. Since each team works only two or three shifts, there's no time to really understand what is going on, to think about it, and to really take possession of the work. Second, there is no time (only two nights at most) to let the concepts cognitively develop. Third, each team will have to spend at least an hour getting caught up with what happened since it was last involved. Fourth, no matter how in synch the teams are, each shift team is going to wander a bit off track, leaving the next shift to redo the work or continue with something it does not understand very well or agree with. Finally, it is a law of nature at the level of quantum mechanics that night shifts do not get as much work done as day shifts. The reasons are many: They do not get as much supervision, the workers are typically less experienced, and they are often younger and less work-world savvy. As a result, there almost always is some animosity or jealousy between shifts, leading to disruption of the planned improvement effort (not to mention the normal work).

This across-the-shifts approach can work with various types of scrambles because there is much less opportunity to misinterpret what should be done. In fact, an across-the-shifts approach for 5S activities can do a lot to reduce shift conflicts. Of course, even if the activity is relatively brief, it is always important to have experienced coaches present to make sure the focus is maintained and there is continuity between shits; supervisors are often not capable of spending enough time on the floor with the workers to provide adequate coaching.

NUMBER OF TEAMS

This chapter assumes that the event being discussed has only one team of five to seven people pursuing one charter. But as coaches gain more experience and there are more of them, a single event may have as many as five teams, each working on its own charter. The presence of many teams at the daily report-outs provides a great learning opportunity because teams will see a lot of different tools and methods used, some of which they are not using themselves. Teams will also see different styles of collecting and displaying data, which will help them improve their technique. For these reasons, it is always better to have more than one team working during an event, assuming there are enough experienced coaches and the size of the organization supports it. Plus, more teams will generate more excitement throughout the organization.

GENERAL STRUCTURE OF AN EVENT

A weeklong improvement event has five phases:

1. Making introductions and getting organized

2. Collecting information about the present state of the process

3. Developing and testing improvement ideas

4. Developing the desired future state and then implementing improvements and the necessary structures to keep them in place

5. Preparing and delivering a final presentation that describes what has been done and what the next steps are

Figure 13.1 illustrates where these events fall during a typical weeklong event. As the figure shows, there is considerable overlap between some of the activities. While the terms *current state* and *future state* are used here, the analyses and formulations of these conditions are often nowhere near as detailed as in a formal VSMapping exercise. Often, it is sufficient to simply implement improvements and note their before-and-after impacts on the metrics listed on a kaizen target sheet (KTS; explained later in the chapter).

In a weeklong kaizen event aimed at a small work group or area, both a current state VSM (CS-VSM) and a future state VSM (FS-VSM) may be relatively easy to construct as part of the initial data collection if there are not too many activities involved. However, this is only the case if the majority of team members are experienced in VSMapping methods. Otherwise, a good chunk

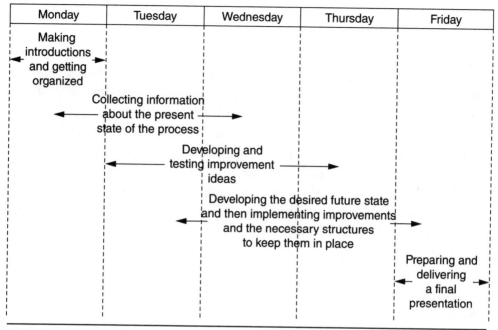

Monday	Tuesday	Wednesday	Thursday	Friday

Making introductions and getting organized

Collecting information about the present state of the process

Developing and testing improvement ideas

Developing the desired future state and then implementing improvements and the necessary structures to keep them in place

Preparing and delivering a final presentation

Figure 13.1 General structure of a weeklong event.

of time may have to be devoted to VSMapping training and explanations on day one. Also, if only one or two people are VSMapping savvy, they will be assigned all VSMapping duties and will have fewer chances to participate in broader group exercises. Exactly which approach is used will be a function of whether a larger-scale VSMapping exercise has already studied the process, the complexity of the process, and the site's kaizen event philosophy. If the process is long and/or complex, there will not be time to do VSMapping and implementation of improvement suggestions in the same week.

Only a couple of rigid guidelines are implied by Figure 13.1. First of all, it is important that team members not make any assumptions about what must be done "to fix the process" until Tuesday at the earliest. While they should be continually encouraged to fill out a kaizen action sheet (KAS; see Chapter 6) anytime they have an improvement idea, try to keep them from getting ahead of themselves. It is important to forestall any discussions among them about solutions until at least the second day. Otherwise, they may overtly and preconsciously promote their ideas and perhaps self-veto or denigrate many worthwhile improvement suggestions that conflict with the "fixes" that first came to mind. Remind the team often on day one to focus on data collection and analysis and let the findings generate the improvement ideas.

The second issue is more important. It has to do with bells and whistles and the waste removal philosophy of an improvement event. These two items are diametrically opposed. Far too many organizations require elaborate Microsoft PowerPoint presentations of event activities. Some teams spend all day Thursday and Friday morning putting them together. It seems ironic (and, let's be candid, stupid) to waste a lot of time developing a computerized presentation with sexy graphics during an event whose very purpose is to eliminate waste.

Don't get me wrong. I love PowerPoint (well, it's more of a love–hate relationship, well, maybe hate–love . . .). I use Microsoft PowerPoint to generate many figures that I can't create with Microsoft Word or Excel. However, I hope that management teams realize that it's far better for a team to spend time creating value through waste elimination than it is to spend time creating more waste disguised as eyewash. It is more productive to have the team speak to its brown paper creations during the presentations than to waste time playing with computers. Everybody can see everything at once, and it's easier to answer questions by walking and pointing to various analyses on the walls than it is to leaf through a computer presentation. And the brown papers already exist—not one additional keystroke is required! And, as Chapter 14 explains, the brown papers are invaluable for presenting in a dramatic and effective fashion information that a computer presentation can't match.

On the other hand, computer-presented information can be useful in some cases. It is always good to show digital photos of dramatic before-and-after conditions as a teaching tool. They seem to have more impact when shown large and crisp on a screen than when printed and taped to a brown paper (although it's harder, if not nearly impossible, to use a computer display in informal hallway expositions of results; see Chapter 14). Sometimes video is the most effective way to illustrate something that is difficult to explain to an audience that may not be familiar with a particular process element. In some cases, it may be necessary to use a computer to project a complex financial or operational analysis that was created in a spreadsheet. Additionally, it would be wasteful to duplicate a vast array of numbers on a brown paper than to show the original spreadsheet. The best course is to use brown papers and posted data as much as you can, and fall back on Microsoft PowerPoint and its kin only when you have to. Of course, if management expects bells and whistles, it may be a poor career move to defy previously established expectations. In that case, use brown papers along with Microsoft PowerPoint and try to break management's electronic addiction gradually over time.

I recommend that the team spend only two hours, say 9:00 a.m. to 11:00 a.m. on Friday, preparing for its presentation (assuming an 8:00 a.m. start and an 11:00 a.m. presentation). The details of this preparation are discussed later in this chapter.

DETAILED GENERAL SCHEDULE FOR THE WEEK

This section presents generic schedule guidelines by day for a typical kaizen event. While events may vary a bit and times will never be exact in practice, the sequence of activities should be maintained as much as possible.

Monday (day one)

Noon	*Kickoff:* The event begins with a welcome by the champion. Safety guidelines for the site and the event are reviewed. This includes any required safety equipment, such as breathing equipment when in areas with halon fire systems, escape routes, fire alarm signals, location of first-responder telephone numbers, and nearest phones. A key executive or two may also welcome the participants.
12:15 p.m.	*Introductions:* The team leader has each person introduce himself or herself (e.g., name, department, any prior kaizen event experience). If there are multiple teams, each team leader can have his or her team introduce itself.
12:35 p.m.	*Hygiene issues:* Explain morning coffee/snacks, lunch arrangements, and electronic communications policy (turn all devices to vibrate and do not leave the room to take messages or return messages until the designated 15-minute personal time during lunch, unless there is an emergency). Point out locations of restrooms and copy machines. Explain the use and location of the message board.
12:45 p.m.	*Review of agenda:* The team leader gives an overview of the week's agenda. The times and main activities are printed on a couple of flip chart pages taped to the wall or brown paper. Do not use a video screen to display the agenda; you might as well get them used to brown papers and wall hangings right from the start. The team leader highlights daily report-outs and final presentation times.

1:00 p.m.	*Overview of kaizen principles:* This is a short discussion of the concepts of waste and a few examples of low-technology waste elimination. Do not go into great depth; the team members can learn most of what they need through hands-on work. Be sure to introduce the KAS (Chapter 6) and explain and encourage its use. Also, designate an area where each team will place its completed KASs.
1:30 p.m.	*Review of the team charter:* Each team member is given a copy of the charter and the team leader reviews it with the team. If there are any modifications, they can be made only with the approval of the coach. If the coach cannot decide, the champion must be brought in.
1:45 p.m.	*Walk-through of the work area(s) involved:* The team visits the work area(s) where the event will be focused. Introductions are made to managers, supervisors, and key personnel who are in the area.
2:15 p.m.	*Break:* Have the teams return to the meeting/work room for a quick 10-minute break. Emphasize that everyone must return from the break on time.
2:25 p.m.	*Work assignment explained:* The exact nature of the first work assignment will depend to a certain extent on the focus of the event and the amount of still-current information available to the team. Assuming that the team is starting from scratch (i.e., no prior VSM, spaghetti diagrams, or other tools are available), it will have to become familiar with the work area. The best approach is to start by showing the teams an example of each of the following tools and discussing how to complete each:

1. Spaghetti diagram.
2. Handoff diagram.
3. Waste checklist. An Office Kaizen waste checklist is shown in Figure 13.2. One should be used for each area of the process, that is, a group of nearby or colocated activities.
4. Activity list (explained in Chapter 9).
5. KTS. An example of a KTS for an office environment is shown in Figure 13.3.

Office Kaizen Waste Checklist				
Process			**Date**	
Operation			**Analyst**	

Possible waste symptom	**Status**	**Comments (submit KAS with improvements)**
1. Difficulty in task		
2. Seeking next item to work on		
3. Needing help		
4. Presence of defects/errors		
5. Inspecting		
6. Reworking/repairing		
7. No designated locations for work		
8. Searching for materials		
9. Moving materials		
10. Searching for information		
11. Moving information		
12. Searching for tools/aids		
13. Searching for a person		
14. Obtaining/providing signature		
15. Waiting		
16. Walking		
17. Attending meeting		
18. Making/receiving phone call		
19. Sending/receiving fax		
20. Sending/receiving e-mail		
21. Work-in-process inventory		
22. No marked inventory locations		
23. Finished inventory		
24. Incoming inventory		
25. Calculating		
26. Making notes		
27. Translating data/rekeying		
28. Other _____		

Status symbols: ◎ Can fix this week   ○ Needs planned improvement   ✓ Okay for now

Figure 13.2   Example of an Office Kaizen waste checklist.

Office Kaizen Target Sheet

Date: Page   of

Department or area	Process name		Average output required					
			Total time available (sec)			Takt time (sec)		
Performance parameter	Starting value	Target	1st effort	2nd effort	3rd effort	Change* (units)	Change* (%)	
Number completed per day								
Work-in-process (WIP)								
Number of process steps								
Total number of touches								
Number of different people who touch it								
Number of people required								
Number of people trained to do it								
Number of signatures required								
Total walking distance (ft.)								
Total number of pages/screens required								
Number of calls/faxes required								
Total hands-on work (manual) time								
Lead time (sum of waiting by a single piece of work at all steps)								
Total waiting time (of people in all steps to process one piece)								
Best possible time**								

Remarks: *Compared with starting value

**Summed optimum activity times with no waiting, WIP, waste, defects, etc.

Figure 13.3 An example of a KTS.

6. A RACI (responsible, authorize, consult, inform; see Chapter 7) chart of the team's assignments. The purpose and structure of a RACI chart should be explained at this point and each team directed to construct one that shows what each team member will be doing during the event. Tasks are added to the RACI chart as they are assigned. The chart can also be used to track progress. When each person who has an *R* completes the task he or she has been assigned, the *R* should be circled, as should the *C*s and *I*s when the *R* consults with and informs, respectively, other team members. Once updated, such a chart provides an easily understandable visual signal as to how a team is doing. It is best if the team members' names are placed in the first column and the team tasks placed from right to left on the top row. This format makes it easy to add additional tasks. The RACI chart should be updated as needed every time team members return to the work room.

2:45 p.m.   *Begin data collection and analyses:* The team visits the work area(s), walks the process, observes the workers, and collects the information shown in the following list for the work area(s) being studied. The coach has the team leader make specific assignments for pairs of people (most always two but sometimes three, if it's an uneven number). These assignments are noted in the RACI chart.

1. *Sequence of activities:* This is a numbered list of actions that starts with the first activity in the process being studied and goes to the end of the process. The list usually has several columns, which show the name of the action, what it does (often the same), and any observations (e.g., workplace organization issues, problems, or quality levels). Other columns can be added and used as the team wishes.

2. *Handoff chart:* One for paper files, one for parts (if any), and one for electronic data.

3. *Waste checklist:* This forces the team to begin looking for specific waste categories.

> 4. *KTS:* As was shown in Figure 13.3, this is a master summary sheet of general metrics for the area/process. The team should start thinking about it right from the start; the best way to make that happen is to have team members start collecting data. If the metrics shown on the example are not sufficient, adjust them as required.

4:00 p.m.	*Quick debriefing of initial data collection:* Poll the team as to how it went and any obstacles they ran into. Update the team RACI chart and circle those items that have been completed.
4:15 p.m.	*Discuss, clean up the information, and plan for tomorrow:* Teams spend some time evaluating where they are on the data collection and what they must do tomorrow.
4:45 p.m.	*Review of tomorrow's agenda:* Work sequence, starting and stopping times, and lunch and continental breakfast arrangement.
4:50 p.m.	*Benefits and concerns:* Participants call out what went well (benefits) and what could have been done better (concerns) and the coach writes these on a flip chart. Always do benefits first. After no more ideas are forthcoming, the coach should address the concerns in terms of what can be changed, what has to be that way, suggestions, and so on. If the champion wishes to make a positive comment and/or observation, it should be made here. If the champion or a member of management thinks something is not working properly, it should *not* be discussed in front of the group until he or she has discussed it privately with the coach.
5:00 p.m.	*End of day one.*

Tuesday (day two)

Note: It is normal for the coach and observers to feel that things are not coming together fast enough by Tuesday afternoon. This happens so often that it sometimes seems as if it is a law of nature. When I am coaching events and I don't have this feeling, I get nervous. Assuming that the advice in this chapter is being heeded, there is a tremendous amount of work going on, but it takes a while for it to come together in visible products. It's really an instance of the chaos cycle presented in Chapter 1. Monday is the descent into chaos, and

Tuesday morning is the beginning of reintegration. By Wednesday noon, the team will be at a new state of equilibrium. From that point on, the coach and the team leader must labor to keep the team in a state of persistent disequilibrium. That is why the demands of new requirements, forms, and methods are continually presented to the team—to keep it thinking and adapting and creating.

8:00 a.m.   *Day two kickoff:* The champion or the coach welcomes back the group. The team leader or the coach reviews safety guidelines, escape routes, fire alarm signals, location of first-responder telephone numbers, and nearest phones.

8:15 a.m.   *Thumbnail report-outs:* If there is more than one team, each team leader and his or her team takes five minutes to discuss how the data collection has gone so far. If there is only one team, the discussion can take 10–15 minutes if needed.

8:30 a.m.   *Additional data collection assignments and expectations:* The coach explains the need for a RACI chart of the people and the process being studied. The team leader then assigns a pair of team members to develop the chart for the tasks being studied (see Chapter 7). This RACI chart has two functions: (1) It determines who is involved in each activity, and (2) it serves as a low-tech cross-training matrix insofar as the *R*s are those who can do a particular task. This is important if tasks need to be moved, adjusted, given more help or more training, and so on. There may be other additional assignments due to the particular nature of the process or the event. Some of them may also be made at this time, and some may wait until Wednesday morning for assignment. The team will also come up with new data collection and/or analysis items of its own. Over the next day, the coach should encourage the team leader to begin managing his or her team's work, and the coach can "manage and coach" the team's work by coaching the team leader. The coach informs the teams that they should begin placing data on their brown papers by 11:00 a.m. This sets the expectation that while there is still a lot of data to collect, the teams must begin thinking about posting things on the walls. If the brown paper process is new to most of the team members, the coach should review brown paper construction principles at this time (see Chapter 7).

8:45 a.m.   *Continue data collection and analyses:* The team returns to the target area and continues to collect data and conduct analyses. If it seems that the amount of work is large, it is. The intent is to keep the teams very busy so that they can learn a lot about the process and how to use the tools. It is far better to work them very hard than to give them too little to do (idle hands are the coffee break's workshop). Remind the teams to keep the RACI chart of their work assignments current. The teams should return to the meeting/work room for a break at 10:50 a.m.

10:50 a.m.   *Break:* Take a 10-minute break. Emphasize that everyone must return from the break on time.

11:00 a.m.   *Status briefing and begin brown paper construction:* Each team gives a five-minute report on its progress and the tasks it will be addressing when it returns to the target area. The champion and a member or two from management should be present. They don't have to say anything unless they have a question. Some of the team members begin to put data on various brown papers.

11:20 a.m.   *Continue data collection, analyses, and brown paper construction:* At this point, each team's members will be working in disparate locations, as some visit the work area and some work in the team room. It is important that the coach circulate widely to assess progress, give tips and guidance, and keep people on task. Tell the teams to return for a working lunch. Pick a time between noon and 1:00 p.m.

Noon to   *Working lunch:* Lunch should be available when they
1:00 p.m.   return. Tell the team members they may take 15 minutes to handle phone calls, stare at a computer screen (for those suffering from withdrawal), and so on. They are then to have a working lunch with their team for another 45 minutes in which they can discuss their work.

1:00 p.m.   *Continue data collection, analyses, and brown paper construction:* The team continues to work. Tell them to incorporate their break into the afternoon when the team leader wishes. The coach should have examined the status of the KASs during the morning and at lunch. If it seems there are too few, the coach should encourage the team members to fill out a KAS whenever they have an idea. Tell the team it is expected to have the following items mostly complete and on brown paper by 4:15 p.m.:

1. Spaghetti diagram

2. Handoff diagram

3. Waste checklist

4. Activity list

The following items should be well under way and at least designed, if not already being transferred from notes to a brown paper:

5. KTS

6. RACI chart

Note: Stand-alone data and the analysis items shown in the list (in contrast to a VSM, which requires more than one "sheet") are easier to read and more aesthetically pleasing if they are constructed on a sheet or two of flip chart paper and then attached to the brown paper. At this time, the team members may be working in disparate locations, as some members will be working on brown paper construction and others will be collecting data. The coach(es) should circulate widely, making sure to keep everyone working, and providing advice when it appears to be required.

4:15 p.m.   *Status briefing:* This session starts by having the team leader review the RACI chart for the team members' data collection and analysis activities. The team leader must make sure that all items are on schedule or have a recovery plan that will start on Wednesday. Team members then take turns explaining the various analyses. Make sure that every team member presents something; this is good practice for Friday. The team should discuss improvement ideas that the analyses suggest. If a suggestion is not accompanied by a KAS, the coach must reinforce the necessity of completing a KAS for every improvement idea. If the team is lagging in generating KASs, the coach must tell the team that at least 20 KASs are expected by end of business on Wednesday.

4:45 p.m.	*Review of tomorrow's agenda:* See Monday at 4:45 p.m.
4:50 p.m.	*Benefits and concerns:* See Monday at 4:50 p.m.
5:00 p.m.	*End of day two.*

Wednesday (day three)

8:00 a.m.	*Day three kickoff:* See Tuesday at 8:00 a.m.
8:10 a.m.	*Discussion of expectations:* The coach (or the team leader if the coach has prepared him or her in advance) explains to the team that it must generate the bulk of its improvement ideas by the end of the day so that it can begin to test and implement them. The coach also points out that the group must have a clear picture by midmorning on Thursday of everything it plans to do. Of course, an additional idea or two may appear at the last moment and be amenable to rapid implementation, but don't depend on these to make a large contribution. The team must also be told that the process workers not on the team must be brought to the workroom (they don't all have to visit at once) sometime today and have the findings and potential improvements explained to them in order to get their reactions and input.
8:30 a.m.	*Introduction of the kaizen to-do list:* Figure 10.2 in Chapter 10 presented an example of a summary table of KAS contributions that might be used to determine the overall impact of improvements in a VSMapping exercise. In a one-week event, it is usually not necessary to track individual KAS contributions to a process in as much detail as Figure 10.2 uses. You could do it, but it might look like overkill (i.e., too much "playing" with the numbers and not enough waste elimination). Typically, it is sufficient in a one-week event to simply show the overall impacts of waste reduction on a KTS (Figure 13.3) for the process or area. However, it is still important to track the selection of to-be-implemented KASs and their implementation status. This is often done on a kaizen to-do list (KTDL). An example of a KTDL is shown in Figure 13.4. Adapted from Toyota, where it is often called a *Kaizen Shimbum* (kaizen newspaper), the KTDL summarizes the status of each KAS.

Kaizen To-Do List **Date:** 6/21/2010 **Page 1 of 1**

Manager or team leader	Area or process name				Person doing this sheet
John Bigboote	Medical Claims Processing				John Smallberries

KAS #	Problem	Corrective action	Person responsible	Date due	Percent complete
3	No ready supply of sorted forms	Install rack with copies of all commonly used forms	John Bigboote	6/22	(100%)
4	Not using FIFO with incoming claims; some sitting too long	Install stand-up FIFO rack; instruct mail handlers on proper use	John Smallberries	6/23	(~90%)
8	Condition coders cannot keep up at end of the week	Cross-train 3 approval coders to do condition coding	John Tem	6/25	(100%)
10	Correspondents use different boilerplate templates	Create a single boilerplate source file and train correspondents	John Orson	6/23	(100%)
11	Number of files moved between workers varies randomly	Create a standard lot size between each activity	John Wells	6/24	(~50%)
14	Files are pushed to next person	Design and install a pull system	John Wells	6/24	(~50%)
15	Approval signatures for deviations are difficult to obtain quickly	Design and install a "sign-off" supermarket rack	John Brothers	6/23	(~75%)

Figure 13.4 An example of a KTDL.

As Figure 13.4 shows, the KTDL makes it easy to track the status of a number of KASs with a single glance. If the KTDL is more than one page, display the pages side by side so that everything is visible without having to flip pages. While the example is shown with printed content for ease of reading, it is always best if the KTDL is hand-written, at least during the event—it keeps the team away from laptops and focused on waste elimination. There is no formal system for determining when a KAS is 25%, 50%, or 75% complete. Use your finely honed kaizen skills and take a guess.

8:45 a.m.   *Selection of KASs for implementation:* Teams usually don't have too much difficulty deciding whether to implement a KAS improvement idea. The vast majority of KAS improvement ideas will be small and low tech; most can be easily implemented within the week. A few may require longer periods due to time delays in order to obtain resources, get higher-level approvals, work out complex process issues, and the like. These KASs can be presented in the "next steps" section of the final presentation on Friday. If the team is having difficulty selecting and prioritizing a large number of KASs, review with them the procedures presented in step 19 of Chapter 9 (pp. 178–181) and coach them to develop a criterion or two with which to evaluate each KAS. As with the VSMapping procedures outlined in Chapter 9, the reference number of each KAS can be attached to the appropriate element of a brown paper to which they pertain. In many cases, the best spot may be on the spaghetti diagram of the area under study (since there may be no other "map" of the process or area shown in the analysis).

Note: As you can see, once a number of improvement events have been run, a great deal of time can be saved by not having to explain how to use forms and general kaizen event procedures. If a team has two or three people who understand and have used all of the forms and procedures, these members can explain the forms and procedures to the others as needed. All the coach has to do is mention at the right time that certain forms should be introduced, and the team leaders can take it from there.

9:00 a.m.   *Continue data collection, analyses, and brown paper construction:* The team continues to collect data and complete its analyses. At this point, each team should be beginning to implement some of the no-brainer KASs. In every case, however, it is important that the changes be communicated to the workers in the area by explaining how and why each improvement was selected. It is always effective if the team member from the area being studied makes the explanations. Tell the team to return to the meeting room at 10:30 a.m. for a break and a quick progress review.

10:30 a.m.   *Break.*

10:40 a.m.   *Status review:* The coach or the team leader, preferably, should review the team's RACI chart with the team and determine the status of each deliverable element of the event. Among them will be the following:

1. Spaghetti diagram
2. Handoff diagram
3. Waste checklist
4. Activity list
5. RACI chart of the process
6. KTS
7. KTDL with KASs selected so far for implementation

The team leader should add any other analyses and assignments to the team RACI chart and determine the status of those items as well.

11:00 a.m.   *Continue data collection, analyses, and brown paper construction:* Have the team return at 12:30 p.m. for lunch. Emphasize that it is important to begin testing some of the improvements by Thursday morning at the latest.

Noon to 12:30 p.m.   *Working lunch:* See Tuesday Noon to 12:30 p.m.

12:30 p.m.   *Continue data collection and analyses:* Tell the team to return at 3:00 p.m. for a break and a status check. Again emphasize that it is important to begin testing some of the improvements by Thursday morning at the latest. All of the implemented suggestions must be in place no later than 9:00 a.m. Friday. Also, have the team schedule a review of its findings and suggestions with some of the workers from the process being studied. Have them schedule this during their working time this afternoon or tomorrow morning in the team's work room.

3:00 p.m.   *Break.*

3:10 p.m.   *Status check:* Once again, have the team leader review the team's RACI assignments with the entire team.

3:20 p.m.   *Continue data collection and analyses:* Tell the team to return at 4:30 p.m. for the daily wrap-up.

4:30 p.m.   *Status review:* Since only one full day of work remains, it is a good idea to have the champion and a few members of senior management present to see how things are going and to give their support to the team. Have the team do a quick review of the completed and still-in-process work.

4:45 p.m.   *Review of tomorrow's agenda:* See Monday at 4:45 p.m.

4:50 p.m.   *Benefits and concerns:* See Monday at 4:50 p.m.

5:00 p.m.   *End of day three.*

Thursday (day four)

Before Thursday (or after hours on Wednesday), the coach and the champion should meet with the team leader and discuss what each of them needs to do in order to ensure that the team achieves its objectives for the week. They must develop an action plan for any work that is behind schedule. The presence of the champion is important for more than "showing the flag." Many champions, especially in organizations just getting started with continuous improvement, do not understand the amount of effort, adjustments, and coaching that goes into creating a successful weeklong CIE. Having the champion present at coaching sessions not only shows the team that the champion (and thus management) is involved but also teaches the champion valuable skills and develops insights that will help him or her support continuous improvement in the future. Of course, nothing teaches better than actual involvement; that is why it is very important to have all members of management participate as CIE team members in at least two events each year. They learn what is really going on in part of the organization, they sharpen their skills in improvement methods and tools, and keep up to date with the types of tools the teams are using. Most important, their preconscious assumptions begin to change in a way that helps make continuous improvement part of their daily leadership approach rather than an occasional activity.

8:00 a.m.   *Day four kickoff:* See Tuesday at 8:00 a.m.

8:10 a.m.   *Discussion of expectations:* The team leader and the coach tell the team that it must have all of its selected improvements implemented by the end of the day. Thus, all of its analysis items and brown papers concerning the current state of the process must be done by noon. While some of the work may require a little more time, such as updating the KTDL after improvements are made, it is important to maintain focus and a sense of urgency. The team leader should quickly review his or her team's RACI chart and give the team any instructions or coaching that was identified during the presession assessment discussion by the team leader, the champion, and the coach.

8:30 a.m.   *Continue to work on brown papers and implement improvements:* Tell the team to return at 10:30 a.m. for a break and a status check.

10:30 a.m. *Break.*

10:40 a.m. *Status check and sustainment action planning:* The team leader must review the status of the KTDL and the RACI chart with the team. The following questions must be asked:

1. Has every change and idea been entered on a KAS?
2. Have all of the KASs selected for implementation been entered on the KTDL?
3. Is every KAS listed on the KTDL also assigned to a specific person(s) and listed on the RACI chart?
4. Is there a specific completion time on the KTDL for each KAS?
5. Has each KAS on the KTDL been explained to the involved workers?

At this point, the coach or the team leader instructs the team to begin thinking about what must be done to support and sustain the implemented improvements. For example, if the team were to implement a new "first in, first out"

(FIFO) lane for incoming claims, what must be done and by whom to ensure that the FIFO lane is used and maintained in the future? And what must be done if something is amiss? The team leader or the coach must introduce the kaizen sustainment action plan (KSAP) and the kaizen follow-up check list (KFCL), which are shown in Figures 13.5 and 13.6, respectively. The KSAP identifies a sustainment action, the date it begins (which is almost always the next Monday), a team member and a worker from the area who will perform the sustainment action, and the frequency with which the action will be performed.

For example, Figure 13.5 shows that KAS 14 will be sustained by team member J. Wells visually examining inventory movement every day within the claims department starting on June 28. Since no frequency is mentioned, once a day is the default inspection frequency. Generally, an event team member does the checking for the first week. After that, F. Tevie, a worker from the area, will conduct the inspections two times a week, on a varying schedule. This sustainment plan is developed and reviewed with the appropriate process workers and supervision in the area and is explained during the final presentation.

Figure 13.6 shows the KFCL. This list presents the follow-up actions, the persons involved, and the specific dates on which the follow-up actions must be performed. It is developed with the participation of the area being studied. It is especially important to have the manager of the area involved insofar as he or she is ultimately responsible for seeing that the area sustains the improvements. The KFCL is posted on the visual metrics display (VMD; see Chapter 6) of the work group to which it applies.

For example, the improvement required by KAS 11 will be inspected by J. Wells each day from June 28 to July 2. When the inspection is performed, the date is circled. When an inspection is missed, the circle is absent. This serves as a gentle rebuke for the person who missed the assignment. As the figure shows, J. Bigboote missed an inspection for KAS 3 on July 1, as did J. Wells on June 30 for KAS 14 and J. Brothers on June 29 for

Kaizen Sustainment Action Plan

| | | Date: 6/24/2010 | Page 1 of 1 |

Manager or team leader

John Bigboote

Area or process name

Medical Claims Processing

Person doing this sheet

John Wells

KAS #	Corrective action	Sustainment action	Begin	Persons responsible	Assignments
3	Install rack with copies of all commonly used forms	Visually inspect rack	6/28	TM: J. Bigboote Area: A. Nho	TM: Daily 1st wk A: 2nd wk on; 2X wk
4	Install stand-up FIFO rack and instruct mail handlers on proper use	Visually inspect rack and observe handlers	6/28	TM: J. Smallberries Area: B. Whein	TM: Daily 1st wk A: 2nd wk on; 2X wk
8	Cross-train 3 approval coders to do condition coding	Review coding staffing and performance	6/28	TM: J. Tem Area: C. Befour	TM: Daily 1st wk A: 2nd wk on; 2X wk
10	Create a single boilerplate source file and train correspondents	Review correspondence for consistency	6/28	TM: J. Orson Area: D. Itz	TM: 2 X wk 1st wk A: 2nd wk on; 2X wk
11	Create a standard lot size between each activity	Visually examine lot sizes	6/28	TM: J. Wells Area: E. Thyme	TM: Daily 1st wk A: 2nd wk on; 2X wk
14	Design and install a pull system	Visually examine inventory movement	6/28	TM: J. Wells Area: F. Tevie	TM: Daily 1st wk A: 2nd wk on; 2X wk
15	Design and install a "sign-off" supermarket rack	Visually examine rack inventory; check aging of forms	6/28	TM: J. Brothers Area: G. Ahde	TM: Daily 1st wk A: 2nd wk on; 2X wk

Figure 13.5   An example of a KSAP.

Kaizen Follow-up Check List			Date: 6/28/2010	Page 1 of 1
Area manager or supervisor Sally Jones	**Area or process name** Medical Claims Processing		**Person responsible for this sheet** Billy Bobby Joe Mohammed	
KAS #	**Sustainment action**	**Persons responsible**	**Dates** (circle if okay; add "X" if deficient)	**Action taken if deficient**
3	Visually inspect rack at claims correspondence	J. Bigboote A. Nho	6/28 29 30 7/1 ⊗ 7/5 9 12 14 20 23 27 30	Inform lead correspondent
4	Visually inspect FIFO rack at and observe handlers at mail entry	J. Smallberries B. Whein	6/28 29 30 7/1 2 7/5 9 12 14 20 23 27 30	Inform mail room supervisor
8	Review condition coding staffing and performance	J. Tem C. Befour	6/28 29 30 7/1 2 7/5 9 12 14 20 23 27 30	Inform Sally Jones
10	Review boilerplate correspondence in customer service for consistency	J. Orson D. Itz	6/28 29 30 ⊗ 2 7/5 9 12 14 20 23 27 30	Inform lead correspondent
11	Visually examine lot sizes in claims	J. Wells E. Thyme	6/28 ⊗ ⊗ 7/1 2 7/5 9 12 14 20 23 27 30	Inform claims supervisor
14	Visually examine inventory movement in claims	J. Wells F. Tevie	6/28 29 30 7/1 2 7/5 9 12 14 20 23 27 30	Inform claims supervisor
15	Visually examine rack inventory; check aging of forms	J. Brothers G. Ahde	6/28 29 ⊗ 7/1 2 7/5 9 12 14 20 23 27 30	Inform Sally Jones

Figure 13.6 An example of a KFCL.

KAS 15. When an inspection discovers that a KAS improvement action is not being sustained, an "X" is placed over the inspection circle. As the figure displays, lot sizes relative to KAS 11 were a frequent problem. Each time, the claims supervisor would be informed, and remedial action (which would have been discussed with the area supervision beforehand) would be instituted.

11:10 a.m.   *Continue to work on brown papers and implement improvements:* Tell the team to return at 12:30 p.m. for lunch and a status check.

12:30 to 1:00 p.m.   *Working lunch:* See Tuesday Noon to 12:30 p.m.

1:00 p.m.   *Status check:* The team leader quickly reviews the status of all work products. These would include most of the following:

1. Spaghetti diagram

2. Handoff diagram

3. Waste checklist

4. Activity list

5. RACI chart of the process

6. KTS

7. KAS selection criteria if a significant number of sheets were not selected for reasons that might not be obvious

8. KTDL with KASs selected so far for implementation

9. KSAP

10. KFCL

Also included would be any one-point lessons developed, charts, and other analysis data. The team leader must remind the group that these items must not only be completed by the end of the day, meaning implementations as well as the information about them, but also be put into a format for presentation on Friday. The coach should emphasize that Microsoft PowerPoint and other computer presentations should be limited to absolutely essential items. The team leader must ensure that final assignments for team members are placed on the team's RACI chart so that each person knows exactly what he or she must do by the end of the day.

1:20 p.m.   *Continue to work on brown papers and implement improvements:* The team is told to return to the team room at 3:00 p.m. for a break and a status check.

3:00 p.m.   *Break.*

3:10 p.m.   *Status check:* The team leader reviews each of the day's *R*s on the RACI chart with the team. Adjustments are made as necessary.

3:30 p.m.   *Continue to work on brown papers and implement improvements:* The team is told to return at 4:30 p.m. for a final status check.

4:30 p.m.   *Status check:* The team leader reviews each of the day's *R*s on the RACI chart with the team. The team leader also reviews the status of the presentation materials for Friday. That is, are all of the necessary brown papers done? If the team does not have all of its work done, the coach can inform the members that they can stay later if they wish, come in a little earlier on Friday morning, or come in at the normal start time and hope they can get it all done in an hour or so. It's up to them. While it is not a good idea most of the time to keep team members later than a nine-hour day (8:00 a.m. to 5:00 p.m.) during an event, they can work longer if they are excited or if they need to and want to. The team leader, however, must make sure that those putting in the extra time are working on items that fit in with the overall plan. All too often, a lone worker or two will waste hours on something that they are interested in but that does not focus on a critical team task. The coach or team leader reviews with the team the schedule for Friday and explains the following agenda items so that the team can think about getting ready for Friday:

8:00 a.m.   *Normal kickoff.*

8:15 a.m.   *Teams put finishing touches on all materials:* If it is not done by 8:45 a.m., it doesn't get done.

8:45 a.m.   *Teams decide who will present each part of the analyses, findings, and improvements:* Everyone on the team must present something, in approximately equal face time with the audience.

9:00 a.m.   *Teams rehearse presentations:* This can be a delicate subject in some organizations. You know yours best. While the purpose of an improvement event is not to create skilled public speakers, there's no doubt that smoother presentations create better impressions and reflect more strongly on continuous improvement (and thus future management support and participation). Also, preparation reduces the stress level of the presenters. Therefore, it's a good idea to have each team go through the entire presentation from start to finish at least twice. And each person should rehearse his or her portion in front of one or two team members at least twice more. I have found that the following sequence works best:

1.   *Entire team presentation from beginning to end*

2.   *Team commentary/discussion of key points*

3.   *Individuals make notes and rehearse to one or two team members at least twice:* Have each person prepare a single sheet or notes with key points that the team thinks are important about each item discussed

4.   *Entire team presentation from beginning to end*

It is important that the champion and the coach be very active and supportive during this phase, as many of the team members may be nervous. Everyone should have an agreed-upon time limit that will be placed on the agenda (which will be on a flip chart sheet). The team leader and the coach must make sure that the time limits are followed (so that one or two people don't talk too long and make it difficult for other team members to cover their material).

	10:50 a.m. *Break.*
	11:00 a.m. *Final presentation.*
4:50 p.m.	*Benefits and concerns:* See Monday at 4:50 p.m.
5:00 p.m.	*End of day four.*

Friday (day five)

8:00 a.m.	*Final day kickoff:* See Tuesday at 8:00 a.m.
8:15 a.m.	*Teams put finishing touches on all materials.*
8:45 a.m.	*Teams decide who will present each part of the analyses, findings, and improvements:* See the team schedule given earlier.
9:00 a.m.	*Teams rehearse presentations:* The general sequence of items for commonly used tools is usually as shown in the following lists. Other items such as one-point lessons, standard work, special analyses, VSMapping, and so on, must be inserted where they fit best.

Current State

Spaghetti diagram (before improvements)

Handoff diagram (before improvements)

Waste checklist

Activity list (before improvements)

RACI chart of the process (before improvements)

KTS (showing metrics before improvement)

Improvements

Explanation of KAS selection criteria (if any)

KTDL

Future State

Spaghetti diagram (after improvements)

Handoff diagram (after improvements)

Activity list (after improvements)

RACI chart of the process (after improvements)

KTS (showing metrics after improvements)

Follow-Up Actions

KSAP

KFCL

Benefits

This can be nothing more than the improvement portion of the KTS if the sheet is particularly detailed with before-and-after costs of labor and materials. In many cases, the benefits will be in terms of faster and higher-quality customer service. In general, let the charter be your guide as to what the management team thinks are the important benefits that should be targeted. If there are any doubts about the charter's focus, have the champion work with the management team before the event to make sure everyone is focused on the correct metrics. It's very disheartening to have a great improvement event that's a little off target and you don't find out until the presentation. That's why it's essential to have some members of upper management attend each of the status review sessions of the team.

11:00 a.m.	*Final presentation:* If there is enough room, people and management from the area studied should attend the presentation. The team should prepare an agenda that lists each item, who will present it, and the time span assigned to the item. The champion should kick it off by introducing the team leader, who then introduces the entire team by name as they stand in front of the room. The team leader then introduces the first presentation topic, and each presenter then introduces the person who follows him or her on the agenda.
11:30 a.m.	*Questions and answers.*
11:45 to Noon	*End of the event:* Final thanks from the champion and comments by management and executives.

FINAL COMMENTS ON CONDUCTING WEEKLONG IMPROVEMENT EVENTS

The procedures described in this chapter may seem overly structured and detailed. Do not be misled: There is a large and positive correlation between the degree of structure applied to a CIE and the magnitude of attained results. When you're conducting an event, you have a lot of forces working against you:

- Everyone is bringing his or her normal work attitudes and approaches to the event. These methods are not typically designed for speed and intense focus over a period of five days. Yet, in a CIE, the people must move from analysis to understanding to implementation in one week.

- The majority of participants do not know one another well or at all. In this environment, some people will be more tentative in expressing opinions, thus wasting time and/or depriving the team of the benefits of worthwhile insights. Other team members will tend to be more direct with strangers, potentially alienating others who might feel they are being bossed around. This can lead to withdrawal or squabbles, which waste time and limit information flow.

- Most of the participants, at least in the first dozen or so events that the organization runs, will not have experience with the majority of tools and methods used. The participants need to be exposed to a lot of tools quickly and efficiently. Never forget that an event has two purposes: (1) results and (2) training people to be more effective in future events (which improves future results).

- The team member's work assignments are numerous and often overlapping. Without specific, sequenced assignments, frequent status checks, and quick reviews right from the start, the team runs the risk of not completing a significant portion of the work. Once things fall behind, it is almost impossible to get back on schedule.

The two things that can counter these influences are structure and coaching. Do not shortchange either one if you want to get the most out of your events.

14

Conducting Follow-Up Actions on Events That Last a Week or Less

Aweeklong (or shorter) improvement event cannot be determined to be a success at the end of the week. Everything typically looks and feels good on the last day of a well-run event. Management is happy because it is dreaming of the bottom-line impacts to come and because "its" continuous improvement program is working. The team members/participants are happy because they worked hard and are proud of their achievements (and they are relieved that the hard work is over). The coach is happy because he or she kept yet another event on track when at times it seemed that everything was teetering on the edge of chaos (and not the good kind of chaos!). The manager/supervisor in the work area that was helped is happy because he or she is hoping that a lot of the problems have been fixed and that he or she can get back to focusing on "normal" issues. The workers in the area are happy because they were glad to get some help and attention, be involved, and be asked their opinions about what should be done. Yet, despite all the happy feelings, the event is not yet a success. In fact, it could, and often does, turn out to be a complete failure despite every sign to the contrary.

Even in events in which a great many improvements are installed and are generating benefits in the week of the event, failure is a more likely outcome than success. This is because follow-up is commonly poor. Across all industries and all event types (including 5S and other types of events with few easily measurable bottom-line benefits), I have found that the average event with good follow-up returns about $50,000 over the 52 weeks following the event. This amounts to about $961 per week. Yet, if the event's benefits last only a few weeks before the improvements wither away, the total benefits are only a few thousand dollars and the event can't be called anything but a failure.

In fact, if improvements are allowed to wither away, the event is worse than a failure; it causes immense harm to the work area and its workers, the participants, and the organization. If improvements are not maintained, everyone involved feels betrayed and tricked. They see themselves as having once again fallen prey to the false hope of the latest flavor of the month being promoted by management, the continuous improvement office, and so on. The next time they are asked to "help," they will be more cynical and harder to convince. In essence, their most negative preconscious assumptions about work, management, and organizations will have been dramatically reinforced.

The bottom line (both financially and logically) is that an event can be termed a success only if the improvements are sustained indefinitely. This requires that the supervisor of the area that was helped and the management team of the site take responsibility for keeping the improvements in place (and hopefully improve things even further). This requires a number of specific actions:

1. *Executive Steering Committee (ESC) or management reviews:* If the site does not have an ESC, one must be formed (see Chapter 6). If one cannot be formed at the time, a management team must be brought together to review the metrics from each event (every event conducted in the last six months) once a week. This is simply a one- to two-minute look of the event metrics being tracked on the kaizen target sheet (KTS; see Figure 13.3) for the event. If things are not where they should be, the management team must take action and get things back on track.

2. *Maintenance of the kaizen follow-up check list (KFCL):* This worksheet, displayed in Figure 13.6, must be monitored by area management every day and reviewed by the ESC or management team every week. This is over and above the requirements of the scheduled reviews by the appointed team member and the area employee assigned during the event. As many readers are no doubt speculating, this means that various members of management will have to do a little walking around and checking things out once a few improvement events have been conducted. The process to structure these visits is discussed in detail in Chapter 15. This could amount to as much as 30–60 minutes per day per manager/executive. This is a small price to pay for creating excellence, but many will say they do not have the time. If the maintenance activities of the KFCL are well maintained for the first month after the event, the KFCL can be discontinued as long as the appropriate KTS metrics of the area are

okay. If things start to deteriorate, another KFCL must be installed and tracked. While one can hope that the area supervision would take responsibility for this action, it will probably have to be directed by the ESC or its equivalent until the organization and its supervision mature.

3. *Daily checking of uncompleted items on the kaizen to-do list (KTDL):* The KTDL (see Figure 13.4) is used during the event to track the status of planned improvements. Almost invariably, there will be anything from a few to many kaizen action sheets (KASs; see Figure 6.5) that cannot be completed during the event. These must be monitored on a weekly basis by an assigned team member from the event until they are completed. Each week, the ESC or its equivalent should review the status of all uncompleted KASs from all past events. This list should be maintained by the site improvement facilitator (SIF; see Chapter 6) or his or her equivalent.

4. *Exposition reviews with the organization:* This is the easiest follow-up action. The brown papers from the event must be taken on a road show around the organization. Typically, this means that a set of dates, places, and times are established, and then the brown papers are hung up. A member of the event team, accompanied by the champion and maybe a worker or two from the area that was helped, explains what was done and then answers questions from people who visit. These expositions work best in a large, open room, a portion of the cafeteria, a large lobby area, and so on, where people can move around as the various brown papers are discussed. Try to keep group sizes under 30. These events do not work well with very large groups (many of the people can't get close to the brown paper). They also don't work well in auditoriums where people are seated (same problem with viewing the brown papers). The expositions should start the Monday or Tuesday after the event (assuming it ends on Friday) and continue for at least a week with at least one exposition per day. More may be needed in larger organizations. In some cases, it helps to schedule certain exposition times for certain parts of the organization in order to keep the number of attendees under control. It is great if departments ask for a special showing. Of course, it is an extra benefit if one of the expositions is videoed and then placed on the company intranet so that those who missed it can see what happened if they wish. If the organi-

zation has a company paper, stories about the event and the exposition should be published.

These follow-up activities may seem like a lot of drudge work after the excitement of the event. They *are* drudge work. But it's always the drudge work that yields the benefits. That's the nature of human organizations and change; keeping things going is always 10 times harder than starting them.

PART IV

The Leadership of Significant Office Kaizen Transformation Efforts

Most systems are more than the sum of their parts. If the average person was provided all the parts of a disassembled automobile, as well as all the necessary tools and consumables (e.g., adhesives, lubricants), what are the odds that he or she could reassemble the car properly? Almost zero. A successful Office Kaizen transformation requires more than the capacity to understand and apply all the methods, tools, and processes described in Parts I, II, and III of this book. It is just as important to know when and in what sequence to apply the various structural configurations, improvement tools, and continuous improvement events (CIEs). Part IV describes exactly how to integrate everything presented in the earlier sections in order to transform anything from a single work group to a multisite organization.

In addition, Part IV describes action leadership (AL), a method to specifically focus leadership efforts at all levels of an organization. AL provides an approach that actively supports all aspects of an Office Kaizen transformation every day with objective, defined actions that can be measured and assessed.

15

The Secret Ingredient to Excellence: Action Leadership

If an organization does everything that's recommended in the earlier chapters, wonderful things will happen. However, the probability of complete success—that is, the probability of becoming an outstanding and perhaps world-class organization—is not 100% or even close to it. I'd say it's only 10%. Why? Because the most important element, more important than dozens of continuous improvement events (CIEs), more valuable than wall-to-wall value stream mapping (VSMapping) with good follow-up, more essential than handfuls of successful Six Sigma projects, and more important than pull systems, is almost always missing. This critical element, the absolutely essential catalyst of world-class change, is focused and structured leadership that empowers all world-class methods, tools, and approaches to realize their full potential as sustainable elements of a smoothly functioning system. The easiest and fastest way to begin creating this level of leadership is called action leadership (AL). This chapter explains how and why AL works and shows you how to get AL started for yourself and your organization.

Please keep in mind that while AL can be applied to any leadership situation, this chapter focuses on using AL to promote Office Kaizen success (and the success of analogous factory situations). That is, this chapter focuses AL on implementing and sustaining the methods and approaches presented in earlier chapters. It is beyond the scope of this book to explain the details of applying AL to other areas of business endeavors such as strategic planning, product development, visioning, and so on. However, the insightful reader should be able to use the content of this chapter to make an intuitive leap and tailor his or her AL efforts to specific scenarios.

Most managers want to be outstanding leaders (or at least they want to get the results that outstanding leadership creates). Every manager who's been around for a while can generate a wish list of leadership end-state objectives (just think of the ubiquitous "vision, mission, values, etc." proclamations on most organizations' conference room walls); the intent of such statements is all good stuff, but how do you get there? Figure 15.1 illustrates the situation faced by would-be leaders of Office Kaizen. Immediately below the arrow with the "1" are four objectives that readers of this book might generate at this point (I hope) as appropriate leadership end-states. Once again, these are all good, but the problem, illustrated by the question marks beneath the four objectives, is that, prior to reading *Office Kaizen 1 (OK1)* or *Office Kaizen 2 (OK2)*, few would-be leaders would know specifically what actions to take within the leadership black box (LBB; see Chapter 6) to realize the objectives. The consequence is that most leaders take the route labeled "1" and apply bits and pieces of theory, examples of previous bosses' leadership styles, and recent fads when they need better results. It takes incredible "one-in-a-million" luck for this approach to work.

Readers of *OK2* know that structural configurations are a mandatory element in any effective leadership system (see Chapter 6). This is illustrated on the left side of Figure 15.1, beneath the strategy arrow labeled "2." As the figure implies, this approach mandates the implementation of nonnegotiable, specific mechanisms and conditions (the white boxes within the "the organization" LBB) as part of standard, day-to-day operating processes. Unfortunately, structural configurations, while extremely effective and essential in creating value, are not sufficiently powerful to transform an organization and keep it that way. As Chapters 3, 4, and 5 showed, the innate tendencies of human beings cause us to continually create pressures that constrain efficiency and erode world-class practices. We are not inherently designed to operate effectively in large organizations. If nature is allowed to take its normal course, it will encourage the formation of competitive cliques that compete with others, hide information, battle for status, and stifle communication (sound familiar?). Even the best-implemented structural configurations by themselves are not up to the task of resisting these innate and powerful tendencies.

However, a core element of basic human nature can be harnessed to turn the tide against the suboptimizing human tendencies that compromise effective organizations. The answer, the cavalry coming over the hill with bugles sounding, is leadership defined by actions, or AL. The AL strategy is illustrated in Figure 15.1 by the arrow labeled "3." As the gray shading in the figure indicates, AL provides a leadership presence that fills the organization and surrounds and supports the structural configurations as well as everything else that happens. Note that the structural configuration boxes are drawn with dashed lines.

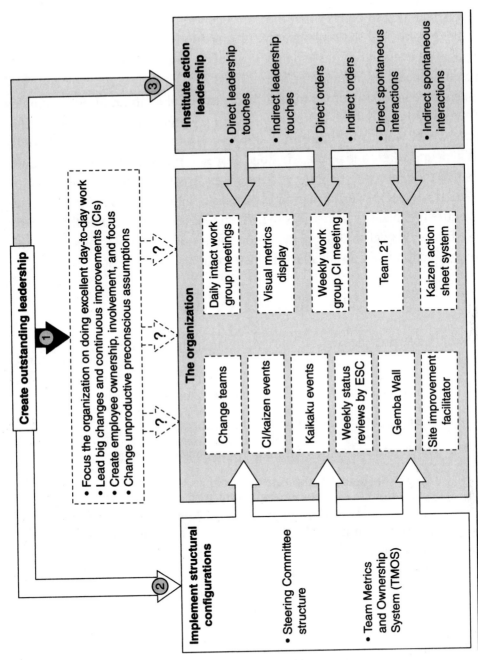

Figure 15.1 The challenge of creating outstanding leadership.

This is intended to convey that they are open to, absorb, and are affected by all the dynamics of the organization. Leadership is one of the most important impacts on everything that happens in an organization. Without AL, the ever-present impacts of human small-group and organization dynamics and poor leadership continually erode the ability of structural configurations. Examples of the erosion include the Executive Steering Committee (ESC) not meeting every week, work group meetings skipped, visual metrics displays (VMDs) not kept up to date, and so on. AL, done properly, provides a counterbalancing, positive influence that sustains and improves structural configurations. Think of AL as a super powerful marinade that soaks into every nook and cranny of the entire organization and raises the effectiveness of all activities that it soaks into. Before we get into the detailed mechanics of AL, let's explore the criticality of action itself as a leadership instrument.

THE PRIMACY OF ACTION

Control theory provides a useful description of behavior. It posits that there are four components of every discrete behavior:

1. The action itself (e.g., talking, moving, reaching, throwing)

2. The thought that accompanies the action

3. The emotional response that accompanies the action

4. The physiological responses that occur with the action

When a behavior takes place, all four components occur simultaneously or in close succession. In normal daily life, most of the components of behavior occur as conditioned responses of the preconscious to prior similar situations. The only part of behavior that can be reliably controlled is action. Emotional and physiological responses are almost impossible to control, especially in spontaneous situations such as when someone sneaks up behind you and says, "Boo!" Thought isn't any easier to control; try keeping your mind perfectly blank for 30 seconds.

The only weapon leaders have is action. It can be their most powerful leadership tool. Action is all that employees can see. In traditional environments, employees possess many negative preconscious expectations about management, leadership, and their organization: "Nothing will change," "They want to work us to death," "They only care about their bonuses," and "Nobody listens to us." The only thing that can change these employee expectations and the reactions they generate is a continuous stream of observable actions from leaders who demonstrate that these assumptions are incorrect. This has to occur often enough over a period of months to force the preconscious expectations to "I" processing so they can be changed and begin to form new, world-class "me" assumptions (see Chapter 3). Only action can force this process.

While action can be the most powerful tool of a leader, it is most leaders' worst enemy. The problem is that action is often trumped by the preconscious expectations of leaders. For example, let's say that Fred is a manager who has just gotten back from a conference about getting employees more involved in process improvements. One of the things he learned was that it is important to visit with workers and ask about the status of key processes.

The next day at work, he decides to visit a work group to try the technique. He worries (his thought) about the reception he will get and how the employees may react. When he engages Liz, she is surprised because Fred has never stopped to talk with her before. She is suspicious and worries that her supervisor, Sally, who reports directly to Fred, might think Liz has gone behind her back. As Fred asks how things are going, Liz says very little and acts disinterested because she doesn't want her boss to hear that she reported any problems. This frustrates Fred, who thought it would be easy. He decides to try someone else.

Fred stops to talk to Yogi as he walks through the sales department. Yogi is an outspoken, aggressive top salesperson. Fred assumes (his thought) that Yogi will have no issues with speaking freely. When Fred asks him how things are going in the sales department, Yogi gets angry: "Going? Going!? It's not going anywhere! You've got to be kidding me! We get nothing but bad numbers from pricing, customer service never gets back to us, and IT is always changing the specs of what we promised. I've sent you e-mails and . . . blah, blah . . . nothing happens . . . I don't know why I even try to keep selling . . . blah, blah, blah." It takes Fred 10 minutes to calm Yogi down before he can get out of the area. Fred never expected this kind of reaction, but it reinforces his preconscious assumptions that it's difficult to deal with employees. The next time he thinks about another such visit, his negative preconscious (and conscious) expectations will act to deter him. He will probably use the slightest excuse to convince himself that it's not a priority, such as, "I've got other more important work to do," "It won't work anyway," "That's what I pay supervisors for," and so on.

The key, as we shall see shortly, is *not to think* at all. It's not necessary. All that needs to be done is the action, without any qualifying thoughts. And, because any action must be justified by the leader's preconscious so that his or her self-image is maintained (see Chapter 4), completed actions create self-satisfaction, increasing the likelihood of future similar actions being performed by the leader.

TYPES OF LEADERSHIP ACTION

Every action conducted by anyone with influence in the organization that is observed by someone else is a leadership action (LAct). While this chapter focuses on formal, appointed leaders (i.e., executives, managers, supervisors, and leads), the process applies to anyone who is viewed as having any influence on anyone within the organization (i.e., influential employees, union representatives, etc.). There are no exceptions, because every observed action provides information that is used to support or challenge existing preconscious assumptions. Figure 15.2 classifies and characterizes the different kinds of LActs.

There are three general categories of LAct: leadership touches, spontaneous interactions, and orders. Each of these can be delivered either directly or indirectly. A *direct action* is one in which the leader and each member of the audience could easily be personally involved in the exchange. Due to personality factors, current mood, and so on, an audience member may not feel involved or may not want to be involved, but the group is small enough and the group members close enough to be part of the interaction. An *indirect action* is one in which the audience does not feel personally involved (as when workers watch a leader doing something from a distance). An order is a mandatory instruction to do something. If the order is given in person to one or a few people, it's direct. If it's given by speech to a large group, or by phone, fax, e-mail, memo, and/or posted flyer, and so on, it's an indirect order.

The definitions of the LAct characteristics on the left side of Figure 15.2 are divided into two groups:

- *Transmission mechanics:* The mechanisms by which the action is delivered and received

- *Effectiveness parameters:* The extent to which the action satisfies conditions required to maximally impact the preconscious expectations and assumptions of the recipients

The subcategories of transmission mechanics and effectiveness parameters are described in the following sections.

Characteristics		Leadership touches (LTs)		Spontaneous interactions (SIs)		Orders (Rds)	
		Direct (DLT)	Indirect (ILT)	Direct (DSI)	Indirect (ISI)	Direct (Drd)	Indirect (Ird)
Transmission mechanics	No. of recipients	1 to 10	1 to 25	1 to 10	1 to 25	1 to 25	1 to 1,000
	How presented	Face-to-face	Observation	Face-to-face	Observation	Face-to-face	Any means
	How interpreted	Auditory with nonverbal cues and preconscious	Nonverbal cues and preconscious	Auditory with nonverbal cues and preconscious	Nonverbal cues and preconscious	Auditory with nonverbal cues and preconscious	Preconscious
Effectiveness parameters	Planned	Yes	Maybe	No	No	Maybe	Maybe
	Scheduled	Yes	Maybe	No	No	Maybe	Maybe
	Monitored daily	Yes	Maybe	No	No	Maybe	Maybe
	Consistent	Yes	Maybe	No	No	No	Maybe
	Repeated	Yes	Maybe	No	No	No	No
	Valid	Yes	Maybe	Maybe	Maybe	Maybe	Maybe

Figure 15.2 Types of LActs: leadership touches, spontaneous interactions, and orders.

Transmission Mechanics

Number of recipients: The approximate size of the audience in which the action can be effective and/or performed. It is difficult to have a direct action with more than 10 people because it is hard for people in a bigger group to be close enough to the leader to feel personally involved. A slightly larger group is possible with a direct order because there is usually little two-way communication.

How presented: The manner in which the action is delivered.

How interpreted: The elements in the communication to which the audience is attending. Note that the first element interpreted by the audience is "preconscious": Never forget that the preconscious is the bedrock of an organization's culture and that existing preconscious expectations must be challenged, broken down, and then recast in order to create a world-class culture.

Effectiveness Parameters

Planned: The action is arranged at least a week ahead of time as to type, location, person/audience, and approximate time.

Scheduled: The action to be performed is written down at least a week ahead of time on a chart or a calendar.

Monitored daily: The action and its occurrence or nonoccurrence are recorded on a stoplight chart or checkoff list.

Consistent: The action is done in a more or less standard manner; that is, participants/viewers recognize what the action is and appreciate, perhaps preconsciously, that the action is the same as other past actions.

Repeated: The action is repeated many, many times every day, week, and/or month and more or less indefinitely.

Valid: The action does what it is intended to do to the preconscious expectations of the recipient.

An examination of Figure 15.2 shows that direct leadership touches (DLTs) satisfy all of the effectiveness parameters. If one is compromised, the LAct is not a DLT and will not have the desired effect over time. DLTs are the workhorses of outstanding leadership. They are the actions that are purposely integrated into the daily schedules of leaders.

For example, when a manager regularly visits a work group's weekly continuous improvement (CI) meeting in his or her department and asks a question or two, coaches a bit, and compliments the group on how well it's doing according to a schedule that has been developed ahead of time, the action is a DLT.

An indirect leadership touch (ILT) is planned and scheduled just like a DLT, but it is observed by recipients rather than directly involving them. Since the number and type of observers cannot always be planned, the assessments of the effectiveness characteristics for an ILT are "maybe." That is, some people may see a specific ILT only 5% of the time it is performed in their area, whereas the planned and expected DLT recipients always experience it (i.e., when a leader plans to talk to one of the employees, it doesn't matter which one it is). ILTs are often an extra benefit that accompanies a DLT if there is an observer. For example, if a supervisor performs the DLT of asking an employee to explain a metric on the work group's primary visual display (PVD), any other employees who see it but do not feel personally involved are receiving an ILT.

While not as effective as a DLT on a one-to-one basis, an ILT has significant impact since many more employees may see one compared with the number receiving the same DLT. In some cases, an ILT is performed without an intended, accompanying DLT. This would be the case if a manager planned to visit a department and count the number of files waiting in an outbox to be picked up without planning to directly engage any employees in conversation. This would send a message (after a number of repetitions) that the manager was interested, that the number of files waiting was important to the manager, and that the issue may need some attention. If someone engaged the manager in conversation, the interaction would not be a DLT (because it was not planned) but a direct spontaneous interaction (DSI).

A spontaneous interaction (SI) is just what the name implies: a somewhat random leadership action that does not meet all (or usually, most) of the effectiveness parameters in Figure 15.2. In fact, a well-intended SI done by one leader may very well be a DLT for another. Most self-trained good leaders have learned instinctively that SIs work better when delivered frequently. While the leaders may not consciously be aware of their strategy, they begin to deliver certain SIs so often and so consistently that many of their SIs almost become DLTs. The drawback to many otherwise great SIs is that they are not DLTs (i.e., they are not planned, scheduled, monitored/charted, consistent, repeated, reliable, and valid). As a result, their impact on employees' preconscious expectations is very limited. In fact, as we know from Chapter 4, if a leader does a good thing inconsistently, it actually reinforces negative (to world class) preconscious assumptions that employees have.

Consider the instance in which a leader visits a work group on a whim and makes a positive comment to the workers about how the group's metrics are moving in the right direction. This is a DSI. The first time this is done in a traditional environment, the employees will assume the leader wants something and is softening them up. Thus, the impact of the DSI may actually be negative despite an honest intention. If the DSI does not meet all the conditions of a DLT, it is by definition a DSI. If people see a DSI occurring, it is an indirect spontaneous interaction (ISI) for them. The thought behind a good SI is laudable, but a lone SI is not effective, because it can't change preconscious expectations enough to overcome normal day-to-day negative impacts.

If the same leader visits that work group three times a week for the next four months and engages an employee or a few employees in a discussion concerning their processes (and all of the other effectiveness parameters are met), the actions are a DLT and will begin to change employee perceptions and decision making if other conditions are at least neutral.

Sadly, some traditional leaders are so out of touch with their employees and the existing culture of their organization that their intended DSIs often function as damaging ISIs. This occurs because the existing "me" assumptions of employees blind them to just about anything a leader says or does; the employees appear to be listening, but they will have tuned out the leader after the first few words. Once this occurs, the sound patterns of the leader only serve to reinforce the employees' most negative preconscious "me" assumptions about management (e.g., "Here we go again," "Blah, blah, blah, do they think we're stupid?"). The stereotypical example of this occurs when a leader gives a pep talk to a group of employees about how the latest "flavor of the month" improvement program is vitally important, will change the company, is supported wholeheartedly by management, and so on. Having heard the same type of speech many times in the past without having experienced any subsequent changes taking place, the employees have completely tuned out the leader's DSI.

This should not be construed to imply that leaders should not give pep talks about a new program or randomly visit work groups. They should talk openly and frequently about any important news. They should visit with work groups over and above their DLTs. How else would employees come to believe that leaders were actively supporting the events? It's a fact of organization life that, in a traditionally run organization, the almost automatic first response of employees to management speeches and talks about anything will be "here we go again" at the "me" level. It's up to management to visibly demonstrate support for the new programs and events often enough in speech *and action* over a span of many months in order to begin to break down these reactions.

Orders are a unique type of action; they have to be given to maintain the structure of an enterprise (e.g., "Get together with Zargon Engineering and make the changes" or "You need to complete all the Frobish account paperwork before end-of-month closing" or "Meet with the work stream team and see if they can install daily work group meetings in all work groups in HR by the end of the quarter"). Generally, "run the business" orders do not cause problems unless they are unrealistic (e.g., "On-time delivery has been running at less than 80%; I want 100% on time this month"). Unless there is a magician on staff, that sort of order is viewed as a joke and devalues management in the eyes of employees. The positive or negative impact of orders depends on what else is happening in the organization. If an order is viewed as being generally supportive of good things that are happening, it's just an order and everything is fine. If the order reinforces bad assumptions (as in the on-time example), it will only do harm.

Figure 15.3 graphically displays the relative impact of the various types of LActs on recipients. The thickness of the dark lines leading from "Leadership actions" is intended to show the relative amount of energy that leaders should devote to each of the action types. As might be expected, DLTs and ILTs should get the lion's share of a leader's time. This does not mean that DSIs and the accompanying ISIs should not be extensively used. SIs will still constitute 70%–90% of any good leader's actions with employees because a large part of what leaders do every day is determined by circumstances and daily events. The thickness of the arrow under the DSIs box may be thin, but they are used 3 to 10 times more often than DLTs; DSIs make up in volume what they lack in impact.

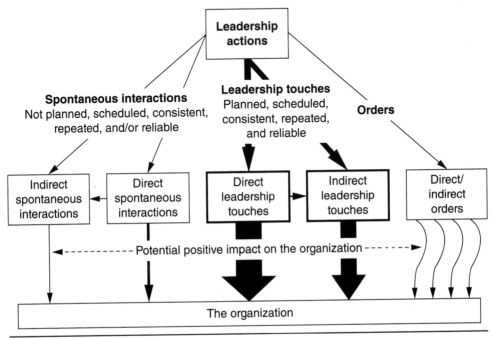

Figure 15.3 The relative impacts of the six types of leadership actions.

Yet, DLTs are still the platinum standard of leadership: The 5%–10% of a leader's actions that are DLTs will generate, as Figure 15.3 shows, a tremendous impact on the organization that is completely out of proportion with the time and energy it takes to perform them. The wavy lines beneath the orders box denotes that their impact, as discussed earlier, varies depending on what else is happening in the organization. The earlier discussion makes it obvious that one of the major limitations of traditional leadership approaches/theory is that LTs and SIs of any kind are hardly ever mandated; leaders do them when and if they are able to and/or in the mood. As a result, very few of them are performed.

IMPLEMENTING ACTION LEADERSHIP

The mechanics of implementing action leadership (AL) are straightforward. The steps are discussed in the following list and reference the flowchart of the process presented in Figure 15.4. This process should be followed if AL is being implemented at a location as part of a formal, recognized change effort that will eventually involve many leaders. Obviously, this won't always be the case. Following the discussion of the formal, larger effort, the particulars of an AL effort for yourself and then your direct reports will be presented.

AL Implementation Steps for a Formal, Sitewide Effort

1. *Meet with the top executive of the site and determine his or her top priorities for (1) everyday work processes, (2) strategic plans, and (3) customer satisfaction.* It's critical to get the support of upper management so that at least two or three actions of each would-be action leader (wbAL) are directly traceable to the concerns of the site's executive staff. While almost any action will support a broad objective such as "improving customer satisfaction" or "cutting costs," be sure that you can draw a straight line from what the top executive wants to some of the wbAL actions. For example, the site leader might state that faster quotes (than the competition) are critical. At least one of each involved wbAL's actions should focus on checking/questioning the status of some part of the quote cycle time and/or being involved with CIEs to improve the process (along with following up on metrics and kaizen target sheet [KTS] progress).

2. *Identify the wbAL candidates.* It's always best to start small and make sure the implementation process is working well before you expand it. Start with four eager, coachable wbALs, get things going for a

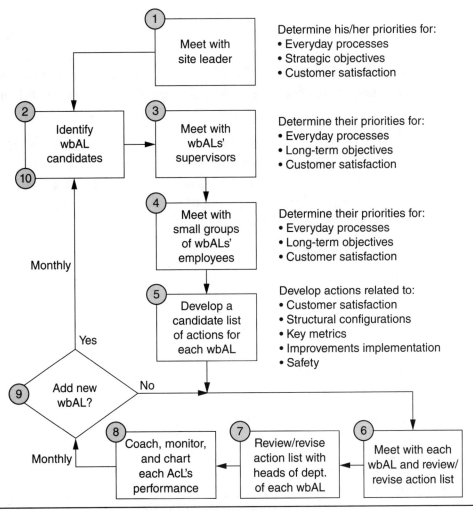

Figure 15.4 The flowchart of AL implementation.

month or so, and then add more wbALs to the initiative if things are going well.

3. *Develop a list of the supervisors of the wbALs and meet with each of them in order to determine his or her top priorities for (1) everyday work processes, (2) long-term goals, and (3) customer satisfaction.* Here, the goal is to make sure that one or two of each wbAL's actions are directly supportive of what his or her boss is worried about. This will ensure that the supervisor will support the effort.

4. *Meet with small groups of employees from the department of each wbAL and determine what sorts of actions the employees require from the wbAL to help them do their jobs better.* Make sure you get approval from the supervisors of the areas to talk with the personnel who work

for each wbAL. You will be talking informally with one or a couple of two- to four-person groups at a time for 5–10 minutes (the number of groups depends on the size of the wbAL's work group). Ask the employees to tell you what their boss could do better or more of in order to help them do a better job. Make sure that at least one of their concerns is included in their boss's (the wbAL) actions.

5. *Develop a candidate list of daily and weekly actions and a planned schedule.* This is called a leadership action matrix (LAM). There is a different LAM for each wbAL based on information provided earlier from the site executive, the department heads, and employees as well as generic actions that deal with the following:

—Daily work group meetings (WGMs)

—PVDs

—Kaizen action sheet system (KASS)

—Work group weekly CI meetings

—Work group Team 21 status and plans

—Customer satisfaction

—CIE status and follow-up

—Attention to and maintenance of metrics

—Focus on safety

As this list of items suggests, there could be as few as 9 actions (one per area) or as many as 27 actions (three per topic) for each wbAL. Some might be scheduled every day, and some might be scheduled two or more times a day if the urgency of the issue is particularly high (such as a visit to a problematic point in a process to check on status). Others might be scheduled one to three times per week.

Figure 15.5 presents a portion of a LAM as it might appear after Thursday's actions have been entered. The figure shows a black-and-white legend, but it could also be shown in color, as color can quickly convey status from a distance (such as circles filled in with green when an action is performed, and red when it is not performed). Making copies of colored figures, however, can be a problem.

The LAM is maintained by the wbAL and updated whenever an action is completed or missed. Ideally, it should be prominently displayed where it can be seen by at least some of the workforce. There will be those in management who contend that it is "embarrassing" for

		Day						
Leader: Leonardo D. Frobish				**Week ending:** July 24, 2010				
Action no.	**Action description**	Sunday	Monday	Tuesday	Wednesday	Thursday	Friday	Saturday
1	Attend daily WGM in acct. rec.	○	✓	○	○	○	◎	○
2	Attend daily WGM in investments	○	○	✓	○	○	○	○
3	Attend daily WGM in acct. pay.	○	○	○	✓	✓	○	○
4	Ask about schedule performance in audit	○	○	✓	○	○	◎	○
5	Visit acct. rec. weekly CI mtg.	○	○	○	○	✓	○	○
6	Visit acct. pay. weekly CI mtg.	○	○	○	✗	○	○	○
7	Examine KAS folders in acct. pay.	○	✗	○	○	○	◎	○
8	Examine KAS folders in acct. rec.	○	○	✓	○	✓	○	○
9	Visit mail room and make positive safety comment	○	✓	○	○	○	◎	○
10	Ask employee about rework in money mgt.	○	○	○	✓	○	○	○
11	Ask employee about key metric in money mgt.	○	○	✓	○	○	◎	○
12	Examine PVD in money mgt.	○	✗	○	○	✓	○	○

○ = Not scheduled   ◎ = Scheduled   ✓ = Performed   ✗ = Not performed

Figure 15.5 An example of a LAM.

leadership performance to be shown publicly. What else is leadership supposed to be doing? Everybody else gets publicly assessed with performance data (i.e., cost, quality, on-time performance, margins, etc.), so there is no reason why the most important element to success should not also be measured and displayed.

6. *Meet with each wbAL and review/discuss/revise the proposed LAM.* This step gets the feedback from the wbAL that enables him or her to craft the LAM to his or her specific situation. The tweaking of the LAM is also important for building ownership of and commitment to the LAM (hands-on involvement builds commitment). It's important not to have all of the LActs in a work group (such as actions 1, 3, 6, and 7 in Figure 15.5) happen on one day. There is a tendency for new wbALs to "bunch up" DLTs in order to save time and visits. This is exactly what must not happen. By spreading out the DLTs to a work group over a week, the impact on preconscious assumptions is kept high. Doing five or six DLTs at one time functions as only one large DLT.

7. *Meet with department heads of each wbAL and review the final version of the LAM.* This step provides an opportunity to build more support with key management personnel and also helps them understand the relationship between their goals and the wbAL's actions. For example, the chief financial officer is the department head of the wbAL whose matrix is shown in Figure 15.5. Action 4 in the matrix is "Ask about schedule performance in audit." This helps the CFO see a direct connection between his or her concerns and a specific hands-on action.

8. *Coach/observe each of the action leaders.* In this step, the wbALs become action leaders (AcLs). Each AcL should be observed and given feedback as he or she performs every action in the first week. This is a lot of trouble (which is why it is recommended that only four wbALs be included in the first wave), but it is essential. It demonstrates to the AcL that each action is important, and it also provides coaching right away before bad habits can start. It is important that the observer or coach be sufficiently skilled and tactful to provide meaningful and timely feedback. After the first week, each AcL should be observed/coached for at least five randomly selected (by the coach) actions each week for the next three weeks. After the first four weeks, the coach should observe at least three actions each week. A key part of the coach's duties is to examine each AcL's LAM at least twice a week to determine whether the AcL is updating his or her LAM right after the actions are done.

At all costs, the tactic of updating the LAM every couple of days must be avoided; there is always a lurking tendency for an AcL to simply check off actions as having been performed even if they weren't after a couple of days have passed. If the LAM cannot be maintained honestly and accurately, the effort will be severely compromised.

As the reader is no doubt thinking, once there are 8–12 or more wbALs and AcLs in the program, the coach will be quite busy. It becomes a full-time job for one person until a number of AcLs have three to four months of solid experience. They can then begin to coach some of the new wbALs. The intent is to eventually have the organization's leaders (at all levels) run the entire program. After all, what better way for a site or department leader to develop his or her personnel than to participate as the coach of his or her own leaders? AL actually creates all the "coaching" that every personnel appraisal system on earth talks about but hardly ever requires.

9. *Add more wbALs or maintain the numbers for another month.* This step questions whether the existing AcLs are performing adequately or whether more wbALs should be added. If more coaching is needed, delay the addition of new wbALs for at least two weeks and conduct additional coaching. It is important to not add wbALs until the current AcLs are performing adequately. If at any time the performance of existing AcLs is not as good as it should be, hold off on adding wbALs and implement remedial coaching for as long as it takes to get things back on track.

Implementing AL for Yourself and/or Your Direct Reports

The process for installing AL for yourself and/or your direct reports is simpler, but you have to do most of the work yourself. The procedure is as follows (using the prior steps as reference points):

1. *Meet with the top executive of the site.* You'll have to determine whether this sort of attention is appropriate. If you're doing AL for yourself, you should probably just get on with it and let the results speak for themselves.

2. *Identify the wbAL candidates.* If it's just you, it's done. If you have several direct reports who will be wbALs, you'll have to decide how many to work with at the same time. It's better to start slow so you can give them all the attention they need. Start with the person whose work group needs the most improvement.

3. *Develop a list of wbAL supervisors and meet with them.* This step is easy—it's you. You should already know what you need from each of the candidate wbALs, but you may not have put it in defined terms. Think about it a bit or, better yet, speak with each wbAL about it.

4. *Meet with small groups of employees from the department of each wbAL.* This is always a good idea and easy to do since you'll only have to do a few groups at most if you start with one or two wbALs.

5. *Develop a candidate list of daily and weekly actions and a planned schedule.* Most of the actions will come directly from the employees and your requirements. Don't forget to include some actions that support the stated requirements of your boss and the top site executive on the wbAL's LAM. This will serve you well if your AL program works well and you are called on to explain how it works. If the wbAL is proactive, you can explain the process ahead of time and have him or her submit a proposed LAM that you can merge with your LAM in the next step.

6. *Meet with each wbAL and review/discuss/revise the proposed LAM.* This works just like before.

7. *Meet with department heads of each AcL and review the final version of the LAM.* It's you, so it's already done.

8. *Coach/observe each of the AcLs.* This step works just as it was explained earlier, except that it's all you. You will have to place actions concerning the daily observing and coaching on your LAM—never, ever miss one!

9. *Add more wbALs or maintain the numbers for another month.* You should be able to add another wbAL each month because you are so close to the coaching. If an AcL is having problems, increase the DLTs and the observation/coaching. Since you'll only have one or two AcLs (if you do as I say), it should be easy to increase the coaching without it consuming too much of your time. Once you have a thoroughly trained AcL, he or she can help you with some of the coaching if you have a number of direct reports. If you have only two to four, it's probably best if you do all the observing and coaching for a while to keep things consistent. If you decide to have someone help with this, be sure to rotate the coach(es) with you so that everyone is involved in all phases of the activity.

16

Transforming a Single Work Group, Section, or Department

The earlier chapters presented the concepts, tools, structural configurations, and building blocks that a leader needs to get started with Office Kaizen. The next three chapters outline how to put all of those elements together in a comprehensive change effort. This chapter presents the procedures for implementing Office Kaizen in (1) a single intact work group (IWG), (2) a section (more than one IWG), and (3) a department (a few to many work groups). Chapters 17 and 18 provide analogous and additional information for transforming a single site and an entire organization (more than one site), respectively. The recommendations in these chapters are based on best practices distilled from dozens of implementations designed and directed by my colleagues and me and from hundreds of other implementations that we have encountered, studied, repaired, been impressed by, and been horrified by as we worked as both external consultants and internal change executives, managers, and champions in many diverse enterprises.

The word *transformation* in the context of this book does not assume or suggest that an IWG, department, or site can be transformed from a state of traditional business practice to a world-class enterprise simply by implementing Office Kaizen. The approaches outlined in Chapters 16–18 will get an organization started, but it is only a start. Much subsequent work and consistent leadership are required to get to sustainable world-class status, or "transformation." It is my hope that the organizations of many readers will ultimately attain such status, but complete transformation takes three to four years at a site, about two years for a department, and a year for an IWG. The hardest part of the journey is not the start—it is the middle. After the excitement has worn off and it's just work, you can't be sure whether you'll make it.

Figure 16.1 shows how Chapters 16–18 are organized. The basic building block of a transformation is the IWG. The IWG is where the hands-on action starts, although it must be planned and led by management at the appropriate

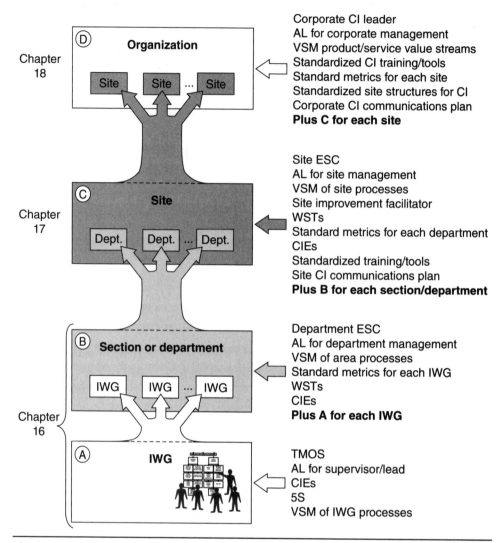

Figure 16.1 Schematic illustrating the organization of Chapters 16–18.

level. Think of the IWG as a brick, a department as a wall, a brick house as a site, and a multisite organization as a neighborhood. The Executive Steering Committee (ESC) is both the architect and the construction superintendent. After the discussion of Figure 16.1, the detailed steps and a schedule for implementation in an IWG are presented.

The IWG is represented at the bottom of the figure by the block labeled with an "A" in the top left corner. The items on the right side list the main elements for transforming a single IWG:

- The Team Metrics and Ownership System (TMOS; Chapter 6).

- Action leadership (AL) for the IWG supervisor/lead (Chapter 15).

- Occasional participation for the IWG members in a continuous improvement event (CIE) involving the IWG personnel/processes.

- A 5S effort within the area (Chapters 12, 13, and 14).

- Value stream mapping (VSMapping) of the IWG processes (Chapters 8, 9, and 10).

The second block from the bottom, labeled "B" (the "brick wall"), illustrates the requirements for transforming a section or department (more than one IWG):

- Implementation of the "A" block items into each individual IWG of the section or department.

- Implementation of a departmental change management team that functions much like a site ESC (see Chapter 6). This "mini ESC" provides a mechanism for the IWG supervisors/leads and the department management to work together to ensure that the work stream teams (WSTs) and CIEs best serve the overall department. This mechanism might not be appropriate for a section with only two or three IWGs, as there might be only one supervisor/lead to compose the mini ESC (although the supervisor or lead is certainly free to confer as much responsibility as he or she wishes to his or her direct reports in planning and conducting IWG activities).

- Implementation of AL for all of the department's management personnel. Many technical managers/specialists in a department don't directly supervise process workers, but they interact with a great many of them each day; they must employ AL in order to assist supervisors in challenging unfavorable preconscious assumptions and reinforcing world-class practices.

- VSMapping of the section or departmental processes that are not adequately dealt with by the VSM the individual IWG would construct.

- Implementation of standard metrics for each IWG.

- Implementation of WSTs to pursue longer-term departmental improvements.

- Implementation of CIEs focused on critical departmental issues.

Block "C" (the "house") illustrates that the transformation of a site (many departments) requires the following:

- Implementation of the "A" items in each IWG.

- Implementation of the "B" block items in each department.

- Establishment of a formal ESC to select, direct, and guide improvements (CIEs and WSTs) that best serve the entire site.

- Implementation of AL for all members of the site management team.

- VSMapping of site processes.

- Selection of a site improvement facilitator manager.

- Implementation of WSTs to address longer-term improvement issues.

- Implementation of standard metrics for each department.

- Implementation of CIEs focused on critical site issues.

- Standardization of a set of CI tools and training.

- Implementation of a site communications plan.

The top block, "D" (the "neighborhood"), displays the transformation requirements of an organization that has more than one site. If the organization has one site, blocks "C" and "D" are equivalent, except for the wording. The transformation of a multisite organization requires the following:

- Implementation of the "A" block items in every IWG in the organization.

- Implementation of the "B" block items in every section and/or department at each site.

- Implementation of the "C" block items at every site.

- Selection of a corporate continuous improvement facilitator (CIF).

- Implementation of AL for corporate management members who visit sites.

- Implementation of global VSMapping of the organization's main product/ service value creation streams.

- Implementation of a corporate standard for CI training/tools.

- Implementation of standard metrics for each site.

- Mandated standardized site structures for CI.

- Development and implementation a corporate CI communications plan.

DETAILED IMPLEMENTATION STEPS AND SCHEDULES

Transforming an IWG

The transformation of a single IWG can be both the easiest change challenge and the most difficult at the same time. It is easy because the manager, supervisor, or lead has only one group to worry about, and typically he or she has a sufficient degree of latitude to modify the group's work environment without having to involve large numbers of people and their requirements. It can be very difficult because there may be little or no support from management. In fact, at first there may be unfavorable observations (e.g., "Who has time to waste on a meeting every day?" "What's the purpose of that board with all the hand-drawn graphs?"). This is because anything that looks different, especially in a traditionally managed organization, presents the threat of change. It's important to make sure that you explain to anyone who asks exactly what you are doing and why. It might not eliminate the initial complaining, but it will help blunt the negative comments until the benefits become apparent.

There are two initial cautions:

1. Do not begin this process unless you will be available for the morning meeting every day for the first week of TMOS (see Chapter 6).

2. Do not begin this process unless you or someone you trust can be present to observe, coach, and/or facilitate the IWG daily meeting every day for two weeks.

Figure 16.2 shows the recommended steps and schedule for implementing Office Kaizen in a single IWG. The following list, whose numbers correspond to the numbers in the figure, provides more details on each step:

1. Carefully read the section on TMOS in Chapter 6.

2. Obtain a temporary visual metrics display (VMD) board (see Chapter 6). This can be a large poster board, a sheet of particleboard, a corkboard, or a whiteboard. I would not spend a lot of money on it at first, because you may not know what you'll eventually want to use. Start low-tech and cheap.

3. Develop an eight-week implementation plan based on this list and your own unique requirements. Read this list first before you do the plan.

4. Develop and post at least one metric on the VMD before the first meeting. Ideally, the metric should be one that can be updated during the day by the work group.

5. Find a place to have the meeting and a place to hang the board. The board should be visible all day in the work area, and the meeting should be a stand-up meeting held in front of the board. If there is no room for the meeting because of narrow walkways, hang the board in the work area and then move it to a nearby office or conference room

No.	Single IWG implementation activity	Week																		
		1	2	3	4	5	6	7	8	9	10	11	12	13	14	15	16	17	18	19
1	Read TMOS section in Chapter 6	█	█	█	█															
2	Obtain a temporary VMD board																			
3	Develop an 8-week implementation plan																			
4	Develop and post at least one metric on the VMD																			
5	Select location for daily WGMs and location of the VMD																			
6	Deal with any flextime issues relative to meeting start time																			
7	Develop a draft topic agenda																			
8	Tell the work group it will have its first meeting tomorrow		█	█																
9	Hold the first daily WGM																			
10	Ask IWG for metric suggestions																			
11	Introduce KASS			█																
12	Introduce RACI chart																			
13	Develop initial LAM				█															
14	Introduce the weekly process improvement meeting					█														
15	Introduce 5S and graph assessment on the VMD						█													
16	Design method and conduct monthly 5S audit							█												
17	Introduce the concept of Team 21 for Office Kaizen								█											
18	Involve IWG in first CIE									█										
19	Introduce the concept of VSMapping										█									
20	Have IWG begin to construct CS-VSM and FS-VSM												█							
21	Do the second iteration of the VSMapping process														Six months →					
22	Introduce skill versatility and track on VMD																			
23	Conduct formal Team 21 audit every four months															█	█			

Figure 16.2 Office Kaizen implementation schedule for a single IWG.

for the meeting. It is important that the board be visible as people move about the work area during the day. *Do not* computerize it; this is a major mistake from which there is no recovery!

6. If flextime is in force, have the meeting when all of the people are typically present. One caution: You must be careful not to allow people to loiter around between the start of their work day and the start of the meeting. In some cases, you may have to move the meeting to midmorning so that people aren't inclined to waste time waiting for the meeting to be conducted before they start their jobs.

7. Develop a draft topic agenda for the meeting. This is simply an ordered list of topics. Write it on a note card and pin it to the VMD so that it can be used by anyone who facilitates the meeting. A draft agenda might be as follows:

   — Any notable changes in the work area (i.e., somebody out for the day, special efforts needing attention, new projects).
   — Review of key metrics' statuses from yesterday.
   — Status of key projects or deliverables (they should be tracked on the VMD).

   Note: The following items won't go on the agenda until the supervisor introduces their content:

   — Mention of RACI (responsible, accountable, consulted, informed) chart (see Chapter 7) responsibilities for metrics updating. This would be left off the agenda until assignments are made.
   — Announcement of new kaizen action sheets (KASs; see Chapter 6) submitted. This would be left off the agenda until week 2.
   — Status of Team 21 improvement plan. This would be left off the agenda until week 4 or 5.

   This draft agenda should be modified as requirements and the VMD evolve. However, always have a current agenda on the VMD so that the meetings stay consistent and organized.

8. Tell the work group about the daily work group meetings (WGMs) and that they will start tomorrow.

9. Hold the first meeting and use your draft agenda. Tell the group that after the first week, anyone who wants to lead the meeting can

volunteer. After the first couple of weeks, the group can decide how to rotate facilitators once a few people have volunteered, tried it, and been coached.

10. In the second meeting, ask the group to submit suggestions (on a special place on the VMD) about other metrics that should be tracked on an hourly, daily, and/or weekly basis.

11. In the second week of the meetings, introduce the kaizen action sheet system (KASS). Hold a 15- to 20-minute meeting in the work area or an office/training room and explain how the KASS works. Have the KAS form already designed and copied and the folders ready to put up after the training. It is important that every time somebody says, "Why don't we . . . ?," "What if . . . ?," "Why can't we . . . ?," and so on, you should tell them, "Fill out a KAS and put it in the submitted folder." Tell them this repeatedly right from the start. Make sure that any new KASs in the submitted folder are announced each day and placed in the "In Process" folder if they are appropriate.

12. By week 3, there should be at least three to five important metrics on the VMD and the facilitator rotation should be established. Introduce the RACI method (see Chapter 7) in a short training session. Have a form already designed and enter the duties for metrics updating and daily meeting facilitation. Add any other important duties to the RACI chart if there are responsibilities that change from day to day or week to week. Unless there are some performance issues or confusion about normal process responsibilities, you don't want to put work duties on this RACI chart. There is nothing wrong with putting work tasks on another RACI chart that would be functioning as a skill versatility matrix. If duties change each day depending on the work content, you could use a simple check-off chart to assign work. This is basically just like a RACI but with a check mark instead of an *R*, *A*, *C*, or *I*.

13. Prior to week 4, develop your initial leadership action matrix (LAM; see Figure 15.5 from Chapter 15). You'll want to include checking metrics maintenance by the group, KAS monitoring, visits to key process points to find out what's going on, and so on. As each new concept is added in the following weeks, modify your LAM to incorporate checks of new configurations and methods.

14. In week 4, introduce the concept of the weekly process improvement meeting of 30–60 minutes. There should be enough submitted KASs

to provide focus for improvement activities. If the nature of the work requires that somebody answer phones, rotate that person each week and then update him or her on what was covered in the meeting.

15. In week 5, introduce 5S. Develop a simple 5S rating sheet in advance and have the work group assess itself and work on some improvement issues. Always insist that the group use KASs for suggestions before it changes anything; this gets the group in the habit of using the KAS for all changes.

16. In week 5, design a 5S audit process and conduct a 5S audit each month. Post the ratings on a graph on the VMD with your comments. It's okay to eventually assign the duties to a rotating pair of IWG employees, but wait at least four months. If you do it earlier, there is a risk that they will be peer-pressured into being too lenient in the audit.

17. In week 6, introduce the concept of Team 21 for Office Kaizen (see Chapter 6) in a short training session. The appendix presents the detailed T-metric descriptions and a chart. Have the generic version already copied and blank rating forms available. Set a four-year goal (70 points is a good level). Ask each work group member to rate the work group separately, and then have everybody post their ratings on a Team 21 graph on a whiteboard or brown paper. Discuss the discrepancies and come to an agreement as to the score of each T-metric. Have the team select the first T-metric it will attack, and use the weekly meeting to work on an action plan. At this point, there should be 5S, Team 21, and KAS issues to work on in the weekly meeting. If you have enough people and they have the time, you can also have one or two mini work stream teams (m-WSTs) in the area where two or three people spend a few hours a week focusing on something that they work on over a period of four to six weeks.

18. In week 8, try to have a CIE in the work area or at least have some of the work group members in a CIE elsewhere at the site. If there are none, confer with some of your colleagues and try to get one sponsored that can be composed of some of your people and some from other areas.

19. In week 10, introduce the concept of VSMapping. It's best to have a number of 15-minute training sessions three or four times a week for two weeks. Each session would present a small piece of the VSMapping procedure. Reserve the weekly improvement meeting for working on

improvements rather than training. Select a key IWG process to use as the teaching example and the first VSMapping effort. Leave the teaching example posted between training sessions so that people see it during the day (to build preconscious focus).

20. Starting in week 12, after two weeks of short training sessions, have the group work on its VSM for 15–30 minutes each day and/or have a couple of people work on it for an hour or so a couple of times per week and then rotate others in. It shouldn't take more than two to three weeks for the work group to finish the current state VSM (CS-VSM) unless it is very complex. Once it is done, use a weekly improvement meeting for the team to recommend improvements (always use KASs), and then use the same approach for constructing the future state VSM (FS-VSM). The FS-VSM should generate lots of additional KASs to work on.

21. After most of the first FS-VSM is implemented (probably about six months), start on another CS-VSM and do it all over again. Once the group is experienced, depending on the amount of time they can spare from their normal work, it should be possible to do another VSM every six months or so (assuming it takes that much time to implement the improvements).

22. After four months, introduce the skill versatility concept and begin to track and display the task coverage using a RACI chart on the VMD.

23. Develop and conduct a formal Team 21 audit every four months and post your scores on the VMD. Discuss with the group at the weekly meeting.

Transforming a Section or a Department

A section or a department can be more than just a collection of IWGs; there are often technicians, managers, and processes that exist outside the constituent IWG but in the orbit of the section or department. In Figure 16.1, these "extra" elements would exist within the "B" box but outside the IWG boxes. For the purposes of this chapter, a *section* is defined as more than one work group that does not have any of the extra processes and personnel of a typical department. A *department* is defined as a part of the organization that has a collection of IWGs plus additional processes and people who are not doing the day-to-day work that occurs in the IWG. As an example of a section, consider a recent banking client of mine that had one supervisor directing three work groups at the processing center. There were no other people other than the supervisor and the three groups of five, seven, and four people. There were no other processes other than those that the three groups worked on individually.

The department in which this section resided had 16 IWGs and four supervisors. Basically, this department appeared to be a section, albeit large. However, the department also had a quality control manager, a quality control technician, an IT programmer, and three assistant VPs who had no supervisory duties but performed a number of cross-departmental technical processes. These "extra" people and their processes make that area a department for our purposes and require some additional Office Kaizen implementation steps if you wish to get maximum benefits. Of course, you can always simply implement IWG structures and omit any additional "department" structures.

The transformation of the 16 IWGs simply required that the elements of box "A" in Figure 16.1 be implemented in each one. The only consideration making the task slightly more complex than the transformation of one IWG was the necessity of conducting concurrent activities among some of the IWGs. If you have strong supervisors and ample time of your own to coach and observe, you could try to have each supervisor do one IWG each week. I would not recommend this tactic, however, as it leaves little maneuvering room if workloads increase or a special project arrives. An effective approach that reduces the workload caused by multiple IWGs with only limited leadership time is to offset the implementation by one to several weeks for each IWG. This adds time to the total implementation effort (which is of little consequence a year later) but compensates by allowing the implementer and the supervisor to learn lessons from each successive implementation that enable them to do a better job with the next IWG implementation. A major consideration of the offset interval is the personal workload of the supervisor and the amount of support he or she can depend on from senior workers in the various IWGs.

The steps presented in this section are for implementing Office Kaizen in a department. Figure 16.3 presents the steps in chart format, using the same step numbers as those in the narrative descriptions. Activities involving the implementation of TMOS, metrics, VSMapping, and so forth, into a single IWG are summarized on one line that represents the 16-week cycle shown for an IWG in Figure 16.2. In the steps, several WSTs (see Chapter 6) are formed to execute portions of the department's Office Kaizen implementation. In smaller departments, there may not be sufficient personnel to form WSTs and/or form them within the recommended schedule. In that case, the department manager may have to assume a larger share of the burden and stretch out the schedule. In a limited-resource situation, it is essential to quickly involve

No.	Department activity	1	2	3	4	5	6	7	8	9	10	11	12	13	14	15	16	17	18	19	20	21	22	23	24
1	Read TMOS, ESC, and WST sections in Chapter 6	█																							
2	Determine d-ESC membership																								
3	Meet with d-ESC; inform them of your plans and assign reading (1)		█	█																					
4	Meet with d-ESC and discuss the readings																								
5	d-ESC members introduce readings to their mgrs., sups., leads			█	█																				
6	Determine d-ESC weekly meeting time and general agenda																								
7	d-ESC develops departmental implementation schedule				█																				
8	d-ESC develops most critical issues and metrics				█	█																			
9	Implement TMOS in 1st IWG (see Figure 16.2)						█	█	█	█	█	█	█1	█	█	█	█	█	█	█	█	█			
10	Introduce the concept of AL to the d-ESC in a training session						█	█																	
11	Work with the d-ESC to develop AL audit system for the dept.							█	█																
12	Formal training session (AL, RACI, 5S, etc.)								█	█															
13	Launch WST to develop weekly proc. imp. mtg. procedures								█	█															
14	Launch WST to design and implement Gemba Wall								█	█															
15	Implement TMOS in 2nd IWG														█	█2	█	█	█	█	█	█	█	█	
16	Have d-ESC members each develop and implement his/her LAM																								

Figure 16.3 Office Kaizen implementation schedule for a department.

No.	Department activity	Week
17	Implement audit system for AL (developed in step 11)	
18	Implement TMOS in 3rd IWG	weeks 8–22, milestone 3 at week 15, → 24
19	Form/launch WST to plan and coach CIE	weeks 9–10
20	WST (step 13) implements wkly. mtgs. in IWG	milestones 1 (wk 10), 2 (wk 12), 3 (wk 14), 4 (wk 16), 5 (wk 18), 6 (wk 20), 7 (wk 22), → 24
21	Train all department leadership in AL concepts and tracking	
22	Each department leader develops/implements his/her LAM	
23	Implement TMOS in 4th IWG	weeks 11–22, milestone 4 at week 16, → 24
24	Formal training session in Team 21 for all leaders	
25	Launch WST to develop Team 21 implementation plan	weeks 12–15
26	Implement TMOS in 5th IWG	weeks 13–22, milestone 5 at week 17, → 24
27	Formal training session to introduce VSM to dept. leaders	week 14
28	Conduct first department CIE	
29	Implement TMOS in 6th IWG	weeks 15–22, milestone 6 at week 18, → 24
30	Form WST to develop/launch dept. 5S program	week 16
31	Launch the 6th IWG	milestone 7 at week 19, weeks 16–22, → 24
32	Launch the departmental 5S program	weeks 17–22, → 24
33	Conduct the 2nd department CIE	week 20
34	Launch WST to develop/implement skill versatility program	weeks 21–22, → 24

Figure 16.3 Office Kaizen implementation schedule for a department. (Continued)

a couple of supervisors or leads or sharp, eager, hands-on process workers as helpers. They almost always rise to the occasion and are able to lift much of the detail burden from the shoulders of the department manager. They learn things faster and take greater ownership as a result of their involvement. However, the department manager must always maintain a highly visible hands-on profile in all facets of the implementation.

It is important not to consider the steps as representing a rigid, one-size-fits-all implementation plan. No two implementations, even of an IWG in the same department, are the same. The main intent of the steps is to serve as food for thought and "check-off" suggestions (i.e., "Did we consider if or when to do step 7?") for your own departmental Office Kaizen implementation plans. While the content of the steps is world-class best practice, the sequence of some of the tool and method implementations can easily be modified. For example, you may decide to do a CIE in the first couple of weeks of your Office Kaizen effort. I have done that many times myself. However, if the transformation you are considering is your first significant one, don't deviate too much from the sequence suggested in this chapter without good cause. As long as you think carefully as you plan and do not attempt to move too quickly, things will work out nicely.

One further observation is important. The steps are developed with a consultant's perspective. That is, while careful planning is critical, clients want results (cultural and bottom line) fast. This is true whether they say so or not. A department manager implementing Office Kaizen has several customers: his or her employees, direct reports, and site management. Whether these customers say anything is not important; the customers have expectations in the form of strong preconscious assumptions that must be dealt with. The employees want to be involved and do a good job but preconsciously expect it to be the same old "flavor of the month" failure. Supervisors want to be real leaders who get to create effective work groups they can be proud of, but preconsciously they don't expect it to happen. Once site management discovers what you are doing, the clock starts ticking; they want results quickly without worry but expect the effort to turn into another failed "all talk and no action" endeavor.

Do not fall prey to the all-too-common in-house change management disease of taking too long to do things because you are afraid of pushing too hard. Don't rush needlessly, but don't dawdle. Everyone is expecting it to fail, and every delay, pause, or slow-up supports their worst preconscious expectations and they'll begin to tune out. Think like a consultant and worry all the time whether you're moving fast enough; keep the fastest pedal to the metal that you can semi-comfortably control. If you ever feel really comfortable in the first year or so, you are probably moving too slow. If you feel like your head is going to explode, slow down a bit.

Following are the steps for installing Office Kaizen in a department:

1. Before you say anything to anyone in the department, carefully reread the sections on TMOS, the ESC, and WSTs in Chapter 6. If there is not enough information, obtain a copy of *Office Kaizen 1 (OK1)* and read its more detailed discussions of these issues.

2. Determine who will be the members of the departmental mini-ESC (d-ESC). If there are fewer than eight or so managers, supervisors, or senior technical people, it is a good idea if they are all on the d-ESC, unless there are significant contraindications (more than eight or nine just won't work). If the department is large and there are more than eight such people, the d-ESC members should be selected from among those who are responsible for the greatest number of people and those whose decisions and concerns most impact the department. If it is necessary to assuage the potentially hurt feelings of some who may not be selected, consider a structure such as the one used by the United Nations Security Council, in which there are permanent members and a number of defined-term rotating members.

3. Meet with the selected d-ESC members and explain what you are doing. At the same time, send out an e-mail or memo to the department (or have an all-hands meeting followed by an e-mail or memo) to explain the situation in general. Assign the d-ESC members the task of reading the sections on TMOS, the ESC, and WSTs in Chapter 6.

4. Meet with d-ESC members and discuss the Chapter 6 material.

5. Assign the d-ESC members the task of introducing the Chapter 6 information discussed in step 4 to their supervisors, leads, and technical personnel. Make sure someone is assigned to introduce the materials to the few in the department who may not report to a d-ESC member. Many of these people may have to do observations and coaching in the next few months.

6. Determine a d-ESC meeting time (the same each week) and establish an agenda for each meeting. Remember, the purpose of the d-ESC is only to establish, coach, and track improvement activities—not to conduct "normal," non-change-related department business. Make sure that the d-ESC meeting is not an extension of the department management meeting and that, ideally, it is not held on the same day.

7. Work with the members of the d-ESC and develop a departmental Office Kaizen implementation schedule. Work with a sense of urgency, but do not create an overly aggressive initial schedule. You can always speed things up later, but it is much more difficult to fix mistakes that were made because you tried to move too fast. It could take several meetings to work out the schedule, as the d-ESC members will need a lot of coaching and discussion. Figure 16.3 should provide a good general starting point. The schedule must include:

— A schedule of TMOS implementation. Be sure to allow at least a week or two between each IWG TMOS installation. The most critical work groups will be those that have the largest performance problems and/or challenges. If there is a reason to expect great amounts of resistance due to union issues (e.g., "It's not our job to solve problems") or to expect meddling constituencies from other functions (e.g., finance worrying about labor charge codes for meeting time, HR concerned about any complaints), it is wise to select an initial IWG or two that will likely be easy to work with. The TMOS schedule will include sequence, timing, and identification of coaches and observers (at least for the first couple of IWGs).

— Development of a priority listing of the department's most critical issues that require attention. This will be used to guide CIEs and WSTs.

— A schedule for at least the first two CIEs and the specification of frequency for conducting CIEs (e.g., one every six weeks).

— A schedule for the development of departmental metrics and a consistent set of metrics for the IWG.

— A schedule for conducting VSMapping of departmental processes as well as a schedule that guides the IWG in mapping its processes.

— A schedule for implementing AL for departmental management.

Note: The following steps provide a schedule that sequences the earlier items. You can make any changes you wish (how would I know, and what could I do about it, anyway?), but I would advise you to stick to the general recommendations unless there are serious contraindications. After all, these are best practices.

8. Determine the department's most critical issues and metrics that assess them at both the department and IWG levels. The department leader

should lead the discussion with the d-ESC and serve as the mentor, coach, and tiebreaker. The metrics for the IWG will be installed into each IWG as TMOS is implemented. While some of these IWG metrics may change, it is important to pick a few that will apply across most IWGs so that each group will have a good starting point from which to start focusing on metrics that assess their performance. Good candidates are the following: total start-to-finish time (cycle time plus lead time; see Chapter 8) of a key process, first-time quality levels of a key process, percentage of "pieces" of work left undone at the end of each day, and percentage of workers cross-trained in at least four other tasks.

9. Begin implementation of TMOS in first IWG in the beginning of week 5. Perform steps 2, 4–13, and 15–23 in Figure 16.2 (and as detailed earlier in this chapter). Assuming adequate resources, the department should be able to launch a new IWG every two to three weeks. You will be tempted to consider one every week, but there is not much of an upside in moving faster; it's far better to do it absolutely right with lots of opportunity for department personnel to observe and learn than to risk missteps and the publicity they create. In a very large department (over 150 people), it may be necessary to establish a WST to do the TMOS implementations. A WST would free up the d-ESC members for other implementation duties and enable faster implementation of TMOS. It is still important that the d-ESC members have a lot of visibility in the process by visiting daily meetings (this type of activity is incorporated into the action leadership [AL] process described in the next step).

10. In week 6, introduce the concept of AL to the d-ESC. Do this in a formal training session so the importance of AL will be apparent.

11. Also in week 6, work with the d-ESC to develop an audit process for coaching, monitoring, and tracking AL activities. AL and auditing will start with the d-ESC in week 8 but will then be introduced to all of the leaders (supervisors, technical experts, leads, managers, and so on).

12. Hold a formal training session with the d-ESC, all managers, significant others, and the supervisors/leads of the first five IWG teams. The session should cover RACI charts (so that the auditing of various LAM and IWG daily meetings and metrics can be easily assigned and charted), 5S, weekly process improvement meetings, WSTs, and CIEs.

13. The d-ESC assigns a champion (from the d-ESC) and selects a team leader to develop procedures and resources for weekly process improvement meetings for each IWG. The team leader should select three or four people from the department (hands-on process workers) to develop the plan (a charter) and bring it back to the d-ESC for approval. The charter must deal with meeting locations, who will coach/facilitate the first four to six meetings, schedules of rooms and coaches, and equipment (i.e., meeting supplies, signing supplies, access to flip charts, projectors) for each IWG. This will be good practice for the d-ESC in directing and coaching the WST. The WST should be able to develop the plan and get d-ESC agreement in three weeks. The meetings won't be implemented until week 8. This same team will be responsible for arranging the implementation of weekly process improvement meetings in IWGs that have yet to be implemented, so it will have to remain active until all IWGs have weekly meetings up and running. If the department is very large, see step 19 in Chapter 17 about scheduling rooms for the meetings.

14. The same formation procedure as step 13, but the WST will design and set up an initial Gemba Wall (see Chapter 6) so that all of the work going on can be charted. In a small department, this can be done by the department manager, although it is always better to involve others in a WST reporting to the d-ESC if possible.

15. In week 7, implement TMOS in the second IWG.

16. In weeks 8 and 9, have each d-ESC member develop and implement a LAM. The d-ESC should review each one of these as a group to maintain a high level of quality, consistency, and coverage.

17. At the same time (weeks 8 and 9) the AL audit system developed in step 11 should be implemented. It is very important that all of the d-ESC members participate as auditors so that they get the experience they will need in order to train and coach other personnel in the department who will be launching their LAM in a couple of weeks. Do not assign auditors in pairs to do each other's audit. This often evolves in a preconscious "easy scoring of each other" strategy. A d-ESC member should never audit someone who audits him or her. Have a department leader who is not yet involved in AL accompany each auditor a few times to see how things work. Not only will this prepare them and get them thinking, it will demonstrate that AL is not just for lower-level management but for every leader in the department.

18. In week 9, implement TMOS for the third IWG.

19. Also in week 9, the d-ESC assigns a champion (from the d-ESC) and selects a team leader to develop procedures and resources to plan, coach, and support departmental CIEs. The team leader should select three or four people from the department (hands-on process workers) to develop the plan (a charter) and bring it back to the d-ESC for approval. The charter must deal with providing a facilitator/coach for each event, selecting and prioritizing issues to address, selecting CIE participants, maintaining open action items (see Chapter 14), and arranging for facilities and equipment (i.e., room reservations, meeting supplies, signing supplies, access to flip charts, projectors) for each CIE. The d-ESC and each team member should read Chapters 12–14 carefully before beginning work with the team. This team must also implement actions to ensure that the facilitators of the upcoming CIE (in week 14) are sufficiently skilled in general tools (see Chapter 7) and in VSMapping techniques (see Chapters 8–10). Some practice work on the processes of one or two IWGs should serve to give them the background they need.

20. In week 10, the WST formed in step 13 implements weekly process improvement meetings for established IWGs and upcoming IWGs.

21. In week 11, hold a formal training session and introduce AL to all departmental leaders not yet involved in it.

22. In weeks 11–13, the d-ESC members should work with each leader to develop and implement AL (including observation, coaching, and tracking as developed in step 11).

23. In week 11, implement TMOS in the fourth IWG.

24. In week 12, hold a formal training session to introduce Team 21 to all leaders. Prior to the training, assign appropriate portions of Chapter 6 and all of the appendix as a reading assignment.

25. In week 12, the d-ESC members must form a WST to plan the introduction, initial scoring, and ongoing auditing of Team 21 to already-formed IWGs and IWGs not yet formed. The plan must include the following:

    — How the concept of Team 21 will be introduced.

    — Having each IWG rate itself and who will facilitate the sessions.

— Standards for the forms for the Team 21 graph and the monthly improvement plans.

— Trial ratings from random employees in various IWGs to determine if any T-metrics need to be dropped, added, or modified to fit specific conditions. This team should be able to complete its work during weeks 12–15.

— Audit systems (including who, how, and how often) for conducting twice yearly or quarterly audits of IWG Team 21 scores and progress in implementing improvement plans.

26. In week 13, introduce TMOS to the fifth IWG.

27. In week 13, hold a formal training session to introduce departmental leaders not involved in the step 12 training efforts to the general concepts of VSMapping. This need not be a detailed how-to, as each leader will eventually be part of a VSMapping effort on a WST or a CIE and learn the mechanics. This training session is to familiarize them with the purpose and general approach of VSMapping and what to look for in a VSM.

28. In week 14, conduct the first departmental CIE. Have the WST (step 19) invite site management to attend the kickoff meeting, daily end-of-day briefings, and end-of-week final report-out. Often, the first CIE is an intensive VSMapping (current state, future state, and improvement plan) of a critical process. If this analysis can't wait and you want to get started earlier, you can do the CIE earlier or have a WST do the VSM over a period of a few weeks by working on it two or three hours a day. In most organizations, VSMapping, 5S, analyses, and process improvements are conducted by a blend of CIEs, WSTs, and scrambles. It's up to you to determine what works best in your department.

29. In week 15, implement TMOS in the sixth IWG.

30. In week 15, form a WST to plan, develop, and implement a departmental 5S approach and process in all formed IWGs and those that will be formed in the future. The d-ESC should instruct the champion to select the team leader and team members from any IWGs that have implemented their own 5S systems. The plan must include the following:

— A rating system with specific definitions of each level of each "S"

— A visual scoring format (see Figure 7.13) for the VMD of each IWG

— Trial assessments of the proposed rating system to see how well the scoring format can be understood and used consistently by auditors

— A weekly auditing process within each IWG by its own members

— A monthly auditing process by a cross-functional departmental team of hands-on workers (two or three people) that rotates membership by one person or so every couple of months

— A twice-yearly auditing process by a departmental management team to provide a higher level of praise and motivation than the monthly audits and to also get department management more involved

— Integration of the 5S items needing attention into the daily meeting agenda

This team should be able to have a system ready to go in four to six weeks. The biggest challenge is coming up with a system that is easy to use and reasonably consistent across different auditors. Don't try for perfection. Human ratings of subjective conditions are fraught with variance. Just get something that works okay and rely on the discussions between the auditors to make it work.

31. In week 17, launch the seventh IWG.

32. In week 19, launch the departmental 5S program (developed in step 30).

33. In week 20, conduct the second departmental CIE.

34. In week 21, the d-ESC should form a WST to develop and launch a skill versatility/cross-training program for the department (see Chapter 7). This is always a long-term, complex, and difficult assignment. It has been deliberately delayed until this point so that department management and workers will have developed a more integrated and nuanced appreciation of the tasks they perform. Their insights from CIEs, WSTs, TMOS, and so on will provide them with critical insights supporting the importance of skill versatility and the criticality of well-controlled tasks and balanced work flows. This WST could require six months to a year to complete this task in a department with 10–20 IWGs. It could take longer if the work is conceptual.

    In some cases where the work is highly conceptual and the job skills require specialized education and experience, the feasibility of implementing a full-scale cross-training program is very low. For example, in an engineering department with graduate-school-trained electrical, mechanical, and software engineers, it would not usually be cost-effective or even possible to transfer technical skills. These sorts of determinations and the omission of such areas/personnel should be made by the d-ESC before this WST team is formed.

Do not try to rush the work or the skill versatility analysis. If possible, gradually rotate a new person onto the team every eight weeks or so to keep things fresh. The team will have to:

— Define the tasks that will be tracked in each IWG and within the department but outside the IWG. This requires that each person's daily work be "chunked" into tasks. For example, an HR recruiter doesn't "recruit": He or she develops requisitions, determines salary and grade levels for a position, schedules interviews, conducts background checks, checks references, places ads, works with executive recruiters in various ways, prepares offers, and so on.

— Develop a method to help each employee and his or her supervisor with the "chunking" of each job. A good approach is to begin by having each employee maintain an informal day-in-the-life-of (DILO; see Chapter 7) log for a few weeks. Another method is to have the employee construct a simple VSM (with just the activity boxes; time is not important for this purpose) to see where a specific task ends and could be handed off (see Chapter 8).

— Develop a final list of tasks for each employee that will be included on the skill versatility matrix and targeted for cross-training.

— Develop standard work for each task—that is, how the task is done now (or how it should be done if it is done incorrectly). Don't get wrapped around the axle with trying to dramatically improve how tasks are done. It is enough to document how a decent level of task performance is currently achieved. This standard work will be used to assess the level of skill versatility that currently exists and to specify the cross-training a person needs in order to attain more versatility in the task.

— Develop a rating format such as one to four, with one representing no mastery and four representing "can do the job as well as a highly trained, experienced worker" or some other scheme.

— Work with the employee and his or her supervisor to assess the level of current skills.

— Determine what tasks are most critical for the improved performance of the IWG/department.

— Implement a training approach (e.g., the number of cross-training hours to be dedicated each week in each group, task priority) for each IWG and other department personnel.

— Develop a visual display of the skill versatility status that can be used on each IWG VMD and on one or more VMDs for non-IWG employees.

This WST faces a very difficult task. There is a great deal of coordination required with the involved supervisors and employees and possibly human resources. If a union is involved, it will have to be included right from the start. The champion, team leader, and team members must be eager, focused, high-energy, "won't take no for an answer" people. The team must get plenty of support and occasional hands-on help from the d-ESC members so that everyone appreciates the importance of the work.

At about this point (or earlier) in the Office Kaizen implementation, the d-ESC or the department manager and his or her key people will probably have begun to put their unique ideas and schedule into practice. New WSTs and additional, regular CIEs will take place, and the department will continue to improve and evolve.

17

Transforming a Site

Taking an organization from traditional practices to a sustainable world-class operation is the ultimate quest of a transformation. Once a site has traveled successfully along the path of world-class practices, there is an opportunity to create a long-term miracle that defies human nature and typical business practice. This miracle is the creation of an organization that produces outstanding products or services over many years because it is founded on the belief that harnessing the best efforts of an engaged and focused workforce using the best tools known is the most important objective of leadership. This miracle can't occur in an independent work group (IWG) or a department, and it can't start from the spark that an IWG or department might provide to a site.

An IWG or department can be outstanding or even the best in the world, but that won't create a site-sized miracle. In 99.999% of organizations, such demonstrations of excellence do not lead other IWG, department, or site executives to even attempt to replicate the excellence right before their eyes—not only can't they see the forest for the trees, they think the trees are rocks. The earlier chapters of this book make it clear how and why this happens—human nature is not designed to operate complex processes efficiently in organizations of any size, especially large ones (finding food, having sex, raising children, sleeping, and avoiding predators are not complex technological tasks).

So, while it makes perfect sense for a manager or supervisor to strive to create a world-class IWG or department in order to produce great results, improve the lives of the employees, and make his or her job easier and more satisfying, such efforts are doomed to be nothing more than small oases of fleeting, cool, refreshing excellence in an endless, arid, sandstorm-whipped desert of business-as-usual. And, sad to say, all such oases are always only temporary; all too soon they are swallowed by the desert of a traditional organization because the oasis creators get beaten down, leave for another job, or get moved to another position. Every drop of their excellence is then sucked back into the desiccating abyss of the organizational desert. If you want to create something special and lasting, your only hope is to transform a site.

A site has a much greater chance of creating and sustaining excellence because of the very same organization dynamics that doom IWGs and departments: the power of a somewhat isolated culture to sustain itself. As earlier chapters discussed, preconscious assumptions sustain themselves. Bad sustains bad. However, if a site as a whole can implement a transformation that is initially successful and sustain it for a while, there is a chance that the same dynamics that sustain bad can be turned to support the good. The tipping point is difficult to get to and the odds of such success are always slim, given human nature, but it can and does once in a great while with strong enough leadership.

For our purposes, a site is defined as a stand-alone operation that has most of the people and resources necessary to produce products or services for its customers. The most common hallmark of a site is that it is a single location to which its employees feel as if they belong. In that humans are territorial and place-oriented, this feeling of belonging is the single best indication of whether an operation or a building is a site. In the manufacturing world, the most common site is a factory with supporting engineering, plant services, human resources, finance, logistics, purchasing, and so on. In the Office Kaizen world, common sites would be insurance administration centers, bank processing operations, large retail stores (i.e., department stores), research centers, hospitals, large law firms, money management/investment firms, order processing centers, large customer service operations, and invoice/billing operations.

Before moving on, it will be helpful to reexamine Figure 16.1 in the last chapter and the related discussion before going further in this chapter.

There are some basic, hard truths about site transformation:

- While the transformation effort will eventually make life easier and more satisfying for everyone, the first six months may require extraordinary levels of effort from the site management team. They will have to do their regular jobs and many, many hours of extra work for the Executive Steering Committee (ESC) each week for months to come. If the site is already familiar with and using continuous improvement tools and processes, the ESC's work will be somewhat easier. However, the willingness of the management team to do this work and the ability and willingness of the site leader to compel the management team to do this work is the first litmus test of whether the transformation might succeed. The instant that the site leader or leadership team blinks in the face of the challenge, the transformation is on the verge of failure. Two blinks and it's gone.

- If the site leader is not 100% eager, enthusiastic, and supportive in word and action for the transformation, it won't work. It doesn't matter how devoted others are; if the leader is not seen by employees to be involved at all times, it can't work.

- If the leader of the site does not understand the content and the implications of the earlier chapters of this book, it won't work. A lot of really smart, hard-working site leaders fail at transformation efforts and even fail to get a reasonably successful "flavor of the month" initiative launched because they do not understand the dynamics of culture change and the impact of leadership actions.

- Site transformation success has almost nothing to do with training. As the earlier chapters show, the central challenge of change is the modification of preconscious assumptions and expectations. Training by itself, even if it is very good, applied, on-the-job, in-the-trenches training, is not capable of getting it done. Training can be a great help, but it's not leadership. Transformation starts, operates, and ends with leadership.

- A site transformation can't be led by a "change specialist" or a consultant— it must be led by the leader and his or her direct reports. If the site leader tries to hand it off so he or she "can focus on the real work," the change effort is doomed from the start. As Chapter 1 explained, every entity in a successfully adapting system must go through the stage of chaos in order to try to move to a new state of reintegration and then equilibrium. If the leader is not roiling around in the chaos with everyone else, discovering and adjusting to the millions of interactions in real time, he or she cannot be a meaningful part of the system. If the site leader is not in the mix in real time, he or she isn't leading the transformation, and every single entity will know it and respond with the standard preconscious assumptions of employees in traditionally managed organizations.

- A site transformation requires practical, hands-on, experienced consulting/coaching/mentoring support. While consultants cannot, by definition, stand in for the site leader or the leadership team, there are few site leaders and/or leadership teams that have or can quickly develop the applied experience and skills to get everything done at the pace that is required once a transformation starts. Without an experienced consultant, there will be too many delays, poorly planned actions, misguided decisions, dead ends, and failed follow-ups. A highly experienced consultant provides the following support that enables an Office Kaizen transformation to move with a sense of confident urgency:

— *Most important:* Provide the site leader and the ESC with candid, truthful feedback on what is happening, what needs to happen, and what needs to be changed. All too often because of status levels, fear, and innate primate social hierarchies, the employees of the organization are reluctant to be candid and frank with those in authority. Such reticence allows problems to continue and cause damage to the transformation. Coaching and feedback shouldn't be mean-spirited, but they must be candid and to the point.

— *Very important:* Provide the site leader and individuals on the ESC with team and individual coaching to improve their daily leadership of the transformation, their championing activities with work stream teams (WSTs), and their action leadership (AL) activities.

— *Very important:* Coach and mentor the site improvement facilitator (SIF). The SIF will eventually replace the consultant, so he or she must get intensive daily coaching, hands-on training, and constant mentoring in how to be the expert in all things transformational, from tools to coaching ESC members. While few SIFs will develop the extensive skills and breadth of experience of a consultant (without additional, follow-on experiences should they leave the organization), they don't have to be expert in many organizations; the SIF only has to be expert in coaching and guiding change in his or her current organization.

— Coach the ESC in meetings and Office Kaizen implementation until the ESC and significant others are performing smoothly.

— Help develop and vet the implementation plan.

— Determine which tools and which methods of training are needed and when they should be provided to support various stages of the implementation plan.

— Provide the trainer with tools and methods training. This is especially important in regard to value stream mapping (VSMapping) because a great deal of existing Office Kaizen VSMapping training is poorly adapted factory VSMapping.

— Help develop the continuous improvement event (CIE) planning, execution, and follow-up process; coach the first couple of CIEs; and train/coach the personnel who will take over the CIE process.

— Help develop the processes and approaches for WST planning, operations, and coaching.

— Help develop and coach the AL implementation and provide train-the-trainer coaching for ESC members and other management so that they can support all of the elements given here.

Frequently, site or corporate management will try to save money by not bringing in expert help and/or not hiring or appointing an exceptional SIF. This is not the place to try to save a little money; every dollar that a site thinks it is saving by not bringing in a consultant or a top-notch SIF will be spent 50 times over in the next couple of years. There may be an in-house expert who has the technical skills. Can he or she coach the management team? Does he or she have all the tools and methods expertise? Will the ESC members see him or her as a mentor and personal coach? The answer is usually no, at least not at the beginning. Simply the fact that he or she probably has a small office (or cube) in a backwater place in the organization is indicative of how his or her status and expertise will be viewed by the very management he or she must coach.

After the SIF has benefited from the transfer effect of status by working with the consultant in coaching and mentoring the ESC, as well as sitting on the ESC as a member, he or she may start to be seen by the ESC and management in general as a coach and mentor. This usually won't happen without a lot of work with someone recognized by the ESC to be an expert and mentor.

GETTING STARTED

The remainder of this chapter directly addresses the site leader since he or she is the one who must lead the transformation. While many others may read this chapter to gain insights and assist the site manager, their buy-in is secondary to that of the site leader. It is important that the site leader never forget this fact, thus the focus on him or her to make the transformation successful.

The following steps for site transformation are displayed in Figure 17.1. It is important that the initial steps be followed in the order given. When there is some leeway for modification to suit local conditions and/or preferences, it is pointed out. Steps that are sufficiently discussed in Chapter 16 (e.g., forming a departmental mini executive steering committee [d-ESC] and a work stream team [WST] and/or installing Team Metrics and Ownership System [TMOS] in an intact work group [IWG]) are not exhaustively detailed in this chapter. The amount of work that can be simultaneously handled by the ESC and the organization is directly related to its size and the intensity of daily work. If the organization is very small and/or barely handling the crush of the

No.	Site activity
	Week 1–24
1	Announce the transformation to mgt. and assign readings
2	Search for, select, and engage a consultant/coach
3	Meet with senior mgt. team twice/week and discuss readings
4	Search for and select an SIF
5	Senior mgt. team selects/develops/prioritizes site metrics
6	Site leader and senior mgt. team select ESC members
7	ESC develops ESC charter, ESC procedures, meeting schedule
8	ESC develops site implementation plan for first six months
9	Launch WST to design site communications plan and processes
10	Implement site communications plan
11	Launch WST to create IWG/TMOS approach and train facilitators
12	Launch WST to install and coach TMOS in IWG
13	Launch WST to develop approach/methods/forms for CIE
14	Conduct CIE
15	Launch WST to develop and implement Team 21 in IWG
16	Review the concept of AL with the ESC in a training session
17	Consultant and SIF work with ESC to launch AL with ESC members
18	Launch WST to develop and implement AL with all leadership
19	Launch WST to install weekly process improvement meetings

No.	Site activity
	Week 18–41
20	Conduct overview VSM training sessions for mgrs. and sups.
21	Launch WST to facilitate, coach, and monitor dept. VSM efforts
22	Launch WST to install skill versatility methods in IWG

Figure 17.1 Office Kaizen implementation schedule for a site.

daily workload, the schedule in Figure 17.1 may have to be extended. On the other hand, things will never get done if they are extended out too far; you can't avoid it—a great deal of pressure, extra work, and suffering are always required for world-class results. Get used to it and learn to love it.

1. Announce the transformation to the senior management team and assign initial readings to get the team familiarized with the concepts of continuous improvement methods, tools, and general change leadership. *Office Kaizen 2 (OK2)* should be the first book they read; *Office Kaizen 1 (OK1)* should be the second. A few other books, shown in the following list, are especially useful for leaders at any level, even if a site transformation is not being attempted. They focus mainly on human behavior, innate tendencies, and primate social practices and structures—factors that shape behavior every second in all situations. I don't include "tools" books in this list, because there are so many of them. Some are good, some are useless, and there is no sense wasting time on dead ends. You will have a consultant and an SIF to provide training, skills, and coaching in the tools and methods. They can recommend books and sources when they are required by various individuals.

   — Kevin Kelly, *Out of Control: The New Biology of Machines, Social Systems, and the Economic World* (New York: Perseus Books, 1994).

   — William F. Allman, *The Stone Age Present* (New York: Simon and Shuster, 1994).

   — Frans de Waal, *Chimpanzee Politics: Power and Sex among the Apes* (Baltimore: Johns Hopkins University Press, 1989).

   — Robert Wright, *The Moral Animal—Why We Are the Way We Are: The New Science of Evolutionary Psychology* (New York: Pantheon Books [Random House], 1994).

   — Tom DeMarco and Timothy Lister, *Peopleware: Productive Projects and Teams*, 2nd ed. (New York: Dorset House Publishing, 1999).

   — Masaaki Imai, *Kaizen: The Key to Japan's Competitive Success* (New York: McGraw-Hill, 1986). Outstanding exploration of the concept of continuous improvement as a management system, not an exhortation. Integrates and surfaces many intuitions and insights that other books in this list have sparked.

   — Masao Memoto, *Total Quality Control for Management: Strategies and Techniques from Toyota and Toyoda Gosei* (Englewood Cliffs, NJ: Prentice Hall, 1987).

— Shigeo Shingo, *A Study of the Toyota Production System* (Portland, OR: Productivity Press, 1989).

— Frans de Waal, *Good Natured: The Origins of Right and Wrong in Humans and Other Animals* (Cambridge, MA: Harvard University Press, 1996).

Assign two books a week. If you don't purchase them and hand them out, the ESC members will drag their feet for another couple of weeks and waste valuable time.

2. Also in the first week, start looking for an Office Kaizen consultant and coach. Do not bring in a consultant as a permanent in-house employee. Because of the normal primate status issues and the necessity of the consultant trying to survive as a group member, his or her influence and ability to be completely candid will be severely compromised very quickly; he or she will "go native" and become part of the problem.

3. In week 2, begin meeting with the senior management team twice a week to assign and discuss the readings. The team should be given a book or two a week and told that the books will be discussed the next week in two separate 60- to 90-minute meetings. As you are likely aware, everyone on the management team will complain about this (which is good; it shows you are challenging their preconscious assumptions). Instead of having them waste time talking, calling, e-mailing, and twittering with one another and you about it, create and hand out a wish list of numbered likely complaints (e.g., "1. I'm too busy," "2. Why are we wasting time discussing this stuff? We have the Frobish proposal to work on," "24. Our business is different," "45. What does this have to do with the annual plan?," "53. It's not in the budget," "74. I agree with the intention but the timing is wrong," and "78. Somebody else should work on this"). Then, instead of wasting time writing long e-mails or complaining for 10 minutes, your staff can simply write or say, "Hey: 1, 5, 6, 14, and 54." An extra added bonus is that the team itself will begin to quote complaint numbers to one another in meetings when people waffle or complain; this will further challenge preconscious assumptions as they begin to raise their awareness of how resistance to change is always lurking. In the discussion of books, always focus the content onto your organization and its practices, issues, and structures; you're not trying to train primatologists (complaint no. 96) or psychologists (complaint no. 68),

you're trying to get the team to really look at what it's up against and why the structures of an Office Kaizen transformation are essential.

One good activity for the first discussion session is to have each person use the Office Kaizen Team 21 (provided in the appendix) to assess a small work group in one of his or her areas. The management team member should assess the work group by himself or herself while sitting in the meeting. This always ends up being a more favorable assessment than the workers would provide (management always rates things better than they are), but it will get them thinking about the status of their areas' processes vis-à-vis the transformation. Save the assessments of the management team members so they can compare them with the later assessments of the IWG when Team 21 is introduced. After a few months, the discussion meetings can be reduced to one per week. After six to seven months, the frequency can go to once a month since most of the management team will be up to their necks in coaching. It's important to always have some sort of compelled management learning and discussion sessions scheduled so that things do not get stale and management is always being exposed to new thinking.

4. In week 3, begin the search for and select an SIF. The delay of two weeks gives the human resources manager and involved others a chance to do a little reading before they try to locate a good candidate. As discussed earlier, the SIF doesn't have to be of the same caliber of experience of the consultant, but he or she must be exceptional in attitude, enthusiastic, and results-oriented. He or she must be eager to learn and be able to work well with others without getting pushed around. Chapter 6 provides more discussion of these qualities, and *OK1* pursues the topic even further. Do not settle for using an existing employee as the SIF simply because he or she is there. If he or she is good, great. If not, find someone else.

5. In weeks 3–5, the senior management team should review existing corporate, site, and department performance metrics. Once the list is developed, the management team must prioritize it for the site. The objective is to develop a final set of metrics that can be used to guide the formation of WSTs, continuous improvement (CI), and the selection of metrics for visual metrics displays (VMDs) in TMOS.

6. In week 6, the site leader and the senior management team select ESC members. The final call is up to the site leader, but it is always a good

exercise to involve the entire senior management team in the discussion. Where there are 10 or fewer direct reports to the site leader, the entire management team plus the SIF will usually be on the team. If there are more than 10 direct reports to the site leader, the number needs to be reduced to no more than 10. A key determinant for membership is how many employees report to the ESC candidate, the criticality of his or her processes to the site's success, and the requirement to involve all senior managers who have to support the Office Kaizen implementation. If necessary, it is possible to have a core ESC and rotating (every six months) members.

7. As soon as ESC members are selected, they must work with the consultant and the SIF to develop the ESC charter, ESC procedures, meeting schedule, the charter format, structure for WSTs, and so on.

8. At the same time that steps 6 and 7 are occurring, the ESC must work with the consultant and the SIF to develop the detailed site implementation plan for the first six months. This chapter gives the broad outlines. The biggest portion of implementation will be conducted by WSTs (described in the following steps). Each team's charter must have an action plan and a schedule that are at least at the level of detail of the plan for IWG transformation that was presented in Chapter 16.

9. In week 7, launch a WST to design, install, and support a site communications activity for Office Kaizen. The communications activity is more than just announcements of what happened last week or what is planned next week. The plan must have the following:

   a. A Gemba Wall (see Chapter 6) that provides the following:

      — Schedules, teams, and locations of upcoming WSTs and CIEs as well as planned and announced audits of 5S, Team 21, and so on.

      — A section for each WST under way. Each labeled section must include the WST charter with action plans and status charts (e.g., "racetrack" charts and "stoplight" charts) and any results so far. A single results sheet that shows the key before-and-after metrics for the activity on a kaizen target sheet (KTS; see Figure 13.3).

      — Status of open action items from all past CIEs (see Figures 13.4 and 13.6).

— Information about where to obtain Office Kaizen forms and materials.

— Results from past CIEs and WSTs. This can get out of hand at the speed of light if not carefully controlled. The Gemba Wall is *not* designed to be an internship program for Pulitzer Prize contestants. The last thing you need is people writing, passing around, editing, and reviewing articles and reports for the Gemba Wall or website (see item "b" below). I suggest that the material for each completed CIE and WST be limited to a copy of the charter, some pictures of the team as a group, and collecting data. The results of past activities should stay up on the Gemba Wall for only one month.

— Descriptions of 5S, Team 21, and any other audit procedures and results of recent audits.

It may be necessary at a larger site to have more than one Gemba Wall. They must all be exactly the same. They must be checked daily to make sure that they have not been tampered with or defaced (this may happen at first). Since the Gemba Wall is not designed for written input from random passersby, it is okay and even advisable in some settings to have a clear plastic cover to protect the material.

b. An intranet site with:

— Schedules, teams . . . (see the first bullet point in "a.").

— A section for each WST . . . (see the second bullet point in "a.").

— Status of open action items . . . (see the third bullet point in "a.").

— Online access to downloadable copies of Office Kaizen forms and materials.

— Results from past CIEs and WSTs. Generally, the same as that shown in the fifth bullet point in "a.," except for the following:

■ Entire charters can be displayed.

■ The results can stay on the site indefinitely (as long as they can be stored in a logical, easily retrievable manner and results aren't just piled together).

■ Without creating Steven Spielberg wannabes, some video of the teams in action is nice. The participants may want to show people at home what they did, and it helps build ownership.

— Descriptions of 5S . . . (see the sixth bullet point in "a.").

— There will be a temptation in larger sites to add every speech and video of the site manager (you!), corporate CEO, and various others holding forth about transformation, their support for the effort, and the need for results. This is sometimes helpful for new hires.

— Video of any tools training that is done on-site. As long as the training content is not out of date (such as when the site's method of using a tool changes), these videos can significantly help people get acclimated to the tools and approaches prior to joining a WST, participating in a CIE, and preparing for a 5S event.

There will be a temptation to include more things on the Gemba Wall(s) and the intranet site. For example, some sites post every IWG Team 21 graph. This consumes a lot of time and effort and few people look at them. After all, every IWG knows its own score and has an improvement plan. Trying to promote competition is a waste of time and dangerous since management and supervisors should be coaching each IWG to get a point or so each month, not compete with one another. I would not want anyone cutting corners just to beat another IWG; the supervisors and managers will be the main offenders.

The communications system must include processes for designing the Gemba Wall(s) and the intranet site, launching the site, preparing formats for all graphics and forms, maintaining the Gemba Wall(s) and the intranet site, and finding/assigning and rotating those who do the ongoing work. An approach that works well is to have a permanent WST that rotates members so new people can learn some of the technical web skills.

10. After the communications plan is complete, install the Gemba Wall(s) and turn on the website. Place a notice about the website on the Gemba Wall(s) and have supervisors and managers mention it to employees whenever an opportunity presents itself.

11. In week 8, launch a WST to create the site's IWG/TMOS approach and train the coaches/facilitators who will install TMOS in the next step. Team 21, weekly process improvement meetings, and skill versatility tracking will be installed by other WSTs. Therefore, this WST will have to design the VMD format, obtain materials for the displays and install them in the test groups, develop a rough agenda for each

daily meeting, and develop a few metrics for the IWG to track. Have each person on the WST read Chapter 16. The charter for this WST should include:

— Selection of work groups that will be used as beta test subjects to evaluate TMOS formats and serve as installation learning examples for the facilitators who will be trained.

— Training approach for the TMOS facilitators. It's usually best if the facilitators work in pairs. They can learn from each other and the work can continue if one of them is absent. A pair of facilitators who installs TMOS in two IWGs and coaches the work group for two weeks under the guidance of the SIF and the consultant will be sufficiently experienced to do the installations on their own (with periodic observation by the SIF and the consultant, of course).

12. In week 11, launch a WST to install and coach TMOS in the IWG. The facilitators who were trained in step 11 must be on the team, along with a supervisor or two from the first couple of departments where the implementations will take place. If the site is very large, it may be necessary to train two or three pairs of facilitators in order to cover the site within six months to a year. Even if there is more than one team of facilitators, keep them on one WST. If you form more than one IWG/TMOS implementation team, they will begin to develop slightly different approaches that will become larger as time goes on. Using one team will help maintain consistency, especially if facilitator pairs are shuffled every few weeks.

13. In week 11, launch a WST to develop approaches, administrative procedures, support mechanisms, methods, and forms for CIEs. This WST will function almost exactly like the WST for CIEs described in step 19 of the Chapter 16 description of a departmental transformation. As was described in Chapter 16, this team must set up a system to train itself and CIE facilitators, staff each CIE with facilitators/coaches, compel the ESC to select upcoming CIEs for the next six weeks, make arrangements for the event, select participants, and support and follow up on all CIEs. The only difference for a site is that the suggestions for CIEs will come from all parts of the site. The ESC must develop a very organized approach for logging in, accepting, holding, rejecting, prioritizing, and updating the status on both planned and completed CIEs. It is especially important that the

CIE process include a mechanism where the ESC is updated weekly as to as-yet-uncompleted action items from past CIEs. This list of uncompleted actions would be compiled from the kaizen to-do lists (KTDLs; see Figure 13.4) of all prior CIEs. Rather than compile and maintain a separate spreadsheet (and risk the ever-present tendency to include more and more on the spreadsheet and thus devote more time to waste), I prefer to simply use copies of the actual KTDL with completed items crossed off. There's something about old forms that are gradually disintegrating but still not completed that gets more attention from site management than just another spreadsheet update.

One other issue requires a slightly different approach from the departmental CIE discussed in Chapter 16. With a department focus, unless the department is huge (200 or more people), the department manager will know most everything that is going on; there won't be any improvement efforts that fly under the radar. The department WST and CIE will encompass almost all of the improvement activities outside of IWG efforts on Team 21 plans and kaizen action sheet (KAS) activities. The same is not true of sites. Lots of things go on inside departments that the site management team is not aware of. This can be a problem.

That is why the ESC comprises most, if not all, of the management team, along with the SIF and perhaps a union leader; it is critical that the ESC understand how, when, why, and how many improvement resources are being allocated at the site. If things are happening that the entire ESC has not approved, resources are being expended when they might be put to better use on the priorities set by the ESC. Therefore, the CIE administration process must include provisions that all activities that occur outside of the IWG be charted and approved by the ESC. This does not mean that departments can't do what they need to do on their own. It only means that they can't do anything without getting ESC approval in case the ESC needs the resources to pursue actions that are critical to the site. This procedure also helps avoid "our plates are full" excuses that areas and departments often use when they do not want to or cannot support site programs—everybody will know whether it's true and will have been part of the decisions that filled the plates in the first place.

14. In week 14, the first site CIE is conducted. Thereafter, the Figure 17.1 plan shows a CIE every other week. If the site is small (fewer than 250 people), it may only be able to handle a CIE every three weeks. If it is hard to get enough people off the job for a CIE, you can supplement

the team by inviting a couple of nearby businesses to send a person over for Office Kaizen training. You'll get a free body with an independent perspective, and he or she will get some useful information that could be advantageous. Be sure to have a really good facilitator if you are bringing in very green outside participants.

15. In week 11, launch a WST to develop and implement Team 21 into the IWG. In addition to developing the implementation processes, this WST will also determine the T-level definitions to be used in the Team 21 for each IWG. For the majority of IWGs in office environments, the Office Kaizen Team 21 T-metric definitions will be appropriate for use just as they are presented in the appendix. In perhaps 10% of cases, however, one or two T-metrics may have to be modified and/or completely swapped out to provide a better fit for the work processes of the IWG. This WST will have to identify the needed modifications and develop new content that the ESC can review. It is easy for the perceived requirement for Team 21 modifications to get out of control: Every one of the T-metrics could be modified for every work group on earth to make them a bit better. The definitions in the appendix have been used in thousands of office work groups of every type over the years and have worked just fine. Small changes are not worth the trouble. After five weeks of preparing materials and procedures and doing trial-run implementations in a few IWGs, the WST will begin to install Team 21 into the IWG in the order in which TMOS (step 12) was implemented into the groups. This will ensure that each IWG will have had time to get accustomed to the VMD, daily meetings, and the kaizen action sheet system (KASS) before dealing with its Team 21 assessment and plan development.

16. In week 11, the ESC is given a 60- to 90-minute overview of the concepts, forms, and general audit and coaching processes of AL. It is good if you, the site leader, deliver this presentation with support from the consultant and the SIF. It will reinforce your position as the leader and help reduce complaining (a lot) and resistance (a little).

17. Right after the ESC training session, the consultant and the SIF develop proposed forms and processes for AL (see Chapter 15) for the ESC and present them to the ESC for review and approval. Essentially, the consultant and the SIF (and perhaps the site leader) are working as a two-person (or three-person) WST. The processes and materials developed in this activity will be used to extend AL to the rest of the

site management. After modifications (if any) and approval, the consultant and the SIF begin working with ESC members to develop and implement their leadership action matrices (LAMs).

18. In week 15, after the ESC has had four weeks of experience in implementing, tracking, and coaching its own LAM, launch a WST to implement AL with the remaining leaders at the site. This includes formal leaders (executives, management, supervision, and leads) and informal leaders (anyone who interacts with the general employee population on a daily basis and is viewed as representing "management" to any degree). Depending on the number of these candidates, this process could take two to four months. It is important to do the process one department or area at a time from top to bottom, in that order, before moving onto another department. This provides peer pressure, support, and a "we're all in this together" feeling among those in the department. It also makes other areas that may not even like the concept (after all, it's a change) a little jealous that they have to wait to get their AL. This team should use all of the same forms and procedures that were used with the ESC. The only change might be the location of the displayed LAM. The ESC may display its LAM in a spot near the ESC meetings, while each department's leaders might display their LAM in a common central area of a department.

19. In week 17, launch a WST to install weekly process improvement meetings (see Chapter 6) in each IWG. This process involves arranging for meeting rooms for one hour (perhaps starting with 30 minutes for the first month or so) each week for each IWG. Each work group *must* have the same time and the same room each week so that no time is wasted chasing room availability and location every week (and nothing demonstrates the unimportance of these meetings to management than seeing teams wandering the halls looking for a place to meet because their meeting room got scheduled for a weight-loss or bowling league meeting). Having the same room each week also allows the IWG to store its supplies in one place, allowing more of the meeting time to be spent solving problems rather than chasing down flip charts, brown paper, tape, and so on. Assuming a normal eight-hour day and leaving the first and last hours alone, a single conference or meeting room can, if allocated six hours a day to IWG process improvement meetings, handle 30 one-hour meetings each week (allocate rooms based on 60 minutes so that there is not a massive disruption when

the meetings go from 30 to 60 minutes). The implementation process must include facilitation of the weekly meetings every week for at least the first six weeks. After that, the meetings should be audited at least once a month. The team must develop a facilitation schedule and assign specific individuals. The assignments must be posted on the respective individuals' LAM. The WST must also provide a mechanism for an IWG to request specific problem-solving support when it needs it to resolve a problem at an upcoming meeting.

20. In week 18, begin conducting a 60- to 90-minute VSMapping overview for all leaders. This could be done by a WST, but they would have to learn VSMapping first and a lot of time would be wasted developing training materials. The consultant, working with the SIF, can easily deliver the sessions. The sessions should be delivered in department sequence. Two to four sessions per department, assuming 15–30 leaders in each training session, should handle all but the most enormous areas.

21. In week 18, launch a WST to facilitate, coach, and monitor departmental VSMapping efforts. Quite a bit of VSMapping activity will take place as the ESC forms various WSTs to address particular problems. Other VSMapping activity will take place during CIEs, all of which are approved by the ESC to focus on important issues. Despite this VSMapping activity, a great many opportunities will not come to the attention of the ESC (or even a department's management). It is important to create a plan and some assistance and coaching that drive VSMapping efforts within departments. This WST will work with each department to identify and prioritize key processes and establish a schedule to create a current state VSM (CS-VSM), future state VSM (FS-VSM), and improvement plans for each key process. Keep in mind that the ESC reviews and approves all charters and reviews WST progress each week. This ensures that the priorities and the plans within departments will be integrated with the overall objectives of site leadership (the ESC). And since most of the department leaders are on the ESC, all VSMapping activities are part of one plan for the site's long-term improvement. This WST will train and coach department personnel to do the VSM and will work with them to ensure that the work is done correctly. This WST may require four to eight months to get the work done, and therefore it might be desirable to rotate new members onto the team.

22. In week 22, launch a WST to install skill versatility tracking (see Chapter 7) and cross-training (SVCT) improvement methods in all IWGs. This WST can take as long as 12 months to complete the job (or, more accurately, coach the job to completion). In the schedule presented in Figure 17.1, the WST has five weeks to develop processes and materials and then implement SVCT in one IWG every two weeks. This means that in one year, this WST could install SVCT in about 22 IWGs (assuming that partial weeks around major holidays would not be used). Given an average of 7 people in the typical IWG, this WST would involve 154 people in SVCTs in a year. Such a rate may be too slow for larger sites. An approach often used to accelerate the process with larger employee populations is to charter a WST to develop the standards for identifying tasks, specifications of levels of mastery, forms, tracking, displays, and audit procedures. When the ESC approves the basic structure of the SVCT, the original WST is split into two or three implementation teams that are augmented with additional people. Each WST then uses the same processes and standards and reports separately to the ESC each week.

After reading this chapter, a leader might be thinking, "There's an awful lot of activity going on to create a world-class structure and change existing preconscious assumptions, but when do we address the problems we know we have?" Keep in mind that the CIEs (step 14) are intended to be focused on critical items that the ESC targets. Also, the departmental VSMapping efforts (step 21) will directly address a lot of critical issues in their improvement plans. Since the ESC controls and approves the charters for both of these activities, it will have plenty of resources to fix the critical operational issues it faces. In addition, the ESC is free to charter additional WSTs if the site can handle it. And don't forget that Team 21, IWG weekly process improvement meetings, and the KASS all work together to take the rust out of the gears of every work group, all the time.

18

Transforming an Organization with Multiple Sites

As the earlier chapters, especially Chapter 17, demonstrate, Office Kaizen employs a site-based implementation model; everything is focused on creating a world-class site. While you can "Office Kaizen" a single intact work group (IWG), section, or department, as presented in Chapter 16, the full power of Office Kaizen to transform lives and improve profits is realized only when the enterprise being transformed is a site. If you wish to transform an organization with many sites, you must see that every site performs the steps recommended in Chapter 17. This sounds easy enough in concept, but its implementation is fraught with hazards that have severely limited the potential of hundreds of multisite efforts and compromised the prospects of many hundreds more. This chapter briefly describes the most common failed approaches and then outlines the steps that the leader of a multisite enterprise must take to create world-class Office Kaizen in multiple sites. Two different approaches are detailed: (1) Steps for transforming a multisite enterprise with stand-alone sites as sites are characterized in Chapter 17, and (2) steps for transforming a multisite enterprise with sites that consist primarily of one or more IWGs and/or small departments.

APPROACHES THAT GUARANTEE FAILURE

The following approaches are so common that it is important for leadership to recognize and avoid them at all costs. There are two reasons why these approaches are popular: (1) They are easier than doing what must be done, and (2) they are used so often that leaders assume they must work. They don't work. However, most organizations, for obvious public relations and leadership ego reasons, do not discuss problems and/or failures publicly; everyone puts on a good face. Just ask yourself, if the following approaches worked, wouldn't most enterprises, including yours, already be outstanding?

Visit, See, Try

The "visit, see, try" approach requires leaders of sites needing transformation to visit a successful site and then copy what they have seen when they return to their own site. This is much like taking inner-city children who only see trees in parks out to the deep north woods for a visit and then expecting them to function as reforestation biologists when they return. It brings to mind the true story about the GM site management team from a failing plant that visited NUMMI. Until it closed in March 2010 due to partnership issues between GM and Toyota, the NUMMI plant in Fremont, California, was one of the top-performing auto plants in the world. It used most of the techniques presented in this book. The visitors from the failing plant were seeing, in their own corporation, the system that could have saved their horribly performing plant. The successful system, the Toyota Production System (TPS), was being used in a plant that had formerly been even worse than theirs. NUMMI was using former GM employees who were hired when the plant started, and it was managed by people who had worked for GM and other auto companies. What's not to love? Yet, with the blueprint of their site's salvation right before their eyes, the visitors whined, "This plant must be a sham. It's impossible to run a car plant with so little inventory. There must be hidden warehouses nearby." Of course, nothing was hidden. Not understanding the principles of lean and kaizen and not being familiar with continuous improvement (CI) tools, the visitors not only could not see the trees for the forest, they were blind to the fact that they were standing in a magical, enchanted forest that could have saved their wretched plant. Taking teams and executives out to see world-class operations before they understand what they are looking at is a waste of time and money and achieves nothing.

Read/Watch, Try

In the "read/watch, try" approach, corporate sends general exhortations in person or on video, often accompanied by vision, mission, values, and guiding principles proclamations, and then orders site leaders to "do something to live up to what we are describing." This is similar to the "visit, see, try" approach, but instead of the visit to the forest, they get a speech and/or a video about trees and a list of forest and tree characteristics. They are then told to get busy planting. As Deming used to say, "How could they know?"

Hear, Learn (a bit), Orate, Try

Senior executives launch the "hear, learn (a bit), orate, try" approach by delivering an overview "rollout" speech to senior site executives at an important meeting with perhaps a subsequent introductory overview workshop. Everyone is then told to go back to his or her site, give a similar speech, and get busy doing their transformations. Sometimes, the "road show" is taken to sites and a speech is given to the assembled employees and next steps are promised. Once, when I worked with one of the former Big Three auto companies, giant circus tents (management never realized the irony of the type of tent it was using, I'm sure) were set up in the parking lots of each plant, and a team of senior corporate and union leaders helicoptered in (it was a car company!) to give rousing speeches and show sagging quality data for 90 minutes. They then jumped back into the helicopters and flew off. There was no follow-up and no change in site leadership personnel or actions. Even if the management team had been inclined to try something new after 30 years of running the plant with traditional authoritarian approaches, how could it begin to imagine what to do after a few speeches and a slide show?

Learn (a little), Try

The "learn (a little), try" approach involves sending corporate trainers to the sites (or sending training materials to the sites for use by on-site trainers) to present sessions on CI and/or CI tools. The hope is that somehow the transformation will begin. Change doesn't happen from tools. This is akin to shoveling wheat kernels from an airplane over a city and expecting to come back in 120 days and find amber waves of grain over thousands of acres. Ninety-nine percent of the seeds would fall on cement, asphalt, and roofs or be eaten by surprised but very happy pigeons and squirrels. The few wheat plants that would grow would be lost among the weeds in unkempt yards, in the vegetation abutting railroad tracks, and in clogged rain gutters. Without preparation of the ground, the wheat is wasted; without structural configurations, tools training is useless.

Read Metrics, Report, Try

The "read metrics, report, try" approach has had a bit of a rebirth in the last few years with the popularity of "metrics" as an attractive instant-pudding flavor. A site is sent a list of CI-related metrics (e.g., number of continuous improvement events [CIEs] completed, number of suggestions submitted, number of processes examined with value stream mapping [VSMapping], number of problem-solving teams formed) and is then required to submit regular metrics reports. The sites are told to do what they have to in order to improve the metrics every month. Two fallacious assumptions are made by those asking for the metrics: (1) Good numbers on a metrics report indicate that the site is making transformational progress, and (2) the management teams at the site will understand what they have to do to improve and sustain the metrics. What chance is there that a site leader would understand how to implement a large number of the activities described in this book in order to move the metrics in the right direction in a sustainable manner? How close can you get to zero without actually touching it? So what happens? The site leaders do whatever seems logical to them and then send in whatever they can cobble together to "get corporate off our backs so we can do our jobs." It's a time-honored business tradition that goes back to early Chinese dynasties; the Chinese expression is

山高皇帝远

Shan Gao Huang-di Yuan

meaning, "The mountains are high and the emperor is far away." I've been working in this field for almost 30 years, and almost every underperforming site I've been called into could generate a decent-looking CI metrics report. The reports showed lots of teams, lots of suggestions, regular CIEs being held, and tons of VSMapping. Yet, it was all smoke and mirrors—*Shan Gao Huang-di Yuan.*

See Kaizen (CIE), Try

After "read metrics, report, try," "see kaizen (CIE), try" is probably the most popular failed approach of the last 10 years. It requires that someone go to a site, coach a CIE or two, and then leave. The site leadership team is supposed to magically select and run more CIEs until the site is world class. This approach is popular because two to four CIEs usually generate some impressive returns for a small investment, and they require almost no participation from site leadership other than attending a couple of status reports and a final briefing. Employees enjoy the CIE, the work areas actually feel that someone cares about their work for a week or two, and most people depart a CIE with a good feeling. Of course, astute readers will recognize several problems with this approach as a means of transformation. First of all, simply conducting the CIE requires few if any implementations of structural configurations. Without follow-through involving IWGs, kaizen sustainment action plans (KSAPs; see Figure 13.5), kaizen follow-up check lists (KFCLs; see Figure 13.6), and so on, even good CIE results that occur will deteriorate. Also, site leadership is not required to do anything different; they change none of their leadership actions.

The workers get quickly disillusioned because they got excited about the CIE, expected additional things to happen, and, in 99% of the cases, nothing did. This strategy is more of a gimmick that provides tremendous reinforcement for existing negative preconscious assumptions about leadership and change in general. All of these violate the "encourage and require controlled chaos among all entities in a system" rule. Read my keyboard: "You can't get to world class with CIE alone."

WHAT HAS TO HAPPEN AT A SITE

No matter how a site is transformed in terms of step-by-step tactics and timing, there is one central, immutable, mandatory, implacable requirement that must guide all that occurs at a site:

> A new set of rules must be mandated for the site and the site leader and everyone at the site must experience the chaos of figuring out the most effective ways to perform the almost infinite number of daily interactions amongst themselves within the boundaries of the new, mandated rules.

Of course, it is not wild, out-of-control, cubicles-on-fire chaos that we seek; it is the controlled chaos that occurs within the prescribed boundaries of the rules on which the system is based (as explained in Chapter 1). The old rules were traditional management rules. The new rules that must guide and limit the actions of the site employees are those presented in this book. The multiple-site challenge for the initiative-launching executive (the executive mandating and owning the transformation [EXMOT] with the power to back it up) is how to ferment and focus controlled chaos (hopefully followed by reintegration, then equilibrium, and finally persistent disequilibrium) at the sites.

THE RECOMMENDED APPROACH FOR ENTERPRISES WITH MULTIPLE STAND-ALONE SITES

The approach discussed in this section focuses on moving all of the sites in an organization toward world-class status as soon as possible, as opposed to a strategy that takes its time by working with each site in sequence. This "simultaneous sites" approach not only maximizes financial results but avoids a potential problem by leveraging the energy of corporate leadership while it is still enthusiastic and excited. No matter how much leadership wants the transformation, needs it, and believes in it, about two years after it starts the transformation, something called initiative fatigue always sets in. Sometimes, it happens sooner. It always happens without exception, and it's always apparent to everyone. Where corporate leadership was bright-eyed and bushy-tailed when the initiative was first launched, at about the two-year mark the fire goes out of their eyes. While site leaders are sustained indefinitely by everything good that is happening around them at their sites, corporate leaders have to proselytize without getting a great deal of direct feedback and team pride from the employees around them; they usually don't have their offices at actual sites. They see what's happening and they like it, but it is difficult for them to fully experience the fellowship and feelings of pride. Their ownership of the initiative is less personal and more transactional. As a result, the gleam goes out of their eyes and they can no longer even feign the excitement they felt in the first two years.

Therefore, before initiative fatigue sets in, it is important to have implemented and integrated all of the structural configurations at as many sites as possible. This doesn't mean that success at all sites is ensured, but it does mean that the sites can keep on improving unless something really bad happens. If an unenlightened site leader takes over or the site is sold to an organization that doesn't support what this book is about, the site will rapidly deteriorate back to traditional management practices and the employees will be even more resistant to future attempts to improve things. However, if the sites have a good two years of Office Kaizen progress under their belts, there is a good chance that a fully engaged site leadership team can take the site all the way to world class and perhaps even carry a new site leader along with them (especially if the EXMOT is still there and keeps pushing).

If the implementation is strung out past two years, the leaders of the sites that are just starting their Office Kaizen journey at that time will accurately perceive that corporate leaders are less involved and less excited about the transformation. As a result, the leaders of the sites getting started later will tend to cut corners and bend the rules a bit. The corporate leaders, being fatigued, will not notice and/or will let more minor violations pass. The result is that the later implementations often get a poor start and stop trying after about six months. A multisite enterprise has a window of opportunity of about two years to get all the sites moving along the path of transformation before the impetus flags.

Note: The steps presented in this section assume that a "site" is large (i.e., 75–100 or more people) and has many functions; that is, it is a stand-alone site as described in Chapter 17. If this is not the case, as in a company with many small locations (e.g., bank branches, insurance company branch offices, state motor vehicle department branch offices, firehouses, police substations, post office branches, and real estate offices), each of these "offices" must be treated either as one or more IWGs or as a department. If this is the case, a full-time SIF would likely not be assigned. With a little training, a lot of structured implementation materials, and some follow-up coaching, the manager or supervisor could handle the implementation activities. This approach works well with smaller offices because the processes are usually less numerous and less complex, and a larger portion of the "transformation work" can be laid out in detail for the manager ahead of time. The steps for dealing with this type of situation are provided toward the end of this chapter. In some cases, an organization will have a mixture of locations, some with small staffs and some that truly are sites with multiple functions and many complex processes. If this is the case, the CIF will have to implement the appropriate blend of both approaches presented in this chapter.

The following steps are displayed in Figure 18.1:

1. Bring a contract consultant on board for six months to a year (depending on the number of sites that must be dealt with) to advise and guide the transformation. The reasons detailed in Chapter 17 are even more important here since the success of more than one site is involved. Many corporate officers are led (or lead themselves) to believe that the organization can manage a multisite transformation without a consultant. It's understandable how this happens. An EXMOT is typically surrounded by all manners of people and functions that will assure him or her that they are ready, willing, and able to provide expert guidance. Plus, there is always the natural inclination to keep out "outsiders" (caused by the natural compulsion among primates to form tight groups). Internal resources are usually not the best option. One drawback is that they are part of the command chain and cannot risk being totally candid and highly assertive with the EXMOT and other executives when necessary. Another reason is that they must maintain cordial relationships with other areas. Even if an internal resource had written this book and has years of experience in guiding transformations, he or she would not be able to resist all of the compromises insisted upon by the various interest groups at corporate and at the sites. This person would have to violate his or her better judgment in all sorts of areas simply to survive politically and "get along" in the organization (i.e., "Look, the executives have given you your way on these 10 things; why can't you just go with them on these 2 things . . . what could it hurt?").

No.	Multisite implementation activity	1	2	3	4	5	6	7	8	9	10	11	12	13	14	15	16	17	18	19	20	21	22	23	24
1	Hire a contract consultant					■																			
2	Hire a CIM							■																	
3	CIM and consultant develop SIF training materials/develop policies								■	■	■	■													
4	EXMOT announces initiatives to site leaders/asks for SIF candidates								■																
5	Site leaders provide SIF candidate names									■															
6	CIM and consultant interview SIF candidates										■														
7	First wave of SIF training													CIE		CIE		CIE	CIE						
8	CIM, consultant, EXMOT, and IT design communication plan																								
9	First eight sites launch Office Kaizen initiative																			■	■	■	■		
10	Coaching of first wave of SIF graduates in the field																							■	■

Week

No.	Site activity	21	22	23	24	25	26	27	28	29	30	31	32	33	34	35	36	37	38	39	40	41	42	43	44
11	Review of feedback and revision of materials			■																					
12	Second group of sites asked to submit SIF candidates				■																				
13	Site leaders provide SIF candidate names																								
14	CIM and consultant interview SIF candidates by phone/in person																								
15	Second wave of SIF training					CIE		CIE		CIE		CIE													
16	Sites 9–16 launch Office Kaizen initiative														■										
17	Coaching of second wave of SIF graduates in the field												■	■	■	■									
18	If third wave of SIF training required, repeat steps 11–17																	■							

Week

Figure 18.1 Office Kaizen implementation schedule for a multisite organization with large sites.

Another important reason why internal experts cannot provide guidance is that few of them have applied experience in structuring and implementing even a single-site transformation, much less one involving multiple sites. Most will suggest a variant of one of the failed approaches described earlier because that is all they have seen.

Do not hire a consulting company to provide a consultant. Hire an independent consultant. A consulting company will try to pack more consultants into the project at every opportunity in order to increase billings; that is the primary objective of most consulting companies. Further, if you use a consulting company, you won't get its best person. A one-person project is not attractive to consulting companies; it gets the lowest priority because it makes the least money. As a result, the company will assign a less seasoned, less experienced consultant because it reserves its best people for projects where the top performers can help manage the work of junior consultants (new MBAs) and attempt to increase billings by adding more "heads." Also, you will pay twice as much or more for a consultant from a consulting company than a single, independent contractor would charge per week. And it doesn't end there; you'll pay for project directors and consulting company brass who will visit you regularly (and bill you for the time and travel expenses) to "work with you to make sure things are going well" (i.e., to try to convince you to hire more consultants).

2. Hire a corporate improvement manager (CIM). This person reports directly to the EXMOT and has a dotted-line relationship to all of the site improvement facilitators (SIFs). The CIM will provide the SIF with coaching, mentoring, support, standard work for structural configuration implementation, training materials, and formats for various forms such as kaizen action sheets (KASs), action leadership (AL) charts, and so on. The CIM will need an experienced, skilled, full-time administrative person who can make arrangements, roll out training programs, travel, send out and update training materials, and so on.

   The chosen CIM must have broad knowledge of continuous improvement methods and understand and appreciate the reality of human motivations, preconscious expectations, and organization change. He or she will work with the consultant to design the implementation of the recommendations in Chapters 16 and 17 and this chapter. Launch the search for the CIM about two weeks after you begin the search for the consultant. Try to get the list of potential CIM candidates down to about six people whom the consultant and the EXMOT will interview once the consultant comes on board.

The consultant and the CIM develop the structure of the initiative and get the EXMOT's approval. The structure will consist primarily of the steps in this chapter (and incorporate the Chapter 17 site transformation details). Such a plan should take only two to three weeks to develop in sufficient detail to get started. One area that might require a bit of thought at this point is how to "brand" the transformation. I believe that it is a big mistake to give transformations rah-rah names such as "Lean Sigma 2015," "Race to Excellence," and so on; such names unnecessarily burden the initiative with a massive, rub-on seasoning of "flavor of the month." However, it is important to organize under one umbrella all of the structural configurations, processes for implementing and sustaining the structural configurations, standard processes, training, and so forth. Many companies simply use a name such as "The (insert your company name here) Operating System" or "The (insert your company name here) Business Operating System." Once it gets fleshed out, it can be used to orient new employees and organize information on the corporate intranet site (which will also have the sites' information on it; see step 8). Having one such "operating system" also helps ensure that all sites use the same techniques and processes and thus don't waste resources doing their own development work or wander off track and try failed approaches that seem reasonable to them. Plus, when people move between sites or move up the management ladder, all sites will be using the same tools and approaches.

An additional element must be decided at this point. In step 4, site leaders are told to provide candidates from their site for SIF training. It is important, before this is done, to determine what the career path will be for the SIFs so this can be explained to the "draftees." If the thought is simply to enlist them, send them to training, place them as SIFs, and then leave them to their own devices about what to do after a couple of years, you are not going to get or keep good people, especially in the second wave of training that replaces people who quit or get promoted (experienced SIFs will be highly attractive to other organizations). Few people are willing to risk leaving their normal career ladder in order to take a chance with a tough new job in an endeavor that may not be successful (that's the existing preconscious assumption that many will have). The SIF position is key to transformational success and sustaining gains; it is critical that it be staffed at each site with high-energy, high-potential personnel who are expected to have a shot at many very good jobs in the organization. I always recommend that the SIF position be a two-year assignment, with the next job being assistant department head, department head, assistant site manager, site manager, or similar type of responsible leadership position at a site, group, or at corporate, depending on the SIF's current level of experience and expertise. If this career path is defined up front, you'll get much better people. In fact, if the EXMOT is really committed to making "The (insert our company name here) Business Operating System" a new way of working, he or she should work with human resources and decree that future department and site managers, say in three years (in order to fill the pipeline), must be individuals who have served at least one full year as a full-time SIF. If this were to be done, you would have to stand clear of the door when asking for volunteers—you'd get trampled as people rushed in to sign up. This would also mean that many of the volunteers would be more seasoned personnel who are already expecting to move up the management ladder—just the kind you want for the SIF position.

3. By about week 8, the CIM should be onboard, and he or she and the consultant begin to develop the SIF training materials, forms, and procedures for launching a Chapter 17 site transformation at each site (without hiring a consultant at each site). The training materials don't need to be as finely tuned as commercially available materials. You're not running a training company; you're implementing a transformation. The consultant will probably have a library of easily adaptable materials. The SIF training is not a minor affair. It takes a minimum of eight weeks to properly train an SIF if you start with high-caliber personnel. If you try to get by with less training, it will not work. You are essentially creating highly specialized internal consultants who can act as true consultants and guide, coach, and direct (but not lead, that's the site leader's job) the implementation at his or her home site. Step 7 describes the training in more detail.

4. In week 9, the EXMOT announces to the site leaders that a new business direction is going to occur. It's best if this is done at one time and in one place so every site gets the same message. After the speech announcing the new direction, a two- or three-hour overview of the general concepts of the transformation should be provided.

The overview covers the general structure of these steps. The site leaders should be instructed not to take any action when they return to their sites, except for picking one or two of their best, high-potential people for SIF training. If the boss of the chosen SIF candidate doesn't respond, "Oh, no, we can't afford to lose her! Pick somebody else!," the person selected is not good enough. All too often, organizations select people who can be spared or who will not be missed. Those types of people are well known and even if they are liked, they will not command the respect of management and/or employees and cannot perform the role of an SIF adequately. Do not accept people who can be spared. Those who successfully complete the training (it's not automatic) will become SIFs. Each site will send two people to SIF training unless the site is very, very small (if the site has fewer than 75 people, it should send only 1). One of the site's graduates (designated in advance) will serve as the SIF, and the other person will serve as a part-time (10 hours per week) SIF advisor so that if the SIF leaves or is ill, the part-time SIF can step in right away. The SIF advisors will also assist the consultant and the SIF in the second and third waves of the training program if the organization has more than 8–16 sites.

5. In week 10, site leaders provide the names of SIF training candidates. If there is any hint of a site leader putting forth the name of a candidate who is less than outstanding, the EXMOT must step in immediately and instruct the site leader to find someone else. Once this happens, word will spread like wildfire through the site manager rumor line and other site managers will be less likely to try the same tactic.

6. As the names of proposed SIF candidates begin to arrive in week 10, the consultant and the CIM conduct detailed interviews by phone or in person. In the interests of time, those who cannot be quickly seen in person must be interviewed by phone. If an interviewee is not appropriate, notify the site leader immediately and request another candidate.

7. In week 12, the first wave of SIF training occurs. The SIF training program (SIFTP) is an intensive, hands-on, real-time training immersion for eight weeks. It is a boot-camp-style, high-workload, baptism-by-fire exercise. It will be the most exhausting business experience they have ever had. A maximum of 16 trainees can attend any one training session (with only the consultant and the CIM running the sessions, this is the largest number that can be provided with the type

of coaching that is required); this means that 8–10 sites will have their SIF trained in the first wave. It takes the eight weeks of training and another four weeks of follow-on coaching to get a class of SIFs up and running at their sites. Thus, about eight sites can be launched every 12 weeks. This means that the consultant and the CIM can complete four waves of training and installations, or 32 sites, in one year. If you have more than 50 sites (not IWG or department sites, these are discussed at the end of this chapter), you will be approaching the initiative fatigue limit described earlier with the later sites and may have to consider using a few of the top-graduate SIFs to help the CIM and the consultant deliver two simultaneous training sessions at once.

Each training wave is usually conducted at one location. In order to provide richness of content, the site should have many processes, and a number of them should be complex. The more problems the site has, the better the training experience will be and the greater the benefits to the site. In essence, the SIFTP provides the hosting site with eight weeks of intense process improvement and structural configuration installation. In a very short time, the host site will be significantly propelled along the road to success. In order to not waste this opportunity, it is essential that the EXMOT, the CIM, and the consultant work closely with the site leader ahead of time to prepare him or her for taking full advantage of the effort.

The eight weeks of the training program consist of four weeks of what I call "see-do" training, separated by four weeks of CIEs. In the "see-do" weeks (one, three, five, and seven), a method, tool, or approach is learned in a group classroom session of 30 minutes to one hour, and then the trainees break into teams of two to four to apply the method or tool to an area or process at the site. Critical processes, selected in concert by the CIM, the consultant, and the site manager, are targeted with as wide an array of tools as required in order to improve efficiency, quality, and costs. For example, if design engineering cycle time and quality (errors on drawings) were to be selected for improvement, various portions of the training might guide the trainees through detailed flowcharting, Pareto charting of error types, VSMapping, task analysis, handoff charts, skill versatility charting, implementation of standard work, implementation of waste removal actions, implementation of a cross-training program, and so on.

The intervening weeks are CIE weeks (two, four, six, eight). Teams of trainees and site workers blitz processes and apply whatever tools the CIM and the consultant believe are necessary to fix the problems. In each successive CIE week, the SIF trainees assume more of a leadership role as the CIE teams add more on-site workers. The objective is to have the trainees leading CIEs in the third and fourth CIE weeks (training weeks six and eight) with the consultant and the CIM observing and coaching. By weeks three and four, there may be two to four CIEs taking place simultaneously as pairs of SIFs co-coach teams of site employees. The end result is that the hosting site benefits from as many as 16 CIEs, not counting the structural configuration and process improvement activities conducted in the "see-do" weeks.

In the course of the "see-do" weeks, the trainees guide the establishment of the ESC, implement all TMOS elements in a selection of IWGs, coach the ESC to establish and charter several WSTs, apply VSMapping to several key processes, and apply whatever other methods are required to address issues selected by the site. The CIE weeks would simply focus more intensity on the same or other issues. Of course, every day, before the new CIE or "see-do" tasks begin, the trainees perform follow-up checks of every improvement action they have already installed at the site. During the final three weeks, each of the SIF trainees also works on detailing an implementation plan for Office Kaizen at his or her home site. The consultant and the CIM provide templates as part of the training materials and coach the trainees through the construction process. Each SIF and his or her site leader pass the proposed plan back and forth via e-mail so that by the time the training is over, the site is ready to launch its initiative. As the plan is being developed, the consultant and the coach carefully review it and work with the trainees and the site managers to refine and focus it. Most of the plans will closely follow the schedule presented in Figure 18.1 unless there are significant contraindications that present themselves to the trainee, the site manager, the CIM, and/or the consultant.

8. Also in week 12, the development and implementation of the communication plan for the operating system begins. The EXMOT, the CIM, the consultant, human resources, and the IT department work together on the plan. The content is almost exactly the same as that detailed in step 9 in Chapter 17. The only difference is that a single corporate site will have sections for each of the sites. If the corporate office does not have the capacity for such a project, it should be assigned to one of

the sites and supervised by the same people noted earlier in this step. Each site should be able to update its information from the site. All of the site locations on the website should have the same consistent appearance and formatting so that it is easy for everyone to navigate through them. The implementation must also specify designs and formats of information for both the hard-copy on-site Gemba Walls and the electronic versions of them on the website. If the corporate location is a site itself (with business processes aside from corporate governance), it should have all of the same elements (SIF, Gemba Wall, implementation plan, etc.) as a "regular" site. The implementation of the communications plan (at least the electronic versions) should occur in week 20, when the SIF graduates return to their sites to begin transformation. The actual placement of the hard-copy Gemba Walls at the sites will take place according to each detailed site plan.

9. The trainees return to their sites and launch the Office Kaizen initiative in the first eight sites.

10. Each site's SIF and its ESC are coached for a week or so by the consultant or the CIM (each will handle four sites). If some sites need additional coaching, one or two associate SIFs (the number-two SIF person at a two-person site) can be assigned to help out various sites for another week or two. It will give them good experience and will help sites having difficulty to stay on target. If a site or two is having a very tough time, the consultant could spend more time and have his or her place backfilled in the second wave of SIFs by one or two associate SIFs.

11. The CIM and the consultant review the feedback from the first wave of training and review materials as appropriate.

12. The site leaders of the second wave of sites are asked to submit SIF candidates' names.

13. In week 22, the same as step 5.

14. In week 22, the same as step 6.

15. In week 24, the second wave of SIF training starts.

16. In week 32, sites 9–16 launch their Office Kaizen initiative.

17. In week 32, the same as step 9.

THE RECOMMENDED APPROACH FOR ENTERPRISES WITH MANY SITES THAT ARE IWGS OR DEPARTMENTS

Many organizations have a significant number of locations that resemble IWGs or small departments more than they do sites as defined in Chapter 17. It is easier to implement Office Kaizen in these locations because there are fewer and less complex structural configurations required. There will be no formal ESC, very few (if any) formal WSTs and champions, and not many unique processes that have to be studied with VSMapping.

A further note about VSMapping is important at this point. In most organizations with many locations, the work is fairly standardized. Rather than teach location leaders about VSMapping, it is more operationally effective, cost-effective, and easier to have a separate team conduct VSMapping of the most important processes and develop revised processes that are distributed to the sites as standard work. The last thing any multilocation organization can afford is 50 location leaders taking a lot of time away from customers to develop 50 different approaches for the same process. The locations' job is to serve customers first. They should already be given the best standard work for processes possible. If not, corporate or regional management should develop the optimum processes (using some location personnel) and then distribute them as ready-to-go, mandated standard work.

Also, there will be very few, if any, five-day CIEs. Instead, four-hour to one-day scrambles with two or three people would likely be used. In essence, the Office Kaizen effort at most of these smaller locations will consist primarily of implementing TMOS and enough training to facilitate problem solving and waste elimination in from one to four IWGs. In the cases of locations that are not true sites but have more than 25–30 people, the Office Kaizen effort will likely be that of a department as described in Chapter 16.

While an initiative at a site (let's use *location* for the remainder of this chapter for small sites) with a small staff is less complex to operate and maintain once it is up and running, it presents in many ways a much more complex training and start-up challenge. The management team at a small site is often only one person who has no one else with whom to share the leadership burden. In some industries, the leader may not have extensive business experience or much familiarity with management concepts or project implementation techniques aside from his or her site's day-to-day business operations. Most locations will not have the necessary personnel to do the day-to-day work and operate even part-time WSTs to handle portions of the implementation as would be the usual procedure at a site.

Therefore, the approach for the small location must be a turnkey (or plug-and-play) model of implementation. With a turnkey approach, the location leader must be able, with very little training, to implement, lead, monitor, and sustain the initiative. In effect, the organization must provide the location leaders with a complete system of formats, charts, visual metrics display (VMD) templates, procedures, processes, instructions, and job aids that are almost self-explanatory. This requires a bit more development work up front, but it pays off big later in direct proportion to the number of locations because every location will be able to use almost exactly, if not exactly, the same materials with little modification. And such a turnkey approach means that the organization does not have to provide the leader of each location with the type of advanced training that an SIF would receive in the site model.

Figure 18.2 shows the recommended steps and schedule for implementing Office Kaizen in an enterprise with many locations. The following list provides more details on each step:

1. Find someone with the technical skills to develop procedures, forms, processes, templates, and so on, for the implementation. This might be a contract consultant or it might be an in-house training resource. If the organization has a sophisticated, in-house training function that provides instruction and development of various technical and/or management training subjects, it should be able to develop most of the materials using this book's content as long as the materials do not wander too far from the recommendations. The individuals developing the materials should be provided with copies of *OK1* and this book and tasked to understand the contents and concepts. If there is some doubt as to the ability of the in-house training department to handle this task, hire a contract consultant for six to eight weeks to work with the training department in developing and testing the turnkey TMOS, problem-solving, and waste elimination materials.

2. If there are sites (per Chapter 17) as well as locations in the organization that will have to be transformed, it will be necessary to hire a CIM at corporate and one SIF for each site. If a CIM is hired, have the training resource report to him or her in reference to all location and site Office Kaizen materials development; the last thing you need is a territorial dispute over who is in charge (it is the EXMOT, with the CIM acting as his or her agent in matters relating to Office Kaizen).

No.	Multilocation implementation activity	Week																						
		1	2	3	4	5	6	7	8	9	10	11	12	13	14	15	16	17	18	19	20	21	22	23
1	Hire a contract consultant or task the training department																							
2	**Hire a CIM if sites are also present**					█																		
3	Develop approach and policies for locations																							
4	Develop location training materials/job aids																							
5	**Develop approach and policies for sites**																							
6	CIM and consultant conduct train-the-trainer sessions																							
7	CIM, consultant, EXMOT, and IT design location communication plan																							
8	EXMOT announces initiative to all locations																							
9	Schedule first five waves and make arrangements																							
10	First wave of manager/supervisor training/launch of five sites																							
11	Communications plan launched																							
12	Follow-on coaching visits																							
13	Second wave of manager/supervisor training/launch of five sites																							
14	Repeat steps 9, 10, 11, 13, 14, 15, 16 as required																							

No.	Multilocation implementation activity	Week																						
		14	15	16	17	18	19	20	21	22	23	24	25	26	27	28	29	30	31	32	33	34	35	36
15	**EXMOT asks site leaders/ask for SIF candidates**																							
16	**Site leaders provide SIF candidate names**																							
17	**CIM and consultant interview candidates/arrange travel**																							
18	**First wave of SIF training**							CIE		CIE		CIE		CIE										
19	**CIM, consultant, EXMOT, and IT design site communication plan**																							
20	**First eight sites launch Office Kaizen initiative**																							
21	**Coaching of first wave of SIF graduates in the field**																							
22	**Review feedback/revise materials**																							
23	**Repeat steps 15–22 as required**																							

Figure 18.2 Office Kaizen implementation schedule for a multisite organization with locations that consist of IWGs and/or small departments.

Note: The remaining steps assume that there are sites as well as locations to be transformed. Activities that denote events for the steps that are specific to sites are in bold type in Figure 18.2.

3. In week 6, the EXMOT, CIM (or training department), and consultant begin to develop policies, procedures, timing, and schedules of the implementation plan (which expands and details these steps).

4. Also in week 6, the consultant and the training department (and CIM, if one is hired) develop the training materials for location (IWG) leaders' training and implementation. These materials must be able to train leaders in three or four days and be designed so that a sharp location leader could read the documentation and/or watch the videos and then use the materials even if he or she had not been to the training. People often forget a lot of what they learn in a training session, so it is important that there be ample step-by-step documentation with photographs and/or video for each element of the implementation so that location leaders can study them. The location materials must include standard work, ready-to-use charts, templates, forms, displays, and procedures for the following:

   — The daily work group meeting (WGM).
   — VMD board. Each location leader must leave the training with a VMD board ready to use (or they can be shipped to arrive before the leader returns).
   — AL. It will be important to leave each location leader with a defined list of actions and the necessary forms so that when he or she returns to the site, AL can be implemented right away.
   — Kaizen action sheet system (KASS).
   — Metrics. It is critical that each location be given three or four metrics, with blank charts and definitions/procedures, so that the site can immediately get busy with metrics right after training. The EXMOT, consultant, and the CIM will have to develop a candidate list of metrics from which to pick for each location. The EXMOT may want to have each location use the same basic set of metrics (it's a judgment call for the EXMOT and depends on the range of variability across locations).
   — Team 21. Depending on the exact nature of your business, the generic Office Kaizen Team 21 shown in the appendix may have a few or several T-metrics that don't fit well. These will have to

be modified during training program development per procedures outlined in *OK1*. If it can be avoided, try not to modify Team 21 T-metrics for slight differences between locations. Any minor issues can be dealt with after the transformation has been rolled out and is working smoothly.

— Weekly process improvement meeting. This would include instructions for common tools such as cause-and-effect (C&E) diagrams, Pareto charts, modified affinity diagramming (MAD), spaghetti diagrams, cross-training matrices, and whatever other tools are appropriate to the processes and likely issues at the location.

5. In week 6, the CIM, the consultant, and the EXMOT develop policies and approaches for the initiative at the sites (if there are any).

6. In week 6, the CIM and the consultant begin train-the-trainer sessions and finalize materials. If there are only a few locations, only one selected individual will be trained to assist the consultant. If there are many locations, as with retail outlets, insurance offices, and restaurant franchises, additional trainers may be needed so that after the first few training sessions, simultaneous training sessions can be run in different regions. There will also likely be some internal training specialists who can be trained to deliver some of the sessions.

7. Also in week 6, the EXMOT, the CIM, the consultant, and IT personnel design the communications plan for weeks 11–17. The purpose of the training plan with many small "IWG locations" is different from that for the transformation of large sites. In the larger sites, a key function of the website is to provide a central resource for all materials, processes, and forms for the "operating system." This is not the case for an organization with many small sites. First of all, almost all the materials and processes relate to the operation and content of the locations' TMOS, so there is not much to put on the website. Another challenge for organizations with many locations is ensuring that they are maintaining their efforts related to improvement and customer satisfaction. The central website will require the location managers/supervisors to update the website daily to show changes in the three or four key metrics being tracked on the primary visual display (PVD) of each location, as well as its Team 21 status. If properly designed, the updating chore should take each manager/supervisor only five minutes per day. The location reports and built-in analyses of the data

(e.g., showing the distribution of Team 21 performance across units) will permit the EXMOT to focus on both outstanding units and those needing extra coaching.

8. In week 8, the EXMOT announces the upcoming initiative. If there are a great many sites, this can be done by teleconference with location leaders and/or video.

9. In weeks 9 and 10, arrangements are made for the leaders of the first five locations to attend a three- to four-day training session at a selected location. The training class is kept to five in these steps because more than that would likely be too disruptive in a small location. It is good if a hotel within close walking distance to the site can be used for the classroom elements of the training and still allow the trainees to move quickly back and forth between the training room and the site. If this is not possible, the training will have to be handled on-site.

10. The first wave of training is given in week 11. The training consists of actual installation and coaching of TMOS into all of the IWGs of the host site. Every element of TMOS is put in place. While it is better to space out the Team 21 installation, a second training session requires extra travel expense and manager/supervisor time away from their locations. If another trip can be accommodated, it is better to have Team 21 be introduced four to six weeks after the initial training. However, if this extra trip would be a burden (when is it not?), the IWG can be introduced to Team 21, allowed to assess itself, and then wait four to six weeks before they begin working on the T-metrics. The five trainees are coached in every aspect of TMOS installation, including metric development and data posting and updating. The trainees learn by coaching the location leader under the guidance of the trainer.

11. In week 12, the communications plan is launched.

12. Also in week 12, follow-on audits and coaching visits begin at the six locations (the host location and the five visiting locations) in the first wave. Each location is visited once a week for a few hours for the first month. After the first month, each location is visited once a month. If this auditing/coaching is not done, the implementation will fail. The auditor/coach attends a morning meeting, interviews a few employees about how TMOS is going, and checks metrics charting and the KASS. Any needed coaching is given.

13. In week 13, the next wave of five locations (plus the host location) is launched. From this point on, a new wave is started every week until all locations are done. An occasional resting week may be used to give the trainers a respite and time to review/update their materials. The follow-on coaching starts up in each location in the week after the training week.

14. Repeat steps 9–11 and 13–16 as required.

15. Same as step 4 in Figure 18.1.

16. Same as step 5 in Figure 18.1.

17. Same as step 6 in Figure 18.1.

18. Same as step 7 in Figure 18.1.

19. Almost the same as step 8 in Figure 18.1. While the location portion of the central website is already up and running, the site portions would be integrated in this step.

20. Same as step 9 in Figure 18.1.

21. Same as step 10 in Figure 18.1.

22. Same as step 11 in Figure 18.1.

23. Repeat steps 15–22 as required.

19

What's Next?

If you read this book in just a few days, you may feel that you have drunk
from a fire hose at full pressure when you only wanted a sip of sparkling
Eau de Office Kaizen. That's a natural reaction. Don't worry about it.
This book presents the distillation of hundreds of years of Office Kaizen
implementation experience from many practitioners, as well as thousands
of years of insights from hundreds of researchers studying organizations,
groups, individual human behavior, and business. You can't expect to automatically absorb and integrate all of the information into your cognitive
map right away.

You have two challenges to overcome in order to best use the material in
this book. The first is that you must logically understand what you have read.
The best way to facilitate this understanding is to reread a chapter a couple of
times, think about it, and talk about it with a colleague or friend. The concepts
and the relationships among the chapters will integrate and arrange themselves
automatically once you have processed them a bit more than was possible
from reading or skimming through the pages.

The second challenge is tougher. Even if you understand the concepts
fully, you may not accept them. You can't be sure if this is due to a pure logical conclusion or to a preconscious assumption that "tells you" the concepts
don't work. The only way to determine what is driving your conclusion or
feeling is to challenge your preconscious by taking some action that compels
your preconscious to react. The best way to do this is to try out some of the
concepts in real time. If you have an intact work group (IWG) reporting to
you, implement Team Metrics and Ownership System (TMOS) for the IWG
and action leadership (AL) for yourself. You will see that your employees
will work better and feel better after a couple of weeks. This should cause
your preconscious to begin to shift its assumptions about Office Kaizen
effectiveness.

If you don't have anyone reporting to you, start up your own personal visual metrics display (VMD) with a RACI (responsible, accountable, consulted, informed) chart of your key responsibilities and a racetrack graph or stoplight chart for important deadlines and tasks. Implement AL to structure how often and when you check on things, report results, make visits to maintain relationships, answer e-mails (only at scheduled times unless it's a main part of your job's communication flow), and so on. You'll see that you'll feel better and begin to feel a sense of satisfaction from seeing the graphs and charts move in the right direction. If and when you have people reporting to you, you'll be primed to take a bigger step with Office Kaizen.

If you have a department or site or more, try out the IWG implementation as a first step. Remember, never risk putting the entire system in chaos. Do a little VSMapping with a team on an important process. The key is to repeatedly and continually push little parts of the system toward persistent disequilibrium to compel the team members to try new things. This will work on their and your preconscious assumptions and teach them some new things. As they get more comfortable with being in persistent disequilibrium, you can increase the pressure and begin to more aggressively implement Office Kaizen.

Remember, without strong, purposeful leadership, nothing will change for the better. You need to get started doing something today, even if it is just rereading. Always keep moving forward, with a plan, and you can make Office Kaizen work in your organization or part of it. The people who work with you are counting on you, even if they don't know it. Good luck.

Appendix

The Office Kaizen Team 21

Level	T-metric 1—Leadership
2	The work group leader is viewed as the group leader by all members of the work group. A work group vision is defined.
3	A plan to achieve objectives is developed. Associates have input to decisions but the leader makes final approval.
4	Everyone in the work group understands the plan to achieve objectives. Decisions are made by group consensus facilitated by the leader, whose main role is that of a coach.
5	Everyone understands the vision, the plan, and the road map to get there. Associates are empowered to make decisions to achieve objectives. The leader/coach provides guidance when needed and his/her input is always appropriate and welcomed.

Level	T-metric 2—Daily work group meetings
2	Daily work group meetings (DWGMs) have begun but are not attended by all work group members. Some meetings are missed, and some meetings seem pointless and/or disorganized.
3	DWGMs are held at least four days out of five and attended by most work group members. Efforts are under way to make the DWGM relevant to all group members.
4	DWGMs are held every day, without exception. Attendance is 100% and most work group members participate actively.
5	The DWGM is viewed as an essential and critical element of the job by every work group member. All work group members participate with interest and actively.

Level	T-metric 3—Team metrics display
2	The work group has a primary visual display (PVD), and it displays some information that is important to the group. The information that is displayed is kept up to date most (about 80%) of the time.
3	The work group PVD is comprehensive and has been extensively improved by work group members. The information is almost always up to date (95% of the time).
4	The PVD visually displays every critical element that the work group must track. Work group members have most of the responsibility for keeping the PVD up to date. It is currently at better than 99%.
5	The PVD display and the performances it tracks are viewed by the work group as the heart and soul of their pride and commitment. Data are always current.

Level	T-metric 4—Metrics and measurements
2	Initial efforts are under way to identify key performance indicators (KPIs) for critical processes in the work group.
3	The work group tracks and displays KPIs for all critical processes and has developed and displayed plans for improvements.
4	The work group tracks and displays the KPIs of all major and most minor processes as well as progress against plans for improvements.
5	The KPIs of all appropriate processes are monitored on a continuous basis, and corrective action is seamlessly integrated into the work group's daily activities.

Level	T-metric 5—Roles and responsibilities
2	Roles and responsibilities (R&Rs) for each work group member are specified by a member of management without any discussion.
3	The supervisor or leader of the work group meets individually with each group member to jointly develop the member's specific R&Rs.
4	Through group brainstorming and discussion by the entire group, each person's specific R&Rs are negotiated and defined (or redefined) in detail at least every six months.
5	As in 4 above, all R&Rs are continually monitored and modified as required through discussion among the work group members.

Level	T-metric 6—Documentation management
2	Elimination of outdated, redundant, and unnecessary documentation has begun. A storage area for shared documents has been established but is not always used.
3	No personal storage areas for work group documentation remain. Occasionally, documents are still misplaced, duplicated, and/or lost.
4	All associates in the work group use the central area for work group documents, and very seldom is a document misplaced and/or found to be out of date or in two places at once.
5	Documents are always where they are supposed to be and they are up to date and accurate. All documents are quickly available to any work group member on demand.

Level	T-metric 7—Deadlines and commitments
2	The work group begins to document and measure deadlines and commitments. Commitments and deadlines (C&Ds) are regularly missed.
3	The work group implements a structured system to manage C&Ds. C&D deadlines are met at least 90% of the time.
4	The work group is skilled in using a structured system to manage C&Ds. Every aspect of managing C&Ds is defined and understood. C&Ds are met at least 98% of the time.
5	Firm schedules are always set and are never missed. Internal and external customers have full confidence that delivery will be on time, every time.

Level	T-metric 8—Competence
2	The work group defines functional/technical competency (FTC) requirements for itself. Associates begin to improve current skill sets through training and education.
3	The work group begins measuring FTC against best practices in their industry/field. All work group members attend at least 3 relevant inside/outside technical workshops each year.
4	Work group FTC is on par with the best in the industry/field. The area associates have the ability to teach FTC skills to other associates.
5	Some members of the work group conduct workshops in their industry/field, and at least one is published as an FTC innovator in their industry/field.

Level	T-metric 9—Time management
2	An efficient, consistent, and standard time management (ECSTM) system is in place and is used by at least half of the members of the work group.
3	An ECSTM system is used by at least 80% of work group members. Work group members can access one another's schedules and plans. Overtime and long days occur no more than once a week.
4	An ECSTM system is used by all work group members, but there are occasional mistakes and omissions in using the system. Long days are rare, and time is rarely wasted due to poor time management.
5	All group members are expert in using the ECSTM system. Long days and overtime are never required to recover from poor time management.

Level	T-metric 10—Workplace arrangement
2	Work group members construct a diagram of the current layout and begin to think about alternative arrangements.
3	The work area arrangement has been modified to improve work flow and communications. There are still some issues that have not been resolved, but they are being explored.
4	Work group equipment is placed to support T-metric processes and work flow. Workspace is flexible and highly mobile. The work group can reconfigure their area as necessary.
5	All floor space is fully utilized to maximum effectiveness. The work group members believe that they have a near-perfect arrangement to be productive without wasted space or motion.

Level	T-metric 11—Skill flexibility
2	The work group begins to define tasks and display skill flexibility charts in the work area.
3	Skill flexibility for all appropriate tasks in the work group is tracked and displayed visually. Goals for work group flexibility are established. At least 50% of the work group members are skilled in three critical tasks.
4	Work group has training plans for each member's skill development. Every task can be done by at least two work group members. At least 75% of the work group members can do all tasks in the work group. Beginning to learn tasks of upstream/downstream work groups.
5	Except for recent hires, all work group members can do 90% of the work group's tasks. Members visually track their mastery of tasks of the immediately adjacent and upstream/downstream work groups and can do 50% of those tasks.

Level	T-metric 12—Problem solving
2	A majority of the work group members understand a few problem-solving tools (PSTs), but they are applied inconsistently. A plan is developed to identify key tools and teach them to the work group.
3	All work group members understand a small set of basic PSTs. The proper PSTs are used for significant problems, but there is still much "subjective" analysis of minor problems.
4	All work group members understand and apply appropriate PSTs for all problem solving. Tool usage skills are tracked on cross-training displays.
5	The work group members (except new hires) are expert in all of the basic PSTs that might be used in the work group. Additional skill development plans are always in process.

Level	T-metric 13—Ownership of objectives
2	The work group identifies and displays short-term (daily and weekly) goals with milestones, completion dates, and accountabilities (MCDAs). Medium-term goals (monthly and quarterly) are being added to the visual display.
3	Short- and medium-term goals are displayed and tracked with MCDAs. Occasional missed goals are quickly dealt with by the group. Changes in the plan create some problems.
4	Short-, medium-, and long-term (annual to several years) goals are tracked and displayed with MCDAs. Work group totally accountable for objective attainment and adjusting to changes. Almost no problems.
5	Work group has full ownership for all objectives, handles changes easily, and adjusts proactively to potential problems. Objectives are always met.

Level	T-metric 14—Cleaning and organizing
2	Plan to improve cleaning and organizing (C/O) is in development. Loose trash is removed by the end of each day by work group members. Unused equipment and out-of-date materials, supplies, and files (MSFs) have been removed.
3	C/O performance is assessed with check lists that are visually displayed and reviewed at least twice per week. MSFs are labeled in both work area and storage areas.
4	C/O activities are conducted during the day by work group members. Audits show near-perfect C/O performance. Only rarely is an item out of place or clutter present. Members begin to plan for optimum placement of MSFs.
5	99.99999% C/O performance. Work area MSFs are stored, labeled, and arranged for optimum ease of use.

Level	T-metric 15—Time control and commitment
2	Attendance is charted and displayed.
3	Work group members generally arrive on time. People are willing to work late when it is required, unless personal commitments are pressing. Unexcused absenteeism is less than 3%. Annual turnover (not counting promotions) is less than 7%.
4	Work group members arrive on time 99% of the time. Absenteeism less than 2%. Annual turnover (not counting promotions) is less than 5%.
5	Group members on time 99.9% of the time and willing to work late when it is very rarely required. Absenteeism is less than 1% and turnover (not counting promotions) is less than 3%.

Level	T-metric 16—Budgets and costs
2	Work group costs are displayed to the work group. Periodically (at least quarterly), work group performance against budget is reported and posted visually to the work group.
3	The work group budget is established at year start and posted. Performance against budget is posted monthly, and the work group discusses among itself how to resolve major discrepancies.
4	The work group participates in development of its annual budget. Performance is tracked and displayed, and the work group is primarily responsible for budget performance with management approval/review.
5	All aspects of cost and budget development and performance are the responsibility of the work group with only minimal management coaching.

Level	T-metric 17—Internal customer service
2	Work group asks internal customers (ICs) to measure and/or report on its performance. Issues are identified and displayed for improvement planning. Many problems still exist.
3	Metrics are in place and displayed to formally monitor IC satisfaction. Continuous improvement plans are defined to address root causes of the most serious problems. Small problems occur regularly but are dealt with quickly.
4	All major and many minor root causes of IC dissatisfaction have been eliminated. Almost all potential problems have been proactively eliminated.
5	Customers' satisfaction is near perfect. IC satisfaction metrics are consistently at the very top of the scale.

Level	T-metric 18—Work standards
2	All work group members are familiar with what a good work standard should look like. A few activities have such work standards that all group members have reviewed.
3	Eighty percent of the work group's primary tasks have work standards, and they are used in cross-training activities.
4	All critical activities and most minor activities (95% of the group's tasks) have standards that the entire work group helped to develop, understands, and uses.
5	Standards for all work group activities, major and minor, have been established, and the work group continually strives to improve them.

Level	T-metric 19—Priority management
2	Priorities are imposed on the group. While there is a little discussion as to how to meet them, the primary strategy is to work harder with little collaboration and planning.
3	There is a good level of work group discussion involved in deciding how to meet imposed priorities. The work group begins to set many of its own priorities and develops and displays plans to manage them.
4	The work group begins to take ownership of all of its priorities and develops and displays plans for them. Management reviews and approves the work group's plans but seldom makes any changes.
5	The work group develops all of its own priorities after being given broader organization priorities. The work group priorities are 100% in line with organization priorities and need no management approval.

Level	T-metric 20—External customer awareness
2	External customer (EC) data relevant to the work group's performance are posted in the work group. Work group begins to make plans to address the most critical issues.
3	The work group has a posted plan with MCDAs for dealing with all major EC issues. Many major issues have been resolved.
4	All major EC issues have been resolved, and the work group is addressing the minor issues with posted plans that have MCDAs.
5	The work group has corrected all EC issues and can resolve any new issue under its control within 24 hours. ECs view the work group as a world-class unit.

Level	Mood	T-metric 21—Description of the prior week's efforts
1	☹	No action taken on a plan to improve on any of the T-metrics (a plan is a posted list of team-developed actions that must be completed to improve by at least one level on one of the T-metrics)
2	☹	At least one action item on one plan was completed
3	😐	At least three action items on a plan were completed
4	🙂	One T-metric was improved by at least one level
5	😊	One T-metric was improved by two levels, *or* two T-metrics were improved by at least one level each

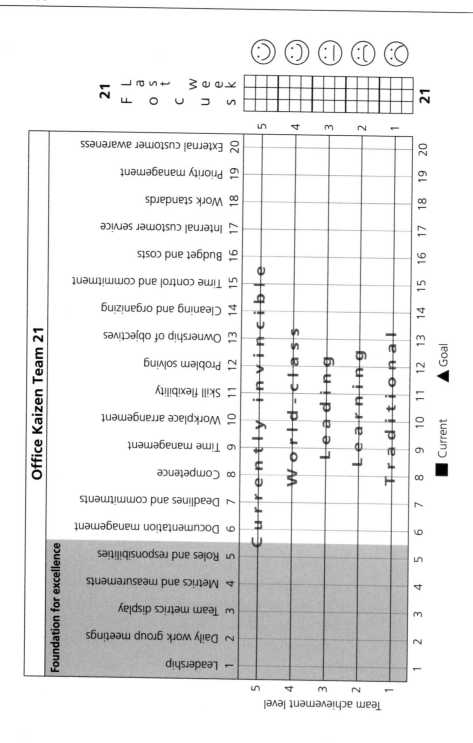

Office Kaizen Team 21

Team achievement level

Foundation for excellence

1 Leadership
2 Daily work group meetings
3 Team metrics display
4 Metrics and measurements
5 Roles and responsibilities
6 Documentation management
7 Deadlines and commitments
8 Competence
9 Time management
10 Workplace arrangement
11 Skill flexibility
12 Problem solving
13 Ownership of objectives
14 Cleaning and organizing
15 Time control and commitment
16 Budget and costs
17 Internal customer service
18 Work standards
19 Priority management
20 External customer awareness

Currently invincible
World-class
Leading
Learning
Traditional

■ Current   ▲ Goal

Team Focus Last Week 21

List of Abbreviations

AcL	action leader
AL	action leadership
AP	action plan
C&E	cause and effect
CI	continuous improvement
CIE	continuous improvement event
CIF	continuous improvement facilitator
CIM	corporate improvement manager
CS-VSM	current state value stream map
CT	cycle time
d-ESC	departmental mini-executive steering committee
DILO	day in the life of
DLT	direct leadership touch
DMAIC	define, measure, analyze, improve, control
DOI	drop off interval
DSI	direct spontaneous interaction
ESC	Executive Steering Committee
EXMOT	executive mandating and owning the transformation
FIFO	first in, first out
FS-VSM	future state value stream map
ILT	indirect leadership touch
ISI	indirect spontaneous interaction
IWG	intact work group
KAS	kaizen action sheet
KASS	kaizen action sheet system
KFCL	kaizen follow-up check list

KGVFC	key goals visual focus chart
KSAP	kaizen sustainment action plan
KTDL	kaizen to-do list
KTS	kaizen target sheet
LAct	leadership action
LAM	leadership action matrix
LBB	leadership black box
LDMS	Lead Daily Management System
MAD	modified affinity diagramming
m-WST	mini work stream team
OK1	*Office Kaizen 1*
OK2	*Office Kaizen 2*
PM	preventive maintenance
PVD	primary visual display
RACI	responsible, accountable, consulted, informed
RIE	rapid improvement event
SI	spontaneous interaction
SIF	site improvement facilitator
SIFTP	SIF training program
SMED	single minute exchange of die
SPC	statistical process control
SSBB	Six Sigma Black Belt
SSMBB	Six Sigma Master Black Belt
SVCT	skill versatility tracking and cross-training
TC	team champion
TMOS	Team Metrics and Ownership System
TPM	total preventive maintenance
TPS	Toyota Production System
TT	takt time
VMD	visual metrics display
VSM	value stream map
VSMapping	value stream mapping
wbAL	would-be action leader
WGM	work group meeting
WST	work stream team
WSTL	work stream team leader

Index

Note: Page numbers followed by f *refer to figures.*

A

Abilene Paradox, 72–73
abnormal variability, 117
action, primacy of, 258–260
action leaders (AcLs), 270–271
action leadership (AL), 253, 255–258. *See also*
        leadership; leadership action (LAct)
    implementing, 266–272, 267f
actions
    direct, 260
    indirect, 260
affinity diagramming, 109–110. *See also*
        modified affinity diagramming (MAD)
attraction, 69–70
attribution effects, power of, 69
attribution theories, 68–69
automatic processing, 37–39

B

behavior, components of, 258
belonging, as human need, 29
brainstorming methods, group, 109–136
    cause-and-effect (C&E) diagrams, 114–115,
        115f
    cross-training matrix, 131–134, 133f
    day-in-the-life-of (DILO) studies, 134–136,
        135f
    5S, 128–131, 129f, 130f, 131f
    flowcharts, 120–122, 121f
    handoff charts, 124, 125f
    histograms, 119, 120f
    line/run charts, 116–117, 116f
    modified affinity diagramming (MAD),
        109–114, 110f, 111f, 114f
    Pareto charts, 127–128, 127f
    RACI charts, 124–127, 126f
    spaghetti diagrams, 122–124, 123f
    statistical process control (SPC) charts,
        117–119, 118f
brown paper approach, 108–109

C

cause-and-effect (C&E) diagrams, 114–115,
        115f
change
    guidelines for increasing, 12
    stages of, in systems, 4, 4f
    structures of managing, 84–85
chaos stage, in systems, 4f, 5–6
chaos theory, 3
charters, 90–91
cognitive maps, 43–52, 46f
communication diagramming, 158–160
conformity, 63–65
confronters, 33
continuous improvement, 13
continuous improvement events (CIEs or kaizen
        events/blitzes), 92–93, 201
    conducting follow-up actions for,
        249–252
    conducting one week or less, 219
    detailed general, 225–248
    general structure of, 222–224
    length of, 220–221
    teams for, 222
control theory, 27–28, 258
corporate culture, 57
    challenge of frozen tundra of, 53–55
corporate improvement managers (CIMs),
        323–329
cross-training matrix, 131–134, 133f
current state VSM (CS-VSM), 139
    steps for constructing, 165–182

D

daily work group meetings (WGMs), 95–96
day-in-the-life-of (DILO) studies, 134–136,
    135*f*
Deming, W. Edwards, 117
departments
    recommended approach for transforming
        multiple, at multiple sites, 330–336
    transforming, 282–295
direct actions, 260
direct leadership touches (DLTs), 262–263, 265
direct spontaneous interactions (DSIs), 264,
    265
DMAIC (define, measure, analyze, improve,
    control) method, 24
drop off interval (DOI), 160

E

effectiveness parameters, 260–262
80-20 rule, 127–128
enacted roles, 66
Enneagram theory, 33
entities, 4
equilibrium, 5
executive mandating and owning the
    transformation (EXMOT), 319, 321
Executive Steering Committee (ESC), 86–88,
    274
expected roles, 66
experimentation, 7

F

first in, first out (FIFO) lane, 162–163, 163*f*
fishbone diagrams. *See* cause-and-effect (C&E)
    diagrams
5S, 127–131, 129*f*, 130*f*, 131*f*
flowcharts, 120–122, 121*f*
follow-up actions, conducting, 249–252
freedom, as human need, 32
fun, as human need, 31–32
future state VSM (FS-VSM), 139
    steps for constructing, 183–200

G

Gemba Wall, 94–95
goals, 65
group dynamics, 57
group formation, 58–59
groups
    Abilene Paradox and, 72–73
    attraction and, 69–70

attribution effects and, 68–69
goals and, 65
idiosyncrasy credits and, 73–74
norms and, 67–68
operating parameters of, 65–68
polarization and, 70–71
roles and, 65–67
social loafing and, 71
groupthink, 74–75

H

handoff charts, 124, 125*f*
Harvey, Jerry B., 72–73
helpers, 33
Hierarchy of Needs (Maslow), 28
histograms, 119, 120*f*

I

"I" consciousness, 43–52
idiosyncrasy credits, 73–74
improvement actions, 203–207. *See also*
        continuous improvement events (CIEs
        or kaizen events/blitzes); kaizen events/
        blitzes
    conduct, that last one week or less,
        219–220
indirect actions, 260
indirect leadership touches (ILTs), 263
indirect spontaneous interactions (ISIs), 264
information processing, levels of, 39–43, 39*f*
innovation
    defined, 14
    reasons for liking, 14–15
intact work groups (IWGs), xiv, 59, 102–103
    recommended approach for transforming
        multiple, 330–336
    transforming, 273–282

J

Janis, Irving, 74

K

kaikaku events, 93–94, 204*f*
kaizen, 13. *See also* Office Kaizen
    defined, xiii
kaizen action sheet system (KASS), 98–100,
    99*f*
kaizen events/blitzes, 92–93, 205. *See also*
        continuous improvement events (CIEs or
        kaizen events/blitzes)
    preparing for, 209–216

kanban, 21–22
kanban boards, 160–161
Kaufman, Stuart, 3
Kelly, Kevin, 3
key goals visual focus chart (KGVFC),
96–98, 97*f*

L

Langton, Christopher G., 3
leaders, 52–53
respect and latitude to, 62–63
leadership, 257*f. See also* action leadership
(AL)
respect and, 61–63
world-class organizations and, 61–63
leadership action (LAct), types of, 260–266. *See
also* action leadership (AL)
leadership action matrices (LAMs), 94–95,
268–271, 269*f*
leadership black box (LBB), 80–84, 80*f*, 83*f*
Leadership of Significant Change, 85, 85*f.*
See also Team Metrics and Ownership
System (TMOS)
charters, 90–91
continuous improvement events (CIEs),
92–93
Executive Steering Committee (ESC),
86–88
Gemba Wall, 94–95
kaikaku events, 93–94
site improvement facilitator (SIF), 91–92
team champions (TCs), 89–90
work stream team leaders (WSTLs), 89
work stream teams (WSTs), 88
Lean Daily Management System (LDMS),
85–86
lean manufacturing, 13, 22–23
line/run charts, 116–117, 116*f*

M

Maslow, Abraham, 28
matrix-organizations, 61
modified affinity diagramming (MAD),
109–114, 110*f*, 111*f*
motivators, 33
muda, 15
multiple site transformations. *See also* site
transformations
approaches that guarantee failure of,
315–319
recommended approach for, 319–329

recommended approach for IWGs or
departments, 330–336
requirement for guiding, 319
Myers-Briggs Temperament Typology, 33–34

N

needs, human, 28*f*
belonging, 29
freedom, 32
fun, 31–32
self-power, 30–31
self-worth, 30
sex, 29
survival, 28
norms, groups and, 67–68

O

Office Kaizen, 13
defined, xiii
overcoming challenges in implementing,
337–338
Office Kaizen implementation schedules
for a department, 284–285*f*
for multiple IWGs or department
transformations, 330–336, 332*f*
for multiple site transformations, 319–329,
322*f*
for section or department, 282–295
for single IWG, 273–282, 278*f*
Office Kaizen 1 (OK1), xiv
Office Kaizen 2 (OK2), xiv–xv
objectives of, xv–xvii
Office Kaizen wastes, from *OK1,* 17–18*f*
Ohno, Taiichi, 16
one-point lessons, 137–138
one-point methods, 137–138
organization dynamics, 57

P

Pareto, Vilfredo, 127
Pareto charts, 127–128, 127*f*
perceived roles, 66
persistent disequilibrium, 10–11, 11*f*
personality conflict, 66
polarization, 70–71
preconscious pilot, 40–41
preconscious processing, 40–42
process-centered work groups, 60–61
processes, ways of improving, 14–15
propinquity, 59–61
push vs. pull, 20–22, 20*f*

R

RACI (responsible, accountable, consulted, and informed) charts, 124–127, 126*f*

rapid improvement events (RIEs), 219. *See also* continuous improvement events (CIEs or kaizen events/blitzes)

reintegration stage, in systems, 4*f*, 6

role ambiguity, 66

role conflict, 66

role expectations, power of, 66–67

roles, groups and, 65–67

S

scrambles, 204*f*, 206

preparing for, 216–218

sections, transforming, 282–295

self-power, as human need, 30–31

self-worth, as human need, 30

7QC

cause-and-effect (C&E) diagrams, 114–115, 115*f*

flowcharts, 120–122, 121*f*

handoff charts, 124, 125*f*

histograms, 119, 120*f*

line/run charts, 116–117, 116*f*

RACI (responsible, accountable, consulted, and informed) charts, 124–127, 126*f*

spaghetti diagrams, 122–124, 123*f*

statistical process control (SPC) charts, 117–119, 118*f*

sex, as human need, 29

Shewhart, Walter, 117

single minute exchange of die (SMED), xvii, 19

site improvement facilitator (SIF), 91–92, 300

site transformations. *See also* multiple site transformations

about, 297–301

implementing single, 301–314

Six Sigma, 13, 23–26

Six Sigma Black Belts (SSBSs), 25

Six Sigma events, 204*f*, 206

preparing for, 209–216

Six Sigma Master Black Belts (SSMBBs), 25

social loafing, 71

spaghetti diagrams, 122–124, 123*f*

spontaneous interactions (SIs), 263–264

standard work, 136–137

statistical process control (SPC) charts, 117–119, 118*f*

structural configurations

defined, 84–85

Leadership of Significant Change, 85–95, 85*f*

Team Metrics and Ownership System (TMOS), 85*f*, 95–105

successive checks, 22

supermarket kanban system, 160–162, 162*f*

survival, as human need, 28

systems, 4*f*

chaos in, 5

chaos stage in, 5–6

entities and, 3

equilibrium in, 5

stages of change in, 4

systems adaptation, law of, 6

T

takt time, xvii

team champions (TCs), 89–90

Team Metrics and Ownership System (TMOS), 85, 85*f*. *See also* Leadership of Significant Change

daily work group meetings (WGMs), 95–96

kaizen action sheet system (KASS), 98–100, 99*f*

key goals visual focus chart (KGVFC), 96–98, 97*f*

Team 21, 96, 100–103, 101*f*, 104*f*, 339–346

visual metrics display (VMD), 96

weekly continuous improvement meeting, 104–105

Team 21, 96, 100–103, 101*f*, 104*f*, 339–346

total preventive maintenance (TPM), xvii, 137

Toyota Production System (TPS), 13, 18–22

principal approaches and methods used in, 19*f*

push vs. pull concept in, 20–22, 20*f*

transformations. *See* multiple site transformations; site transformations

transmission mechanics, 260–262

"type" perspectives, 33–34

U

uncommon variability, 117

V

value stream mapping (VSMapping), xvii, 13, 23, 77, 139–140

communication diagramming, 158–160

concepts and symbols for, 160–163

OK2 approach to, 147–160
  type of information used in, 149–158
value stream maps (VSMs), xvii, 139–140
  basic structure of, 140–147
  current state, 139, 165–182
  future state, 139, 183–200
variability, abnormal, 117
visual metrics display (VMD), 96

W

waste reduction, 13
wastes, 13, 15–18
  defined, 16
  Office Kaizen, from *OK1,* 17–18*f*

Taiichi Ohno's original, 16, 16*f*
  types of, 16*f*
weekly continuous improvement meeting,
  104–105
work stream team leaders (WSTLs), 89
work stream teams (WSTs), xiv, 88
would-be action leaders (wbALs), 266–267,
  270